DAMNED
GOOD COMPANY

TWENTY REBELS WHO BUCKED
THE GOD EXPERTS

BY LUIS GRANADOS

CONTENTS

For my wife, Pat, and son, Paul, who have shown infinite patience.
And for our dog, Rosie, who has not.

INTRODUCTION

I have no problem with God.

I have no problem with the idea that there might be a force our intellect does not understand—and perhaps cannot understand—that was involved with the creation of the universe. This force may have views on the way we humans should live our lives, it may intervene in our affairs, and it may even provide us with an afterlife—or not. Maybe there is nothing but what we see; maybe something simply set things in motion, and doesn't really care whether we covet each other's wives or not. I don't know—and I don't believe anyone else knows either.

The debate about the existence of a god has raged for a long time. There is nothing new to say about it. So I won't.

This is a book about people, not about God. It is about people who have written about God, preached about God, taken money for sharing what they say they know about God, and ordered others about to carry out what they claim to be God's will. "I know about God; therefore you should do as I say" is my working definition of religion.

While I have no problem with God, I do have a problem with God experts who claim they know something about God. I have a problem with people who grab money and power based solely on their insistence that they know who or what God is and how God works. And I have a serious problem with people who claim their God expertise gives them the right to tell me or anyone else how to live our lives.

I am not alone—though it sometimes feels that way. A good 16 percent of Americans tell pollsters they are not affiliated with any religious belief.[1] Not all are outright atheist; many are agnostic, or "don't

1

know," which is pretty much the same thing. (Agnostics know they don't know; others just plain don't know.) That 16 percent is more than any single religious denomination in the United States other than Catholics.[2] There are more unbelieving Americans than there are black Americans. Or Hispanics. Or gays. What's more, we non-believers are a relatively well-educated, high-income group. So why do we get so little respect?

Even larger is the 60 percent of people who told pollsters they don't attend any church on at least a weekly basis.[3] Careful studies show that even the 40 percent regular church attendance figure is exaggerated; the true figure is closer to 25 percent.[4]

Every religion insists that its followers must at least attend church—after all, that's where the money comes from. So we have a vast proportion of Americans who say they believe in a particular version of God, but when it comes to doing the bare minimum necessary to save themselves from everlasting damnation, they can't be bothered. Are they really believers? Or are they just mouthing the words because that is the respectable thing to do?

There is often a terrible opprobrium to admitting lack of belief in God. God is on our money, he's in the middle of our Pledge of Allegiance, he starts every session of Congress, and he worms his way into almost every major political speech. At this writing, there are 535 members of Congress, including several who are overtly homosexual—and exactly one who admits to disbelief in God. (He, by the way, waited until age 75 before "coming out.")[5] George H. W. Bush—the "kinder, gentler" one—insisted that an atheist could not be patriotic: "No, I don't know that atheists should be considered as citizens, nor should they be considered patriots. This is one nation under God."[6]

One method of responding to this is to complain, and periodically to file lawsuits about the Pledge of Allegiance, the faith-based initiative, crucifixes on federal property, etc. As a practicing lawyer, I love it when people file lawsuits—the more the merrier. I hope the plaintiffs start to win more often, but I don't think they will until the culture changes—until it becomes far more socially acceptable to live proudly without religion. Judges don't have any more guts than politicians do.

This book takes a different tack. Rather than complain about how put upon we non-believers are, this book boasts about how courageous we are, and have been, throughout history. It takes backbone to stand up to the God experts because so many people treat doing so as scorning morality itself.

Senator John F. Kennedy wrote *Profiles in Courage* in 1955. Can one little book be credited with emboldening the 1960s generation to take on segregation, imperialism, and male dominance? No—but it helped. It made would-be reformers feel good about themselves. It taught them they were not alone, and instead were part of a proud tradition of men (Kennedy found no courageous women) willing to buck the prevailing wisdom even when it meant probable damage to their own political careers.

The men and women profiled in this book faced consequences more dire than losing an election. Some died for their lack of belief; one who remains alive today does so by grace of round-the-clock security protection. Many of those who made it through to natural deaths faced quite credible death threats from the God experts they challenged. They stood their ground. They knew fraud when they saw it, and they had too much respect for themselves to look the other way just because that's what everyone else was doing.

Very few of the heroes in this book were certain in their disbelief of the supernatural. Some held firm views to the contrary; one was even a priest. All of them, though, had the courage to buck the prevailing wisdom of the leading God experts of their time and place, not because they felt their own expertise was greater, but because they were convinced that the experts themselves knew not whereof they spoke. Their lack of confidence in the experts' hotline to heaven led our heroes, to varying extents, to attitudes of tolerance for a variety of beliefs; to disdain for government promotion of religion; to repugnance at the use of violence to promote supernatural belief; to rejection of divinely-inspired racial or ethnic bigotry; and to greater respect for knowledge gained through scientific observation than for that gained through divine revelation.

The villains, in much of literature, are as interesting as the heroes.

Some of the villains here are notable individual God experts. Some are groups or institutions, whose collective conventional wisdom was more powerful than that of any individual. Some villains are notable primarily as representatives of such institutions, and not for their personal achievements. One villain is not even a human, but a germ, whose spread was enhanced by God experts. On an even lower rung are politicians, who have used religion without believing in it, to advance their own selfish ends.

The stories span the globe and all of recorded history. This is deliberate; resistance to religion has been around as long as religion itself. You won't get a complete picture of the history of religious resistance from reading these 20 stories, anymore than you would get a complete picture of the Amazon by looking at 20 snapshots. But you can get some sense of the grandeur of the Amazon from 20 well-selected photos, and my intention is that you get some sense of how heroic the men and women of all races are who stood up to overbearing religious dogma in parallel ways that can inspire the jaded in the twenty-first century.

Heroism must be measured in relation to its time and place. The list of pre-nineteenth century atheists and agnostics of whom we have substantial knowledge is short; yet there were men and women throughout recorded history who bucked the religious establishment and helped move the ball toward greater tolerance, greater separation of church and state, and greater reliance on scientific thinking than the prevailing supernatural wisdom of the day. Most of the chapters devote considerable attention to setting the stage on which the conflicts were fought, without which they have little meaning.

Be warned: not all of these heroes prevailed. Especially in pre-Enlightenment times, most of them went to their graves believing they failed. Failure does not make their efforts less admirable, or their stories less dramatic. We learn from failure as much as from success, and our respect for those who fought when the odds were hopeless must be as great as for those who benefited from the groundwork laid.

Thanks to the cumulative efforts of these heroes, America and the rest of the Enlightenment-influenced world is now a place where men and women don't face the threat of death for lack of belief. All we face is being political and social pariahs, the burden of lawmaking influenced by superstition, and the aggravation of our own tax money being used against us. This will continue until we start showing one-tenth of the courage of the men and women of this book by standing up and demanding respect, just as blacks, women, and gays have done before us. Doing so will put us in some damned good company.

1 Pew Forum, *Religious Landscape.*
2 Pew Forum, *Religious Composition.*
3 Pew Forum, *Bad Economy.*
4 Peterson, *Church Attendance.*
5 Marinucci, *Stark.*
6 Dawkins, *God Delusion*, 43.

Socrates

CHAPTER 1

SOCRATES VS. EUTHYPHRO

Sacrifice

This is the story of the earliest recorded conflict in the Western world between God experts and those who stood up to them. The story revolves around the concept of religious sacrifice, a central feature of pagan (and later Christian) belief, and pits the fellow who claimed to have the most perfect God expertise in Athens against a teacher who had the audacity to think for himself.

We do not know exactly how religion started. Some artifacts suggest that Neanderthals, an altogether different species from today's *Homo sapiens* who lived 30,000 to 130,000 years ago, had ceremonial burials and some sort of worship involving bears; however, the evidence is not conclusive. There is no doubt, though, that the Cro-Magnon people, the oldest modern humans who lived in Europe 10,000 to 35,000 years ago, had an elaborate religion. There are cave paintings of a Cro-Magnon priest wearing antlers, bear paws, and a horse's tail, summoning the blessing of a god for an upcoming hunt.[1]

The concept of sacrifice to gods made an early appearance, about 15,000 years ago. To get a little, you've got to give a little. South American Indians got their water from melting snow on the mountain peaks; to keep the flow coming, they sacrificed victims at the tops of those peaks. In 1964, climbers reached the summit of Mount Toro in northwestern Argentina, after previous attempts of experienced mountaineers had failed. Most of the climbers used bottled oxygen. At the summit they discovered a massive stone altar, 35 by 20 feet in area and 3 feet high, with the body of a young victim buried beneath it.[2]

Sometimes the problem in West Africa was not a lack of water, but too much of it. How can you get a message to the rain-god to stop already? The accepted procedure was to prepare a woman with special prayers, place a message in her mouth, club her to death, then place her body on the top of a high tree, where the rain-god could see her and read the message.[3]

Each year, Aztecs selected a young man to represent the God of Gods, Tezcatlipoca, who was clothed, fed, and otherwise treated royally throughout the year. For a 20-day period before the annual religious festival of Toxcatl, he was presented with four beautiful brides, designated as the goddesses. At the highlight of the festival, he ascended majestically to the top of a pyramid, where he was seized and held down by the priests upon a block of stone, while one of them cut open his breast, thrust his hand into the wound, wrenched out his heart and held it up before the crowd in sacrifice to the sun. Scholars estimate that between 20,000 and 40,000 people a year were sacrificed to the sun in Mexico, where a still-grateful sun continues to reign supreme.[4]

At this point, paler-skinned readers may be thinking subconsciously, "I'm glad *my* ancestors didn't do that sort of thing." Well, they did. When a Scandinavian or Slavic husband died, his now-useless widow would often be killed along with him. This occurred in Poland as late as the tenth century CE. Arab visitors to southern Russia reported that, if a man died with three wives, his favorite would be selected to be strangled and then burned on the man's funeral pyre. When a Viking ship was launched, victims were bound to the rollers over which it slipped into the sea, in order to redden the keel with human blood. Julius Caesar was sickened by the amount of human sacrifice he witnessed in France. "The Gauls consider that the oblation of such as have been taken in theft, or robbery, or any other offences is more acceptable to the immortal gods; but when a supply of that class is wanting, they have recourse even to the innocent."[5]

Judeo-Christian God experts today are fond of claiming that God's last-minute command to Abraham to cancel the sacrifice of his son, Isaac, ended human sacrifice in their tradition. Their Bible says otherwise. The book of Judges tells us that a thousand years after Abraham,[6] Jephthah promised God that he would sacrifice the first living thing he saw on returning home if he could defeat the Ammonites in battle. He may have been anticipating a sheep, but the first living thing he saw turned out to be his daughter. Undaunted, Jephthah kept his word and carried out the sacrifice; a grateful nation later appointed him as judge over all of Israel, which he ruled for six years. Nor was Jephthah unusual in this. The Phoenician historian Philo of Byblus noted that in time of war the Jewish king would dress his son in royal robes and sacrifice him on an altar.[7] This was apparently in accord with the command of God in the book of Exodus: "Thou shalt not delay to offer the first of thy ripe fruits, and of thy liquors: the firstborn of thy sons shalt thou give unto me." King Ahaz went even further, burning several of his children.[8]

Archeologists have found the remains of decapitated infants under house floors near the Dead Sea, which appear to have been deliberate sacrifices made at the time the foundation of the building was laid to assure its strength. In the sanctuary at Gezer, two burnt skeletons of six-year-old children were found, along with the skulls of two adolescents that had been sawn in half.[9]

Even in Greece, the cradle of democracy and humanist philosophy, human sacrifice flourished. A tablet from the Greek town of Pylos promises the gods an offering of 13 golden vessels, 2 men, and 8 women. In Athens, well-organized God experts kept on hand a group of men and women called the Pharmakoi, maintained at public expense, for a quick sacrifice in case plague, famine, or some other disaster arose. Pharmakoi were equally useful for annual events such as the early summer Thargelia festival, when two men were led out of the city and stoned to death as scapegoats for the wrongs of others.[10]

The Greeks of Anatolia varied the procedure somewhat. Rather than wasting money supporting prospective victims, when a crisis arose they simply selected an ugly or deformed person to take upon himself all the evils that afflicted the community. He was brought to a suitable place, where dried figs, a barley loaf, and cheese were given to him to eat. Then he was beaten seven times upon his genital organs with branches of a wild fig tree, while musicians played a hymn. After he was burnt on a pyre of wood, his ashes were cast into the sea.[11]

Socrates

Not everyone cooperated with the Greek god experts, though. In the fifth century BCE, a man came along who decided he knew as much as they did—or more precisely, as little as they did—about the supernatural. A stubborn man who would not accede to conventional religious wisdom—even when his life depended on it.

We have only a few details about Socrates' life. Born in Athens around 470 BCE, the son of a stone carver and a midwife, Socrates had a wife and three sons, two of them arriving late in life. He was said to be rather ugly, with a snub nose, bulging eyes, and thick lips. Though he earned a decent living as a tutor, he lived like a pauper, going barefoot, bathing rarely, and wearing the same thin cloak year-round.

Socrates was prominent enough in the community to serve on a committee of the Athenian Assembly, where he was the only vote against a motion to put military commanders on trial for failing to retrieve the bodies of the dead after a sea battle. Later, he risked his life by disobeying an order of the "Thirty Tyrants" who had briefly overthrown the Athenian democracy.[12]

His real trouble, though, involved his views on the Greek gods. We cannot tell today exactly what those views were; Socrates left no written record, and contemporary accounts do not paint a full picture. We do know, though, that those views were far outside the mainstream.

The first evidence we have is a satirical play written by Aristophanes, around 423 BCE. Aristophanes' principal goal in writing *Clouds* was to attract a paying crowd by being funny. Learning about Socrates from his depiction in *Clouds* is akin to learning about a modern politician by reading scripts from *Saturday Night Live*–not accurate in every detail, but enough to discover what strikes a responsive chord in an audience.[13]

Aristophanes portrays Socrates as a pointy-headed intellectual, who uses clever words to make men doubt what everyone knows to be true. The plot involves a character who joins Socrates' school, the "Pondertorium," to learn how to avoid paying his debts–*i.e.*, to learn how to dodge straightforward morality. Early on, Socrates is painted as godless; when the prospective student says "Name your price, whatever it takes, I swear by the gods to pay you!" Socrates laughingly replies "Swear by the gods?' We don't give credit to the gods here!" Later, Socrates insists that his student "repudiate all other gods, except those we venerate: the holy trinity of Chaos, Clouds, and a confident tongue"; the student eagerly confirms that "I wouldn't even speak to a god if I met one, and you won't catch me sacrificing, pouring libations, or burning incense on any of their altars."[14]

Aristophanes also has a character call him "Socrates the Melian," an apparent allusion to Diagoras of Melos, who had recently been condemned to death in Athens for scorning traditional religion. We know almost nothing about Diagoras, other than that he managed to disappear before the sentence could be carried out. Cicero, writing several hundred years later, tells of how someone tried to convince Diagoras of the existence of the gods by pointing to all the pictures of those who were saved from storms at sea through the power of prayer; Diagoras replied that "there are nowhere any pictures of those who have been shipwrecked and drowned at sea." Cicero relates another story of Diagoras at sea during a storm; when the angry crew blames the storm on his disrespect for the gods, he asks them why the other boats without a Diagoras on board are being caught in the same wind.[15]

Aristophanes' play skewers Socrates for placing science over religion. When his student mentions Zeus, Socrates scornfully replies "Zeus? Don't be absurd! Zeus doesn't exist." The student asks who makes it rain if Zeus doesn't exist, and Socrates replies "Why, the Clouds of course! I'll prove it to you. Does it ever rain without Clouds? No, and you would have thought that Zeus could have made rain on his own if he so desired, without the help of the Clouds." Then the student's punch line: "And I always thought it was Zeus pissing through a sieve!"[16] (Comedy has come a long way since then.)

But what about thunder, asks the student. After Socrates explains that "The Clouds become full of water and crash into each other, thus they emit a thundering sound because of their sheer density," the student gets more laughs with "The exact same thing happened to me once at the Diasia feast. I was cooking a nice big sausage for the family, and I completely forgot to prick it. Well, it swelled right up and suddenly BANG! It blew up right in my face and showered me with hot blood and fat."[17]

Euthyphro

So much for the SNL version. A more serious take on the objections to Socrates is presented in a dialogue recorded by Socrates' student Plato—between Socrates and a fellow named Euthyphro.

Euthyphro was one of the leading God experts in Socrates' Athens. While we have no direct evidence that he participated in the human sacrifices of the Pharmakoi or Thargelia, it seems certain that he was front and center at all such solemn occasions. He was a "mantis," the Greek word for prophet, deriving from the same root that gives us "mania." Socrates acknowledges, and Euthyphro doesn't deny, that "You say you have a finer knowledge of religious matters than any other human being." Euthyphro also claims to have "exact knowledge" about the position the gods take on what is pious and what is impious.[18]

An important man about town and everyone's friend, Euthyphro expresses shock that Socrates has been indicted, of all things for "corrupting the young." His accuser charges that Socrates is "an inventor of gods." "And because I invent new gods," Socrates replies," and don't acknowledge the old ones, he's indicted me for the latter's sake, so he says." The real problem, adds Socrates, is that he discusses his views with his students. "Athenians, it seems to me, aren't much concerned if they think someone's clever, so long as he doesn't teach his own wisdom. But if they think he's making other people wise like himself, they get angry, whether out of envy, as you say, or for some other reason."[19]

Socrates admits to Euthyphro that there are stories about the gods he simply cannot accept: "That, it seems, is why some people will say I'm a wrongdoer." He asks whether Euthyphro truly believes all the conventional wisdom—especially about "terrible hostilities and battles, and other such things of the sort the poets relate." Indignantly, Euthyphro replies "Not only those, Socrates, but as I mentioned just now, I will, if you like, tell you lots of other things about religious matters that I'm sure you'll be amazed to hear."[20]

Realizing he was not going to get much help from Euthyphro, Socrates decided to pursue his favorite pastime of twisting him into knots—a practice which did little to endear Socrates to the jury of five hundred that ultimately decided his fate. Because he was being accused of "impiety," Socrates asked Euthyphro to explain to him exactly what piety is, so he could better construct his defense.

After a false start in which he gives examples of piety rather than the general definition Socrates is seeking, Euthyphro opines that "What's loved by the gods is pious, and what's not loved by the gods is impious."[21]

But, said Socrates, don't the gods "quarrel and differ with one another?" Even fight battles, as Euthyphro had acknowledged a few moments ago? So what is pleasing to one god is not necessarily pleasing to another. Euthyphro slowly admits that is right; which brings Socrates back to his original question: what exactly is "piety," an inquiry of more than passing interest to a person being criminally charged with the lack of it.

Euthyphro works his way out of that jam, with Socrates' help, by getting to the point that the pious is what all the gods love, and the impious is what all the gods hate, while continuing to claim that he knows exactly which is which. More consternation arises, though, when Socrates asks whether something is pious because the gods love it, or do the gods love something because it is pious. After chasing his tail for a while on that conundrum, a frustrated and embarrassed Euthyphro bursts out: "But Socrates, I have no way of telling you what I have in mind. For whatever proposals we put forward keep somehow moving around and won't stay put."[22] Religion, then as now, was a set of simple answers to hard questions; probing beyond the first layer causes as much indignation in today's God experts as it did with Euthyphro.

At Socrates' insistence, Euthyphro then takes a completely different tack: "If a person knows how to do and say the things that are pleasing to the gods in prayer and sacrifice—those are the ones that are pious. And actions like them preserve both the private welfare of households and the common welfare of the city, whereas those that are the opposite of pleasing are unholy, and they, of course, overturn and destroy everything."[23]

Sacrifice—the pinnacle of which, of course, was the human sacrifice of the Pharmakoi. Socrates bores in on this definition in his irritatingly clever style:

SOCRATES: But tell me, what is this service to the gods? You say it's asking for things from them and giving things to them?

EUTHYPHRO: I do.

SOCRATES: Well then, wouldn't asking in the right way consist of asking for the things we need from them?

EUTHYPHRO: What else could it be?

SOCRATES: And, conversely, giving in the right way would consist of giving them, in turn, the things they need from us? For surely giving someone what he didn't at all need isn't something that an expert in the art of giving would do.

EUTHYPHRO: That's true, Socrates.

SOCRATES: Then piety, Euthyphro, would be a sort of expertise in mutual trading between gods and men.

EUTHYPHRO: Yes, trading, if that's what you prefer to call it.

SOCRATES: I don't prefer anything, if it isn't true. But tell me. What benefit do the gods get from the gifts they receive from us? I mean, what they give is clear to everyone, since we possess nothing good that they don't give us. But how are they benefited by what they receive from us? Or do we get so much the better of them in the trade that we receive all our good things from them while they receive nothing from us?[24]

That was all poor Euthyphro could stand. "Some other time, Socrates. You see, I'm in a hurry to get somewhere, and it's time for me to be off." As he scurries away, Socrates calls out sarcastically: "What a way to treat me, my friend! Going off like that and dashing the high hopes I had that I'd learn from you what things are pious and what aren't. Then I'd escape Meletus' indictment by showing him that Euthyphro had now made me wise in religious matters, and ignorance would no longer cause me to improvise and innovate about them. What's more, I'd live a better way for the rest of my life."[25]

Corrupting the Young

There is no doubt that Socrates was guilty of "corrupting the young," the crime with which he was charged. His knack for confounding the powerful tickled the fancy of young followers, while enraging the victims of his dissection.[26] More than mere embarrassment was often involved, though. The fact that Athens operated as a democracy created the need for skill in argument and rhetoric that had never existed in more primitive times, and a group of proto-lawyers, called "Sophists," earned the same opprobrium that slick lawyers and lobbyists encounter today, especially when their techniques for swaying votes worked against the interests of the powerful.[27]

Young students of Socrates worked out a whole way of living their lives that did not involve gods or sacrifices at all. One of them, named Aristippus, spread the idea that the main purpose of life had nothing to do with serving the gods, and everything to do with simply having a good time.[28] What did the pursuit of true pleasure mean? Well, opinions varied. Aristippus himself was a fan of instant gratification, on Aesop's idea that a bird in the hand is worth two in the bush. Alcohol and sex ranked high in his esteem.[29]

Hangovers and unwanted children were as problematic then as they are now, though; so some of Aristippus' colleagues began exploring the question of how to maximize pleasure more thoughtfully. Concentrating on such matters is a pleasant pastime in itself, like comparing the merits of Cabernet and Merlot. In any case, some followers of this growing school of thought disagreed with Aristippus, holding that pleasure maximization not only meant planning at least a bit further ahead than the next glass of wine, but even involved matters beyond physical sensation, such as friendship, family, and contentment of the mind. Decent treatment of others also played a role, because otherwise one could have no expectation of decent treatment for oneself, resulting in a most unpleasant state of uncertainty and fear. Some even demonstrated the conundrum that a certain degree of asceticism could help yield ultimate pleasure; toning down the level of desires made them easier to satisfy. "To accustom one's self, therefore, to simple and inexpensive habits is a great ingredient in the perfecting of health, and makes a man free from hesitation with respect to the necessary uses of life."[30]

The common thread among all the Socratic philosophies of pleasure, though, was that none of them had anything to do with gods, and in all of them the idea of taking something valuable and deliberately "sacrificing" it made no sense at all. On the contrary: "The beginning and root of all good is the stomach's pleasure." One of Aristippus' followers even became known as "Theodorus the Atheist"; his outspoken denial of the Olympian gods ultimately earned him banishment from Athens.[31] Epicurus, who raised the philosophy of pleasure to its most sophisticated level, did not wish to endure the unpleasantness of banishment, so he acknowledged the gods' existence. He taught, though, that the gods were so far above mankind that they cared nothing about us and did not intervene in our affairs, any more than we care about the affairs of insects, so that prayer and sacrifice were an utter waste of time.[32]

Theodorus and Epicurus lay decades in the future at the time Socrates was indicted, but the city fathers could see where the minds of the young were headed, and they didn't like it. Only a few years earlier, a band of miscreants including five students of Socrates had systematically vandalized the statues of the god Hermes that dotted the city; those who were caught were put to death.[33] A symbiotic relationship between religion and government existed in Athens as it has in many other societies; priests were paid by the state, and in turn "guided" it, that their pay and influence might flourish. The Delphic Oracle answered specific questions of state, such as whether wars should be launched or not. Specific taxes were levied to support the worship of individual gods. Happiness, according to the prevailing wisdom, came from pleasing the gods through prayer and sacrifice. As the indictment of another religious innovator put it: "Our ancestors, who only made the sacrifices prescribed in Solon's code, bequeathed to us a city which was the greatest and happiest in all Greece; and so we ought to perform the same sacrifices as them, if for no other reason, for the good fortune that they brought."[34]

It was bad enough when upstarts introduced new gods, which undermined the authority of those who were paid to mediate between man and the old gods. This practice was made a crime during Socrates' time. But when followers of Socrates went around making statements such as "religion was a deliberate imposture devised by some cunning man for political ends" and attempted to use science rather than the actions of the gods to explain natural phenomena, the ruling God experts were deeply troubled. Rather than put a whole generation on trial, they aimed for the gray head they saw as its inspiration.[35] By taming or exiling Socrates, the elites could perpetuate their control with much less effort than if they had to put up with his irritating *questions* all the time.

There was precedent for this. A contemporary of Socrates named Protagoras had written a book called *On the Gods*, only the first lines of which have survived: "Concerning the gods, I have no means of knowing whether they exist or not or of what sort they may be. Many things prevent knowledge including the obscurity of the subject and the brevity of human life."[36] He was indicted, fled, and was said to have been drowned at sea (by an angry Poseidon). His book was then publicly burned. Diagoras of Melos had also been condemned to death for impiety, as noted above.[37]

Trial

So in 399 BCE, off to trial Socrates went, defying the probable expectations of his accusers who expected him to flee into voluntary exile instead.[38] There are two competing versions of what happened at

17

the trial, given to us by Xenophon and Plato. Xenophon portrays the whole affair as an extended suicide.[39] In his version, Socrates could certainly have been acquitted or convicted of a petty offense if that were his aim; instead, he deliberately antagonized the jurors, because he was worn out and tired of living at the age of 69. Surely there are less stressful, more reliable ways of carrying out a suicide, though. Perhaps the germ of truth in Xenophon's portrayal is that the old curmudgeon Socrates didn't give a damn what people thought; if he had an audience of five hundred attentive listeners, he was going to speak his mind, without concern for the consequences.

Plato's rendition depicts Socrates as a humanist—one who puts man at the center of life, rather than the gods: "a thinker about things in the heavens, an investigator of all things below the earth, and someone who makes the weaker argument the stronger. Those who've spread this rumor, men of Athens, are my dangerous accusers, since the people who hear them believe that those who investigate such things do not acknowledge the gods either."[40]

Plato's Socrates is a deist. Like Epicurus decades later, he readily admits that some supernatural level exists; he just doesn't know or care very much about it. What Socrates does know and care about is human wisdom, rather than superhuman wisdom:

> You see, men of Athens, I've acquired this reputation because of nothing other than a sort of wisdom. What sort of wisdom, you ask, is that? The very sort, perhaps, that is *human* wisdom. For it may just be that I really do have that sort of wisdom, whereas the people I mentioned just now may, perhaps, be wise because they possess *superhuman* wisdom. I don't know what else to call it, since I myself certainly don't possess that knowledge, and whoever says I do is lying and speaking in order to slander me.[41]

Simple enough. Matters become more confusing, both for the Athens jury and modern readers, when Socrates starts talking about his "daimon," a term he never explicitly defines. A daimon is not a demon, as commonly pictured today (though early Christian authorities despised the daimon concept so much they used it to define evil incarnate). It is not a cute form-shifting animal as in the *Golden Compass* books and movie, though author Philip Pullman certainly based that conceit on Socrates. For Socrates' critics, the daimon was a new god that Socrates had invented to override the established gods—blasphemy in itself, punishable by death because of Socrates' insistence on titillating Athens' youth with his heresy.

Socrates' own references to his daimon, though, make it appear less like a god along the lines of Apollo or Athena, and closer to what we would call a "well-developed conscience." A conscience shaped by years of reflection and debate, of the type that so flustered the God expert Euthyphro. A conscience not based on divine revelation, which at the time was principally summarized in the works attributed to Homer, but based on Socrates' human wisdom. Still, Socrates could not resist the opportunity to tie an opponent into knots. First, he induced his prosecutor to allege that Socrates did not believe in gods; then he got him to concede that Socrates' daimon was a god; so how is it possible to believe and disbelieve in gods at the same time?

Socrates' pride elevated the daimon to a status a bit higher than "what I think is right." The closest he comes to a definition is "A divine and daimonic thing comes to me—the very thing Meletus made mocking allusion to in the indictment he wrote. It's something that began happening to me in childhood: a sort of voice comes, which, whenever it does come, always holds me back from what I'm about to do but never urges me forward." It's too bad there wasn't another Socrates around to pester the original Socrates with questions to pin down exactly what he meant by "divine."

A sharp twenty-first century lawyer could have intervened at that point and gotten Socrates to back off from the claim that his daimon was divine, and admit that all he was doing was using human wisdom as a guide for human actions, without making any claims one way or the other about the supernatural—the essence of humanism, which suffered a two thousand year setback in Europe when Socrates blew his defense. Instead, the jury voted by approximately 280 to 220 to convict Socrates of corrupting the young with his talk of daimons.[42]

We do not know whether Euthyphro was in that jury, or if so how he voted—but we can guess.

On to the penalty phase. Even a mediocre twenty-first century lawyer would have advised Socrates at this point to be contrite, promise to be less obnoxious, and suggest for himself a modest punishment allowing both sides to save face. Instead, Socrates proposed that if he were to be given what he truly deserved, it would consist of free meals at the city hall for the rest of his life for the service he had done for the community. We don't know what expletives the Greeks used on hearing those words, but we do know that the majority vote to put him to death after that taunt was higher than the majority to convict in the first place.[43]

Even at death, Socrates did not deny the divine, or even the afterlife. His last words before draining the cup of hemlock were: "But one is, I suppose, permitted to utter a prayer to the gods—and one should do so—that one's journey from this world to the next will prove fortunate. That is my prayer; may it be fulfilled."[44] Had a man with Socrates' respect for precision thought he knew which god to pray to or how, he would have done so. His conviction that neither he nor Euthyphro possessed this knowledge, and his arrogance in proclaiming that conviction, caused his death.

> Is Epicurus too shallow? Is there more to life than just being happy? Or does the point lie in how well you define happiness? Share your thoughts on this and the other questions you'll find at **dgc.humanistpress.com**!

Notes:

1 Walsh, *Role of Religion*, 17-18; but see http://experts.about.com/q/ Anthropology-2291/neanderthal-religion.htm.

2 Walsh, *Role of Religion*, 18; Tierney, *Highest Altar*, 42-46.

3 Gillooly, *Adam and Eve*, 143.

4 Frazer, *Golden Bough*, 186-187; Gillooly, *Adam and Eve*, 143.

5 Davies, *Human Sacrifice*, 45, 103.
6 Russell, *Time Chart*.
7 Frazer, *Golden Bough*, 113.
8 Exodus 22:29; II Chronicles 28:3.
9 Tierney, *Highest Altar*, 372; Davies, *Human Sacrifice*, 61.
10 Davies, *Human Sacrifice*, 54-55; Frazer, *Golden Bough*, 182.
11 Frazer, *Golden Bough*, 183.
12 Reeve, *Trials*, viii.
13 Reeve, *Trials*, 86; Parker, *Athenian*, 203.
14 Aristophanes, *Clouds*, 103.
15 Cicero, *Nature of the Gods*, 143.
16 Aristophanes, *Clouds*, 110.
17 Aristophanes, *Clouds*, 112-114.
18 Plato, *Euthyphro*, 7, 22.
19 Plato, *Euthyphro*, 4, 5.
20 Plato, *Euthyphro*, 9, 10.
21 Plato, *Euthyphro*, 11.
22 Plato, *Euthyphro*, 18.
23 Plato, *Euthyphro*, 22.
24 Plato, *Euthyphro*, 23.
25 Plato, *Euthyphro*, 25.
26 Parker, *Athenian*, 201; Copleston, *Philosophy,* 107.
27 Copleston, *Philosophy*, 122-124.
28 Copleston, *Philosophy*, 121.
29 Long, *Socratic*, 633-634; Annas, *Morality*, 227.
30 Copleston, *Philosophy,* 122-123, 408-410; Annas, *Morality*, 229-230, 232, 236.
31 Erler and Schofield, *Epicurean Ethics*, 648; Parker, *Athenian*, 203.
32 Long, *Socratic*, 636, 639, 648; Copleston, *Philosophy*, 404-407, 412; Murray, *Five Stages*, 129.
33 Burkert, *Greek*, 317; Parker, *Athenian*, 200, 206.
34 Burkert, *Greek*, 95, 116; Parker, *Athenian*, 125, 152; Long, *Socratic*, 622;
35 Burkert, *Greek*, 247, 257; Parker, *Athenian*, 211-212; Long, *Socratic*, 619-620; Annas, *Morality,* 228.
36 Poster, *Protagoras*.
37 Burkert, *Greek*, 313, 316.
38 Copleston, *Philosophy*, 96, 114.
39 Reeve, *Trials*, vii.
40 Plato, *Apology*, 28.
41 Plato, *Apology*, 31.
42 Plato, *Apology*, 53.

43 Plato, *Apology*, 55.
44 Plato, *Phaedo*, 82.

Julian

CHAPTER 2

JULIAN VS. AUGUSTINE

Monotheism

Human sacrifice was the worst aspect of European paganism. Paganism had some bright spots, though, chief among them its high level of tolerance for multiple beliefs. If one person had a special devotion to Apollo, and another had a special devotion to Athena, or Yahweh, or some other god, that wasn't a problem. As best scholars can tell, there were no religious wars among the pagans; there was always room for one more god. That tolerance ended with the rise of totalitarian monotheism, which found its ultimate theoretician in Augustine of Hippo. Tolerant polytheism didn't go down without a fight, though. As we will see, if Rome's Emperor Julian had not died (perhaps at the hands of a Christian assassin) at an early age, the Christian totalitarianism of the Middle Ages, with its incessant violence to enforce proper deference to the agents of the One True God, may never have gotten off the ground.

The cloud on the tolerance horizon arose in Persia, sometime before 500 BCE. A God expert there named Zoroaster, who may have been high on a sacred herb called "haoma,"[1] began teaching that there was a god who was supreme over all the others. Zeus was the strongest of the Greek gods, but he was a first among relative equals; Zoroaster's "Ahriman," the creator of the universe, was on another plane altogether.

There was something about monotheism that fed martial ardor: "We fight not just for land or gold; we fight for the supernatural power that controls the universe, which we understand and you don't." Persia's Zoroastrian King Cyrus conquered today's Iraq sometime around 538 BCE, where he found several thousand Jews whose forebears had been captured 50 years earlier. Iraq's Jews were delighted at this turn of events; many of the glowing references in the book of Isaiah to God's "anointed" that Christians claim are prophecies about Jesus are really paeans to Cyrus.

Persia relied on these Jews to govern the often restive Palestine province. The Temple of Jerusalem was rebuilt with Persian money under the guard of Persian soldiers.[2] More importantly, the new governors brought Zoroastrian monotheist ideas with them, and used them to re-work Judaism from the ground up. Previously, worshipers of Yahweh had been as blissfully polytheist as the rest of the world: "God standeth in the congregation of the mighty; he judgeth among the gods." Archeologists have found figurines of a variety of gods and goddesses at Israeli sites from the Old Testament period.[3] In the new Persian-influenced Judaism, though, there was only one god—all the others were fakes. The Persian Jewish governor Ezra edited and assembled older traditions into a single book to go with the new idea of a single god, and coerced the leaders of the community to sign on to it. The resulting "Bible" was a slapdash job, though; it has two creation stories, two flood stories, even two versions of the Ten Commandments.[4]

Lockstep unity worked for a time. The Jews even achieved independence for about a hundred years after Alexander's conquest of Persia, during which time they busied themselves with forcibly converting their neighbors to the true faith. However, they were unable to withstand the power of republican Rome; Pompey breached the walls of Jerusalem in part because many of its Jewish defenders refused to bear arms on the Sabbath.[5]

Judaism prospered mightily under Roman rule. The Temple was rebuilt on a magnificent scale, far larger than Solomon's original. Monotheism's assertion of moral monopoly won increasing numbers of converts; by the first century CE there were about eight million Jews in the world, comprising about 10 percent of the Roman Empire, and widely dispersed through its eastern portion. Even Emperor

Nero's wife may have converted to Judaism. There was another large group of near-converts called the "God-fearers," who were attracted by monotheism but put off by the need for circumcision and adherence to elaborate dietary and other laws.[6]

Wealthy, respected, and poised to become the dominant religion in the world, the Jews had never had it so good. So how did they respond? They rebelled against the evil of toleration of other gods. Several minor revolts were put down without great difficulty in the first half of the century. The major outbreak occurred in years 66-70 CE, resulting in both terrific slaughter and the demolition of the Temple, which had only been completed 40 years earlier.[7]

Christianity

These continued outbreaks were *not* par for the course in the Roman world. Most provinces liked the peace, refinement, toleration, and prosperity the Romans brought, and could not fathom why the Jews caused so many problems.[8] The sudden unpopularity of mainstream Judaism created an opening exploited by the followers of an oddball God expert named Paul.

Paul was a Turkish Jew who sought political advancement in Jerusalem by working as a hit man for the High Priest. The Jewish hierarchy earned a rich living from the enormous new Temple the Romans had helped rebuild, and had little use for heretics—in fact, one of the first acts of the rebels of 66 was to burn the Temple archives so that records of debts would be destroyed.[9] One Jewish sect, the Essenes, expressed disdain for the Temple hierarchs and, instead of participating in the sacrifices that made the Temple tycoons rich, followed the cheaper expedient of washing away sins in the Jordan River. John the Baptist was a leader of this sect; after he was killed, his cousin Jesus seems to have taken over, followed by his brother James, and then another cousin named Simeon. The earliest Christians, all of whom were of Jewish origin, had beliefs and practices closely paralleling those of the Essenes.[10]

Paul's job was to harass and occasionally murder these Jewish Christians, so they would not threaten the supremacy of the High Priest.

For some reason, Paul switched sides; according to Jewish Christian tradition, he became angry when spurned by the High Priest's daughter.[11] The Jewish Christians, though, did not welcome their tormentor with open arms. Now despised by both sides, Paul began traveling through the eastern Mediterranean, inventing a new religion centered on the executed Jesus as he went. Paul's concept took the moral superiority elements of Jewish monotheism and subtracted the objectionable elements of arcane dietary and other laws along with the great bugaboo, circumcision.[12]

Paul's principal headache was the Jewish Christians who had actually known and heard Jesus. They pursued him with "truth squads" to undo what they regarded as outrageous heresy. When he returned to Jerusalem to beseech them to leave him alone, they tried to kill him. For causing so much disorder, he was arrested and dispatched to Rome.[13]

Paul's cult would have been quickly forgotten, but for the effects of the terrible 66-70 war. Jews became reviled throughout the empire; suddenly, it became quite convenient to say "I'm no Jew—I'm a Christian, which is different. The Jews hate us as much as they hate the Romans." The war halted the growth of Judaism in its tracks; Christianity began to grow in its place.

By the end of the third century, the Emperor Diocletian decided that the empire needed to become more unified. The way to accomplish that, he decided, was to impose the worship of a single god, rather than continuing to put up with a multiplicity of followers of Isis, Jesus, Bacchus, etc. who caused nothing but confusion. The god Diocletian settled on was the sun god Mithra, who was especially popular among Roman soldiers. Repression of Christian and other sects ensued, far worse than the sporadic harassment Christianity had suffered heretofore as it grew in wealth and power.[14]

Often what doesn't kill you makes you stronger. Diocletian's efforts did not exterminate Christianity—they bolstered it. So much so that his successor, the Emperor Constantine, decided that if you can't lick 'em, join 'em. He was clever enough, though, to minimize the making of enemies by essentially engrafting Christianity onto the existing Mithraic structure. The result would have been unrecognizable to the original Essenes, rural Jewish fundamentalists who resented the hierarchy for its wealth and cosmopolitanism; but it was a hardy hybrid nonetheless. Many features of Christianity today bear a striking resemblance to those of Mithraism:

- Worshipers of Mithra addressed their God experts as "Father," and Mithraic bishops wore a pointed hat called a "miter," a word deriving from "Mithra."

- The chief Mithraic bishop, known as the "Father of Fathers," lived in Rome, wore a red cap and garment and a ring, and carried a shepherd's staff. A halo, symbolizing the rays of the sun, adorned the head of Mithra the sun-god.

- Mithraic religious celebrations were held on Sunday—the day of the Sun—instead of on the Sabbath observed by the Jewish Christians.

- A religious holiday occurred on December 25 of each year, shortly after days began lengthening, celebrating the birth of the sun god Mithra.

- Another religious holiday occurred on March 25 of each year, shortly after the spring equinox, celebrating the resurrection of Mithra after he had died and spent three days among the deceased souls of Hades. In Rome, the sun god rites were celebrated on Vatican Hill, where St. Peter's Basilica now stands.

- Priests administered a sacrament of communion with Mithra, consisting of bread and water. The Christian Eucharist uses bread and wine. But it was not always so; early Christians in many areas used bread and water, and it took a special statute enacted at the end of the fourth century to put an end to this practice.[15]

Many long-time Christians were appalled: "Meet your new bishop. You may recall him as the fellow who was executing your fellow parishioners a few years back when he was a Mithraic bishop under Diocletian." When large numbers of North African Christians backed an original bishop named Donatus over his Roman replacement, Constantine responded with overwhelming force. The Emperor Julian noted a few years later that "Many whole communities of so-called heretics were actually butchered, as at Samosata, and Cyzicus in Paphlagonia, Bithynia, and Galatia, and among many other tribes villages were sacked and destroyed."[16]

Constantine threw the vast resources of the state behind the new hybrid religion, but did not go so far as to ban paganism altogether. His son Constantius took that step, enacting a ban on pagan sacrifices in 341. The new law sparked Christian vigilantes to crush tolerant paganism by seizing treasure and temples to exact, in the words of one Firmicius Maternus, "vengeance and punishment for this evil."[17]

Julian

To solidify his hold on power, Constantius systematically murdered members of his extended family who might rise to challenge him. But he skipped over a five-year-old cousin named Julian, instead exiling him to a distant estate. As Julian was later to relate, "He put to death six of our cousins, my father who was his uncle, another of our uncles on my father's side and my eldest brother, without trial."[18]

Julian was raised as a Christian. He survived by being non-threatening, burying himself in books. At some point, Julian turned back to paganism—but he prudently kept quiet about it. Constantius, after all, had decreed the death penalty for all who engaged in pagan liturgies–an early step in a long journey of Christian intolerance.[19]

Lulled by Julian's apparent docility, Constantius sent him on a mission to Gaul, a nearly ungovernable province beset by corruption and barbarian incursions. At the ripe old age of 23, Julian excelled; he even recaptured the city of Cologne from its German occupiers. Julian cultivated the key ingredient to success in Roman politics— loyalty of the army—by spurning the perks of a general, sleeping and eating as the common soldiers did.[20]

By January of 360, a paranoid Constantius ordered Julian to send most of his troops back to the east, to join his own command. If Constantius hoped to clip Julian's wings, he failed; Julian's loyal troops instead rose in revolt, and (with little effort) urged their commander to challenge Constantius for the emperorship. Before battle could be joined, Constantius took ill and dropped dead at the age of 44. Julian, now 28, took command as undisputed emperor.[21]

The new emperor was not shy about proclaiming his pagan beliefs. "I worship the gods openly and the whole mass of the troops who are returning with me worship the gods. ... I have offered many great public sacrifices to the gods as thanks offerings. The gods command me to restore their worship in its utmost purity and I obey them."[22]

Julian knew that persecution of Christianity would fail; what it could not abide, though, was competition in a free marketplace of ideas. He was adamant that there should be no physical harassment: "It is by reason that we ought to persuade and instruct men, not by blows or insults or physical violence." The first step was to allow exiled heretics, including the Donatists and a hodgepodge of others, to return, sowing confusion in the Christian ranks. Julian's protégé Ammianus quipped that "No wild beasts are as dangerous to man as one Christian to another." Julian boasted "I have behaved with such kindness and benevolence to all the Galileans that none of them has suffered violence anywhere or been dragged into a temple or threatened into anything else of the sort against his own will."[23]

This drove the Christians batty. Gregory of Nazianzus harrumphed: "He begrudged the honor of martyrdom to our combatants ... He attacks our religion in a very rascally and ungenerous way, and introduces into his persecution the traps and snares concealed in arguments."[24]

Even worse, in Christian eyes, was the benevolence Julian accorded the Jews. Christian loathing for their monotheist rivals was already building; St. John Chrysostom, a contemporary of Julian's whom today's Catholic Encyclopedia calls "the greatest preacher ever heard in a Christian pulpit," taught in his famous "Sermons Against the Jews" that "the Jewish people were driven by their drunkenness and plumpness to the ultimate evil; they kicked about, they failed to accept the yoke of Christ, nor did they pull the plow of his teaching. ... They live for their bellies, they gape for the things of this world, their condition is not better than that of pigs or goats because of their wanton ways and excessive gluttony." Julian ordered the destroyed Jerusalem temple to be rebuilt, in order to enhance spiritual competition to the Christian monopoly, and to challenge Christian prophecies linking its rebuilding to the end of the world.[25]

Though John Milton in a 1644 pamphlet called Julian "the subtlest enemy to our faith," he could be unsubtle as well. He revoked Constantine's tax exemption for the Christian clergy, and revoked as well the judicial powers they had been given, including the power to enforce wills. When someone burned the temple of Apollo in Antioch, he closed the Christian church there in retaliation. Julian ordered Christians to return all the temples and treasure they had stolen from the pagans, and pay to rebuild pagan temples they had destroyed.[26]

Julian's boldest move was in the field of education. He did nothing to ban Christian education; he simply commanded that pagan works should be taught by people who held pagan beliefs, not by Christians who taught that pagan gods were devils. The restriction applied only to teachers, not to students: "For one must, I think, teach, but not punish, the insane." Since most of the world's knowledge at the time consisted of the works of pagans, and no one could advance in life without being familiar with Homer, Plato, *et al.*, this caused an uproar; over time, it would surely have deflated the Christian balloon.[27]

A scholar as well as a tactician, Julian wrote a three-volume anti-Christian treatise called *Against the Galileans*, in which he explains how "the fabrication of the Galileans is a fiction of men, composed by wickedness." Discussing the Ten Commandments, Julian asks: "Except for the commandment 'Thou shalt not worship other gods,' and 'Remember the Sabbath day,' what nation is there, I ask in the name of the gods, which does not think that it ought to keep the other commandments?" Among other things, it criticized the hypocrisy of the Christians for their idolatrous veneration of relics, pointed out inconsistencies in the Bible, and contrasted the church's vicious attacks on heretics with its lip service to forgiveness and love.[28]

Julian also recognized the need to strengthen a pagan faith that had ossified. "So when I saw that we had a great contempt for the gods, and that all piety for the ruling powers has been driven out by impure and vulgar luxury, I always lamented these things to myself. I observed that those devoted to the impious school of the Jews are thus so fired up that they would choose to die for it. ... [W]hile we treat matters relating to the gods carelessly, so that we forget the customs of our forefathers."[29]

They key, he believed, lay in improving the quality of pagan priests. "Any priest who behaves unjustly to his fellow men and impiously toward the gods or is arrogant, must either be given a warning, or be rebuked with great severity," he wrote. "Warn them that no priest may enter a theater, drink in a pub, trade or run a business that is improper and not respectable." He envied the Christian reputation for charity, and sought to compete with it: "I order that one-fifth of [a corn allotment] be used for the poor who serve the priests and the remainder be distributed by us to strangers and beggars. It is disgraceful that when no Jew ever has to beg and the impious Galileans support not only their own poor but ours as well, all men see that our people lack aid from us."[30]

Ending the Christian monopoly was not Julian's only passion. He was also keenly interested in the rule of law, which should govern the ruler as well as the ruled. "Law is reason exempt from desire," he wrote. It behooves an emperor to "behave toward the people and the magistrates like a citizen who obeys the laws. Not like a king who is above the laws." On one occasion, while hearing a case in Antioch, Julian had independent information as to the guilt of the defendant. But when the prosecutor proved too incompetent to bring forward evidence to establish guilt, Julian let the man go; the integrity of the process itself was more important to Julian than the outcome of a particular case. Another time, after committing an error of procedure, Julian fined himself 10 pounds of gold. Montesquieu wrote of Julian that "there has not been a prince since his reign more worthy to govern mankind."[31]

Julian, now known as "the Apostate," accomplished all this in only 20 months. Leading his armies into Persia at the age of 31, he was felled by a spear, apparently from one of his own men. A debate about whether he was deliberately assassinated by a Christian raged for decades afterward; we do know that the Persian king offered a reward to whomever among his men had killed Julian, and no one claimed it. Accurately or not, Christians took credit; a soldier named Mercurius is said to have received a direct order from Jesus Christ to carry out the fragging, which earned him sainthood. According to legend, Julian's last words were "Thou hast won, O Galilean."[32]

Augustine

When Julian died, a North African boy named Augustine was eight years old. His father was a pagan, his mother a Christian; young Augustine joined the Manichean faith, a hodgepodge that included both Mithra and Jesus. Julian's successors re-tightened the screws on non-Christians, though, and at the age of 30 Augustine found it prudent to take up Christianity (though he later claimed that Mithra and Jesus were the same god).[33]

A prolific writer, Augustine wound up as co-bishop of the African city of Hippo.[34] More than anyone else, Augustine is responsible for sweeping away polytheistic *laissez faire* and ushering in the Christian totalitarian worldview of the Middle Ages. The central theme of his 22-volume *City of God* was that Constantine's revolution had enabled the church to take over the state and run a universal divine kingdom here on earth.[35] Led by God experts like himself, Christianity could transform and perfect all existing bonds of human relations, creating a lockstep Christian society. "It is You," he wrote of the church, "who make wives subject to their husbands." He continues:

> You set husbands over their wives; join sons to their parents by a freely-granted slavery, and set parents above their sons in a pious domination. You link brothers to each other by religious bonds tighter than blood. ... You teach slaves to be loyal to their masters. ... You link citizens to citizen, nation to nation. You bind all men together in remembrance of their first parents, not just by social bonds but by common kinship. You

teach kings to rule for the benefit of their people, and warn the peoples to be subservient to their kings."[36]

Properly established, the theocratic state would command the obedience of all men:

> The reply on the side of justice was that the rule over provincials is just, precisely because servitude is the interest of such men, and is established for their welfare when rightly established; that is, when license to do wrong is taken away from wicked men; and that those subdued will be better off, because when not subdued they were worse off. ... Servitude is the interest of some men, and that service, to God at any rate, is the interest of all.[37]

Augustine commanded that everyone must become a Christian—by force, if necessary. Though he frowned on exotic forms of torture, he encouraged beating people with rods until they saw the light.[38] All this was authorized by the Bible. God had used violence when he knocked Paul to the ground and blinded him for three days in order to convert him.[39] Jesus had said "Go out into the highways and hedges, and compel them to come in, that my house may be filled."[40]

Compulsion could be psychological as well. Jesus had very little to say about hell; Augustine luridly filled in the blanks, describing its ferocious flesh-eating animals, which tore humans to bits slowly and painfully, and were themselves undamaged by the fires. God arranged all this in order to give the elect reasons to be grateful for their happy state.[41]

For the church to fulfill the role Augustine planned, it had to be unified. That meant getting rid of the pesky Donatist heretics, who resisted being ordered about by "Christian" bishops who until quite recently had been persecuting Christians. Augustine used military force to teach the Donatists a proper respect for duly constituted authority, at the price of driving many of them to suicide. As he put it: "By the severity, or one might rather say, by the mercy of God, it is common for treachery to be chastised by the scourge of tribulation ...

the fear of punishment keeps the evil desire from escaping beyond the bounds of thought."[42]

Another recurring theme in Augustine's work that paved the way for the backwardness of the Middle Ages was a disdain for scientific research. In his *Enchiridion* or handbook, he taught that there is no need to be "dismayed if Christians are ignorant about the properties and the number of the basic elements of nature, or about the motion, order, and deviations of the stars, the map of the heavens, the kinds and nature of animals, plants, stones, springs, rivers, and mountains. ... For the Christian, it is enough to believe that the cause of all created things ...is ...the goodness of the Creator."[43]

The thirst for knowledge was downright dangerous:

> There is another form of temptation, even more fraught with danger. This is the disease of Curiosity. It is this which drives us to try and discover the secrets of nature, those secrets which are beyond our understanding, which can avail us nothing and which man should not wish to learn.[44]

He firmly censured "the vain and curious desire of investigation, known as knowledge and science."[45]

For some reason, he had a particular distrust of the science of mathematics: "The good Christian should beware of mathematicians ... the danger already exists that the mathematicians have made a covenant with the devil to darken the spirit and to confine man in the bonds of Hell." Far better simply to rely on God experts: "Nothing is to be accepted save on the authority of Scripture, since greater is that authority than all the powers of the human mind."[46]

Another pet peeve of Augustine that he succeeded in elevating to the will of the Almighty was his loathing of sex. "This diabolical excitement of the genitals," as Augustine called it, was evidence of Adam's original sin which is now transmitted "from the mother's womb, tainting all human beings with sin, and leaving them incapable of choosing good over evil or determining their own destiny." Augustine knew whereof he spoke. At the age of 17, he took a concubine, who bore him a son during their 13-year relationship; but he dropped her like a rock the minute his mother found him a rich Christian to marry.[47]

Augustine amplified the teaching of other early Christians that marriage didn't matter that much–sex was sinful regardless, and should be avoided as much as possible even between married partners. Bishop Ambrose of Milan put it succinctly: "Marriage, then, is honorable, but chastity is more honorable. ... That, then, which is good need not be avoided, but that which is better should be chosen."[48]

Disparagement of sex led inexorably to disparagement of women. According to St. Clement of Alexandria, "Every woman should be filled with shame by the thought that she is a woman." Augustine regarded it as a mystery that God should have created the female sex at all. After all, "If it was good company and conversation that Adam needed, it would have been much better arranged to have two men together as friends, not a man and a woman." If there must be women, they must be subject to men: "A husband is meant to rule over his wife as the spirit rules over the flesh."[49]

The rule of one person over another was not limited to the marital relationship. Augustine was a strong advocate of slavery, which of course was sanctioned by the Bible itself: "The condition of slavery is justly imposed on the sinner. Wherefore we do not read of a slave anywhere in the Scriptures until the just man Noah branded his son's sin with this word; so he earned this name by his fault, not by nature." "Listen, slave:" he wrote elsewhere, "do what you are bidden by him who looks after your welfare, who attends to your safety." In practice, Augustine's church became Europe's largest holder of slaves, who were used to cultivate its enormous estates.[50]

The church's adoption of Augustine's totalitarian society was not a foregone conclusion. His worldview had strong competition, notably from a British priest named Pelagius. Pelagius viewed Christianity as a moral force to improve society, helping men and women to become more socially responsible. He emphasized free will, arguing that men and women are perfectly capable of doing good if they so choose. Pelagian religion de-emphasized the supernatural, and emphasized the moral. His stress on personal morality grew quite popular.[51]

Augustine had no use for Pelagius, calling him a "slantyhead" who "waddles like a turtle." He saw in Pelagius a rebellion against the church by undue stress on man's own powers. According to Augustine, the beginning and end of the duty of the Christian was to obey the church, not to be some sort of freelance do-gooder. Salvation, as Augustine saw it, is entirely in God's hands; there is nothing an individual can do. It is only God's grace administered by God's agents, and not any action on the part of the individual, that leads to salvation.[52]

The final straw for Augustine was when he heard that Pelagius, "that corpulent dog, weighed down with Scotch porridge," had denied Augustine's pet doctrine of original sin: that every baby began life as a sinner because of the sin of Adam, and thus needed the intercession of the church to have any chance of salvation. Though Jesus came and went without mentioning original sin, Augustine knew more about God than Jesus did. Besides, without original sin, there was no need for infant baptism; without infant baptism, how do you have a cradle-to-grave authority of the church? "There is no salvation outside the church," he insisted.[53]

As early as 411, Augustine began attacking Pelagianism, and he had it condemned the same year at the Council of Carthage. He pursued Pelagianism relentlessly until its condemnation by Rome, pronounced in 417. A gratified Augustine proclaimed: "Rome has spoken; the matter is settled."[54]

When the civil authorities seemed too soft on Pelagianism, Augustine resorted to bribery, shipping fine Numidian stallions to Roman cavalry commanders while castigating Pelagians as communists who sought to redistribute property. The legions got the message, and proceeded to smash Pelagians in Britain, Spain, Sicily, Rhodes, and Palestine.[55] Augustine's conception of monotheist totalitarianism, the culmination of Zoroaster's drug-induced vision of a thousand years earlier, dominated Europe for the next thousand years.

Some historians, including Edward Gibbon in his *Decline and Fall of the Roman Empire*, blame Christianity for weakening the Roman Empire to the point where it could be overwhelmed by barbarians.

That is endlessly debatable; what is not debatable is that when Augustine died, 70 years after Julian, he was in hiding while the Vandals were overrunning his portion of the empire.

Some observers today bemoan (or celebrate) the fact that America is reverting to a more polytheistic religious atmosphere, a cafeteria-style spirituality in which individuals pick and choose for themselves from among a smorgasbord of beliefs and values rather than dutifully obeying the God experts of their parents. One scholar quips that we are becoming a nation of "310 million people with 310 million religions."[56] Julian would have loved this; Augustine would have hated it. One of the bigger "what-ifs" of history is "What if Julian had died at 71 rather than at 31?" Would Augustine's Christian monopoly of Europe have been achieved at all? Would science and research have been stifled for a thousand years, or would the free play of ideas Julian encouraged have brought about the scientific revolution of the Enlightenment that much sooner? Would the shock to the conscience of slavery and the subjection of women have survived so long without a regard for the inerrancy of the Bible to prop them up? We don't know—but we can guess.

> Having "310 million religions" is an exaggeration, but do you see any significant difference between that state of affairs and having a religious monopoly (as in Augustine's *City of God*), or an oligopoly of a handful of principal religions as in 19th century America? Share your thoughts on this and the other questions you'll find at **dgc.humanistpress.com**!

Notes:

1 Gillooly, *Adam and Eve*, 73.
2 Johnson, *Jews*, 86.
3 Albright, *Stone Age*, 311.
4 Nehemiah 8:1-3; I Maccabees 9:27; Johnson, *Jews*, 87-93; Walsh, *Role of Religion*, 53; Armstrong, *God*, 54; Fohrer, *Israelite Religion*, 358-359; Genesis 1; Genesis 2:4-7; Exodus 20:1-17; Deuteronomy 5:6-18; Alward, *Flood Stories*.
5 Johnson, *Christianity*, 9, 107.

6 Cate, *Interbiblical Period*, 116, 146; *Encyclopaedia Judaica*, vol.13, 870-871; Johnson, *Jews*, 11, 132.

7 Holman Bible Dictionary, *The Egyptian*; Cate, *Interbiblical Period*, 37-40,151-157.

8 Johnson, *Jews*, 117.

9 Acts 22:4; Johnson, *Jews*, 137.

10 Ellegård, *Jesus*, 169; Armstrong, *God*, 80; Akers, *Lost Religion*, 41-42, 178.

11 Maccoby, *Mythmaker*, 182.

12 Galatians 2:16; Galatians 3:10; Galatians 5:2.

13 Acts 15:1; Acts 21:23-26; Acts 28:14.

14 Grant, *Constantine*, 128; Geffcken, *Last Days*, 33.

15 Psychic Investigator, *Mithras*; Wynne-Tyson, *Mithras*, 66; Walker, *Woman's Encyclopedia*, 155, 665; Weigall, *Paganism*, 123, 155.

16 Johnson, *Christianity*, 86.

17 Geffcken, *Last Days*, 121.

18 Murdoch, *Last Pagan*, 14, 17.

19 Murdoch, *Last Pagan*, 14, 24, 27; Tougher, *Julian*, 54.

20 Murdoch, *Last Pagan*, 38, 49-50. Tougher, *Julian*, 34.

21 Murdoch, *Last Pagan*, 76, 94.

22 Murdoch, *Last Pagan*, 95.

23 Tougher, *Julian*, 56. Murdoch, *Last Pagan*, 134-135; Geffcken, *Last Days*, 141-142.

24 Tougher, *Julian*, 123.

25 Chrysostom, *Homilies*; Tougher, *Julian*, 8, 158.

26 Geffcken, *Last Days*, 143-145; Murdoch, *Last Pagan*, 7, 126-127, 134.

27 Tougher, *Julian*, 57, 93; Geffcken, *Last Days*, 145-146.

28 Geffcken, *Last Days*, 153; Murdoch, *Last Pagan*, 132-133.

29 Tougher, *Julian*, 91.

30 Murdoch, *Last Pagan*, 140-141; Tougher, *Julian*, 58.

31 Murdoch, *Last Pagan*, 105-106, 210; Tougher, *Julian*, 49.

32 Murdoch, *Last Pagan*, 2, 188, 190.

33 Encyclopedia Britannica, *St. Augustine*; Walker, *Woman's Encyclopedia*, 664.

34 Wills, *St. Augustine*, 81.

35 Johnson, *Christianity*, 113.

36 Johnson, *Christianity*, 115.

37 Garnsey, *Ideas of Slavery*, 38.

38 Johnson, *Christianity*, 116.

39 Acts 9:4-8.

40 Luke 14:23.

41 Johnson, *Christianity*, 341; MacCulloch, *Reformation*, 244.

42 Daniel-Rops, *Dark Ages*, 30; Johnson, *Christianity*, 115; Peters, *Inquisition*, 23.

43 Lindberg, *Christian Attitudes*, 51-52.

44 Dawkins, *God Delusion*, 132.

45 Walker, *Woman's Encyclopedia*, 345.

46 Gillooly, *Adam and Eve*, 99.

47 Ellerbe, *Dark Side*, 31; Johnson, *Christianity*, 113; Catholic Encyclopedia, *Adeodatus*.

48 Walker, *Woman's Encyclopedia*, 911; Johnson, *Christianity*, 108; Ambrose of Milan, *Treatise on Widows*, paragraph 72.

49 Ellerbe, *Dark Side*, 7, 114; Armstrong, *God*, 124.

50 Garnsey, *Ideas of Slavery*, 216, 232; Berkhofer, *Slavery*, 555.

51 Johnson, *Christianity*, 118; Daniel-Rops, *Dark Ages*, 31. Catholic Encyclopedia, *Pelagius and Pelagianism*.

52 Wills, *St. Augustine*, 123; Johnson, *Christianity*, 119; Ellerbe, *Dark Side*, 31.

53 Johnson, *Christianity*, 119; Daniel-Rops, *Dark Ages*, 26.

54 Daniel-Rops, *Dark Ages*, 32.

55 Johnson, *Christianity*, 120.

56 Miller, *Hindus*; Colson, "Do It Yourself Religion."

Han Yü

CHAPTER 3

HAN YÜ VS. HSIEN-TSUNG

Confucianism

Julian is noteworthy for his tolerance, but not for his lack of belief in the divine, nor for any notions of separation of church and state. Our next hero, several thousand miles to Julian's east, stood up for the humanist ideals of Confucianism against a politician who put the government at the service of powerful Buddhist God experts.

The earliest forms of religion in China were similar to those found on the rest of the planet. There were multiple gods, magic and sacrifice to end drought, disease, childlessness, and other ills, and an identification of the civil ruler with divinity. Much of this religion survives today, loosely under the rubric of "Taoism."[1]

Eighty years before Socrates, the leading figure of Chinese humanism was born in today's province of Shantung. Confucius arrived at a time of turbulence, when a fractured China suffered from endless feudal wars and famines. Orphaned at an early age, Confucius worked at state-owned parks and granaries while he pursued his self-education. Confucius had no interest in founding a religion or in promoting Taoist superstition; he was a humanist reformer, a self-taught scholar keenly interested in expounding the virtues, both personal and societal, that would result in a more orderly and compassionate world.[2]

Confucius' philosophy centered on:

• Endless striving for self-improvement through study, self-examination, and the giving and receiving of constructive criticism.

• Emphasis on *li*, a Chinese word best translated as "appropriateness." Confucius paid great attention to ritual, not because he believed that adherence to form produced magic effects, but because it conditioned people to the idea of taking proper actions under varying circumstances–somewhat like military drills condition raw recruits into the habit of following officers' orders in the heat of battle.

• Reliance on merit, rather than accident of birth or brute force, as qualification for government service. This seems commonplace today, but in the time of Confucius the implications were enormous–and highly threatening to the establishment.

• Benevolent cooperation, as among members of a well-functioning family, as the guiding principle for organization of society. A good family may be a dictatorship in form, but is flexible and democratic in practice; each member fulfills his or her function, while genuinely caring for the wishes and well-being of the other members, and occasionally letting the children stay up after bedtime.

• Complete disinterest in the supernatural. Confucius did not deny the gods, and he found the observation of rituals including sacrifices to promote good order. But he claimed no divine origin for his teaching, and no special insight into matters of the gods; when asked once about the afterlife, he responded "Not knowing life, how can we know death?"[3]

Confucius badly wanted to win important government office, so that he could put his ideas into practice. In this effort he failed, largely because he lacked aptitude for brownnosing. He died a failure in his own mind, never having been appointed to more than a powerless sinecure. Confucius left behind a devoted following, though, whose members played a key role in the emergence of the powerful Han Dynasty around 200 BCE. The early Han leadership, heavily influenced by the Confucians, created a golden age in China rivaling that of any other civilization in the world.[4] Though we will see in Chapter 6 how later ages perverted the Confucian ideal, the Han system of examinations open to all, with advancement based on demonstrated merit rather than noble birth, had no parallel elsewhere until the European Enlightenment two thousand years later.

Buddhism

At about the same time that Confucius was filtering out the supernatural and concentrating on how humans can best get along with one another, another thinker to the west was taking a rather opposite tack. We think. Humanists today emphasize how little accurate information we have about Jesus and Muhammad, correctly noting that the earliest reports we have were written many decades after the supposed dates of their deaths. Next to the Buddha, though, our picture of Jesus and Muhammad is practically a live webcam—the first biography of any kind was written more than *600 years* after Buddha is supposed to have died. We truly do not have the slightest idea whether this person ever existed, or if he did exist, what he said and did. The description here is thus the legend, not the actual facts.[5]

Supposedly, Siddhartha Gautama was born around 560 BCE, son of a wealthy Hindu prince of Nepal. Sheltered as a boy, he was shocked when he first snuck outside the palace compound and witnessed human misery. For reasons not entirely clear, this experience drove him to try to become miserable himself. After a six-month fast, he sat down under a ficus tree to await illumination. An evil spirit came to him, urging him to give up the fast and get on with life. The spirit's words backfired, though, because they inspired Gautama to the brainstorm that the desire to get on with life was exactly the problem. Instead, he received enlightenment about the nature of suffering, which he framed as the "Four Noble Truths," one of which was the "Eightfold Path." The attainment of this knowledge led his followers to call Gautama "The Awakened One," or the "Buddha."[6]

The gist of Gautama's teaching was simple: life is full of suffering, and the root cause of suffering is wanting things we cannot have, at least not for very long. The idea is not to figure out how to do a better job of getting what we want, but to figure out how to stop wanting things in the first place; then you aren't so disappointed when you don't get them.[7]

Raised as a Hindu, Gautama accepted reincarnation into some novel form of misery as a given. The law of getting what one deserved was inexorable; if a one-day old infant died a painful death, it had to be because he or she had misbehaved in a previous life. The real goal, therefore, was to break out of the cycle altogether by achieving a level of enlightenment such that all desires cease; this "blowing out" of desire was called nirvana. After 40 years of teaching people how to extinguish their miserable lives as thoroughly as possible, Gautama died at the age of 80.[8]

The Buddhist antipathy to "craving" stifled the advancement of human knowledge and the improvement of the human condition. Buddhists taught that the whole sphere of human activity was a great evil, best dealt with by complete abandonment. The most respected Buddhists were the monks who withdrew from life in society altogether, at someone else's expense.[9]

Like Christianity, Buddhism grew slowly on its own, and did not really take off until a secular ruler decided to promote it long after the founder's death. Five hundred years before Constantine, an Indian prince named Asoka fought a number of bloody wars to extend his power from parts of today's Iran all the way to Bangladesh, and most of India's southern peninsula as well. Once he reached the top of the heap, he decided it would be a good idea to spread the Buddhist doctrine of absence of desire throughout his empire; what could be better calculated to keep people docile and uninterested in rebellion? Docility was also to be encouraged in neighboring lands. Asoka sent out missionaries, first to Sri Lanka, then to the rest of Asia, including southern China. Like the Christians, he put a special emphasis on the worship of body parts or other objects associated with Gautama, building (according to one legend) some 84,000 temples to honor them.[10]

Just as Christianity largely disappeared from the place of its birth only to thrive in Rome, Buddhism largely disappeared from India after Asoka's death, but gained a new lease on life in China. When the Han dynasty collapsed in the third century CE, China reverted to the state of permanent civil war that had characterized Confucian times.[11]

Chaos was the perfect environment for the rise of Chinese Buddhism. Outs looking to become ins sought to differentiate themselves as much as possible from the *ancien régime,* which meant among other things promoting an alternative to Confucian orthodoxy. One critical tipping point occurred when a Buddhist missionary to the north used a "miracle" magic trick (making a lotus blossom appear in a bowl of water after saying a spell over it) to impress Lo, the new Hun chieftain of most of north China. For the next 20 years, Lo spread Buddhism throughout his domain.[12]

In a world of disorder and violence, the solace offered by tuning out reality and attempting not to crave material comfort that was now difficult to attain had enhanced appeal. It was easy for Buddhists to argue that Confucianism, which promised nothing other than a better life here on earth, had failed; it was tougher for the Confucians to demonstrate that the Buddhist promise of better times in the next life would fail as well.[13]

Many local warlords promoted Buddhism for quite practical reasons. Confucianism stressed that sons should respect their parents by staying home and working the land. It was above all things a philosophy of peace, not conducive to the recruitment of armies of conquest. By contrast, Buddhists made terrific soldiers. The privations of war were easy to endure for those who craved nothing in this life and concentrated exclusively on moving up a step in the next. Constant propaganda from Buddhist God experts in pay of the state that the best way to do that would be to die the most heroic of deaths in battle had the expected effect (just as it did for Japanese Buddhists in World War II).[14]

Either by amazing coincidence or by some long-distance cross-fertilization, Chinese Buddhism and European Christianity developed quite a few similar features at about the same time: prayer and fasting, renunciation of the world, salvation of the soul, an afterlife of reward and punishment, temples and images, pilgrimages and penances, tonsure and beads, candles and incense, gorgeous vestments, shrines and relics, the chanting of liturgical services, the intercession of saints, baptism, and even special devotion to the mother of the divinity, called "Maya" by the Buddhists.[15]

Buddhism even offered the promise of a messiah. The jolly fat fellow in the little Buddha statues is not Gautama, but Maitreya, a future Buddha, who will come someday to preside over a new and better age.[16]

Buddhism Ascendant

The most important common idea, though, was that of vicarious salvation. The vast majority of the people had to devote their waking hours to farming or other work in order to survive; they had no time to lose themselves in the meditation necessary to achieve a better next life. To the rescue came a class calling itself the "Bodhisattvas": men who were holy enough to enter nirvana, but who selflessly held back at the threshold, so they could instead help others to move up a level or two. As the famed Bodhisattva Sāntideva put it: "May I become an unfailing store for the wretched and be first to supply them with the manifold things of their need. My own self and my pleasures, all my righteousness, past, present, and future, I sacrifice without regard, in order to achieve the welfare of all beings."[17]

Gautama (or at least the earliest works about Gautama) hadn't really said anything about the role of Bodhisattvas, so it became necessary to forge collections of his sayings, in popular Chinese style, to justify what he certainly *would have* taught, had he only thought about it.[18]

Bodhisattvas congregated in vast monasteries, similar to those of Christianity, where they could concentrate their energies on uplifting the souls of their benefactors. Thus they could all march into ultimate nirvana together. At a monastery, sinners could purchase pardon, either for cash or through works of piety. There was even a Buddhist procedure for confession of sins, like the Christian sacrament of penance.[19]

Celibacy was (at least officially) practiced at Buddhist monasteries, sometimes aided by self-mutilation. This was a further irritant to the Confucians, who regarded celibacy as unnatural and anti-family. Buddhist monks enjoyed a status far superior to that of nuns, who were required to stand and bow upon the approach of any monk without regard to relative seniority or rank. The Buddha was reported to have taught that "It is impossible, and it cannot come to pass that a woman perfected can become a fully self-awakened one." The ideal a woman could strive for was rebirth as a man.[20]

As in Europe, the monasteries enjoyed a symbiotic relationship with the earthly powers. Emperors and nobles provided land, money, and slaves; the monasteries taught the people to revere the ruling house. The emperor, Buddhists explained, is the progeny of "the true dragon Son of Heaven," whose personal conduct could be either auspicious or disastrous for his domain.[21] Knowing where their bread was buttered, the monks allowed the civil authorities broad power not only over clerical appointments and temple procedures, but even over core doctrines such as the curriculum of Buddhist schools, the classification of certain doctrines as heresy, and the promotion, demotion, or attribute-assignment of individual gods.[22]

Monasteries grew steadily in wealth and power. The sixth century Chinese Emperor Wu made a practice of periodically "giving himself" to a particular monastery, and then requiring his ministers and nobles to "ransom" him with enormous gifts. Other wealthy Chinese competed with each other in the extravagance of their donations, a form of conspicuous consumption with the added benefit of accumulating brownie points toward future salvation. As permanent economic institutions akin to modern corporations, monasteries invested in water mills, oil presses, money lending, and manufacturing in ways that individual entrepreneurs could not match. Often they came to control entire villages or clusters of villages, whose people became hereditary serfs of the monastery.[23]

With wealth came privilege. Monasteries and their residents were exempt from conscription, exempt from taxes, and exempt from the corvée system of forced labor imposed on those without the cash to pay their tax.[24]

A life of devotion and ease in a temple set amidst lovely scenery had enormous appeal, even aside from what it might do for one's afterlife. Donation (sometimes real, sometimes fraudulent) of land to monasteries to escape the land tax was also a common practice.[25] Some monks came to regard their enlightened selves as superior to civil rulers, and refused to kowtow to them as other subjects did. After all, they wouldn't even be monks unless they had lived exemplary former lives, and they had power over future afterlives far greater than any earthly prerogative a mere emperor enjoyed.[26]

The controversy over whether the monks should pay homage to the emperor lasted for nearly four centuries. The Tang Emperor Gaozong's edict ultimately exempted clerics from the obligation of performing ceremonious acts toward the emperor. Having won this victory, monks were known to speak disparagingly of crass worldly rulers who lacked their own inner merit.[27]

The privileges and arrogance of the Buddhist elite were too much for some emperors to bear. The loss of productivity of hundreds of thousands of able-bodied men and women, the removal of vast tracts of land from the tax base, and the investment of huge sums to construct sacred objects and buildings were bad enough; but having these parasites look down their noses at the emperor himself crossed the line.[28]

The first official actions against the Buddhists were taken by the northern Emperor Taiwu in 438, banning all persons under the age of 50 from becoming monks or nuns. A few years later, after discovering Buddhist weapons caches, he had 11 monks executed. On a roll, the following year he ordered that all Buddhist temples be destroyed, all Buddhist scriptures burned, and that "all priests, young or old, be buried alive." Bureaucrats dragged their feet in carrying out this order until Taiwu died, though, and his successor relented.[29]

In the next century, a northern emperor commissioned a series of debates among Taoists, Confucians, and Buddhists on the relative merits of their beliefs, from which (in his mind) emerged a clear winner: "Confucianism must be ranked first because it represented the traditional ideology of the land," with Taoism ranking second and Buddhism a distant third. The following year, he banned both Buddhism and Taoism and authorized the complete destruction of their scriptures and images. Although the figure may be exaggerated, one chronicler insists that 40,000 temples were confiscated by the state at this time.[30]

Han Yü and the Bone

The most dramatic confrontation between Confucian humanists and Buddhist God experts occurred early in the ninth century. Han Yü, born as a peasant in 768, was a talented writer and administrator who passed his examinations and rose steadily through the ranks of Chinese government–exactly as Confucius had in mind. In 809, he was assigned to supervise the Buddhist monasteries in the capital, a task he pursued with a zeal that made him quite unpopular. One chronicler wrote that "By expelling unworthy monks, regulating their activities, and forbidding noisy assemblies, he put the Buddhists in order!" In a report to his superior, Han Yü wrote that his duties "have brought me into daily conflict ... they wait for me to make a mistake, utter calumnies and slander against me, and create disorder among the official documents." He requested an investigation, but instead was transferred to the magistracy of Honan county.[31]

The new assignment did not end his conflict with the Buddhist clergy. When he discovered local officials engaged in a lucrative trade of selling ordination certificates to persons far more interested in the monastic tax exemption than in the Eightfold Path, he had them arrested and flogged. He was transferred again, but this time moved up to the position of imperial palace secretary in the capital, with direct access to the emperor himself. There he advocated a firm though unpopular stand against rebels to the north. He walked the walk as well as talking the talk, participating in a military campaign that proved quite successful.[32]

A triumphant Han Yü, now age 50, was awarded the important post of vice-president of the Ministry of Justice, and lived at the center of the cabinet surrounding Emperor Hsien-tsung that actually ran the government.[33] Life was good. Unfortunately for Han Yü, his humanist common sense got him in a world of trouble.

The source of Han Yü's catastrophe was, of all things, a human finger-bone. Like the Christians to the west, Buddhists regarded relics as having powerful magic, and a finger-bone that was thought to be Gautama's was the number one relic in the land.[34] (Even in this century, Buddha relics rake in the bucks; 60,000 donors contributed $30 million to build a temple in Singapore to house an object purported to be Gautama's tooth, even though dental experts who have examined it are certain that it is the tooth of a cow or a water buffalo.[35] In Han Yü's day, a Japanese monk named Ennin recorded in his journal that "People tossed cash like rain toward the storied hall of the Buddha's tooth."[36]) The fanatical Empress Wu had encased this particular finger-bone in a gold and silver reliquary in 660, and devout Buddhists were known to express their piety by burning off their own fingers in its honor. In 742, another emperor responded to an insurrection by bringing the finger-bone to the palace, where it could be worshipped 24/7 by several hundred monks. They chanted with such energy that a minister was forced to complain they were disturbing residents outside the palace walls.[37]

In 819, the Emperor Hsien-tsung decided to bring the finger-bone to the palace once again. Whether he did so because of genuine personal devotion, a desire to appease his Buddhist subjects, or a baser desire to line the pockets of the local Buddhist clergy is not entirely clear. He was not known as a fanatical Buddhist; he was simply a politician, of the type we will see repeatedly in subsequent chapters, anxious to reap short-term gain by caving in to the wishes of the prevailing God expert class without a thought for the long-term disadvantages of having civil government honor superstition over common sense. In any case, he created a sensation. A rash of bodily mutilation broke out, and the local economy was disrupted as peasants abandoned their farms and poured into the capital.[38]

Han Yü was appalled. He was not the only humanist who thought this circus a disgrace, but he was the only one courageous (or foolish) enough to say so publicly. In an open letter to the emperor, the eloquence of which shines through even today, he minced no words:

> Now one hears that Your Majesty has ordered monks to welcome a bone of Buddha at Feng-hsiang and is preparing to watch from a tower its entry into the palace. Moreover, every monastery has been ordered to reverence it in turn. Although

your servant is most ignorant, even he certainly knows Your Majesty is not so deluded about Buddhism that you would worship this relic to seek blessings. Rather, because this is a year of prosperity and happiness, you accord with the people's wishes in allowing the population of the capital this weird and perverse spectacle. For how could a sage intelligence as yours believe in this?

The minds of ordinary people, however, are easy to mislead but difficult to enlighten. They see Your Majesty acting in this manner, they will think you are really worshiping the Buddha. All will say, 'If the Son of Heaven, a great sage, believes with all his heart, then how can we ordinary people begrudge our bodies and our lives?' Thus, they will cauterize their scalps and burn off their fingers, by the tens and the hundreds they will throw off their clothes and disperse their wealth, and from dawn to dusk they will follow each other in fear of being left behind. Old and young in restless waves will discard their trades and professions and if they are not immediately stopped, will go from monastery to monastery cutting off their arms and mutilating their bodies as a form of sacrifice! Such immoral behavior, which will make us a laughing stock to the world, is not a trifling matter. ...

Should [Gautama] be alive and come to court as an envoy of his country, Your Majesty would admit him and grant a single audience in the reception hall, a single banquet, and a single suit of clothing. He would then be escorted to the border and not be allowed to delude the multitudes. ... Given that he has been dead for such a long time, how is it possible that this rotten and decayed bone, this evil and filthy relic, is allowed to enter the private apartments of the palace? ...

I am deeply ashamed. I entreat you to hand this bone over to the proper authorities so it can be thrown into fire and water so that it be destroyed forever, ending the world's confusion and halting the delusions of future generations.[39]

He further traced the history of emperors who supported Buddhism, noting that their reigns were generally short; of one particular predecessor, he concluded that "In the end he was driven out and died of hunger. His dynasty likewise came to an untimely end. In serving the Buddha he was seeking good fortune, but the disaster that overtook him was only the greater. Viewed in the light of this, it is obvious that the Buddha is not worth serving."[40]

What Han Yü was really arguing for would today be called "the separation of church and state." Civil government should stick to its basic duties, and not encourage "the delusions of future generations." There is little discernible difference between honoring a finger-bone by displaying it in the palace and honoring a crucifix by displaying it on public land.

Compared to modern political diatribe, this all seems pretty tame. In 819, it was the equivalent of peeing on the emperor's shoes. Emperor Hsien-tsung's response was instant: Han Yü must be put to death.[41]

Only with the most valiant efforts did Han Yü's former comrades in arms persuade Hsien-tsung that Han Yü had meant well, that he was only trying to look out for the emperor's interests, that he had given a lifetime of tireless service to the state, and that—well, everyone is entitled to one mistake. (It is doubtful whether anyone tried arguing that Han Yü was actually right.) Finally, the emperor's resolve was worn down, and Han Yü's life was spared. However, Hsien-tsung never wanted to see Han Yü or hear his cutting truth again. Han Yü was banished from the pinnacle of power to a minor position in the remotest of China's provinces.

Han Yü had to have been a shrewd operator to go from farm boy to mover and shaker. How could he have made such a colossal blunder? It is difficult enough to isolate a cause for things that happened last week in the full glare of television, much less events that occurred 1200 years ago where only scraps of evidence remain. A theory that connects the facts relates to a poem Han Yü wrote a decade before his fall from grace:

The reason I like to drink is to write poems waiting to get high.

The wine has a delicate clear taste and a good strong bouquet.

Our spirits slowly turn boundless, till laughter and joking and poems are everywhere.

This really gets at the idea of wine, anything else is just being rowdy. ...

Now I and my several friends are really all about equally matched.

Rough words that terrify even ghosts, exalted diction that matches the Three Emperors.

The best treasures need no refining.[42]

So maybe he was drunk. *In vino veritas.*

Far worse was yet to come. Han Yü had to depart immediately, his family to follow his arduous trek a few weeks later. The light of Han Yü's life, his 11-year old daughter Han Na, was ill when the grueling 2,500 mile journey began, and succumbed along the way. When he ultimately reached her grave, Han Yü poured out his grief:

Strands of vine bound round the tree-bark coffin rudely in-terred in desolate hills. Your white bones cold. Panic pierced your heart, your palanquin carried down the road whose hard-ships were known to all. ... Thus did my crimes bring you guiltless to this. And for me a hundred years of shame, re-morse, and tears.[43]

Shattered by his daughter's death, Han Yü took up the cause of ending child slavery at his new outpost in Yüan-chou. It was com-mon practice in that region to pledge children as collateral for loans; if payments were missed, the child became a slave–as Han Yü put it, "being whipped and flogged and finding no rest until death." By far the largest slaveholders and money-lenders were the Buddhist mon-asteries, just as the Christian monasteries were the major slaveholders of Europe. Han Yü personally intervened to free 731 children in his jurisdiction. After Hsien-tsung died a year later and Han Yü was allowed to return to the capital, he petitioned the new emperor to put an end to this evil.[44]

After Han Yü

Han Yü died four years after returning to the capital, and like his role model Confucius he may have thought himself a failure.[45] Yet, like Confucius, he had a following, that two decades later exacted revenge. When the Emperor Wu-tsung took power in 840, he went after Buddhism with a vengeance:

> On matters of due reverence and support they abandon both ruler and parents; on the basis of prohibitions and command-ments they transgress against their spouses. No other religion surpasses this one in wrecking the laws and injuring humans. Furthermore, if a single man does not plow, someone will be hungry because of it; if one single woman does not weave, someone will be cold because of it. Now, there are numberless monks and nuns in the empire, but they all feed while relying on others to farm, and they clothe themselves while relying on others to weave. Monasteries, temples and all living quarters reflect the ignorance of any rules or regulations. Their elabo-rate designs and ornamentations indicate their pretension to imperial palaces and halls.[46]

When a courtier made the mistake of offering Wu-tsung two Bud-dhist scrolls, he received a scathing dose of imperial rage:

> But he is drowned in evil doctrines, which stir up depraved customs. He has opened the door to delusions and has gone completely against the doctrines of the sages. How deep is the depravity among those of high office! ... Why should foreign religions be propagated? We should like to overlook [his of-fense], but this may do injury to public morality. He is to be demoted, and We are still to be called magnanimous [in doing this].[47]

To be sure, Wu-tsung was motivated less by Confucian humanist ideals and more by a xenophobic preference for "Chinese" Taoism over "foreign" Buddhism.[48] He died at age 31 after consuming a magical Taoist elixir for good health–quite a few emperors were poisoned this way.[49] His attack on Buddhism was certainly egged on by humanists inspired by Han Yü, though, even though they declined his call to take up Taoism. Over 50,000 Buddhist monasteries were dismantled, and a quarter of a million ostensible monks and nuns were required to return to the world of work–though many of them turned to crime instead. Even more importantly, Wu-tsung freed some 150,000 slaves who supported these parasites, while returning millions of acres of fertile land to taxable status. The Japanese pilgrim Ennin reported that giving or receiving contributions in honor of the Buddha's fingerbone became punishable by 20 lashes.[50]

Wu-tsung crowed:

> Alas that this was never done before! It appears to have waited for Us to do. How could it be called untimely that We have at last wiped them out? We have driven away the lazy and idle fellows to a number of more than ten millions. We have done away with their gorgeous but useless buildings to a number not less than a myriad. Thenceforth, purity will guide the people, who will esteem Our effortless rule. Simplicity will be Our policy, which will achieve the merits of a common culture.[51]

Wu-tsung's successors swung the pendulum massively back toward Buddhism. In particular, the Emperor I-tsung not only returned the finger-bone to the palace but exhausted the state treasury on a massive re-Buddhification program of monastery-building and monk ordination, neglecting his day-to-day work while lost in prayer. I-tsung's religious excess broke the back of the Tang dynasty. His death was followed by a decade of civil war, during which rebels systematically completed the destruction of monasteries Wu-tsung had begun. What is sometimes called a "Confucian Renaissance" characterized the Sung Dynasty that followed, with an abandonment of mystical otherworldliness for a humanist focus on the needs of this world: public clinics, hostels for the aged, and homes for orphans, which was ended only by the Mongol invasion of the thirteenth century.[52]

Am I too hard on Buddhism? Or too soft? Share your thoughts on this and the other questions you'll find at **dgc.humanistpress.com!**

Notes:

1 Wright, *Buddhism*, 32; Barrett, *Taoism,* 16.

2 Messadié, *Devil,* 63.

3 Clennell, *Religion in China,* 47.

4 Creel, *Confucius,* 3, 234.

5 Skilton, *Buddhism,* 20; Messadié, *Devil,* 44; Yamamoto, *Eastern Religions,* 7.

6 Yamamoto, *Eastern Religions,* 7-8; Messadié, *Devil,* 43; Basham, *Hinduism,* 60.

7 Walsh, *Role of Religion,* 35.

8 Basham, *Hinduism,* 60; Clennell, *Religion in China,* 93; Yamamoto, *Eastern Religions,* 9, 30.

9 Clennell, *Religion in China,* 103.

10 Basham, *Hinduism,* 68; Messadié, *Devil,* 65; Yu, *State and Religion,* 91.

11 Clennell, *Religion in China,* 93.

12 Wright, *Buddhism,* 31, 57; Yu, *State and Religion,* 86.

13 Clennell, *Religion in China,* 93; Wright, *Buddhism,* 25.

14 Wright, *Buddhism,* 75.

15 Clennell, *Religion in China,* 113; Reischauer, *Ennin,* 177.

16 Wright, *Buddhism,* 82.

17 Armstrong, *God,* 84; Wright, *Buddhism,* 93.

18 Wright, *Buddhism,* 81.

19 Walsh, *Role of Religion,* 39; Clennell, *Religion in China,* 96; Gillooly, *Adam and Eve,* 95.

20 Mather, *Conflict of Buddhism,* 135; Yu, *State and Religion,* 97; Crandall, *Gender,* 62.

21 Wright, *Buddhism,* 58; Yu, *State and Religion,* 108.

22 Yu, *State and Religion,* 111; Wright, *Buddhism,* 99.

23 Wright, *Buddhism,* 51, 52, 59.

24 Wright, *Buddhism,* 60.

25 Wright, *Buddhism,* 53, 60.

26 Mather, *Conflict of Buddhism*, 133-134; Walsh, *Role of Religion*, 39.

27 Yu, *State and Religion*, 105, 111.

28 Mather, *Conflict of Buddhism*, 132.

29 Yu, *State and Religion*, 119; Mather, *Conflict of Buddhism*, 132.

30 Yu, *State and Religion*, 121.

31 Hartman, *Han Yü*, 20, 56, 73, 74.

32 Hartman, *Han Yü*, 75, 80, 83.

33 Hartman, *Han Yü*, 83.

34 Clennell, *Religion in China*, 98.

35 Deutsche Presse Agentur, "Experts Claim."

36 Reischauer, *Ennin*, 190.

37 Weinstein, *Buddhism*, 46, 58.

38 Weinstein, *Buddhism*, 102-103.

39 Mather, *Conflict of Buddhism*, 165.

40 Reischauer, *Ennin*, 222.

41 Hartman, *Han Yü*, 85.

42 Hartman, *Han Yü*, 70.

43 Hartman, *Han Yü*, 101.

44 Hartman, *Han Yü*, 93, 102.

45 Hartman, *Han Yü*, 114.

46 Yu, *State and Religion*, 123.

47 Reischauer, *Ennin*, 243.

48 Reischauer, *Ennin*, 29.

49 Weinstein, Buddhism, 136; Clennell, *Religion in China*, 120.

50 Reischauer, *Ennin*, 242, 246, 270; Yu, *State and Religion*, 126.

51 Reischauer, *Ennin*, 227.

52 Clennell, *Religion in China*, 132; Wright, *Buddhism*, 90-94.

Umayyad philosopher Ibn Rushd

CHAPTER 4

UMAYYAD VS. HASHIMITE

Barbarians from the South

Unlike most of the other chapters that pair two individuals, this is the story of two competing royal dynasties, with sharply differing views on the proper role of God experts in society. The winners of this struggle gave us most of what is wrong with Islam today. The losers gave Europe a fleeting vision of what a tolerant, secular, knowledge-hungry humanist society could look like.

There is an elaborate Muslim legend about the birth of Islam, almost all of which is demonstrably false. If you've heard something in popular culture about Islam's origins, please put it out of your mind, and make room for some facts.

The Arabian Peninsula south of Palestine was never conquered by the Roman Empire. A Roman expedition attempted once to capture Yemen, but failed. The Romans most likely could have conquered Arabia if they had tried, but it never seemed terribly valuable.[1]

No single religion dominated Arabia during the Roman era. Zoroastrianism and Christianity competed with older pagan cults, while a number of prominent Jewish communities thrived throughout the peninsula. The Roman Diodorus Siculus, writing in 60 BCE, mentions the Kaaba, a pagan shrine in the town of Mecca, which today attracts millions of Muslim pilgrims every year.[2] From the standpoint of the future development of Islam, the most interesting Arabian religion of the time was described by a fifth century Palestinian Christian named Sozomenus as a form of Arab monotheism similar to Judaism, whose followers were sometimes called the "Hanifs." Sozomenus

61

thought that these "Arabs who live in the Jewish way" were the spiritual descendants of Abraham's son Ishmael as described in Genesis 17:20.[3]

Rome grew steadily more Christian, and steadily weaker, in the decades that followed the death of Augustine in 430. Barbarian incursions undercut its revenues, which in turn undercut its ability to pay soldiers to fight the barbarians, a downward spiral ending with the demise of the last Western emperor less than 40 years later.[4] The Eastern portion of the Empire, which became known as Byzantium, lasted another millennium in shrunken form.

Byzantium and Persia fought a series of draining wars against each other for supremacy in the fifth and sixth centuries. The cost of fighting the Persians, when added to the cost of defending themselves against barbarians from the north, took a heavy toll on the Byzantines and caused them to lower their guard elsewhere. An archeological survey of the Byzantine border defense system against Arab invaders, including excavations of the forts along the defensive line, shows that Byzantium abandoned most of these fortifications during these centuries.[5]

Muhammad

If you leave valuable items in an unlocked car, they will disappear. If you abandon your border defenses against barbarians, you will be invaded. Before they could take full advantage of Byzantine weakness, though, the Arabs needed to get their own act together. This is where Muhammad took advantage.

Unlike Jesus and Buddha, for whom the evidence is scant, there is no plausible doubt that Muhammad existed. Several outside sources from the early to mid-seventh century discuss him—though more as an Arab king than as a religious figure.[6]

For example, a Persian writer in the 670s mentions Muhammad simply as the ruler of the Arabs, without indicating that he had any religious significance. An Armenian source, who had no reason to be biased, describes Muhammad as establishing a community of Arabs and Jews, with descent from Abraham as their unifying force—just like the Hanifs of Sozomenus. These allies then set off to conquer Palestine from the Byzantines, with rapid success. A Byzantine writer tells of a prophet who appeared among the Arabs proclaiming the coming of the Jewish messiah, while warning of the danger of falling into the hands of these combined Jews and Arabs.[7]

There are no Arab documents from this time period, and many stories about Muhammad were manufactured centuries later. One such story that has the ring of truth, though, and is supported by independent evidence, tells of the conflict between the Hashimite family, whose most famous member was Muhammad, and another family known as the Umayyads, beginning with a confrontation between Muhammad and an Umayyad elder named Abu Sufyan.[8]

Simply put, Abu Sufyan wasn't buying the new message from God that Muhammad was selling. Mecca made a lot of money from pilgrims to the Kaaba, a temple housing some 369 pagan idols. The last thing Abu Sufyan and the other city fathers wanted was some new God expert debunking their main source of revenue. The locals expressed their displeasure by leaving pots of excrement outside Muhammad's door.[9]

Muhammad fled Mecca altogether for the city of Medina. There he found more success and acceptance, and ultimately led a military campaign against his tormentors back in Mecca. To make a long and probably inaccurate story short, he won, and once again confronted Abu Sufyan—this time as a conqueror rather than as an eccentric. "Well, Abu Sufyan," he is reported to have gloated, "do you now admit that there is no other god but Allah?" "Yes," replied Abu Sufyan. Muhammad continued: "Would you also not confess that I am the messenger of God?" "Forgive my outspokenness," replied Abu Sufyan, "but on that point I still have some doubts."[10] Umayyad doubts about Hashimite pretensions persisted for the next 350 years.

After Muhammad's death, leadership of the Mecca/Medina region was assumed by Abu Bakr, the father of one of his many wives. He took the title "caliph," meaning "the prophet's representative."[11]

Abu Bakr's main headache was the ease with which it was possible to gain a political following in Arabia by claiming a special relationship with God. Whether the rivals were copycats of Muhammad, or whether Muhammad was a copycat of someone else, we will never know. We do know that Abu Bakr conducted a series of what were called the "Apostasy Wars" against a constellation of competing God experts:

- Al-Aswad Al-Ansi, who killed the ruler of Yemen and married his wife. She was unimpressed and successfully conspired to have him assassinated in his bedroom.

- Tulayah, of the Banu Asad tribe, who said he received a vision of a holy book from the angel Gabriel just like Muhammad did. During the climactic battle, he stayed inside his tent talking to the angel Gabriel. When his military commander suspected that he was actually muttering gibberish, resistance collapsed.

- Musaylimah, of the Banu Haneefah tribe, another supposed confidante of the angel Gabriel, who came within an inch of ultimate victory. When Abu Bakr finally defeated him, he celebrated by slaughtering seven thousand prisoners.[12]

By the time of his death only two years after taking power, the entire Arabian Peninsula was under Abu Bakr's control. On his deathbed, Abu Bakr selected as his successor Umar, another of Muhammad's Hashimite fathers-in-law. Umar reigned for 10 years, during which time he discovered how weak the Christian Byzantines had become. Syria, Iraq, and the plum of Jerusalem itself soon fell under his control.[13]

Being king of the hill has certain disadvantages, though—Umar was assassinated in 644. Then a strange thing happened: a quickly convened council of elders selected a man named Uthman, the nephew of Muhammad's old antagonist Abu Sufyan, to be the new caliph. The Umayyad dynasty was back on top.

Umayyad Rule

Uthman expanded the Arab conquests well beyond the easy pickings of the unguarded Byzantine territories. The ancient empire of

Egypt fell under his control, as did mighty Persia–a feat even the Romans were never able to achieve.[14]

The interesting thing about these early conquests is that, contrary to conventional wisdom, they were *not* done for the purpose of propagating Islam. Non-Muslim soldiers fought side-by-side with Muslims. There are many written records of Christians living in Palestine, Syria, and Egypt describing the conquest itself–but not a word about attempts on the part of the conquerors to spread Islam as they went. In fact quite a few Christians welcomed the change. Not only were taxes under Arab rule lower, but there was greater freedom of religious belief than there was under Augustine's "City of God." The conquerors didn't care what anyone believed. Like the pre-Christian Romans, they wanted to preserve order and collect taxes, without the slightest interest in what their subjects did or did not believe about the supernatural. The Christian Patriarch of Jerusalem, writing at the time of its Arab conquest, characterizes them simply as godless barbarians committing gruesome atrocities, not as bringers of any new religion.[15]

In 656, Hashimite operatives murdered Uthman. This set off a civil war between the Umayyads and the Hashimites, who claimed to be fighting for God and who were led by Muhammad's nephew and son-in-law Ali. (Despite having many wives, Muhammad supposedly had no living sons, so Ali was his principal heir.) Ali's supporters were called the "partisans of Ali," or "*shiat Ali,*" the forerunners of today's Shiites.[16] Ali claimed a precarious control over Mecca and Medina after his victory at what became known as "The Battle of the Camel," but his reign was brief. Abu Sufyan's son (and Uthman's cousin) Muawiya, who had been governor of Syria, never acknowledged Ali's right to power, and adopted the war cry of "Vengeance for Uthman against Ali." After Ali in turn was assassinated in 661, Muawiya became caliph, as did his heirs after him. However, the powers Muawiya and his Umayyad successors assumed were strictly secular, with no religious authority at all.[17]

The Umayyad monarchs, like their forebear Abu Sufyan, were not enamored with the religion associated with Muhammad. The documentary evidence that survives from Muawiya's 20-year reign (661-680) makes no mention of Muhammad at all. There are references to the single Hanif god Muawiya's father Abu Sufyan believed in, but not a word about Muhammad. In fact, Muawiya hounded Muhammad's heirs, and succeeded in killing off Ali's two sons, Husayn and Hasan. With one exception, Muhammad's daughters had difficulties finding suitable husbands; several of his grandchildren died in obscurity. The bier that had held Muhammad's corpse was auctioned off for cash; throughout the first hundred years after his death his tomb was neglected and his house attracted no special attention.[18]

Later Umayyad leaders were downright irreverent. According to Caliph Alwaleed Ibn Yazid, "Muhammad the Hashimite manipulated people by his claim that he was a prophet without true inspiration or an inspired book." Caliph Abd-Almalik Ibn Marawan, who held a copy of Islam's holy book the Koran on his lap when he was appointed, later folded it and said "This is the last time I will ever use you." Caliph Walid II is said to have stuck the Koran on a lance and shot it to pieces with arrows.[19]

Umayyad law was almost entirely secular, based on what humans thought made sense rather than on what Muhammad said God intended. Some Umayyad rulings were directly contrary to the explicit wording of today's Koran, causing scholars to suspect that today's Koran was not fully formed until post-Umayyad times. There is strong evidence of competing early versions of the Koran, not at all the image of the Koran as the verbatim word of God (or even of Muhammad) that modern Islamic teaching presents.[20]

In some cases, Umayyad provincial governors actively *discouraged* conversion to Islam. Non-Muslims were required to pay a tax for the benefit of their Muslim superiors. But if everyone became a Muslim, the financial benefit of being a Muslim would disappear. Thus, the rules for qualifying as a tax-exempt Muslim began to multiply.[21] Other than this modest tax, there is no record of Umayyad persecution of other religions; archeologists have discovered and dated 30 pagan sites in the Negev desert region of southern Israel, proving that paganism flourished there throughout Umayyad times.[22] In fact, the most devout Muslims were suspected by the authorities (not without reason) of being closet Hashimite supporters.[23]

The Abbasids Invent Islam

During the Umayyad years, Arabia grew rich off the plunder of conquered lands. Wealth facilitated the growth of a class of parasites called theologians, who spent their days pondering deep issues about God and man, and developing a body of religious thinking. The Umayyads tried to co-opt this class by supporting their scholarship, especially when it served to cement the legitimacy of their rule.[24]

But life was no more perfect in the seventh century than it is today, and these theologians believed they knew the reason why: the godless Umayyads had usurped the right of Muhammad's dynasty to rule, making God terribly unhappy.[25] They soon "discovered" a prediction of Muhammad to validate their distress:

> You will eventually be ruled by emirs, who will dispose of your daily bread and will refuse it unless you admit their lies to be true and support them in their unbelief: give unto them what is theirs by law as long as they accept the same from you, but if they act as traitors in this, fight them, and he who is killed because of such conduct will be deemed a martyr.[26]

In 680, a serious revolt against Muawiya's son broke out in what is now Iraq among the supporters of Ali's son and Muhammad's grandson, Husayn ibn Ali. Much of the clergy sided with the Hashimites because of Husayn's blood connection with Muhammad and their disapproval of Umayyad secularism. Husayn was killed at the battle of Karbala, but his supporters never gave up and the battle is still commemorated annually by enormous Shiite pilgrimages.[27]

In 747 another revolt broke out against allegedly decadent Umayyad rule. This one succeeded, but with a last-minute twist. The general who commanded the successful rebel army had reason to distrust the chief claimant who was a direct descendant of Muhammad, and instead installed as caliph a different Hashimite, whose descent was from Muhammad's uncle al-Abbas. Ironically, al-Abbas himself had been a relatively late convert to Islam, but at least he was a Hashimite. The new caliph styled his dynasty "Abbasid" to emphasize the link to al-Abbas; he also consolidated his grip on power by executing both the general who had installed him and the Shiite claimant he had leapfrogged.[28]

The descendants of Ali and their Shiite backers who had carried the water against Umayyad rule for over a century were outraged at having their triumph melt into defeat; they still haven't gotten over it.[29]

In part to differentiate themselves from the ruling house they had displaced, and in part to pacify the restive Shiites, the Abbasids exaggerated the differences between themselves and the Umayyads, and proclaimed their intent to establish the rule of God on earth. Some of the differentiation was symbolic; Abbasid caliphs frequently donned what they alleged was the cloak worn by Muhammad, literally wrapping themselves in his authority. Propagandists proclaimed that "the light of prophecy" shone from the forehead of the Abbasid caliph, who liked being called "God's shadow on earth."[30]

But there was substance to go with the show. Abbasids recognized religious law, as it was being developed by the God experts, as the only legitimate law on earth; all Abbasid judges (who exercised administrative as well as judicial authority) had to be experts in religious law. Gone was the religious tolerance of the Umayyads; according to another newly discovered "tradition," Muhammad on his deathbed had given a command that all non-Muslims be expelled from Arabia, which was now duly enforced.[31]

God experts heaped praise on the new Abbasid regime, which responded by heaping money and power on the religious leaders.[32] (Today, such a relationship is called a "faith-based initiative.")

It was under the Abbasids that Islam as we see it today took shape. The conventional doctrine today is that Islam's central text, the Koran, exists on a special table in heaven, was dictated by God to Muhammad, and then was orally passed on by Muhammad to his followers, who later wrote it down. However, although we have good evidence that Muhammad existed, we have no such evidence for the Koran; there is no reference to its existence anywhere until nearly the end of the seventh century, 60 years after Muhammad died. Moreover, the earliest evidence we have, consisting of coins and inscriptions, contains sayings *different* from those appearing in today's Koran. Important Arabic legal documents from as much as a century after the Koran was supposed to have been assembled do not even mention its existence, as we would presume they would have if in fact it existed at that time. Legal decisions from Umayyad times require that the terms of contracts be proven by oral evidence of witnesses, not by written instruments–in direct contradiction to the plain words of the Koran. Many scholars therefore conclude that the Koran was assembled as a composite of competing traditions, over a period of several generations, achieving its current form only during Abbasid times.[33]

Even more important than the Koran to the development of Islam was the fabrication of the "Sunna," or the "way" of Muhammad, which derives from traditions of the words and actions of Muhammad (and sometimes of his companions) called "hadiths." When the Abbasids first came to power, the scholar Malik ibn Anas was able to come up with only 600 sayings of Muhammad relating to Islamic law. Within a couple of centuries, though, the number exploded into the hundreds of thousands.[34] Why? In part, because people would pay to hear them, just as Americans of a later age paid to buy Parson Weems' "biographies" of George Washington filled with myths about his chopping down the cherry tree.[35] In part, because the Koran itself had relatively few hard rules of law; Abbasid judges under orders to rule in accordance with God's will were eager to accept evidence of what that will might be, especially when it fit their own predilections. For example, nearly a century after Muhammad is supposed to have died, the age for determining when a child became an adult had still not been decided. No problem: a legal scholar named Nafi succeeded in "finding" a hadith that Muhammad had refused a youth of 14 the rights of adulthood, but granted them a year later when he had attained the age of 15.[36]

Nothing in the Koran even remotely suggested that Muhammad's god intended there to be any earthly manifestation of his will other than the Koran, the Torah, and the Gospels, or that the way Muhammad lived his life was intended by his god to be an example for the rest of humanity. It wouldn't have been difficult for a god to have said so, if that's what was meant; a sentence would have sufficed. But it isn't there. In fact, the Koran repeatedly describes Muhammad as "a plain warner," not as an eternal role model for mankind.[37] Undeterred by the mere "Word of God," though, Abbasid God experts such as Muhammad ibn Idris al-Shafi'i announced that the collective example of Muhammad and his companions was to be accepted as binding divine authority along side the actual Word of God itself. In fact, the principle was ultimately announced that: "The Sunna is the judge of the Koran, and not vice versa."[38]

Hadiths covered almost everything. Generals tried to fight battles at the times of day during which Muhammad had once fought the unbelievers. In deciding whether it was permissible to wear a gold signet ring, the sole criterion was to find out whether Muhammad had worn such jewelry. Some Muslim theologians as late as the 1890s were not entirely reconciled to the use of the knife and fork, which Muhammad had not used. An unimpressed early commentator named al-Nasai observed that "Your comrade Muhammad teaches you how to relieve yourselves."[39]

The fact that hadiths were being fraudulently manufactured right and left was an open ninth century secret. The response was to fabricate more, to counteract the previous fabrications. In some, Muhammad himself warns against fakery: "In the later days of my community, there will be those who will hand you communications which neither you nor your forefathers have ever heard. Beware of them." Then again, according to another hadith, some fakes were ok: "After my departure," Muhammad is reported to have said, "the number of sayings ascribed to me will increase in the same way as sayings have been ascribed to previous prophets. What therefore is told to you as a saying of mine you will have to compare with the Book of God, and what is in accordance with it is by me, whether I have in fact said it myself or not." Asim al-Nabil, a specialist in the study of tradition who died in Basra in 834, admitted openly: "I have come to the conclusion that a pious man is never so ready to lie as in matters of the hadith."[40]

The study of the hadiths imagined by Abbasid God experts still forms the core of Islam today. At this writing, a team of 80 God experts at the University of Ankara is busily sorting through 170,000 hadiths–with the aid of a computer!–to sort the wheat from the chaff, and to come up with a version of Islam to fit their own predilections.[41]

Andalusia

The Umayyad role was far from finished, though. In 711, Umayyad forces had crossed into Iberia, and over the next several years brought most of Spain and Portugal under their control. This turned out to be fortuitous. Following their victory in 750, the Abbasids began rounding up every member of the Umayyad family they could find, including women and children, and torturing them before putting them to a well-publicized death. After the Abbasids declared an amnesty, 70 Umayyad family members ventured out of hiding; this made them much easier to catch and then execute.[42]

Abd al-Rahman ibn Mu'awiya, grandson of a former Umayyad caliph, was wise enough not to fall for this ruse, but remained instead at his farm in Iraq. When Abbasid soldiers appeared, he swam for his life across the Euphrates River, accompanied by his 13-year-old brother, who did not survive the crossing. After a series of harrowing adventures, he wound up in Andalusia, as the Umayyad-controlled portion of Spain and Portugal was known. Shrewdly taking advantage of political divisions–and with a little luck–Abd al-Rahman displaced the provincial governor, and established a second Umayyad dynasty in Andalusia that ruled for another three centuries. Even the Abbasid caliph back in Baghdad expressed grudging admiration for the man "who first by cunning escaped from among the spears and swords of his enemies, traversed the desert and crossed the sea, entered a land of unbelievers, founded cities, gathered armies and with his good government and firmness of character built an empire in a lawless country ... with nothing to aid him but his wits, and no supporter but his unshakable will."[43]

Umayyad Andalusia became a vastly different place than the Middle East under the Abbasids. The later Umayyads were by no means atheists, and they were quite capable of harshness. But they were not nearly as driven by what the God experts told them as the Abbasid regime they escaped.

Islamic law, for example, is divided into four main "schools" of interpretation (or five, if you count the Shiites as a separate school). Andalusia followed the "Maliki" school, which is based largely on the common law prevailing in Medina in pre-Islamic times, as opposed to laws based on hadiths that were dreamed up in Abbasid times.[44]

For Andalusia to be considered Muslim at all, laws on the books had to forbid the consumption of alcohol. But as with the American experiment with Prohibition, these laws were nearly universally ignored. We are told of a Muslim on his deathbed, praying not for salvation, but saying with his last breath, "Oh Lord of all things in Paradise, I only ask thee for a draught of Malaga wine." An Umayyad prince sang, "I have passed my life among drinkers and lovely faces; I have not wasted one evening or dawn: My nights I spend awake in drunken revels, and I never hear the morning muezzin call me to fresh pleasures."[45]

As noted above, an Abbasid-discovered hadith commanded the expulsion of all non-Muslims from Arabia.[46] Andalusia, by contrast, became a model of religious tolerance. Non-Muslims had to pay an extra tax, but the overall tax burden was still lower than it had been under Christian rule. Christians and Muslims mixed freely, learned each other's languages, gave their children each other's names, and attended each other's religious celebrations. Intermarriage was common, even at the highest levels; later Umayyad kings wound up with blonde hair and blue eyes. There were no restrictions on the building of new Christian churches as there was in the Abbasid world. Christian God experts even invented stories about miracles performed by the Blessed Virgin on behalf of Muslims.[47]

Tolerance also extended to another important minority, the Jews, who accounted for about a third of the population. Arab mapmakers, in fact, referred to Granada, Lucena, and Tarragon as "Jewish cities." Jews had provided valuable assistance when the Umayyads first invaded Spain, because they had no use for their Christian rulers: 90,000

Jews had been forcibly baptized in the preceding decades, and a 681 decree (never enforced) gave Jews 12 months to convert to Christianity or leave the country. The grateful Umayyads allowed Jews greater freedom and respect than they were to enjoy anywhere in Europe until the Enlightenment broke the Christian stranglehold. Jews became prominent in all the professions, in the diplomatic service, and in international trade; two Jews even served as prime ministers to the king.[48]

Women also fared better under the Umayyads then they did under the Abbasids or the Christians. The level of equality did not approach that of the twenty-first century, but women under several of the Umayyad kings were free to travel the streets alone, to work as publishers, doctors, lawyers, and professors, and to run their own businesses.[49]

Scholarship, music, and art–especially poetry–thrived. Stories are told of quick-witted young men who escaped decapitation for transgressions by coming up with a clever verse to delight their judges.[50] The regime was friendly to science as well–mathematics, geology, horology, and cartography all flourished. Andalusia's astronomers remained unsurpassed in some areas until the twentieth century; Galileo, Copernicus, Kepler and Tycho Brahe all acknowledged their debt to them. Andalusia's medical reputation was so outstanding that Christian kings traveled there for treatment. In 875, some 600 years before Leonardo da Vinci, a Cordoban inventor named Ibn Firnas– who had already developed a new form of water clock and a method for processing cut crystal glass from sand–leapt from a wall in a glider he developed by studying birds, traveling over a hundred yards before encountering greater-than-anticipated problems with his landing. The library at Cordoba housed some four hundred thousand books, at a time when that of Paris held two thousand.[51]

The heady combination of tolerance, high culture, and science produced philosophical breakthroughs as well. A Jew named Maimonides and a Muslim named Ibn Rushd both attempted a similar feat: reconciling reason with the tenets of the religions into which they had been born. Maimonides searched for logical reasons behind

73

hundreds of Jewish laws. For example, the various sexual prohibitions of the Torah were there "to inculcate the lesson that we ought to limit sexual intercourse altogether, hold it in contempt, and only desire it very rarely." "Circumcision," he explained, "simply counteracts excessive lust, for there is not doubt that circumcision weakens the power of sexual excitement and sometimes lessens the natural enjoyment."[52] Ibn Rushd (known in Europe as Averroës) wrote commentaries on the works of Aristotle, the champion of reason, who had disappeared from European consciousness. Ibn Rushd's massive work *On the Harmony of Religions and Philosophy* is a complex attempt to accommodate religious belief with Aristotelian rationalism.[53]

True God experts were appalled by both men. Their knowledge came from revelation, not from reason; thinking could lead to all sorts of problems they did not want to deal with. French Jews prevailed on the Christian authorities to burn the works of Maimonides, only to discover that the taste for burning Hebrew texts spread far beyond what they had in mind.[54] Ibn Rushd was forced into exile by Muslim fundamentalists who displaced the Umayyads (as was Maimonides). The idea that philosophical thought could exist independently of religion was known as "Averroism" in Europe right up until the time that the nineteenth century agnostic writer George Holyoake renamed it "secularism."[55] Many humanists today regard the effort to reconcile reason with religion as a waste of energy, and prefer to concentrate on reason without the shackles of religious tradition. They are probably right; but somebody had to work the reconciliation angle first, at least to establish that it would lead to a dead end.

Constantly pressed from the north by the Spanish Christians, the Umayyad dynasty finally came to a violent end at the hands of fundamentalist Muslims from Morocco in 1094.[56] So did the spirit of tolerance, and so did the vast library of human knowledge at Cordoba. Andalusia's Jews despised the new regime and worked to undermine it—only to discover, after completion of the Christian re-conquest in 1492, what real oppression was all about.

It is a bit disingenuous to contrast centuries worth of Hashimites with centuries worth of Umayyads. There was more diversity among members of both dynasties than there is space here to talk about. It is equally disingenuous to stereotype all the Umayyads as kind and gentle humanists; "greedy thugs" is closer to the mark for some of them. Compared to some religion, though, greedy thuggery has its advantages. Once the basic demands of the rulers are satiated, it can create an environment of freedom, peace, prosperity, and intellectual growth, in contrast to the rule of God experts who know everything about how the rest of us should live our lives.

> People like Bill Maher and Sam Harris say that Islam is the greatest obstacle to humanist values in the world today. Is it a good idea to offend militant Muslim sensibilities, as this chapter undoubtedly does? Share your thoughts on this and the other questions you'll find at **dgc.humanistpress.com**!

Notes:

1 Trifkovic, *Sword*, 16.
2 Donner, *Muhammad*, 4; St. Clair-Tisdall, *Sources*, 233.
3 Walsh, *Role of Religion*, 81; Koran 2:173; Cook, *Muhammad*, 81; Al-Rawandi, *Origins*, 112.
4 Encyclopedia Britannica, *Later Roman Empire*.
5 Donner, *Muhammad*, 3; Koren, *Methodological Approaches*, 434.
6 Al-Rawandi, *Origins*, 102.
7 Warraq, *Quest*, 32; Cook, *Muhammad*, 74.
8 Ismail, *Politics*, 108-109.
9 Mikhail, *Islam*, 17; Walsh, *Role of Religion*, 83.
10 Renan, *Muhammad*, 147.
11 Sonn, *Islam*, 23.
12 Donner, *Muhammad*, 11; Jad'an, *Abu Bakr As-Siddeeq*, Chapter 3.
13 Donner, *Muhammad*, 11-12; Trifkovic, *Sword*, 91.
14 Encyclopedia Britannica, *Uthman ibn 'Affan*.
15 Shaban, *Abbasid*, 65; Koren, *Methodological Approaches*, 432; Warraq, *Quest*, 32.
16 Sonn, *Islam*, 27-28.
17 Shaban, *Abbasid*, 144-146.

18 Al-Rawandi, *Origins*, 97, 103; Renan, *Muhammad*, 147; Lammens, *Koran*, 182.

19 Mikhail, *Islam*, 116; Warraq, *Not a Muslim*, 243.

20 Goldziher, *Muslim Studies*, Vol. 2, 40; Koren, *Methodological Approaches*, 429; Nöldeke, *Koran*, 40; Al-Rawandi, *Origins*, 110; Jeffery, *Materials*, 119.

21 Schacht, *Islamic Law*, 131-132; Shaban, *Abbasid*, 111; Cornell, *Fruit*, 76.

22 Koren, *Methodological Approaches*, 435.

23 Goldziher, *Muslim Studies*, Vol. 2, 38.

24 Goldziher, *Muslim Studies*, Vol. 2, 41-42; Donner, *Muhammad*, 23-24.

25 Shaban, *Abbasid*, 157.

26 Goldziher, *Muslim Studies*, Vol. 2, 90.

27 Trifkovic, *Sword*, 93.

28 Encyclopedia Britannica, *Abbasid Dynasty*; Goldziher, *Muslim Studies*, Vol. 2, 59; Shaban, *Abbasid*, 150, 164, 167.

29 Shaban, *Abbasid*, 166.

30 Shaban, *Abbasid*, 165; Goldziher, *Muslim Studies*, Vol. 2, 60, 61, 67.

31 Schacht, *Islamic Law*, 49-50; Goldziher, *Muslim Studies*, Vol. 2, 61; Cook, *Muhammad*, 23.

32 Goldziher, *Muslim Studies*, Vol. 2, 61, 71.

33 Cook, *Muhammad*, 74; Schacht, *Islamic Law*, 18-19; Wansbrough, *Quranic Studies*, 44-47.

34 Warraq, *Quest*, 44.

35 Weems, *History*, chapter 2.

36 Goldziher, *Muslim Studies*, vol. 2, 29.

37 *See, e.g.*, Koran 7:184, 15:89, 22:49, 29:50, 38:70.

38 Cornell, *Fruit*, 74; Goldziher, *Muslim Studies*, Vol. 2, 31.

39 Goldziher, *Muslim Studies*, Vol. 2, 29, 33-34, 128.

40 Goldziher, *Muslim Studies*, Vol. 2, 52, 56.

41 Dickey, "New Face."

42 Hole, *Andalus*, 153.

43 Hole, *Andalus*, 154-158.

44 Hole, *Andalus*, 38; Schwartz, *Shari'a*, 20.

45 Hole, *Andalus*, 148-149.

46 Cook, *Muhammad*, 23.

47 Hole, *Andalus*, 21, 23, 30.

48 Johnson, *Jews*, 177; Hole, *Andalus*, 21, 50-52.

49 Hole, *Andalus*, 125, 150; Gill, *Andalucia*, 100.

50 Hole, *Andalus*, 24, 103.

51 Hole, *Andalus*, 30; Gill, *Andalucia*, 76-77, 99, 109.

52 Sigal, *Emergence*, 184.

53 Gill, *Andalucia,* 111.
54 Popper, *Censorship,* 7.
55 Gill, *Andalucia,* 112.
56 Hole, *Andalus,* 25.

Emperor Frederick II

CHAPTER 5

FREDERICK VS. GREGORY

The Medieval Church

When we left Augustine on his deathbed at the end of Chapter 2, his town was being overrun by Vandal barbarians. Still, his ideas of a church-dominated society held sway for the next thousand years. The most serious challenge to the church's stranglehold arose from a thirteenth century monarch who believed that human reason provided a more peaceful, more pleasant, more satisfying way to run a society than the rigid orthodoxy of the Augustine-inspired medieval church.

The western portion of the Roman Empire lasted only another 46 years after Augustine's death. The barbarian conquerors, most of whom had already converted to some version of Christianity, kept the church structure in place as an efficient tool for administering their new domains.[1]

Church leaders aspired to more than just a secondary position in the new kingdoms, though. Sometime around 750, they produced documentation establishing a much broader legal basis for power. A collection of ancient documents said to have been assembled by the famous scholar Isidore of Seville was presented to Europe's monarchs, some stretching all the way back to the first century Pope Clement, the immediate successor to St. Peter himself. The most important of these documents, known as the *Donation of Constantine*, proved that the emperor who converted the Roman Empire to Christianity had made an outright gift of Rome and its surrounding territories to the pope and his successors. Other documents in the collection justified a broad view of the power of bishops and the pope, at the expense of the secular authorities. For example: "In the bishops you should venerate God, and love them as your own souls," and "You (bishops) are given us as gods by God." The documents repeatedly insisted that bishops who were accused of wrongdoing could not be tried by kings or other secular authorities, but only by fellow bishops, with a right of appeal to the pope.[2]

The letters and decrees had the desired effect of enhancing the clergy's already substantial secular power, especially in central Italy. No one had the temerity to question their authenticity—for nearly 600 years. Upon closer examination, most of them turned out to be forgeries—crude ones at that—cleverly mixed in with some that were previously known to be authentic, to enhance their overall credibility. Popes of the first and second centuries were writing in Frankish Latin of the ninth century. Documents were quoted before they had been written, and rulings were issued on questions that had not yet arisen.[3]

Meanwhile, the church was using its power to grow fabulously rich. In England, the clergy, with 1 percent of the population, disposed of about 25 percent of the gross national product. This was not at all unusual. In some parts of France and Germany, the church was even wealthier and owned a third to a half of all real estate. The papacy skimmed off about 10 percent of the church's total income, in addition to direct payments from the public.[4]

Church lands were generally exempt from taxation, which gave churches a tremendous competitive advantage, and allowed them to improve and acquire even more land. Private land owners would frequently transfer their property to the church to escape taxation, since vows of poverty by the "clerics" who remained on the land either did not exist or were not taken seriously.[5] This was a ploy that modern tax planners can only envy.

The church had no patience for those who suggested it should part with any of its hard-earned wealth. John Ball, an English priest of the fourteenth century, preached against class and privilege, including that of the church. He demanded agrarian reform, insisting that the landholdings of the church be redistributed among the people. He was arrested by church authorities a number of times, then excommunicated, then hanged.[6]

Church-owned land by itself did not produce income. Someone had to work it, and the sons and daughters of the nobility who became bishops, monks, priests, and nuns were not about to get their hands dirty. Instead, they purchased slaves to do the work. There is no good count of exactly how many slaves the church owned, but the number was probably in the millions. One eighth century French monastery alone owned over 20,000 slaves.[7]

Gaudri, bishop of Laon, enjoyed showing off black African slaves as a novelty.[8] The majority of the church's slaves, though, were European. Since it was easier on the church's delicate conscience to have non-Christians as slaves, the eastern edges of Christendom became the great source of pagans who could be captured and sold into servitude. In fact, the etymology of the word "slave" shows it derives from "Slav," referring to the Slavic people living to the east of Christendom who were fair game to be taken and sold.[9]

Something about the buying and selling of human beings troubled the consciences of those lacking a full understanding of God's will as the church understood it, and they often found themselves on the defensive in justifying this practice. Christian Bibles go on and on about it. Slavery was created by Noah, with God's blessing, in the book of Genesis. God himself told Moses that an owner could beat a slave to within an inch of his life, "since the slave is his property."[10] In the New Testament, the apostle Paul was as explicit as he could be, ordering slaves to obey their masters "as you would obey Christ," and dispatching a runaway slave back to his owner.[11] Augustine explained to the squeamish that "The prime cause of slavery then, is sin, so that man was put under man in a state of bondage; and this can be only by a judgment of God, in whom there is no unrighteousness, and who knows how to assign divers punishments according to the deserts of the sinners."[12]

The church wrote the legal codes governing the master-slave relationship, which was quite convenient since the church itself was by far the largest slaveholder. These codes prescribed how many blows a master could inflict on animals and slaves for various offenses; animals generally got off lighter than humans. Masters were also legally allowed to punish slaves by amputation and facial scarring.[13]

The one thing the church could not abide was anyone questioning its wellspring of power: its monopoly on the truth. Especially dangerous were those who employed the devil's trick of empirical observation of facts, which could turn out to be at odds with church teaching and thereby undermine the whole house of cards. Paul himself was the first to warn of the danger: "Beware lest any man spoil you through philosophy and vain deceit, after the tradition of men, after the rudiments of the world, and not after Christ." To the Corinthians, he wrote: "Let no man deceive himself. If any man among you seemeth to be wise in this world, let him become a fool, that he may be wise. For the wisdom of this world is foolishness with God."[14]

The prolific Christian author Tertullian in the second century declared:

> We want no curious disputation after possessing Christ Jesus, no inquisition after enjoying the Gospel! With our faith, we desire no further belief. For once we believe this, there is nothing else that we ought to believe. ... It therefore served Thales of Miletus quite right, when, stargazing as he walked, . . he had the mortification of falling into a well. ... His fall, therefore, is a figurative picture of the philosophers; of those, I mean, who persist in applying their studies to a vain purpose, since they indulge a stupid curiosity on natural objects.[15]

As always, the authoritative voice was that of Augustine: "Nothing is to be accepted save on the authority of scripture, since greater is that authority than all the powers of the human mind." Augustine taught that there was no need to be "dismayed if Christians are ignorant about the properties and the number of the basic elements of nature, or about the motion, order, and deviations of the stars, the map of the heavens, the kinds and nature of animals, plants, stones, springs, rivers, and mountains. ... For the Christian, it is enough to believe that the cause of all created things ... is ... the goodness of the Creator."[16]

Crusades

With the wealth and political power of much of Europe securely under its thumb, the church sought to expand its political reach through a series of military adventures called the Crusades. God experts relied on the explicit words of Jesus: "Think not that I am come to send peace on earth: I came not to send peace, but a sword." ... "He that hath no sword, let him sell his garment, and buy one."[17]

As a Crusade recruiter put it:

> The aim of Christianity is not to fill the earth, but to fill heaven. Why should one worry if the number of Christians is lessened in the world by deaths endured for God? By this kind of death people make their way to heaven who perhaps would never reach it by another road.[18]

Not all Crusades involved expeditions to Palestine; military campaigns to impose Christianity by force in the Baltic territories, in Muslim Spain, and on the Cathar heretics of southern France were all described as Crusades, and those who signed up to kill heathens received a papal indulgence forgiving all their sins for their efforts. The main event, though, was the struggle to capture the land of Jesus. Muslims had conquered Palestine in the seventh century; in 1096, Pope Urban II announced that he wanted it back. Over a hundred thousand men trekked across Europe to embarkation points to heed the pope's call. Along the way, quite a few of them honed their combat skills by killing defenseless Jews.[19]

Under the primitive communications and transportation conditions of the age, it was no easy task to put this polyglot force into a position to achieve positive results. When those who got as far as Antioch found themselves surrounded by angry Muslim armies, morale sagged—until someone reported that St. Andrew appeared to him in a vision and revealed the location of the Holy Lance which had been used to pierce the side of Jesus. That, plus stories of another appearance by Jesus himself to assure the soldiers that they would prevail if they repented of their sins, gave the troops the boost they needed to break through the siege and head on toward Jerusalem.[20]

On July 14, 1099, the Crusaders captured Jerusalem, and celebrated with a rampage of holy butchery. Raymond of Aguilers exulted:

> Wonderful things were to be seen. Numbers of the Saracens were beheaded. ... Others were shot with arrows, or forced to jump from the towers; others were tortured for several days, then burned with flames. In the streets were seen piles of heads and hands and feet. One rode about everywhere amid the corpses of men and horses. In the temple of Solomon, the horses waded in the blood up to their knees, nay, up to the bridle. It was a just and marvelous judgment of God, that this place should be filled with the blood of unbelievers.[21]

Raymond also quoted Psalm 118: "This is the day the Lord has made. Let us rejoice and be glad in it."[22]

Rumor spread that the local Muslims sometimes swallowed their gold as the surest way to hide it, so disemboweling became a common practice in the search for plunder. Hoping to avoid the slaughter, Jews crowded into their principal synagogue to give notice that they were not Muslims. The Crusaders burnt down the synagogue, killing them all.[23]

Christians ruled what became known as the Kingdom of Jerusalem for nearly a century. Little attempt was made to convert the Muslims who comprised most of the population; instead, they were simply enserfed to their new Christian masters. In 1187, the surrounding Arabs got their act together under their great leader Saladin, and drove the Christians back out of Jerusalem and nearly all the rest of Palestine.[24]

Immediately, the popes set about the effort to regain what they had lost. Richard the Lionhearted led a Crusade that failed in 1192. In 1201, a mighty Fourth Crusade was launched from Venice. Its leaders were far more interested in plunder than in winning heavenly favor, though; after sacking Christian Constantinople, then the wealthiest and most renowned city on earth, they turned around and went home.[25]

The Reluctant Crusader

This set the stage for Frederick II of the Hohenstaufen family. Frederick was born to the queen of Sicily in 1194. Orphaned at age 4, he was put under the guardianship of the pope, who coolly wrote to him that: "God ... has taken away your father and your mother; yet He has given you a worthier father, His Vicar, and a better mother, the church."[26] In 1211, the pope supported his ward's election as Holy Roman emperor, and backed Frederick in a messy civil war across Germany to defend his crown against a rival claimant. After many difficult years, Frederick prevailed. At a magnificent coronation ceremony where he received the crown of Charlemagne, Frederick promised Count Ugolino, who doubled as the Cardinal of Ostia, to undertake a new Crusade to recapture Jerusalem. Ugolino was then appointed by the pope to drum up support for the Crusade across northern and central Italy.[27]

Years rolled by, but Frederick's Crusade kept failing to materialize. This was not a complete surprise because Frederick had already displayed disturbing signs of having a mind of his own. As soon as he became independent at age 15, he had dismissed several church officials who displeased him. The pope was shocked: "We are amazed at the conduct of your advisers. Do not usurp our office in things spiritual: be content with the temporal power you hold from us." Frederick backed down, but a year later he dismissed the pope's financial representative, who was stealing from him, causing more consternation.[28]

That pope died, then his successor died, and still Frederick served up an endless stream of excuses rather than a crusading army. The real trouble was, Frederick didn't really *want* to crusade. He was engrossed with launching a humanist revolution, as described below, and he feared (correctly) that his absence would tempt rebels back home. In 1227, though, a cloud darkened Frederick's horizon. Count Ugolino, to whom Frederick had made his vow, and who had devoted the succeeding years to recruiting support for a Crusade that Frederick would not launch, was elected pope. Now 82 years old, he was full of piss and vinegar, most of it aimed at the ungrateful young whippersnapper who occupied the imperial throne. Ugolino, now called Pope Gregory IX, immediately laid down the law: start the Crusade *now*, or face excommunication.[29]

Later that year, Frederick and an army finally set sail for Jerusalem. But his ships returned three days later because Frederick claimed he felt ill. Gregory was not amused–he immediately excommunicated Frederick, declaring him in league with the devil:

> But he (Frederick) breaking all his promises, bursting every bond, trampling under foot the fear of God, despising all reverence for Christ Jesus, scorning the censures of the church, deserting the Christian army, abandoning the Holy Land to the unbelievers, to his own disgrace and that of all Christendom, withdrew to the luxuries and wonted delights of his kingdom, seeking to palliate his offense by frivolous excuses of simulated sickness.[30]

To increase the pressure, the pope banned the administering of sacraments in Frederick's domains: no couples could marry, no infants could be baptized, and no one dying could be comforted by a priest.

Monarchs before Frederick had groveled before such harsh treatment by a pope. Frederick's own ancestor, the Emperor Henry IV, had once stood barefoot three days in the snow to beg the pope's forgiveness.[31] Frederick did not. Instead, he ordered all the clergy within the empire to continue administering sacraments, with the explicit threat of imprisonment and confiscation of property for those who refused. Most complied. Frederick then calmly levied a special tax on all churches within the kingdom, proceeds to be used for a Crusade in the spring.[32]

Tax the church? To pay for the church's war? Gregory was apoplectic. Frederick responded by seeking support from the other monarchs of Europe, warning them that if he were beaten, they would be next. He wrote to king Henry of England:

> The church of Rome, as though she were the true church, calls herself my mother and my nurse while all her acts have been

those of a stepmother. The whole world pays tribute to the avarice of the Romans. ... The Romans are now rolling in wealth; what wonder that the walls of the church are undermined to the base and threaten utter ruin. ... Your house is in danger when that of your neighbor is on fire.[33]

In March 1228, not knowing what else to do, Gregory excommunicated Frederick again, upping the ante this time to take away his kingdom, while threatening excommunication to anyone who paid his blasphemous taxes. Nonetheless, Frederick set sail for Palestine three months later. He took only a token force, leaving most of his army behind to defend Naples and Sicily against an expected attack from papal armies.[34]

Upon arriving in Palestine, Frederick (who was fluent in Arabic, having been raised among Sicily's Muslims) began listening and learning about political divisions in the Arab world, rather than fighting.[35] Amazingly, after a few months of negotiation with Kemal, sultan of Egypt, he succeeded in signing the Treaty of Jaffa in February 1229, giving the Christians exactly what they wanted without any bloodshed. Jerusalem, Bethlehem, Nazareth, and other towns were returned to Christian control. The Church of the Sepulcher, which is supposed to stand on the burial place of Jesus, was also returned, while the Muslim Dome of the Rock and Mosque of al-Aqsa remained in the hands of the Muslims. Freedom of worship for both Christians and Muslims was guaranteed. Frederick himself was crowned King of Jerusalem, and both sides promised to refrain from violence for the next 10 years.[36]

Was Gregory thrilled that Christian rule had been peacefully restored to Christianity's holy places? No! If anything, he was even angrier than he had been before since success had been achieved in the face of his opposition. The Christian patriarch of Jerusalem was outraged as well because the treaty accorded Muslims actual rights, and because Frederick had crowned himself King of Jerusalem after the patriarch had ordered him not to. Some openly lamented that it was not by blood and the sword that Jerusalem had been regained. Muslim clergy were furious with their peace-making sultan as well.[37]

Frederick left Palestine behind to defend his Italian possessions from the pope the very next day after his coronation. He tried to leave secretly, but his departure was discovered and he was pelted with tripe as he passed the Christian meat markets on his way down to the port.[38]

Back home, Frederick's reputation soared. Beating the Muslims and the pope at the same time was seen as quite a feat. Many commoners came to believe he was somehow super-human, especially since the church had been spreading rumors that he was dead. Although Gregory's army had in fact been invading Frederick's kingdom in southern Italy the very day he was crowning himself King of Jerusalem, Frederick quickly expelled it. The unimaginative Gregory excommunicated Frederick yet again, this time on the additional grounds of having captured Jerusalem without official permission.[39]

But Gregory was now dealing with a star, and he had to back down. In 1230, Frederick and the pope concluded a peace treaty, in which Frederick agreed to stop taxing churches while the pope agreed to recognize him as King of Jerusalem.[40]

Camelot

Frederick's maternal grandfather had established Sicily (recently re-taken from the Muslims) as a tolerant, multicultural, wealthy island kingdom where Christians, Jews, and Muslims could enjoy security and protection in the practice of their religious customs.[41] After Frederick returned from Palestine, his court enjoyed a golden age such as Europe had not witnessed in a thousand years. While the church at this time was bent on restraining scientific investigation and the arts, Frederick was eagerly embracing new teaching wherever he could find it:

> We have always loved knowledge from our youth; whatever time we can steal from state affairs we cheerfully dedicate to reading the many volumes stored in our library. We have stripped the works written by the Greek and Arabic philosophers of their garb; we have had them translated by chosen men, maintaining faithfully the virginity of the words. We do not wish to keep them all to ourselves. ... Do you make them

public for the use of your students, to the glory of your Caesar. We do not wish to keep them all for ourselves.[42]

One of Frederick's favorite pastimes was mathematics. When the great mathematician Leonardo Fibonacci dedicated his treatise to Frederick, Frederick responded by giving Fibonacci some problems to solve, which Fibonacci ultimately did. While negotiating with the sultan in Palestine, Frederick did him the honor of sending a gift of mathematical problems to ponder, while requesting in return the honor of hosting Arab astronomers at his court.[43]

The intellectual freedom of Frederick's circle attracted an ever increasing number of travelers and scholars. With the founding of the University of Naples, Frederick's court became the established center of a great educational movement and his imperial seat became the principal destination of teachers and scholars from Europe and the Middle East—Christians, Muslims, and Jews. He turned the medical school at the University of Salerno into the foremost institution of its kind in the world; a condition of receiving a license to practice medicine was taking an oath to serve the poor, for free.[44]

Frederick did more than encourage science; he pursued it himself, writing an extensive treatise on ornithology that stood as the leading work in the field for centuries. His interest was sparked by the sport of falconry, but his six-volume *De Arte Venandi cum Avibus* became arguably the most impressive work of empirical science of any kind during the entire Middle Ages. He resolutely rejected conventional lore, recording only observations that he himself or his trusted associates made: "We have followed Aristotle when it was opportune. But in many cases, especially in that which regards the nature of some birds, he appears to have departed from the truth. That is why we have not always followed the prince of the philosophers because rarely, or never, had he experience of hunting which we have loved and practiced always." The church, by contrast, had forbidden all study of Aristotle in 1209.[45]

If the facts were not available on a particular issue he drew no conclusions but left the question open. He observed that birds who obtain their food by scratching the earth have the inner face of the claw on the middle toe of each foot serrated for the purpose: that cranes have the inner front toe of each foot curved like those of birds of prey, and that in order to preserve their sharpness these toes lie sideways on the ground. He advanced a theory that vultures have no feathers on their necks because they thrust their heads into the carcasses of dead animals while they are feeding. It was Frederick who first discovered the nesting habits of cuckoos; he noticed a strange chick in a nest and brought it home to be reared with great care, and found that it grew up into a cuckoo. One of Pope Gregory's many denunciations of Frederick was that he would only believe what was proved by force of reason and nature.[46]

The free and open atmosphere that Frederick encouraged led him to another astonishing conclusion for its time: that his people deserved to have a written constitution, spelling out their rights. On September 1, 1231, Frederick proclaimed the Constitution of the Kingdom of Sicily, one of the great legal codes of history. Among other things, the Constitution:

• Abolished serfdom and gave peasants the right to inherit land. Frederick was fond of saying that "nothing is more odious than the oppression of the poor by the rich."

• Stripped the clergy of their jurisdiction in criminal cases, which were to be tried in the king's courts.

• Increased penalties for crimes against women, and allowed women to inherit estates.

• Provided for a representative assembly, with each town sending two delegates to inform the king about local needs.

• Allowed the government to legitimize the illegitimate children of priests.

• Banned trial by ordeal, a practice in which guilt or innocence was established by subjecting a defendant to various forms of torture to see whether God would protect him or not.

• Ensured freedom of worship for Muslims and Jews.[47]

Gregory, of course, was outraged, and issued a ringing denunciation of the entire Constitution as soon as he heard about it.[48]

Frederick surrounded himself not only with scholars, sculptors, and scientists, but with troubadours and dancers, a menagerie of exotic animals, carnivals and jousting tournaments in which the knights of France were eager to participate. His cosmopolitan court had an air of Eastern splendor and magnificence, graced by poets, musicians, and artists. Dante Alighieri later called Frederick the father of Italian poetry: not for his financial support, but for his own written work.[49] He was said by his enemies to maintain a harem, a charge which may have contained more than a kernel of truth, given the number of illegitimate children he acknowledged and supported. He even took a bath every day, in an age when dirt was considered to be an outward sign of Christian humility.[50]

War

The final breach with Rome resulted from Frederick's efforts to consolidate his rule over rebellious cities of northern Italy. Success would mean that Gregory would be hemmed in by Frederick and his dangerous ideas on all sides; indeed, Frederick seems to have intended to end papal rule over central Italy and create a unified secular Italian state. Combined with his rule over most of Germany, this would truly have re-created the pre-Augustine Roman Empire.[51]

A war of words accompanied the war on the battlefield, with the pope claiming that Frederick had turned a holy altar into a public latrine, had used churches as brothels, had practiced sodomy openly, had blasphemed by calling Christ, Moses, and Muhammad "three impostors," and had said of the Eucharist: "How long will this hocus-pocus continue?" He was "a beast filled with blasphemous words ...with the feet of a bear, the mouth of an outraged lion, the rest of the body shaped like a panther ... the creator of lies, oblivious of modesty, untouched by the blush of shame."[52]

Name-calling was a two-way street. Frederick called the clergy "insatiable leeches ... disguised in sheep's clothing, these ravenous wolves send legates hither and thither to excommunicate, to suspend, to punish—not as sowers of seed, that is the word of God, but to extort money, to harvest and reap that which they did not sow."[53]

Pope Gregory, now nearly a hundred years old, excommunicated Frederick once again in 1239, absolving all subjects of allegiance to him. When Frederick turned his army toward Rome, the pope played his ace: he led a solemn procession through Rome supposedly carrying the heads of both St. Peter and St. Paul, and then before an enormous crowd removed his tiara and placed it on the head of St. Peter. How was a mere emperor supposed to match *that*? There was more ammunition where that came from; the pope had at his disposal items purporting to be the ark of the covenant; the tablets of Moses; the rod of Aaron; an urn of manna; the virgin Mary's tunic; John the Baptist's hair shirt; the five loaves and two fishes from the feeding of the five thousand; the table used at the Last Supper; and, to cap it all off, the foreskin and umbilical cord of Jesus himself. Wisely or unwisely, Frederick backed down and ordered his army away from the gates of Rome.[54]

In 1241, Gregory called for a council, apparently for the purpose of mobilizing the entire church behind the effort to destroy Frederick. Frederick could not allow this to happen; after a successful naval battle, he captured three cardinals, four archbishops, six bishops, and other assorted clergy on their way to the council. News of this outrage may have helped finish off Gregory, who finally died in August 1241. Reconciliation seemed within reach when a new pope to Frederick's liking was elected.[55]

Two weeks later, the new pope was dead, under suspicious circumstances. This time the cardinals haggled for two years before finally agreeing on a successor; the winner, who became Innocent IV, turned out to be as adamantly anti-Frederick as Gregory had been. What was worse, Innocent snuck out of Rome by night and set sail for France, where Frederick could not control him. There he raised vast sums of money to foment insurrections against Frederick, with no interest in compromise:

His sentence is absolutely irrevocable! His probation is the voice of God by the church: he is condemned and forever! His viper progeny are included under this unmitigable proscription. Whoever then loves justice should rejoice that vengeance is thus declared against the common enemy and wash his hands in the blood of the transgressor.[56]

Civil war dragged on inconclusively for five years, while papal agents (including the pope's brother in-law) attempted to assassinate Frederick. In the days before mass media, Frederick had no way of countering the vituperation that poured from every pulpit, week after week, from clergy who did not like being called "insatiable leeches." Frederick grimly hung on, but did not prosper; while he was preoccupied in Germany, the Jerusalem truce expired, and the Muslims once again drove out the Christian army—this time, for 700 years. When a frustrated and embittered Frederick died in 1250, the pope exclaimed "Let the heavens rejoice and the earth exult!"[57]

The church had no intention of putting up with any more insolence from the Hohenstaufen family. All 10 of Frederick's "viper progeny" children and grandchildren were either exterminated by the pope or died in his dungeons.[58] Europe's Enlightenment, which Frederick seemed about to launch, was delayed for 500 years.

As warned at the outset, pre-Enlightenment heroes didn't fare too well. Those who champion peace rather than violence, reason rather than revelation, and tolerance rather than bigotry still deserve applause, whether or not they win their battles.

Wouldn't Frederick's story make a great movie? Who's going to play Frederick? Who plays Gregory? Who's in the harem? How do you stage the naval battle? How do we get this project funded? Share your thoughts on this and the other questions you'll find at **dgc.humanistpress.com!**

Notes:

1 Daniel-Rops, *Dark Ages*, 90, 110; Johnson, *Christianity*, 128; Southern, *Western Society*, 98.

2 Seckel, *Decretals*; Davenport, *Decretals*, 23, 87.

3 Davenport, *Decretals*, 68.

4 Norwich, *Absolute Monarchs*, 43; Masson, *Frederick*, 53; Johnson, *Christianity*, 220.

5 Johnson, *Christianity*, 139.

6 Robinson, *Blood*, 14.

7 Berkhofer, *Slavery*, 555; Sylvester, *Slavery,* 62.

8 Bloch, *Slavery*, 29.

9 Online Etymology Dictionary, *Slave.*

10 Exodus 21:21.

11 Ephesians 6:5; Philemon 1:15.

12 Garnsey, *Ideas of Slavery,* 47.

13 Berkhofer, *Slavery*, 595.

14 Colossians 2:8; I Cor. 3:18-19.

15 Lindberg, *Christian Attitudes*, 48-50.

16 Gillooly, *Adam and Eve*, 99; Lindberg, *Christian Attitudes*, 51-52.

17 Matt. 10:34; Luke 22:36.

18 Riley-Smith, *Crusades*, 257.

19 Logan, *Middle Ages*, 120-122; Martin, *Cathars*, 84; Riley-Smith, *Crusades*, 11, 161, 213; Johnson, *Christianity*, 245; Robinson, *Blood*, 5; Armstrong, *God*, 197.

20 Riley-Smith, *Crusades*, 30.

21 Logan, *Middle Ages*, 125; Ellerbe, *Dark Side*, 65.

22 Robinson, *Blood*, 65.

23 Robinson, *Blood*, 65.

24 Riley-Smith, *Crusades*, 61, 86.

25 Riley-Smith, *Crusades*, 118, 129.

26 Masson, *Frederick*, 28; Einstein, *Emperor Frederick*, 77.

27 Masson, *Frederick*, 44, 72; Catholic Encyclopedia, *Pope Gregory IX.*

28 Einstein, *Emperor Frederick*, 99-100.

29 Norwich, *Absolute Monarchs*, 182; Masson, *Frederick*, 87; Einstein, *Emperor Frederick*, 155, 211.

30 Norwich, *Absolute Monarchs*, 184; Einstein, *Emperor Frederick*, 215, 219.

31 Einstein, *Emperor Frederick*, 33.

32 Einstein, *Emperor Frederick*, 221.

33 Masson, *Frederick*, 124; Einstein, *Emperor Frederick*, 222.

34 Einstein, *Emperor Frederick*, 227, 235.

35 Masson, *Frederick*, 32, 119.

36 Norwich, *Absolute Monarchs*, 186; Einstein, *Emperor Frederick*, 238, 242.

37 Norwich, *Absolute Monarchs*, 186; Einstein, *Emperor Frederick*, 244; Masson, *Frederick*, 139; Logan, *Middle Ages*, 187.

38 Norwich, *Absolute Monarchs*, 187; Riley-Smith, *Crusades*, 151.

39 Norwich, *Absolute Monarchs*, 188; Einstein, *Emperor Frederick*, 240, 246, 260; Masson, *Frederick*, 147.

40 Norwich, *Absolute Monarchs*, 188; Masson, *Frederick*, 151; Einstein, *Emperor Frederick*, 264.

41 Norwich, *Absolute Monarchs*, 130; Encyclopedia Britannica Online, *Roger II*. Einstein, *Emperor Frederick*, 59.

42 Einstein, *Emperor Frederick*,154, 291.

43 Masson, *Frederick*, 112, 143.

44 Masson, *Frederick*, 224-225; Einstein, *Emperor Frederick*, 275.

45 Masson, *Frederick*, 216, 235.

46 Masson, *Frederick*, 217, 229.

47 Masson, *Frederick*, 156, 161; Einstein, *Emperor Frederick*, 272-274; Catholic Encyclopedia, *Ordeals*.

48 Encyclopedia Britannica online, *Gregory IX*.

49 Masson, *Frederick*, 93, 186, 206, 207.

50 Einstein, *Emperor Frederick*, 207, 268; Masson, *Frederick*, 93, 197.

51 Norwich, *Absolute Monarchs*, 189; Einstein, *Emperor Frederick*, 323; Masson, *Frederick*, 284.

52 Johnson, *Christianity*, 201.

53 Johnson, *Christianity*, 202.

54 Johnson, *Christianity*, 200; Einstein, *Emperor Frederick*, 346, 337-339; Masson, *Frederick*, 305.

55 Norwich, *Absolute Monarchs*, 190; Einstein, *Emperor Frederick*, 336, 358.

56 Norwich, *Absolute Monarchs*, 190; Einstein, *Emperor Frederick*, 362, 381, 402.

57 Norwich, *Absolute Monarchs*, 191; Logan, *Middle Ages*, 187.

58 Johnson, *Christianity*, 202.

Emperor Zhu Di

CHAPTER 6

ZHU DI VS. THE MANDARINS

Confucianism Perverted

In 2003 the Library of Congress paid a record $10 million for a Portuguese map.[1] What's so special about it is that it depicts the western coast of South America with uncanny accuracy. Of course, maps available for a lot less than $10 million do that as well—but this map was drawn in 1507, before Europeans had ever visited the western coast of South America. So how did the Portuguese mapmaker know what it looked like?

To suggest an answer to that question, this chapter first provides more information about the early humanist Confucius, and how his work was later twisted beyond recognition by God experts and politicians for their own ends. Then it tells of the magnificent Chinese Emperor Zhu Di, whose efforts to advance the world's knowledge by leaps and bounds may well have been responsible for creation of the map, only to have his work later destroyed by God experts relying on the warped version of Confucius.

As described in Chapter 3, Confucius had no interest in founding a religion, though later generations have claimed otherwise. His interest was simply in improving the world around him, by encouraging constructive thought about the best way for humans to live together. As part of his ultimately futile drive for power in his own right, Confucius assembled a party of talented individuals around himself. They talked; they plotted; they argued. They learned from each other and from the master himself, whom they came to revere. Many of these men did go on to achieve high office for themselves, but they never forgot Confucius.[2] A modern comparison might be Ralph Nader, who never achieved office himself but whose disciples have become influential throughout the government.

Unlike Nader, Confucius did not leave a body of written work. After he died, his followers collected some of the things he used to talk about in a compendium called the *Analects* or "literary gleanings" of Confucius.

Summarizing the ideas of Confucius in a few words is not possible, in part because he dwelt less on *what* to think than on *how* to think. He stressed flexibility, cooperation, and treating others as you wish to be treated yourself.[3] He disliked mysticism in all its forms, while intentionally avoiding any discussion about heavenly beings in his teachings.[4] Although he participated in religious ceremonies, he did so simply as an exhibition of respect, while energetically condemning mystics who promised specific results for specific prayers or sacraments. He once said "As for what follows in the imperial ancestral sacrifice once the libation has been made, I do not desire to watch it." He never made the slightest effort to preach to a congregation or to create an ecclesiastical organization. He valued truthfulness, which meant not expounding on things he knew nothing about. "Zilu asked how to serve the spirits and the gods. The Master replied, 'Not yet being able to serve other people, how would you be able to serve the spirits?'"[5] After his death, his followers recalled that "The Master had nothing to say about strange happenings, the use of force, disorder, or the spirits." Mo Tzu, a critic born about the time that Confucius died, charged that the Confucians considered "Heaven to be without intelligence, and the spirits of the dead to be without consciousness."[6]

In 221 BCE a brutal dictator usurped the ruling dynasty and established a rigid, highly unpopular regime. Members of the Confucian party refused to cooperate, and actively fomented conspiracies that, within less than 20 years, succeeded in ousting the oppressive rulers. Confucians then played a prominent part in installing the new Han dynasty, which was to last more than four hundred years.[7]

The earliest Han rulers warmly embraced the ideas of their Confucian supporters. Kao Tsu, the first Han emperor, appointed ministers chosen on the basis of merit to administer his domain, rather than ruling through the hereditary nobility as his predecessors had done. His successor, Emperor Wen, asked the common people for constructive criticism of his policies, freed government-owned slaves, and abolished punishment by mutilation. Another successor, Emperor Wu, created the system of examination that became a permanent feature of Chinese government thereafter, so that those of greatest merit would be awarded positions of power within the administration—an idea not copied in the West until the nineteenth century. He appointed a former swineherd to the highest office in the land based on his reputation for scholarship. Hereditary aristocracy virtually ceased to exist in China.[8]

As the years wore on, though, Wu and later Han emperors chafed under Confucian restrictions on their arbitrary power. Condemning Confucianism would never have worked because of its overwhelming popularity with the people. Instead they began to edit and alter it. Ideas utterly contrary to the spirit of Confucius worked their way into the *Analects*, and into fabricated histories of the man and his ideas—forgery on the order of what the Christians perpetrated in the *Donation of Constantine* documents revealed in the previous chapter. These "histories" recite dialogues between Confucius and various men who had been dead for as much as a hundred years before Confucius lived, list as his first disciples men who were born after Confucius died, and portray other absurdities such as a plot to assassinate the Master by chopping down a tree to fall on his head. An eminent Chinese scholar of the nineteenth century, after exhaustive study, called the Han era biography of Confucius "70 or 80 percent slander."[9] Han Yü, the dedicated Confucian we met in Chapter 3, lamented in the ninth century that "the great classics are lost beyond recovery; the great doctrines decayed beyond recognition. Only one part in a hundred remains of what once was."[10]

Attributing rigid orthodoxy to the people's hero Confucius—putting totalitarian ideas and even the practice of magic into his mouth—made life much easier for the later Han emperors, while making life much worse for the Chinese people. Wu and others also lavished the leading Confucian scholars with rewards, buying their loyalty for a regime that was "Confucian" in name only.[11] Perhaps the greatest insult of all to the memory of Confucius, though, was turning him into a god. Temples in his honor, perhaps as many as a thousand, were built in prefectures and market-towns throughout the empire, where worshipers prostrated themselves and offered sacrifices to obtain his favor. A decree in the year 59 CE ordered the worship of Confucius in every state school, and declared this warped Confucianism the state religion.[12]

No single individual was solely responsible for turning Confucianism into an instrument of repression, but one who did more than his share was a writer named Hsün Tzü, who had a far lower opinion of human capacity than did Confucius. Confucius pressed his students toward a relentless search for knowledge; Hsün Tzü said that proper study "begins with reciting the Classics and ends with learning ritual procedure," echoing the Taoist doctrine of the danger of too much knowledge: "Our life has a limit, but knowledge has no limit. To use the limited to seek the unlimited is indeed dangerous." In Hsün Tzü's perversion of Confucianism, men were to be herded like sheep, with every movement strictly regulated by law.[13]

By the time the Sung dynasty took power in 960, Confucianism had become so altered from Confucius' original simple humanism that modern scholars now refer to the Sung dynasty's leading lights as "Neo-Confucians." Neo-Confucianism featured metaphysical speculation, rigid adherence to societal hierarchy, blind obedience to the emperor, and insistence that the heavily doctored writings attributed to Confucius and other ancient sages constituted the equivalent of biblical revealed truth—everything worth knowing was in there somewhere to find for those with the scholarly achievement necessary to know where to look. What Confucius thought of as a sensible way to approach the ordering of human affairs morphed into unchangeable, divine principles of the cosmos.[14] The simple, flexible humanist of the *Analects* would have been appalled.

The examination system for appointing government administrators created the "mandarin," or bureaucrat, in Chinese society. Mandarins were dominated by Neo-Confucians during the Sung dynasty.[15] In 1280, the Mongols conquered China, and installed a regime that distrusted the loyalty of the mandarins, stripping them of their tax exemptions and social status. Mandarin scholar-bureaucrats moaned that they ranked next-to-last in Chinese society—between prostitutes and beggars.[16]

Zhu Di

Mongol rule was intensely unpopular in China. It lasted less than a century before being overthrown in 1368 by a peasant soldier named Zhu Yuanzhang, who established what came to be known as the Ming ("enlightened") dynasty.[17] The mandarin class who had chafed under the Mongols prayed that Zhu Yuanzhang would restore their influence, and for the most part they got their wish. The emperor's sons received a proper Neo-Confucian education under the mandarins, and the eldest son in line to succeed his father to the throne was a mild-mannered classical scholar.[18]

The emperor's fourth son, Zhu Di, was not. He was a brilliant soldier like his peasant father, who felt far more at home among the troops on the northern frontier than among the effete mandarins of the capital. He sometimes dressed as an ordinary soldier and mingled with the villagers, learning first-hand about their concerns. Later, he wrote that "Stability depends on superior and inferior communicating; there is none when they do not. From ancient times, many a state has fallen because a ruler does not know the affairs of the people." Though there is some indication that Zhu Di may have been his father's favorite, the emperor obeyed the traditions of primogeniture. Even though his oldest son pre-deceased him, the emperor had made clear that his grandson was to follow him to the throne.[19]

Zhu Di accepted this outcome at first, but his conviction of his own superior merits led him to launch a civil war against his nephew within a year of the coronation. The effort succeeded, and Zhu Di became emperor of China in 1402.

The new emperor was not magnanimous toward the mandarins

who had supported his rival, who he feared intended to undermine his own rule. Several thousand were executed or banished, including 870 associates of the Neo-Confucian thinker Fan Xiaoru.[20] With his most dangerous political opponents out of the way, though, Zhu Di sought to ingratiate himself with what remained of the academic class.

This program took the form of assembling a great encyclopedia of human knowledge—all of it. Over three hundred years before Diderot undertook a similar effort during the French Enlightenment, Zhu Di set two thousand scholars to work compiling a massive collection, ultimately containing four thousand volumes and fifty million words, of all known literature and knowledge—the largest scholarly enterprise ever undertaken. The compilation included material on classical texts, history, institutions, ritual, codes of law, military affairs, philosophy, Buddhism, Taoism, astronomy, mathematics, geography, medicine, animals, plants, novels, fiction, and drama.[21]

Zhu Di wrote the preface himself:

> Ever since I succeeded to my father's throne, I have thought about writing and publication as a means of unifying confusing systems and standardizing government regulations and social customs. But it is indeed very difficult to write introductions to the biographies of hundreds of rulers, to summarize classics from every dynasty, to record continuing events of so many centuries, and to simplify and edit so many complex topics. ... Nevertheless, I ordered my officials to compile the Four Treasuries, to purchase lost books from the four corners of the country, to search and to collect whatever they could find, to assemble and classify them according to both topical and phonetic order, and to make them into enduring classics. The fruit of their labor is this encyclopedia, which includes the breadth of the universe and all the texts from antiquity to the present time, whether they are big or small, polished or crude.[22]

Far from honoring Zhu Di for his encouragement of knowledge, though, many mandarins scoffed at the inclusion of scientific and technological material alongside the works of their revered ancient sages. Some complained that out of the 22,877 entries in the work, only 4,946 were "real wheat," with the rest nothing but chaff and banality. Some were upset at the emperor's insistence that controversial interpretations of the classics be included, implying approval of the dangerous idea that settled tradition should be open to later innovation. Other "chaff and banality" dealt with cutting-edge technologies in civil and hydraulic engineering, the use of new construction materials, and the design of new kinds of canal gates and locks for a massive canal Zhu Di built linking the Yangzi delta with north China. Zhu Di also advanced military science, using prototype cannons and blunderbusses in his campaigns against the Mongols that could deliver a projectile as far as a mile and a half away. Europe had nothing so advanced.[23]

The second great work of Zhu Di's reign was moving the imperial capital from Nanjing to Beijing in the north, and building the magnificent Forbidden City to house it. Zhu Di wanted his capital closer to the northern frontier, where barbarians and Mongols posed a constant threat; and he wanted to escape the decadent atmosphere of Nanjing. Over two hundred thousand skilled workers were directly employed onsite; counting those involved in lumbering, quarrying, and transport there were probably a million Chinese at work on the world's most spectacular construction project since the Egyptian pyramids.[24]

The Treasure Fleets

The mandarins hated being uprooted and packed off to the bleak north. They despised even more, though, Zhu Di's third great undertaking: the construction of the mightiest navy the world had ever seen, and the dispatch of that fleet on voyages of exploration to the far corners of the world.

Why would the mandarins object to such a project? Well, their god Confucius was reported to have said "When your father and mother are alive, do not journey far, and when you do travel, be sure to have a specific destination."[25] The likeliest meaning of the passage is something like "Don't be an aimless bum"; it is quite unlikely that Confucius had in mind an organized mission of overseas exploration at a time before the technology enabling such an effort existed. The mandarin God experts, though, took it as a "Thou shalt not."[26] Moreover, all true wisdom was held to be already contained or implied in the works of the sages; Mandarins looked down their nose at any knowledge other than the classics of Chinese literature in which they were already expert, especially mundane subjects such as the physical sciences and mathematics. Besides, interest in contact with the outside world implied that China itself was not already at the pinnacle of perfection; China had no need of interaction with inferior neighbors, which only sullied its dignity.[27]

Fire destroyed several buildings in the Forbidden City in 1421; a plague broke out at the same time, killing 174,000 in the province of Fujian alone. Clearly, the gods were unhappy about something— mandarins pointed their fingers at Zhu Di and his innovations.[28]

None of these misgivings deterred Zhu Di. He was driven in part by the thirst for knowledge, as he was when he sponsored the encyclopedia. Writing once about his rigorous daily schedule, he noted that "Whenever I can find the time, I read history books and the classics so as to avoid idle living. I constantly remind myself that the world is so vast and state affairs so important that I cannot succumb to laziness and complacency for even a moment. Once one has succumbed to laziness and complacency, everything will become stagnant."[29] Zhu Di also felt pride in ruling the most powerful empire on earth, and sought to enhance his glory by disseminating some of the world's most advanced culture. On a more mundane level, he believed his government could profit from overseas trade.

Zhu Di built enormous ships. Some of his vessels were nine-masted junks, 444 feet long—nearly a football field and a half. By contrast, Christopher Columbus sailed the ocean blue 70 years later in vessels that were less than 60 feet long.[30] Voyages of exploration carried some 27,000 sailors, roughly the same as the number of men who fought at the same time—on both sides, on land—in Europe's momentous battle of Agincourt.[31] In total, Zhu Di's navy had some

3,500 vessels; today's United States Navy, by far the largest in the world, has 283.[32] So Zhu Di's intention to explore and to project Chinese influence was not a lark; it was a fantastic undertaking.

To command his fleets, Zhu Di selected an irreligious Muslim eunuch named Zheng He. The practice of castrating young boys to be brought up to serve as government officials was not unique to China; it was common throughout Asia, and not unknown even in Europe. Eunuchs were safer around the royal women, and were thought to be less avaricious since they would never have a family to support or heirs to endow. Thus, they often achieved positions of great power within the government without having learned the niceties of classical literature.[33]

Zheng He and his enormous fleet undertook six major voyages of exploration, spreading Chinese influence throughout southeast Asia, Indonesia, India, Persia, and Arabia. These expeditions were massive projects involving as many as three hundred ships at a time, taking as much as a year to prepare and two years to sail. He reached as far as east Africa and Madagascar on two of his voyages. Mogadishu, capital of Somalia, was described by a member of one expedition as "intolerably hot ... because of the torrid weather only a few plants can grow ... and if anyone wandered over this country he would have met with only sad glances. An entire land having nothing but sand."[34]

The voyages accomplished more than just pushing back the edges of the map. The Chinese planted ambassadors in the countries they visited, and returned foreign ambassadors to Beijing. Soon after Zhu Di moved his capital to Beijing in 1423, he received, in one day alone, an audience of 1,200 envoys from 16 countries, including delegates from Malacca and Mogadishu. "Now all within the four seas are as one family," said Zhu Di.[35]

As important as the diplomatic exchanges was the creation of trading relationships between China and the lands bordering the Indian Ocean. Zheng He's ships were often called the "treasure fleet" because they left home loaded with Chinese goods to sell abroad. According to one report, the mountain of Chinese goods unloaded at an Indian port was so great that it took three months just to price everything.

They returned with exotic items for domestic consumption, along with curiosities such as ostriches, rhinoceroses, leopards, zebras, and giraffes—Zhu Di was especially enthralled with the giraffes. Zhu Di threw China's doors open to foreigners and foreign merchants, decreeing "Let there be mutual trade at the frontier barriers in order to supply the country's needs and to encourage distant people to come." Zhu Di's China maintained trade relationships with some 38 foreign nations in all; the wealth generated from the trade missions financed the building of the Forbidden City.[36] Zheng He also helped clear the sea of pirates who preyed on trade, killing five thousand who had dominated the straits of Malacca in a single battle off Sumatra.[37]

Though many historians disagree, there is evidence suggesting that Chinese navigators in Zhu Di's time also visited Australia, the west coast of Africa, and the Americas.[38] This is where the $10 million map mentioned at the beginning of the chapter comes in. The map dates from 1507—more than a decade *before* Ferdinand Magellan set off on his voyage around the globe, becoming the person your fifth grade history book probably told you was the first European ever to visit the western coast of South America. What's more, using a mathematical technique called "polynomial warping," scholars who compare the shape of South America's actual western coastline with that of the 1507 map declare it to be approximately 75 percent accurate. "The idea that this was a total guess is far-fetched," says the man who ran the analysis.[39] What some historians believe is more likely is that the Chinese did in fact explore the Americas, and the information they gathered found its way (legally or otherwise) into the hands of Europe's 1507 mapmaker. This hypothesis is supported by pre-Columbian artifacts unearthed by archeologists in the Americas that appear to be of Chinese origin, by genetic studies of Central American Indians indicating a linkage to the Chinese province of Kwantung, and by wreckage of what appears to be a fifteenth century Chinese junk in San Francisco bay.[40]

None of the evidence is smoking-gun conclusive, and some scholars dismiss it all as pseudo-history.[41] Skeptics pose a simple question: if this theory is true, then why didn't China have an ongoing connection to this new land? Surely China would not have discovered the New World and then just forgotten about it?

The response is just as simple: never underestimate the intransigence of a God expert.

The Humanist Emperor

Zhu Di was not an atheist, though he did once write that "Fortune or calamity, good or bad luck do not originate from heaven; they are caused by people." But he deliberately played different categories of God experts against one another, so that none would grow too powerful; for example, at one ceremony he simultaneously donned a Confucian cap, a Taoist robe, and Buddhist sandals. Though he sponsored the publication of Buddhist texts, when the number of applicants registering to become Buddhist monks started to get out of hand, he banished them to a distant province. He also treated formal religious observance with disdain, occasionally sending a delegate to take his place at rites that only the emperor was supposed to perform.[42]

Rather than concentrate on metaphysical or theological issues, such as reincarnation or proper forms of sacrifice, Zhu Di was what would later be described in the West as a "deist," who acknowledged divine power but paid little attention to what the God experts taught. Instead he thought for himself, and cherry-picked what he saw as the best elements of the three principal streams of Chinese religious thought to build a more humane society, at least by comparison to the Mongol regime that had preceded his father's revolt. His humanist thinking is best reflected in a book he compiled called *Do Charities Anonymously*, which consisted of 165 biographies of persons he thought worth emulating. In the preface he explained that: "The Book of History says that heaven protects and benefits those who do charities anonymously. When a person performs virtuous deeds and gives charities, but prefers not to be recognized or to receive anything in return, heaven, which governs all creation, will respond like an echo to a sound." Here and in other writings, Zhu Di stressed the importance of the individual conscience, as opposed to mindlessly following the dictates either of one's ancestors or the God experts.[43]

Zhu Di's humanism was echoed by his wife, the Empress Xu, who authored two books on her own:

> His Majesty has also resolved to help the people live longer, happier, richer, kinder, and gentler lives. He often says that when the emperor works harder, the whole world will enjoy more leisure. I usually have bowed and echoed his belief that diligence is the foundation of politics and humanism is the source of bliss. ... But humanism is born out of kindness, while kindness is the bedrock of bliss. Therefore, if one is seeking bliss and good fortune, one ought to first practice kindness and charity.[44]

At the same time, Zhu Di cracked down hard on religious secret societies and Buddhist messiahs who sprang up in the countryside. According to one of his decrees:

> Some [shamans] may secretly possess charts and images; burn incense to gather a crowd; assemble at night and disperse at daybreak; deceptively appear to be engaged in good works; and arouse and mislead the common people. The leaders are to be strangled while their supporters are to receive one hundred strokes of the heavy bamboo and banishment to three thousand li.[45]

Destroying the Evidence

When Zhu Di died in 1424, his efforts to move China forward came to a screeching halt. His successor, Zhu Gaozhi, surrounded himself with a group of traditional mandarin God experts who were anxious to turn back the clock. The day after he formally ascended the throne, Zhu Gaozhi issued his first edict: "All voyages of the treasure ships are to be stopped. All ships moored at Taicang (near the mouth of the Yangtze River) are ordered back to Nanjing and all goods on the ships are to be turned over to the Department of Internal Affairs and stored. If there were any foreign envoys wishing to return home, they will be provided with a small escort. Those officials who are currently abroad on business are ordered back to the capital immediately. ... The building and repair of all treasure ships is to be stopped immediately." Zhu Gaozhi also began planning to move the capital back to Nanjing.[46]

What the mandarins despised the most was the disruption to the god-created order of things caused by the voyages. It was bad enough to put on display things such as giraffes that the ancient sages had never written about, and to imply that there were things worth learning that the mandarins didn't already know. What was worse was the economic effect of foreign trade, which tended to enrich eunuchs, merchants, entrepreneurs, and other unworthies who had not devoted their lives to the study of classic literature. While it is certainly not uncommon today for academics to scorn business people, in fifteenth century China, the academics had the ear of the emperor, and the gods on their side. Had not Confucius himself said "The mind of a superior man dwells on righteousness; the mind of a little man dwells on profit"?[47] Mandarins believed that the sudden creation of an uncouth nouveau riche class disrupted the natural counterpoise of society, favoring instead a balance which conveniently placed themselves back on top.[48]

The mandarins overlooked, of course, the overwhelming weight of the authentic teaching of Confucius, which opposed rigid doctrines and encouraged people to think for themselves. The followers who compiled the *Analects* recalled that "There were four things the Master abstained from entirely: he did not speculate, he did not claim or demand certainty, he was not inflexible, and he was not self-absorbed," and "The Master said, 'Exemplary persons in making their way in the world are neither bent on nor against anything; rather, they go with what is appropriate.'" They also recalled that "Weisheng Mou said to Confucius, "Why do you flit from perch to perch? Are you aspiring to be an eloquent talker?" Confucius replied, "It is not that I aspire to be an eloquent talker, but rather that I hate inflexibility." Moreover, Confucius never taught envy. On the contrary: "The truly virtuous man," he said, "desiring to be established himself, seeks to establish others; desiring success for himself, he strives to help others succeed."[49]

Zhu Gaozhi died after less than a year on the throne. His successor was not quite as backwards, authorizing Zheng He to make one last grand voyage.[50] There continued to be a political push and pull between the mandarins and those who stood to profit from the expansion of trade, until one day in the middle of the century someone—no one knows who—managed to slip into the imperial archives, locate the carefully preserved charts and voyage logs, and destroy them all.[51] Whether records about voyages to the Americas were caught up in the conflagration is anyone's guess.

This clever maneuver ended the debate. Over decades, since the time of the Mongols, navigators with every expedition had meticulously charted details of their exact position every day, building a knowledge base that made every subsequent voyage that much easier. Now it was all gone, and with it the temptation to learn facts that might call into question the wisdom of the sages. A stream of imperial edicts banned all overseas trade and travel; anyone sailing out of sight from land was to be executed. In 1551 even fishing boats were forbidden to go out to sea. Chinese shipbuilding know-how vanished with the lack of demand for new ships; so did the closely related development of guns and cannons, allowing the Europeans to catch up in the technology of firepower.[52] Not long afterward, Spanish ships began to show up in Chinese ports, followed inexorably by Portuguese, Dutch, and English.[53] Trade began to flourish again—this time under European control, on terms overwhelmingly favorable to the Europeans, who ultimately came to dominate China.

China under mandarin domination settled into a comfortable intellectual backwardness that extended to sciences other than geography and armament. A century after Zhu Di, a self-educated doctor named Li Shih-Chen failed the civil service examinations three times, because the medical knowledge he had learned was irrelevant to the classical literature on which the tests were based. Abandoning his hope of a government career, he instead devoted himself to the expansion of medical knowledge. He didn't just paste together quotations; he analyzed, compared, incorporated empirical observations of efficacy, and did his best thereby to attain new knowledge. Though

Li Shih-Chen was never persecuted for his work, as a European Christian might have been at the time, he was not encouraged or rewarded either. He was never given any money by the government, and although after his death a couple of provincial authorities agreed to reprint his work, the mandarins who dominated the emperors steadfastly refused to acknowledge the significance of knowledge beyond what they had learned to pass their own exams.[54]

Chinese intellectual backwardness was not reversed until a decidedly non-religious regime under Mao Zedong took power five hundred years after Zhu Di. A short 50 years later, a new generation of Chinese explorers began aiming for the moon.

> The mandarins were not the only God experts who stifled the growth of useful human knowledge. We saw that earlier with Augustine, and we'll see it repeatedly in later chapters. What is it about religion that is so opposed to the idea of scientific development? Share your thoughts on this and the other questions you'll find at **dgc.humanistpress.com**!

Notes:

1 Library of Congress, *Waldseemüller*.

2 Creel, *Confucius*, 3, 40.

3 Creel, *Confucius*, 122.

4 Yamamoto, *Eastern Religions*, 60; Clennell, *Religion in China*, 64.

5 Confucius, *Analects*, 84, 115, 144; Yu, *State and Religion*, 19.

6 Creel, *Confucius*, 114.

7 Creel, *Confucius*, 4, 230.

8 Creel, *Confucius*, 1, 229, 232, 234.

9 Clennell, *Religion in China*, 52; Creel, *Confucius*, 7, 245.

10 Hartman, *Han Yü*, 5.

11 Creel, *Confucius*, 4, 5, 111, 242.

12 Watters, "Guide," 121; Yu, *State and Religion*, 49; Yamamoto, *Eastern Religions*, 64.

13 Creel, *Confucius*, 208-209.

14 Tsai, *Happiness*, 136; Chan, *Chien-Wen*, 184; Hartman, *Han Yü*, 10; Peterson, *Confucian*, 710.

15 Peterson, *Confucian*, 709.

16 Levathes, *Seas*, 49.

17 Menzies, *1421*, 45.

18 Tsai, *Happiness*, 28.

19 Brook, *Communications*, 638; Tsai, *Happiness*, 29, 63.

20 Tsai, *Happiness*, 70.

21 Menzies, *1421*, 62; Chan, *Chien-Wen*, 221; Brook, *Communications*, 653.

22 Tsai, *Happiness*, 134.

23 Tsai, *Happiness*, 119, 124, 136, 171; Chan, *Chien-Wen*, 220.

24 Levathes, *Seas*, 144-145.

25 Confucius, *Analects*, 93.

26 Levathes, *Seas*, 33.

27 Clennell, *Religion in China*, 145-148; Levathes, *Seas*, 180; Yu, *State and Religion*, 106.

28 Tsai, *Happiness*, 83; Menzies, *1421*, 77.

29 Tsai, *Happiness*, 102.

30 Chan, *Chien-Wen*, 232; Pickering, *Columbus's Ships*.

31 Chan, *Chien-Wen*, 235; Knights, *Agincourt*.

32 Levathes, *Seas*, 174-175; Naval History Command, *Force Levels*.

33 Levathes, *Seas*, 72, 147.

34 Brook, *Communications*, 616; Levathes, *Seas*, 151.

35 Tsai, *Happiness*, 201; Levathes, *Seas*, 88.

36 Brook, *Communications*, 616; Chan, *Chien-Wen*, 235; Tsai, *Happiness*, 124; Levathes, *Seas*, 88, 144-145.

37 Chan, *Chien-Wen*, 233.

38 *See generally*, Menzies, 1421.

39 Brown, *Mapmaker*.

40 Menzies, *1421*, 246, 265, 267.

41 *See, e.g., The 1421 Myth Exposed*.

42 Tsai, *Happiness*, 8-84, 146; Taylor, *Official Religion*, 857.

43 Tsai, *Happiness*, 145; Chan, *Chien-Wen*, 219.

44 Tsai, *Happiness*, 139.

45 Tsai, *Happiness*, 108; Taylor, *Official Religion*, 889.

46 Tsai, *Happiness*, 98; Levathes, *Seas*, 163-164; Chan, *Chien-Wen*, 282.

47 Levathes, *Seas*, 33, 175, 180.

48 Menzies, *1421*, 50.

49 Confucius, *Analects*, 91, 127, 179; Creel, *Confucius*, 131.

50 Levathes, *Seas*, 165; Brook, *Communications*, 616.

51 Menzies, *1421*, 35.

52 Brook, *Communications*, 619; Geiss, *Chia-Ching*, 495; Levathes, *Seas*, 177.

53 Geiss, *Chia-Ching*, 504.

54 Peterson, *Confucian*, 782-784.

Desiderius Erasmus

CHAPTER 7

ERASMUS VS. LUTHER

Decadence of the Church

After killing off the last of Frederick II's "viper progeny," the church saw its power grow unchecked. Even a schism in 1378 that gave Christendom two (and later three) simultaneous competing popes over a period of four decades did not shake the people's faith.[1] The straw that finally broke the camel's back was the excesses of the Borgia family who captured the papacy for themselves twice and who became notorious for their greed and decadence.

Alfonso di Borgia became Pope Calixtus III in 1455. Though he reigned for only three years, he appointed dozens of family members to various posts, where they quickly developed a reputation for enjoying luxury and an attitude of insolence. In 1458 Calixtus installed his nephew Rodrigo di Borgia to be Bishop of Valencia, then bishop of Cartagena, then bishop of Majorca, and to several other posts as well—all at the same time. Rodrigo was highly industrious, squeezing every penny he could out of his territories.[2]

Rodrigo had seven children by various mothers while he was a cardinal and one or two more after he became Pope Alexander VI in 1492. The mother of four of the children Alexander acknowledged was married to someone else at the time. He paraded his young mistress, Giulia Farnese, openly at papal functions. When Giulia reunited briefly with her husband, the pope demanded that she return to Rome instead, threatening her with excommunication when she delayed. To celebrate the Jubilee Year of 1500, one of Alexander's illegitimate sons gave a banquet for his father at which 50 courtesans danced, first clothed and then naked, ultimately crawling among the feet of the diners to gather chestnuts from the floor.[3]

There were at least 30 Borgia family members in high positions of church and state, all of whom needed money. Alexander was both ruthless and creative about satisfying this need. He excommunicated lords for failing to make their payments to the church on time. He allowed King Ladislaus of Hungary to cast off his wife—for 25,000 ducats. He granted a posthumous absolution to two deceased kings of Portugal—after their successors paid off what he claimed was their debt to the church.[4]

Niccolò Machiavelli, not widely regarded today as a paragon of virtue, had little use for Alexander. "We Italians are irreligious and corrupt above others," Machiavelli wrote, "because the church and her representatives set us the worst example." Other critics were less subtle: "These are the days of Antichrist; the bestiality and savagery of Nero and Caligula are surpassed. Rodrigo Borgia is an abyss of vice, a subverter of all justice, human or divine."[5]

Erasmus' Alternative

Disgust for what the church had become found an articulate spokesman in Desiderius Erasmus, born in 1469 as the bastard son of a Dutch priest.[6] After what seems to have been a miserable child-hood, Erasmus joined an Augustinian monastery, where he was not much happier. Monastic asceticism did not suit him: "Perhaps God wishes to tempt us," he later wrote, "but surely he does not want to torture us." He spent decades in an ultimately successful quest to receive a papal dispensation from his monastic vows.[7]

What he did come to love was the written word, especially the literature of pagan Greece and Rome. These works had been shelved for a thousand years because of the church's insistence that only works of Christian piety were worthy of study. In 1500, while the Borgias cavorted with their nude dancers in the Vatican, Erasmus brought out his first book, the *Adages*. This was simply a collection of 818 quotations from Greek and Roman pagan authors, along with Erasmus' commentary on each. While such an effort would seem trivial today, in 1500 it caused a sensation. Wisdom from non-Christians? What will they think of next! Using the newfangled technology of the printing press, the *Adages* quickly became a bestseller. The book was so successful that Erasmus expanded and republished it several times, with the final edition having grown to more than four thousand items.[8]

The commercial success of the *Adages* brought Erasmus enough attention to enable him to publish his own original work, *The Dagger of the Christian Knight*, a frontal assault on the empty formalism of the church. He offered this observation:

> The salt of the earth has lost its savor. I am ashamed to say how superstitiously the majority of religious observe ceremonies of completely human origin, how hatefully they expect others to conform to them, how implicitly they trust in them, how boldly they condemn others and how cock-sure they are in their expectation of heavenly reward.[9]

He singled out for scathing criticism the practice of selling indulgences for the remission of sins: "You believe, perhaps, all your sins and offenses to be washed away at once with a little paper or parchment sealed with wax. ... You have wandered completely from the path." Between the lines, *The Dagger* implied the rejection of hierarchical authority, encouraging everyone to read the scriptures themselves and form their own conclusions.[10]

In 1510, Erasmus branched into yet another genre: satire. *In Praise of Folly*, the work for which he is best known today, is an oration of the Goddess of Folly in praise of herself, since she thought no one else was willing to recognize her worth. This device allowed Erasmus to poke fun at every profession and class, even every body part:

> As is my fashion, I ask you, is it the head, or the face, or the chest, or the hand, or the ear—all considered respectable parts of the body—is it any of these which generates gods and men? No, I think not. Rather, the human race is propagated by the

part which is so foolish and funny that it cannot even be mentioned without a snicker.[11]

But his sharpest barbs were reserved for the God experts:

> They depict every detail of the infernal regions so exactly that you would think they had spent several years in that commonwealth. … If wisdom would come to the popes, what comforts it would deprive them of! It would deprive them of all wealth, honor and possessions; all the triumphal progress, offices, dispensation, tributes and indulgences; the many horses, mules and retainers; in short, it would deprive them of all their pleasures.[12]

In Praise of Folly became an instant hit all across Europe, and cemented Erasmus' reputation as the preeminent intellectual of the day.[13]

In Erasmus' own mind, though, his most significant work was his retranslation of the New Testament. The Gospels had originally been written in Greek (an interesting tidbit in itself because it is extremely unlikely that the disciples of Jesus spoke Greek, and the Greek-speaking cities of Palestine are conspicuously absent from the list of places the Gospels tell us Jesus visited).[14] But Greek was not widely spoken even by educated people in Rome or the western portion of the Empire, so during the fifth century Jerome had translated the New Testament into Latin, in a text known as the *Vulgate*, which the church had approved as the official version.[15]

As Erasmus became more proficient in the Greek language, he came to realize that much of the translation in the *Vulgate* was simply wrong. How could people interpret the Bible for themselves if the words they were looking at weren't even the actual words of the Bible? So Erasmus gathered what he thought were the earliest Greek texts available, and produced a new translation, correcting errors at a rate exceeding one on every page. He also added provocative commentary, such as his observations that the commission Jesus gave to Peter ("upon this rock I will build my church") said nothing about giving any authority to his successors, and that Luke could not have witnessed the events he described.[16]

The errors weren't just typos, either. For example, the bizarre three-god concept of the Trinity rested almost entirely on a single verse in the Gospel of John. But when Erasmus examined his Greek sources, he discovered that the verse wasn't there; it had apparently been inserted at a later date, perhaps to justify a theory that had been manufactured from whole cloth as a sop to polytheism. So Erasmus, his eye solely on the truth, left it out. This caused such an uproar that one group of industrious traditional God experts set themselves to forging a Greek text of the Gospel of John that put the words back in, and sending it to Erasmus with a demand that he publish a revision. The fraud worked; Erasmus put the forged verse into his next edition.[17]

Even aside from the Trinity verse, Christians were stunned to learn that the Bible was not the Bible. A professor at the Sorbonne College in Paris hysterically burst out that "If in one point the *Vulgate* were in error the entire authority of Holy Scripture would collapse, love and faith would be extinguished, heresies and schisms would abound, blasphemy would be committed against the Holy Spirit, the authority of theologians would be shaken, and indeed the Catholic Church would collapse from the foundations." Erasmus had found not one error, but hundreds. In many places, such as Cambridge, England, his book was banned as soon as it arrived.[18]

Even more profound than his result, though, was his method: looking critically at the text and making informed judgments as to its validity. No one had ever done that in a public way before; Christians had been brainwashed that the *Vulgate* was the be-all and end-all, and the hierarchy's interpretation of it beyond question. After Erasmus, scholars dug deeper and deeper, discovering so many variations among different ancient biblical texts, translation errors, internal discrepancies, and contradictions of known historical facts that the whole "word of God" notion became untenable. Modern biblical scholar Bart Ehrman, for example, has pointed out that there are more variations among the early New Testament manuscripts than there are words in the New Testament. Ehrman and others also note that the Greek manuscripts Erasmus worked from turn out to be among the least authentic available, though Erasmus had no way of knowing that.[19]

Luther's Revolt

The Sorbonne professor's panic at what might happen once the bubble of church credibility was punctured was on the mark.

One person who read Erasmus with intense interest was a fellow Augustinian named Martin Luther. Whether Luther would have had the audacity to reject Rome's authority had Erasmus not blazed the path is unknowable. What we do know is that Luther approached religion from an entirely different standpoint than Erasmus did. He felt no need to determine what the early Scriptures actually said because he believed that he received his revelation directly from God (while seated on the toilet).[20]

Luther's first act of rebellion was against the low-hanging fruit of the sale of indulgences, which Erasmus had ridiculed years earlier. The pope, seeking money for the construction of St. Peter's Basilica in Rome, had authorized the Dominicans to launch a traveling indulgence sales tour through Germany, drawing in crowds by exhibiting a collection of some nine thousand relics including a bone of Isaac, manna from the wilderness, and a jar from Cana (with miracle wine still in it). The Dominican pitch would have done Madison Avenue proud: "The moment the money tinkles in the collecting box, a soul flies out of purgatory."[21]

The road show infuriated Friedrich, the Elector of Saxony. Not because he found such commercialization unseemly, but because he had his own revenue-producing collection of 17,433 relics, including the entire body of one of the Holy Innocents said to have been slaughtered at the time Jesus was born, and he hated the competition. Correctly expecting that Friedrich would protect him from harm, Luther nailed a document he called "Ninety-five Theses Against Indulgences" to the church door of Wittenberg Castle: "The pope has wealth far beyond all other men—why does he not build St. Peter's church with his own money instead of the money of poor Christians?"[22]

The pope at first chalked up Luther's assault to rivalry between the Dominicans, who were authorized to sell indulgences, and the Augustinians, who were not.[23] He underestimated, though, how seriously Erasmus had undermined the foundation of popular confidence in Rome. Once Luther realized he could step on the tiger's tail and live to tell about it, he invented more and more points of difference between the way he imagined God worked and the traditional teaching of the church.

Chief among these was the concept of predestination—if God is *all* powerful, then man must be completely *lacking* in power, including any power to affect his own afterlife. According to Luther, God simply decides on a whim who goes to heaven and who burns in hell, and there is nothing anyone can do about it. No one can possibly *deserve* to be saved because man is so utterly depraved. According to Luther, "God's eternal hatred of man is not only hatred of the shortcomings of the free will, but a hatred which existed even before the creation of the world." Luther believed that only a tiny fraction of humanity would end up being saved, with the rest consigned to the hellfire they so richly deserved. Responding to criticism that such arbitrariness on God's part was unfair, Luther responded majestically that "Since God is true and one, He is utterly incomprehensible and inaccessible to human reason. Therefore His justice also must be incomprehensible."[24]

Luther observed the German political situation astutely. One of his first books was his *Address to the Christian Nobility of the German Nation*. Not an address to the emperor, but an address to the people who actually had the power on the ground. Luther urged the princes to free themselves and their subjects from domination by the pope because the pope was an impostor put in place by the devil. When princes read this, they realized that Luther's doctrine meant they would no longer have to pay taxes to the pope—a prospect with enormous appeal.[25]

In 1520 Luther was condemned for heresy by a papal decree, *Exsurge Domine*. He responded by dramatically burning the decree at the gates of Wittenberg University. The rhetoric then escalated, with Luther calling the pope the anti-Christ, and inviting Christendom to "wash your hands in the blood of these cardinals, popes and other dregs of the Roman Sodom." The Catholic God experts of Louvain responded by calling for the execution of Luther, "that pestilential fart of Satan whose stench reaches to Heaven."[26]

War and Peace

Throughout Germany, average citizens noticed that authority was being challenged without the challengers being immediately consigned to the flames. Peasants and artisans seized the opportunity to turn on their aristocratic oppressors, in what became known as the "Peasants' War" of 1524. There had been populist risings in Europe in the past, which failed in part because they lacked a coherent philosophy. The insurgents of 1524 saw Luther as a fellow rebel, and claimed they were fighting in the cause of "divine law" and "divine justice." The establishment saw things the same way, branding every rabble-rouser as a Lutheran heretic.[27]

Luther sympathized with the rebels at first, but he knew that God experts who allied themselves with peasants tended to have short life-spans. The Peasants' Revolt provided him with a golden opportunity to win the affection of the princes who could nurture him by betraying the peasants who were putting their lives on the line in support of his own ideas. Luther's tract entitled *Against the Robbing and Murderous Hordes of Peasants* relied on Romans 13:1 ("For there is no power but of God: the powers that be are ordained of God") to cast the murderous hordes as sinners:

> Let everyone who can, smite, slay and stab, secretly or openly, remembering that nothing can be more poisonously hurtful or devilish than a rebel. ... These times are so extraordinary that a prince can win heaven more easily by bloodshed than by prayer. ... You cannot meet a rebel with reason. Your best answer is punch him in the face until he has a bloody nose.[28]

Erasmus' response to the uprising was quite different. He urged the abolition of the crushing feudal tax obligations that beset the peasants: "Against this revolt of misery and despair the princes know no remedy but cruelty, which does not cure the evil." Centuries before it became fashionable, Erasmus called for public care of the aged and infirm, state controls over capital to avoid undue concentration of wealth, and reform of the penal system. Long before the outbreak of Lutheran violence, Erasmus had written the first book in European history entirely devoted to the cause of pacifism, aptly titled *War is Sweet to the Inexperienced*.[29] He explicitly rejected the teachings of Augustine and Thomas Aquinas that killing was ok so long as it was done in the context of a "just war"–*i.e.*, a war to promote Christianity against its enemies.

Luther also promoted violence against demons and witches. "Many regions," he said, "are inhabited by devils. Prussia is full of them, and Lapland of witches. In my native country on the top of a high mountain called the Pubelsberg is a lake into which if a stone be thrown a tempest will arise over the whole region because the waters are the abode of captive demons." He personally ordered the burning of four witches at Wittenberg, as well as the killing of a retarded child whom he deemed to be the offspring of Satan.[30] Erasmus flatly condemned the burning of witches, along with the entire institution of the Inquisition.[31]

Truth

Betrayal of his supporters served Luther well; his next step was betrayal of the Bible. Erasmus, we saw above, was so committed to accuracy that he risked prosecution as a heretic to translate the New Testament as it was written. He encouraged others to translate his work into local languages so the common people could read it as well, even though church law flatly prohibited laymen from owning or reading the Bible at all, in any language. Luther accepted the invitation to translate Erasmus' work into German.[32] But contrary to Erasmus, when Luther encountered passages at odds with his own theology, he simply changed them.

One of Luther's central tenets, a corollary of predestination, was that man was powerless to affect his own destiny through acts of kindness or other good works; the only thing man could do for himself was to have faith in the all-encompassing power of God.[33] The Epistle of James was rather at odds with that notion:

What good is it, my brothers, if a man claims to have faith but has no deeds? Can such faith save him? Suppose a brother or sister is without clothes and daily food. If one of you says to him, "Go, I wish you well; keep warm and well fed," but does nothing about his physical needs, what good is it? In the same way, faith by itself, if it is not accompanied by action, is dead. … You believe that there is one God. Good! Even the demons believe that. … You see that a person is justified by what he does and not by faith alone. [34]

Even though the Bible says that James was Jesus' brother, Luther decided that he knew more than James did, so he left out this Epistle altogether. Then, at the critical point of Romans 3:28, "A man is justified by faith without the deeds of the law," he chose to insert the word "only" in front of "faith" since Paul had not gone quite far enough in driving home the point Luther wanted to make.[35]

Luther's disdain for accuracy reached epic proportions in the marital affair of Philip of Hesse, his most powerful backer among the German princes. Luther had little regard for women: "Girls begin to talk and to stand on their feet sooner than boys because weeds always grow up more quickly than good crops." "If [women] become tired or even die, that does not matter. Let them die in childbirth—that is why they are there."[36] Vows were unimportant to Luther. He broke his own vow of chastity in order to marry an ex-nun, who also broke hers, and he authorized divorce for anyone whose spouse was so obtuse as to decline to convert to Lutheranism.[37] When Luther married, Erasmus remarked that what had begun as tragedy was now ending in comedy.[38]

So when Philip's eye wandered from his wife to one of his sister's ladies-in-waiting named Margaret of Saale, Luther was ready to authorize a divorce without hesitation. The trouble was, Philip couldn't readily divorce his wife because she was the daughter of an equally important German prince. But Philip had read Luther's German Bible. He found especially interesting the parts about how many wives the ancient Hebrew kings had enjoyed. Why did he rate only one? Besides, Philip implied, if Luther wouldn't let him have a second wife, maybe he would try asking the pope. That wouldn't do at all; but neither could Luther endure the storm of criticism that would surely accompany his sanction of bigamy. As pressure from Philip grew, Luther conceived a brilliant idea: grant Philip a special dispensation to take a second wife, but keep it a *secret*. Presto—problem solved, everybody happy.[39]

The only loose end was that it may have been a *bit* much to expect that Margaret—and even more importantly, her mother—would keep their part of the bargain. In any event, even in the days before supermarket tabloids, this became the juiciest story to hit Europe in a long time. Philip's spin doctors thought that the best thing to do would be to publish the special dispensation he had received from Luther himself. Luther was aghast; the truth would never do. At a conference in Eisenach in July 1540 Luther recommended that the affair should be dismissed with what he called "a good, strong lie," *i.e.*, by simply disavowing the whole wedding and treating the new bride as a concubine. That didn't really work, either; the tremendous blow to Protestant prestige caused by the whole affair was a key factor emboldening the emperor to launch a military action which came within an inch of eliminating Lutheranism in the 1540s.[40]

Tolerance

More significant for the future of Europe was the difference between Luther and Erasmus on the toleration of competing beliefs. In the early days, when Luther saw himself as a voice in the wilderness, he was all in favor of open debate. He said he did not want to "triumph by fire, but by writings." Luther argued that secular government should "busy itself with its own affairs, and let each one believe this or that as he can and as he chooses, and not use any force with anyone on this account." Once he attained power, though, he changed his tune. By 1525, he had forbidden the Catholic mass, "that this blasphemy may be suppressed by the proper authority." The ban on the mass was soon extended to rival forms of Protestantism: "A secular prince should see to it that his subjects are not led to strife by rival preachers whence factions and disturbances might arise, but in any one place there should be only one kind of preaching."

Luther demanded one hundred percent lockstep support for his cause. "Even if people do not believe, they should be driven to the sermon because of the Ten Commandments, in order to learn at least the outward works of obedience." He insisted that followers of competing sects "should be done to death by the civil authority."[41]

Erasmus, by contrast, objected to forcing any particular system of belief on anyone. He wrote to the duke of Saxony: "Tolerating the sects may appear a great evil to you, but it is still much better than a religious war. If the clergy once succeed in entangling the rulers, it will be a catastrophe for Germany and the church ... ruin and misery everywhere, and destruction under the false pretext of religion." His written advice to the governing council of Basel, where he spent much of the early Reformation period, was that not only should members of different sects be allowed to live next to one another, but that books advocating competing ideas should be permitted as well, so long as "the authors argue temperately, without slander or vituperation."[42]

Erasmus sympathized with Luther's attacks on indulgences and the power of the hierarchy. "What a filthy traffic this is," he exclaimed, "designed to fill coffers rather than to stimulate piety!" But he profoundly disagreed with Luther's doctrine of predestination, which gave God all the power and man none. Erasmus was a theistic humanist, who put humans rather than God at the center of his world, and insisted that the choices they made truly mattered. As Luther correctly observed, "human conditions prevail in him [Erasmus] much more than divine." Erasmus celebrated Jesus more as a proponent of good ideas about how humans should get along with one another than as a divinity who had magically undone the sin of Adam by dying on the cross.[43]

In fact, Erasmus argued that theology should be reduced to the absolute minimum, and should "define as little as possible." On many points, "everyone should be left to follow his own judgment because there is great obscurity in these matters." "All that is of faith," he wrote, "should be condensed into a very few articles. And the same should be done for all that concerns the Christian way of life." The best religion, according to Erasmus, was that which taught least, and which focused on humanist values rather than mystical conceptions of the divine. "You will not be damned for not knowing whether the Holy Ghost precedes the Father and Son as from three premises or from two ... but you will not escape damnation if you do not attempt to acquire... charity, patience and meekness." Before he ever heard of Luther, Erasmus wrote to a friend that "There are many points which it is better to pass over than to examine (and it is a part of knowledge not to know some things). There are many points concerning which it is more salutary to remain in doubt than to make a decision."[44]

He had no patience for the church's mountain of doctrines having nothing to do with improving human life on earth; when Pope Clement VII reprimanded him for his failure to honor the fasting rules, he replied "My heart is Catholic, but my stomach is Protestant." Even on his deathbed, he declined to receive the church's sacrament for the dying.[45]

One of his final books, *On the Sweet Concord of the Church*, pleaded for a council to reunite Catholics and Protestants and avoid further bloodshed, while condemning "the calumniators who twist the language of piety," and "the hot-tempered who shout 'Heresy!' and 'Burn them at the stake!'" What mattered most to Erasmus was maintaining an environment conducive to the advancement of human knowledge, which the war between the Protestant and Catholic God experts was ruining. "I try to stay neutral in order to help the revival of learning as best I can. And it seems to me that more is accomplished by a civil modesty than by impetuosity."[46]

Erasmus' call for minimalist theology brought him nothing but hatred, from both sides. Many in the Catholic hierarchy branded him a heretic, and large portions of his writings were censored by the church. One energetic critic published a pamphlet enumerating some 60,000 counts of heresy against Erasmus. But because the pope feared his influence and was in no position to reject even lukewarm allies, Erasmus was never actually excommunicated. Luther, though, minced no words, calling Erasmus "the incubus of the devil," "a snake," "a piece of shit," the "insane destroyer of the church," the "inflamer of the base passions of young boys," whom he had personally seen walking "arm in arm with the devil in Rome," and "who regards Christ as I regard Klaus Narr" [a sardonic jester of German mythology]. Erasmus replied with the weapon of wit against which Luther was helpless: "I would wish you a better disposition, were you not so marvelously satisfied with the one you have already. Wish me anything you will—except your temper."[47]

Erasmus could not conceal his bitterness, though, that Luther's revolt and the reaction it engendered had destroyed the environment for learning to which he had devoted his life: "Everything that anyone now says, all that a man does, now serves as a pretext for suspicions. On all we had hitherto been free to discuss, we hardly dare open our mouths. The slavery you had thought of suppressing has been redoubled."[48]

When Erasmus died in 1536, his enemies piled on the invective. Luther gloated that he had died "without cross and without God." The Catholics went even further, deciding at the "reforming" Council of Trent that the *Vulgate* was the true Bible, and the Erasmus translation heresy. Pope Paul IV sought a sweeping decree to burn every word "the leader of all heretics" had ever written, even pieces having nothing to do with religion. Mere possession of books written by Erasmus dispatched Spanish and Dutch humanists to the torture chambers of the Inquisition.[49]

Erasmus is the most "religious" of the heroes of this book. His religion, though, was a forerunner of the deism we will see in Spinoza, Paine, and other heroes of the later chapters. He claimed to know far less about God than virtually every other intellectual of his age, and he put humanity, not divine esoterica, at the center of his world. Had Europe listened to Erasmus rather than to Luther and the popes, it would have been a far more peaceful and prosperous place.

Does a religious believer like Erasmus belong as a hero in a book like this? Share your thoughts on this and the other questions you'll find at **dgc.humanistpress.com**!

1 Armstrong, *God*, 272.
2 Johnson, *Borgias*, 48-49, 60.
3 Norwich, *Absolute Monarchs*, 264, 271; Johnson, *Borgias*, 65, 79, 93, 105, 156.
4 Johnson, *Borgias*, 92, 150, 161.
5 Johnson, *Borgias*, 147, 166.
6 Faludy, *Erasmus*, 1.
7 Faludy, *Erasmus*, 1, 26, 29; Jones, *Erasmus & Luther*, 15-16.
8 Faludy, *Erasmus*, 121.
9 Jones, *Erasmus & Luther*, 40; Faludy, *Erasmus*, 90.
10 Jones, *Erasmus & Luther*, 41; Faludy, *Erasmus*, 92.
11 Erasmus, *Folly*, 18.
12 Erasmus, *Folly*, 97; Faludy, *Erasmus*, 124.
13 Faludy, *Erasmus*, 133.
14 Koester, *Hellenistic Age*, 110.
15 Faludy, *Erasmus*, 83.
16 Faludy, *Erasmus*, 157, 160, 162, 163.
17 Koester, *Early Christianity*, 37.
18 Jones, *Erasmus & Luther*, 53; Bainton, *Erasmus*, 135; Faludy, *Erasmus*, 165.
19 Ehrman, *Misquoting*, 10, 78-80.
20 Jones, *Erasmus & Luther*, 60; Johnson, *Christianity*, 281.
21 Chadwick, *Reformation*, 42.
22 Jones, *Erasmus & Luther*, 63; Johnson, *Christianity*, 280.
23 Belloc, *Reformation*, 42.
24 Faludy, *Erasmus*, 204; MacCulloch, *Reformation*, 150; Bainton, *Erasmus*, 189.
25 MacCulloch, *Reformation*, 128.
26 Jones, *Erasmus & Luther*, 69; MacCulloch, *Reformation*, 127; Lau, *Reformation*, 18; Johnson, *Christianity*, 277.
27 Lau, *Reformation*, 52-53.
28 Jones, *Erasmus & Luther*, 79; Chadwick, *Reformation*, 61.
29 Bouyer, *Erasmus*, 120; Faludy, *Erasmus*, 150, 156, 200.
30 Jones, *Erasmus & Luther*, 9; Johnson, *Christianity*, 309; White, *Warfare*, 378.
31 Faludy, *Erasmus*, 219.
32 Johnson, *Christianity*, 273; Koester, *Early Christianity*, 36.
33 Jones, *Erasmus & Luther*, 36.
34 James 2:14-24.
35 MacCulloch, *Reformation*, 134.
36 Ellerbe, *Dark Side*, 99, 134.
37 MacCulloch, *Reformation*, 143, 154.

38 Jones, *Erasmus & Luther*, 77.
39 Chadwick, *Reformation*, 72.
40 Lau, *Reformation*, 157-159.
41 Johnson, *Christianity*, 288-289.
42 Faludy, *Erasmus*, 192, 225; Johnson, Chr*istianity*, 277.
43 Bainton, *Erasmus*, 155; Jones, *Erasmus & Luther*, 84; Faludy, *Erasmus*, 93, 174.
44 Bainton, *Erasmus*, 184; Johnson, *Christianity*, 275; Erasmus, *Folly*, 155.
45 Faludy, *Erasmus*, 195; Encyclopædia Britannica Online, *Desiderius Erasmus*.
46 Jones, *Erasmus & Luther*, 70; Faludy, *Erasmus*, 175, 248.
47 Faludy, *Erasmus*, 177, 182, 209; Johnson, *Christianity*, 278.
48 Bouyer, *Erasmus*, 134.
49 Bainton, *Erasmus*, 278; Faludy, *Erasmus*, 254, 257, 258.

Baruch Spinoza

CHAPTER 8

SPINOZA VS. ZEVI

Kabala

On one point, Martin Luther and the Catholic Church were in agreement: they didn't care for Jews. In his pamphlet *On the Jews and Their Lies*, Luther displayed his customary level of prudence and restraint: "First, their synagogues should be set on fire, and whatever is left should be buried in dirt so that no one may ever be able to see a stone or cinder of it." He continued that Jews should then be banned from the roads and markets, their property seized, and then these "poisonous envenomed worms" should be drafted into forced labor and made to earn their bread "by the sweat of their noses," before being exiled "for all time."[1]

Why the hatred? The chain of events that ultimately resulted in the twentieth century Holocaust goes back a long way, even before the first century events that branded Jews as Christ-killers. Pre-Christian Jews were taught by their God experts that they had been chosen specially by their one and only god, making everyone else their inferiors. Not only were Jews forbidden from marrying Gentiles, they were not even supposed to eat with them.[2] As early as 133 BCE the Greek king of Syria was told by his advisers that the Jews should be annihilated because they were the only people on earth who refused to associate with the rest of humanity.[3]

Even after their Temple was destroyed, forcing a fundamental change in a religion that had revolved entirely around Temple sacrifice, the rabbis assembled a Talmud teaching that Jews should steal from Gentiles, and should not leave their cattle with Gentiles because Gentiles have sex with cattle. Other Talmud passages appear to describe Jesus as an idolator, a fornicator, a sorcerer, and the bastard son of a hairdresser prostitute.[4]

Whatever the provocation, even before the twentieth century Holocaust the Christian response was excessive. The church promoted a series of laws punishing Jews for being Jewish, while encouraging the systematic looting of Jewish property and the expulsion of Jews from most of the territories of Western Europe.[5] Thousands were murdered at the time of the Crusades, more were slaughtered during the time of the Black Death (based on false accusations that Jews poisoned water wells), and yet more during the the Spanish Inquisition. The pope ordered the Jews of Rome and other cities under his control herded into ghettoes, burning 25 Jews alive in the public square of Ancona to encourage compliance.[6]

Perhaps affected by all this hostility, a large segment of Judaism moved in the direction of a mystical creed known as "Kabala," a misnomer meaning "tradition."[7] For Kabala was not tradition at all, but brand-new knowledge, imparted to the world by experts in direct communication with God.

One aspect of Kabala was simple magic tricks: spells, séances, and sleight of hand. The secret to most magic lay in the Bible itself, if only you looked hard enough for it. Rabbi Akiva, who helped to reinvent Judaism after the destruction of the Temple, was deeply convinced that the scriptures were the actual word of God. He figured that God wouldn't use words lightly, so not only must every word be filled with meaning, but every letter of every word must have meaning and value as well, and it was up to scholars to decode these meanings.[8]

Not only was the Bible filled with letters, it was filled with numbers as well. If you equate the first letter of the Hebrew alphabet to one, the second letter to two, and so on, and then start adding up the numbers in words and phrases and doing some arithmetic, you stumble on some seemingly fascinating patterns. For example, a Kabala manual called the *Book of Creation*, purportedly written by Abraham himself, links the word-number science to the various names given to God: "With 32 wondrous paths of wisdom He engraved: Yah, YHWH, Hosts, God of Israel, Living God and Eternal King, El Shaddai, Merciful and Gracious, High and Exalted, Eternally Dwelling, of High and Holy Name, Who created His universe with 32 books, with number, and text, and story."[9]

Why 32 paths? Obviously, because the first letter of the Torah is the Hebrew letter Bet (ב), which carries the numerical value of 2, and the last letter of the Torah is the letter Lamed (ל), which carries a numerical value of 30. Add them up, and there's your proof. Still not convinced? Does the fact that the name for the Hebrew god (Elohim) appears exactly 32 times in the 6-day creation account of Genesis get you there? How about the fact that there are 22 letters in the Hebrew alphabet, plus 10 distinct names for God listed in the passage, which also gets you to 32?[10] Thousands of man-years of study of the names of God and numerical values revealed many other "secrets" as well.

Zevi

The concept of a messiah to save the Jews never appeared in the Old Testament, but it became a central tenet of Kabala. More than a few Jews volunteered for the job; David Alroy proclaimed his messiahship in Kurdistan in 1160, followed by Abraham Abulafia in Sicily a century later.

Despite all these messiahs, conditions for Jews in Christendom continued to grow worse rather than better. The 1648 rebellion of Bogdan Chmelnitzky led to the extermination of tens of thousands of Polish Jews; Poland had previously been one of the few places that welcomed them.[11] The time was ripe for a messiah who would put his predecessors to shame.

Shabbetai Zevi was born in Smyrna, on the southern coast of Turkey, in 1626. He became a rabbi in Jerusalem at the age of 18, and immersed himself in the intricacies of Kabala. He lived alone in a hut by the seashore, entertaining himself with fasting, flagellation, and ice-cold baths. After two marriages that he claimed were never consummated, he "married" the Torah itself, under a wedding canopy.

Later, he also married a prostitute, who seems to have resolved the consummation problem.[12]

Zevi might have passed his life as an obscure nutcase, but for the fact that he stumbled onto what every budding celebrity needs: an agent. Abraham Nathan ben Elisha Hayyim Ashkenazi, known as Nathan of Gaza, saw Zevi's eccentricities as evidence that here indeed was the true messiah.[13]

The more Nathan pumped him up, the bolder Zevi became. He began pronouncing the name of God (Yahweh) in public—the worst blasphemy for ordinary men, but proof that Zevi must be special because no lightning struck him down. He celebrated the principal Jewish feasts all together on the same day. He invented new rituals, and announced that sins could be holy if they were properly blessed. Word was spread that he was capable of miracles, such as an unearthly radiance surrounding his face, and an ability to float in mid-air.[14]

Nathan introduced him to the other rabbis of Gaza, who became enthusiastic supporters. Zevi admonished skeptical rabbis in other places: "You and your like have always failed to recognize, and misunderstood, the true prophets of God. Would you treat me as you treated the Nazarene?" But the rabbis of Zevi's home town of Smyrna, who knew him best, had enough of Zevi's bizarre behavior and excommunicated him.[15]

Meanwhile Nathan was busily sending letters to all corners of Europe proclaiming the arrival of the messiah. After a 1,600-year losing streak, Jews everywhere were ready for some good news:

> The First-begotten Son of God, Shabbetai Zevi, Messiah and Redeemer of the people of Israel, to all the sons of Israel, Peace! Since you have been deemed worthy to behold the great day and the fulfillment of God's word by the prophets, your lament and sorrows must be changed into joy, and your fasting into merriment, for you shall weep no more. Rejoice with song and melody, and change the day formerly spent in sadness and sorrow into a day of jubilee, because I have appeared.[16]

In London, Jewish bookmakers laid odds of 10 to 1 that Zevi

would be recognized as the messiah within two years. In Amsterdam, special prayer books were printed showing Zevi on a throne, six lions on either side of him, with four angels holding a radiant crown over his head. Other books published at the time were dated in "the year of the messiah."[17]

The entire Jewish world was in uproar. From Egypt to London, believers rushed to immersion baths to cleanse their souls for the day of salvation. They lay naked in the snow. They scourged themselves. Many sold their worldly possessions, even their homes, to go on pilgrimage to join the messiah.[18]

Business came to a standstill in many ghettoes; the wealthy distributed their goods among the poor since the messianic age was about to begin. Synagogues were decorated with Shabbatai Zevi's initials under a royal crown, and the 21st Psalm, Israel's thanksgiving for the victory of the messianic king, was inscribed on the walls. "Thou settest a crown of fine gold on his head; his glory is great through Thy salvation." In Hamburg, wealthy Spanish exiles were seen dancing in the synagogue.[19]

Constantinople

In September 1665 Nathan sent out an epistle outlining the messiah's program to all the principal Jewish communities. First he would be crowned at Constantinople, and make the sultan there his servant. Next he would go to the River Sambatyon to gather the lost tribes of Israel and to marry Rebecca, the 13-year-old daughter of Moses, who had come back to life. The Temple would re-arise. There would follow times of desperate straits for Israel and the messiah while the wars of Gog and Magog were fought, but then the year 1670 would be the Year of Jubilee, when the holy soil of Palestine would give up its dead. Forty years later, the general resurrection of the dead would follow and the messianic age of peace would be firmly established.[20]

To fulfill Nathan's prophecy, Zevi began a triumphal procession toward Constantinople, stopping first in Gaza, then Aleppo, and on to Smyrna. Vast crowds accompanied him everywhere; if an unconvinced rabbi protested, the crowd was liable to attack his house.[21]

Zevi returned in triumph to Smyrna, the home town from which he had been ignominiously expelled. The synagogue was still closed to him, so with a crowd at his back he took an axe to the door and forced his way in. He marched down the aisle, grasped the scroll of the Torah, cradled it in his arms, and proceeded to serenade it with an old Spanish love ballad.[22]

Business in Smyrna ground to a halt, to the amazement and dismay of the English and Dutch merchants based there. The chief rabbi fled for his life, along with most of his colleagues. A skeptical merchant, Haim Peña, was attacked by a mob and nearly lynched, being saved only when his daughter began to prophesy.[23]

Feeling his oats, Zevi announced big changes in Judaism. For starters, no more fast days; what used to be fast days were now to be days of merriment. On a roll, Zevi revealed that Jesus had actually been a prophet after all, whose predictions would be fulfilled when he entered Constantinople. June 18, 1666, would be the day the sultan would be deposed. Before sailing for Constantinople, Zevi took the time to reward 26 of his faithful followers with royal titles to prevent future quarrels. Some of the titles were imaginative, none more so than that bestowed on his brother Elias: "King of the King of Kings."[24]

The sultan was well aware of the upheaval in Smyrna, and the danger that Zevi posed. Jews were numerous and prominent throughout his empire, and the last thing the sultan wanted was a general uprising.[25] He also knew how large parts of the world viewed the last ruler who had executed a messiah, and was not keen on sharing that fate. And no doubt somewhere in the back of his mind a small voice asked, "What if this guy is for real?"

Shabbetai Zevi set sail for Constantinople on January 1, 1666, and arrived a few weeks later. Somewhere along the voyage, though, Zevi lost his bravado. Immediately upon landing he was taken into custody by soldiers, and brought before a mid-level bureaucrat. Zevi protested that he was no messiah, but merely a humble rabbi and alms gatherer, who had nothing to do with the crowds that were following him.[26]

The magistrate first assigned Zevi to a debtor's prison, then to more comfortable (and defendable) quarters at the fortress of Abydos. Although he was a prisoner, he was treated like an honored guest, expenses paid by his followers. The warden began charging stiff fees to outsiders for the privilege of a brief audience with Zevi; inns near Abydos raised their rates and made a fortune.[27]

As the months wore on, Zevi began to lose some of his privileges, and grew depressed. June 18 came and went. The sultan sent his personal doctor to Zevi on several occasions, and the doctor succeeded in befriending him. In long conversations, Zevi's new friend would commiserate with him about the horrors he had witnessed in the sultan's torture chambers, and brainstorm about how he might escape this terrible fix. An excellent idea, the doctor suggested, might be to convert to Islam, as the doctor himself had done many years ago. After all, since Zevi had already declared Jesus to be a prophet, how tough would it be to admit that Muhammad had some merit as well?[28]

When Zevi had been reduced to the proper mental state, he was suddenly whisked to the palace, for a trial before the sultan himself. At the trial, the sultan smiled and spoke: "Far be it from me, the Commander of the Faithful, to oppose the will of Allah. I'll offer you a perfectly fair test. You shall be stripped naked, and six of my archers shall shoot poisoned arrows at you. If their darts bounce off your body without harming you, you may assume my throne and I will do homage to you as Allah's anointed. Surely, this is but a small matter for one who is the messiah."[29]

The arrows never had a chance to reach their target. Zevi threw off his Jewish headgear, donned a turban, and agreed to convert to Islam. He took a new name, Aziz Mehmed Effendi, and was appointed "Keeper of the Palace Gates" with a small pension. The relieved sultan even gave him a second wife. Zevi wrote to his brothers: "And now forsake me, for God has made me an Ishmaelite. He who was your brother is now become the king's doorkeeper."[30]

Jews everywhere were shattered. They immediately began re-writing history. "Zevi? We knew he was a fraud all along. Nobody was taken in by him. It was nothing." Records were re-written or

destroyed to downplay the whole embarrassing affair. Only the pains-
taking efforts of modern historians like Gershom Scholem have un-
covered just how pervasive the Zevi boom really was.[31]

Spinoza

One Jew who did not fall for Zevi was Baruch Spinoza of Amsterdam, who can best be understood in the context of his Dutch
environment.

For centuries, Holland and the other territories northeast of France
had been possessions—in fact, the richest possessions—of Spain.
When the wars of the Reformation broke out, the merchants of Holland found themselves heavily taxed, in order to pay the Catholic
side's bills. They also found themselves under the intense scrutiny of
the Inquisition; the church and the emperor could not allow heresy to
cut off such an important revenue stream.[32]

The combination of high taxation and loss of liberty had the effect one might expect: rebellion, which simmered for decades before
resulting in de facto independence for the Netherlands. The resulting
republic was a curious mix of recalcitrant Catholics, militant Calvinist Protestants, and a new phenomenon: people who used their new-
found freedom to skip organized religion altogether.

Calvinism, oversimplified, was a more extreme form of Lutheranism, with a special emphasis on predestination. God had arbitrarily
chosen a select few, maybe one in a hundred, to be saved; everyone
else would burn in hell. Though founded by a Frenchman named
John Calvin, Calvinism was strongest in Switzerland, Scotland, and
England; the English Civil War was instigated by Calvinist "Puritans"
seeking more godliness in England's government. Dutch Calvinism
was also bolstered by 150,000 refugees from religious civil war in
France. As seventeenth century philosopher Gottfried Leibniz put it,
"Every time troubles start up in Germany and in Belgium (as earlier
in France), Holland—the universal refuge of sects and exiles—sees its
population and riches grow."[33]

A significant number of Dutchmen, by contrast, had soured on
paying taxes to support God experts of any stripe, and had grown

downright irate when the "reformers" of the Reformation turned out to be as greedy and intolerant as the regime they replaced. Though there is little indication of a full-blown atheist movement, there is much evidence of decline in respect for those who claim to know the mind of God. "Even here at The Hague," noted another commentator in 1592, "there is not, in the judgment of those who do observe it, a quarter part of the multitude well affected to religion."[34]

Into this mix arrived a fourth ingredient: a small but influential community of Jews, most of whom had been expelled from Portugal. The ruling Calvinists bitterly resisted their efforts to build a synagogue in 1612, but patience and bribery ultimately won out. Some, though not all, became infected with the religious skepticism of their new homeland, including a merchant named Michael d'Espinosa, who is credited with passing on his freethinking spirit to his son, Baruch, born in 1632.[35]

When Michael died in 1654, young Baruch took over operation of the family import-export business. There was a difficulty with the estate, though. His sister was engaged to the son of Amsterdam's leading rabbi, and the rabbinic council with the power to decide such things had awarded her an unduly large portion of his father's assets. Baruch responded by doing the unthinkable: bringing a civil case before the secular authorities, rather than resolving the dispute inside the Jewish community. Both sides were embittered, and Spinoza grew more reckless in his charges that Amsterdam's Jewish God experts did not know what they were talking about—he even expressed doubt that God had chosen the Jews above all other people.[36]

Brash young Spinoza succeeded in exasperating Amsterdam's Jewish leadership, to the point where they threatened to excommunicate him. Excommunication was the gravest of punishments; it meant being cut off entirely from all contact with family, friends, and business associates. Spinoza's challenge was so worrisome that the elders of the synagogue even tried to bribe him into acquiescence with a thousand guilders, which only strengthened his resolve. He responded to the threat of excommunication with a smart-aleck offer to help draft the proper language for it.[37]

This the rabbis did not need; their decree of excommunication is a model of eloquence:

> With the judgment of the angels, and the sentence of the saints, we anathematize, execrate, curse and cast out Baruch de Spinoza ... pronouncing against him ... all the maledictions written in the book of the Law. Let him be accursed by day and accursed by night; accursed in his lying down and his rising up, in going out and in coming in. May the Lord never more pardon or acknowledge him. May the wrath and displeasure of the Lord burn against this man henceforth, load him with all the curses written in the book of the Law, and raze out his name from under the sky. ... Hereby, then, are all admonished that none hold converse with him by word of mouth, or communication by writings, that no one do him any service, abide under the same roof with him, approach within four cubits' length of him, or read any document dictated by him or written by his hand.[38]

While this was being read by Rabbi Aboab, the lights of the synagogue were extinguished, one by one, to simulate the darkening of Spinoza's soul. The synagogue later petitioned the municipal authorities to denounce Spinoza as a "menace to all piety and morals."[39]

Treatise

Spinoza responded with his first written work, his *Apology* or "defense," a conscious allusion to Plato's *Apology of Socrates*.[40] (Modesty was not one of Spinoza's virtues.) That work has now been lost, but much of it found its way into another book, one that made Spinoza infamous across Europe, with the unappetizing title of *Theological-Political Treatise*.

Dutch politics of the day was a war, sometimes of more than words, between the Calvinist God experts and humanists in the tradition of Erasmus led by a mathematician named Jan de Witt, called "the most scientific statesman of his time."[41] Spinoza seems to have believed that the best way to kick the Calvinists in the groin was to apply his considerable intellect to an analysis of what they claimed to be the basis of their authority, the Bible itself. Book by book, he exposed the Bible as riddled with contradictions, while demonstrating that the Torah could not have been written by Moses or any other single individual.[42]

Spinoza had kind words for Jesus, but only as a moral teacher, not as a deity or magician. Like Erasmus, he condemned the greed of the God experts:

> In the religion of the common people, serving the church has been regarded as a worldly career, what should be its unpretentious offices being seen as lucrative positions and its pastors considered great dignitaries. As soon as this abuse began in the church, the worst kind of people came forward to fill the sacred offices and the impulse to spread God's religion degenerated into sordid greed and ambition.[43]

After shattering the credibility of the Bible, Spinoza went on to advocate freedom both of speech and of religion, going even further than Erasmus had before him. He certainly echoed Erasmus in looking forward to the day when "religion is finally separated from philosophical theories and reduced to the extremely few, very simple dogmas that Christ taught to his own."[44]

The Dutch republic of Jan de Witt was Spinoza's ideal:

> Now seeing that we have the rare happiness of living in a republic, where everyone's judgment is free and unshackled, where each may worship God as his conscience dictates, and where freedom is esteemed beyond all things dear and precious, I have believed that I should be undertaking no ungrateful or unprofitable task, in demonstrating that not only can such freedom be granted without prejudice to the public peace, but also, that without such freedom, piety cannot flourish nor the public peace be secure.[45]

Spinoza knew that what he was writing was incendiary. So he published anonymously, and he even had the cover page falsely identify the place of publication as Hamburg, a city he had never visited. His caution was well-founded; the book went through numerous press runs as it grew in popularity among Europe's humanists, while God experts outdid each other in condemnation. The Calvinist Council of Amsterdam called it a "work forged in hell by a renegade Jew and the devil," while another synod called it "the most vile and sacrilegious book the world has ever seen." Its sale was banned in Holland. When Spinoza's authorship became an open secret, a French theologian named him "the most impious and the most dangerous man of the century," and a bishop denounced him as "that insane and evil man, who deserves to be covered with chains and whipped with a rod."[46]

Caution

Since Spinoza could no longer do business in the Jewish community and wasn't much more popular with the Christians, he turned to honest work: he learned the skill of grinding lenses, becoming so proficient that the astronomer Christian Huygens, discoverer of Saturn's rings, preferred Spinoza's lenses to all others.[47]

Some of his critics used more than words; one evening when leaving the theater, Spinoza was attacked by a man wielding a knife. He escaped death only because he was wearing a heavy cloak that absorbed most of the blow. He kept the slashed cloak as a reminder of the need to be careful, while also wearing a signet ring inscribed with the Latin word for "Caution."[48]

That caution kept Spinoza from publishing his most substantial work, *Ethics*, during his lifetime. He bitterly observed that "I have devoted prolonged and much study to the thinking out and writing down of things which now certainly no one will read." His caution was well advised; when the book was published after Spinoza's death, one reviewer called it "a book which . . . surpasses all others in godlessness and which endeavors to do away with all religion and set godlessness on the throne."[49]

Actually, the *Ethics* goes to great length to deny that Spinoza is atheist, but the god it defines is not at all like that of any organized religious tradition. For Spinoza, God is essentially identical with na-

144

ture, not something apart from it, and certainly not anything like a human with magic powers as described in the Old or New Testaments. "To ascribe to God those attributes which make a man perfect would be as wrong as to ascribe to a man the attributes that make perfect an elephant or an ass," Spinoza wrote to one correspondent. "If a triangle could speak," he added, "it would say that God is eminently triangular." Some sagely observed, though, that there is little difference between saying that everything is God and saying that there is no God; according to Spinoza's contemporary Thomas Hobbes, "To say the World is God, is to say, there is no cause of it, that is, no God."[50]

Caution briefly deserted Spinoza in 1672, when a Calvinist crowd attacked Jan de Witt and his brother, tore them to pieces, fed their entrails to the dogs and hung their limbs from lampposts. Why the anger? Among other reasons, one pamphlet charged that de Witt had given "the evil Spinoza" the protection to write and to publish the *Treatise*, "brought forth from hell by the fallen Jew Spinoza, in which it is proven, in an unprecedented, atheistic fashion, that the word of God must be explained and understood through Philosophy, and which was published with the knowledge of Mr. Jan." When Spinoza heard the news, he made up a placard proclaiming "You Are the Greatest of the Barbarians" which he intended to erect at the site of the assassinations. His landlord, who had grown fond of Spinoza's company, locked him inside the house for his own protection.[51]

Modern day atheist activist Ayaan Hirsi Ali, whom we will meet in the final chapter, has made this observation about Spinoza:

[He] was clear-minded and fearless. He was the first modern European to state clearly that the world is not ordained by a separate God. Nature created itself, Spinoza said. Reason, not obedience, should guide our lives. Though it took centuries to crumble, the entire ossified cage of European social hierarchy—from kings to serfs, and between men and women, all of it shored up by the Catholic Church—was destroyed by this thought.[52]

We know that a London correspondent wrote to Spinoza inquiring specifically of his views on the Zevi-mania sweeping Amsterdam. Unfortunately, Spinoza's reply has been lost. Did he mention Abraham Pereira, one of the richest of Amsterdam's Jews, who offered his entire fortune of several million guilders to the messiah? Or the eloquent Rabbi Aboab, who had recited a decade earlier the decree excommunicating Spinoza, who replaced the customary prayer for the civil leadership of Holland with a prayer for "Our Lord the Great King Shabbetai Zevi, the Anointed of the Lord, the Messiah son of David, the Messiah King, the Messiah Redeemer, the Messiah Savior, our Messiah of Righteousness, the Anointed of the God of Jacob"? Did he mention the plan to dig up the corpses in the Jewish cemetery in Ouderkerk so that they could be transported to Jerusalem, there to be resurrected?[53]

We do know of Spinoza's general view of Kabala: "I have also read, and personally know, some people who dabble in Kabalism; the stupidity of whom is beyond belief."[54]

He marveled at their belief "that they alone may be held to possess the secrets of God," and he judged their works as "childish lucubrations." Perhaps he quoted his *Treatise*:

> If men were always able to regulate their affairs with sure judgment, or if fortune always smiled upon them, they would not get caught up in any superstition. But since people are often reduced to such desperate straits that they cannot arrive at any solid judgment and as the good things of fortune for which they have a boundless desire are quite uncertain, they fluctuate wretchedly between hope and fear. This is why most people are quite ready to believe anything.[55]

One would think that Zevi's public conversion to Islam would have been the embarrassing end of his story. But Nathan of Gaza never missed a beat, explaining how God's messiah had always done things that were hard for ordinary people to understand—after all, how could a messiah be ordinary? What a brilliant, unexpected stroke: to endure the shame of apostasy as a final sacrifice before unveiling the full glory of his triumph—much more powerful than a mere crucifixion! Some followers pled that Zevi had tricked his enemies: he had actually been transfigured to heaven and only his material shape remained, in the form of a Muslim.[56]

Even Zevi's death did not slow Nathan down—Zevi had actually ascended to heaven and been absorbed into the supernatural light. The Zevi movement within Judaism continued to thrive for another century, though on a smaller scale than in the glory days of 1665. Some tried to make up for their lack of numbers by the grandiosity of their claims: Rabbi Abraham Cardozo taught that "the Holy One, blessed be He, removed himself upward and Shabbetai Zevi ascended to be God in his place." After all, on the third day after Zevi's death his brother visited Zevi's tomb, and reported that "Neither Our Lord nor anything else was in the cave, but it was full of light." In 1752, a scandal erupted in Hamburg when its highly respected chief rabbi was unmasked as a secret Zevi disciple.[57]

In Turkey, another group remained loyal to Zevi; after his death they decided to honor his example by fraudulently converting to Islam while remaining closet Jews. The sect at one time numbered 20,000 followers and persists to the present day.[58]

Seventeenth century Jews aren't the only people who have fallen for a messiah. What will it take to get people to realize that the best place to look for someone to give them a better life is to themselves alone? Share your thoughts on this and the other questions you'll find at **dgc.humanistpress.com**!

Notes:

1 Johnson, *Jews*, 234.

2 Acts 10:28; Acts 11:1-3; Tacitus, *Histories*, 5:5.

3 Johnson, *Jews*, 134.

4 Babylonian Talmud, *Abodah Zarah 22a-22b, Sanhedrin 43a, Sanhedrin 57a, Sanhedrin 106a, Sanhedrin 107b; Sotah 47a; Shabbath 104b; Gittin 57a; Kallah 51a,* quoted in Herford, *Christianity*, 48-49. Some claim that the Talmud is referring to a person other than the

Christian Jesus; *see, e.g.,* Student, *Jesus Narrative.* Other Orthodox Jews claim exactly the opposite; see, e.g., JAHG-USA, *Who Was Jesus?*

5 Logan, *Middle Ages,* 198; Sigal, *Emergence,* 218; Armstrong, *God,* 264.

6 Norwich, *Absolute Monarchs,* 216; Logan, *Middle Ages,* 284; Sigal, *Emergence,* 270; Johnson, *Jews,* 226, 243.

7 Sigal, *Emergence,* 275.

8 Johnson, *Jews,* 194; Hanson, *Kabbalah,* 65.

9 Johnson, *Jews,* 196; Hanson, *Kabbalah,* 88.

10 Hanson, *Kabbalah,* 90.

11 Schnur, *Mystic Rebels,*170, 174.

12 Schnur, *Mystic Rebels,*167-168; Johnson, *Jews,* 264.

13 Johnson, *Jews,* 267.

14 Sigal, *Emergence,* 305-306; Schnur, *Mystic Rebels,* 170, 194; Johnson, *Jews,* 264.

15 Johnson, *Jews,* 270; Schnur, *Mystic Rebels,*178-180.

16 Hanson, *Kabbalah,* 178.

17 Schnur, *Mystic Rebels,*192; Sigal, *Emergence,* 309.

18 Hanson, *Kabbalah,* 178; Johnson, *Jews,* 271.

19 Schnur, *Mystic Rebels,* 186, 192.

20 Hanson, *Kabbalah,* 178; Schnur, *Mystic Rebels,* 196.

21 Johnson, *Jews,* 270.

22 Hanson, *Kabbalah,* 177.

23 Schnur, *Mystic Rebels,* 195, 200-201.

24 Schnur, *Mystic Rebels,* 193-198, 202; Johnson, *Jews,* 270.

25 Schnur, *Mystic Rebels,* 209.

26 Schnur, *Mystic Rebels,* 204.

27 Schnur, *Mystic Rebels,* 206, 208.

28 Schnur, *Mystic Rebels,* 210.

29 Schnur, *Mystic Rebels,* 211-212.

30 Johnson, *Jews,* 271; Schnur, *Mystic Rebels,* 211-212.

31 Armstrong, *God,* 328.

32 MacCulloch, *Reformation,* 310; Israel, *Dutch Republic,* 82, 99.

33 MacCulloch, *Reformation,* 244; Gorski, *Divergence,* 173; Stewart, *Courtier,* 23.

34 Israel, *Dutch Republic,* 94, 363-366.

35 Goldstein, *Betraying Spinoza,* 3; Israel, *Dutch Republic,* 377; Feuer, *Spinoza,* 18.

36 Goldstein, *Betraying Spinoza,* 252; Johnson, *Jews,* 290; Feuer, *Spinoza,* 17, 36.

37 McKenney, *Spinoza,* 653; Stewart, *Courtier,* 32; Feuer, *Spinoza,* 31.

38 Johnson, *Jews,* 271.

39 Goldstein, *Betraying Spinoza,* 270.

40 Stewart, *Courtier*, 35.

41 Goldstein, *Betraying Spinoza*, 242; Feuer, *Spinoza*, 76.

42 Travis, *Spinoza*, 11; Spinoza, *Treatise*, 132, 190.

43 Spinoza, *Treatise*, xix, 7.

44 Spinoza, *Treatise*, 161.

45 Feuer, *Spinoza*, 65.

46 Spinoza, *Treatise*, xxxi; Goldstein, *Betraying Spinoza*, 271; Stewart, *Courtier*, 11, 104-105.

47 Goldstein, *Betraying Spinoza*, 5.

48 Goldstein, *Betraying Spinoza*, 217, 245-246.

49 Feuer, *Spinoza*, 148, 255; Stewart, *Courtier*, 218.

50 Stewart, *Courtier*, 162; Feuer, *Spinoza*, 247.

51 Stewart, *Courtier*, 122; Goldstein, *Betraying Spinoza*, 245-246.

52 Hirsi Ali, *Infidel*, 282.

53 Yesselman, *Letters*; Goldstein, *Betraying Spinoza*, 225-226, 228.

54 Spinoza, *Treatise*, 137.

55 Feuer, *Spinoza*, 24; Spinoza, *Treatise*, 3.

56 Sigal, *Emergence*, 307.

57 Schnur, *Mystic Rebels*, 213, 219; Johnson, *Jews*, 273; Armstrong, *God*, 331; Sigal, *Emergence*, 309.

58 Armstrong, *God*, 329; Schnur, *Mystic Rebels*, 219.

Queen Caroline

CHAPTER 9

CAROLINE VS. SMALLPOX

Humankind's Greatest Enemy

Smallpox is a virus, whose scientific name is *Variola major.* It affects only humans, not other animals. Like the common cold, it spreads through sneeze and cough emissions, bedding and clothing, or direct contact. Once it enters the nose or mouth, it heads for the lymph glands, where it is given a free ride throughout the body. Unlike the invasion of the common cold, what happens next is catastrophic.[1]

Fever, nausea, vomiting, muscle ache; then a rash of hundreds or thousands of blisters, frequently starting on the forehead before covering the entire body. Sometimes the blisters merge together into sheets, rotting off all the underlying skin when they harden. What it does inside your body is just as bad; some victims die of thirst when it becomes impossible to swallow. The eighteeenth century British noble Lord Dalkeith succumbed after only two days; his limbs fell off while his body was being placed in its coffin.[2]

Like the common cold, smallpox is no respecter of class. Though the urban poor living in cramped conditions were the most susceptible, smallpox cut down nobles and even monarchs—five in the eighteenth century alone. Smallpox is by far the worst infectious deadly disease humanity has ever known: hundreds of millions have died from it, more than the Black Death and all the wars of the twentieth century put together. Surviving smallpox is no picnic either; it can cause blindness, loss of limbs, and horrible deformity, especially of the face.[3]

Smallpox developed an important ally in the first century CE: the Christian church. Man has a powerful intellect; from the smallpox perspective, it was critical that he not use it.

From earliest times, the Christian church taught that all useful knowledge was to be found in Scripture, and not in scientific research. Paul warned the Colossians: "Be sure that no one leads you away with false and empty teaching that is only human, which comes from the ruling spirits of this world, and not from Christ." Augustine of Hippo taught that there was no need to be "dismayed if Christians are ignorant about the properties and the number of the basic elements of nature, or about the motion, order, and deviations of the stars, the map of the heavens, the kinds and nature of animals, plants, stones, springs, rivers, and mountains ... For the Christian, it is enough to believe that the cause of all created things ... is ... the goodness of the Creator."[4]

The story of Galileo is well-known: under threat of torture, he was forced to recant his discovery that the earth revolved around the sun, and to spend the rest of his life under house arrest. Chemistry was nearly as disturbing as astronomy: at the urging of the church, Charles V of France forbade in 1380 "the possession of furnaces and apparatus necessary for chemical processes." An experimenter named John Barrillon was imprisoned and nearly executed for violating this law. In 1163, Pope Alexander III forbade "the study of physics or the laws of the world" to all members of the clergy. At the time, these were the only people in any position to attempt such studies. Even study of the weather was problematic. When Ben Franklin demonstrated that lightning rods could protect church steeples (normally the tallest structures around, often with a large metal bell as an added attraction) from the effects of lightning strikes, he was reviled for atheism. John Adams in 1758 recorded a conversation with a prominent Christian who was incensed about the presumption of using lightning rods to control the power of heaven, comparing them to Peter's presuming to walk on water.[5]

Knowing how the planets move satisfies our curiosity. Knowing how the body works keeps us alive. Greek and Roman pagans, from Hippocrates to Galen, had made important progress in applying the scientific method to the study and treatment of disease.[6] But nothing could be more un-Christian than to focus on natural causes for a supernatural phenomenon. The third century Christian scholar Origen wrote: "It is demons which produce famine, unfruitfulness, corruptions of the air, pestilences; they hover, concealed in clouds in the lower atmosphere, and are attracted by the blood and incense which the heathen offer to them as gods." Augustine added that "All diseases of Christians are to be ascribed to these demons; chiefly do they torment fresh-baptized Christians, yea, even the guiltless, newborn infants." St. Nilus and St. Gregory of Tours stressed the sinfulness of resorting to medicine instead of trusting to the intercession of saints.[7]

In 540, the church declared the whole field of Greek and Roman medicine to be heresy. On this point, Protestants and Catholics were in agreement. Martin Luther said that "Satan produces all the maladies which afflict mankind," and that "he poisons the air." According to John Calvin, no medicine could change the course of events which had already been determined by the Almighty. John Wesley insisted that many bodily diseases are caused by devils because the Bible told him so.[8] He was right about his source; the Book of Chronicles told the sad story of King Asa, who trusted to physicians rather than to the priests of Yahweh, and therefore died.[9]

Viewing disease as a physical rather than as a supernatural phenomenon undermined not only the teaching of the church, but its revenues as well. Sick people wanted help, and were willing to pay for it. If the only officially sanctioned form of help was in the form of prayers and the use of relics, that is what the people would pay for. Water in which St. Remy's ring had been dipped cured fevers; relics of St. Valentine cured epilepsy; relics of St. Christopher cured throat diseases; relics of St. Gervase—rheumatism. St. Nicaise was assigned the task of interceding with God on behalf of smallpox victims.[10]

Smallpox was further assisted by the Christian bias against hygiene. God is so great; man is so small. Next to God, man is worthless. How better to express appropriate humility before God than by living a life of degradation and filth? Such was the thought process of some of the most admired saints in the early centuries of Christianity. St. Hilarion was glorified for never washing his clothes or changing his shirt; his entire holy body was covered with scabs and mange. Athanasius gushed that St. Anthony "neither bathed his body with water to free himself from filth, nor did he ever wash his feet, nor even endure so much as to put them into water, unless compelled by necessity." St. Abraham for 50 years refused to wash either his face or his feet. Abasement of the flesh was strictly enforced by the Portuguese Inquisition, which ranked "bathing the whole body" as a crime of the magnitude of bigamy, denying the virgin birth, and witchcraft. Catholics reproached Erasmus for "having betrayed the Christian norm in his pagan concern for the body," while protesting against his "proposal of washing oneself every day, a disgusting northern idea incompatible with human dignity."[11]

The Ally Crippled

Though few would have predicted it at the time, the death-knell for smallpox sounded when Luther's wars of the Reformation broke out in the 1520s. For two centuries thereafter, Europe was wracked with continuous warfare between adherents of competing God experts. The worst outbreak, the Thirty Years War, devastated central Europe from 1618 through 1648. Responsible estimates of the population decline in central Europe resulting from the Thirty Years War range from 15 to 40 percent.[12]

Even though the Thirty Years War was kicked off by the ejection of the daughter of England's King James I from the throne of Bohemia, both James and his successor Charles I kept England largely out of the war. James, in fact, deliberately found a Catholic bride for his Protestant son, while trying to tone down religious bickering within his domain. In 1623 James issued a proclamation banning discussion of the favorite Calvinist doctrine of predestination because sermons about the subject were getting contentious and causing trouble. He published a *Book of Sports* to prevent Calvinist interference with harmless games on Sunday; preachers foamed that bowling on Sundays was as great a sin as murder.[13]

All this infuriated England's Protestant God experts no end. By the 1640s, rebellion broke out against James' successor Charles I, who lacked his father's engaging personality. Though the English Civil War was no match for the Thirty Years War in intensity, it had its moments; the reprisals of the victorious Calvinist General Oliver Cromwell not only cost Charles I his head, but Ireland approximately 40 percent of its recalcitrant Catholic population. Cromwell proceeded to impose on England a decade of Calvinist theocracy. He closed theatres, alehouses, and racetracks, took down maypoles and ordered shopkeepers to stay open on all pagan holidays, including Christmas. Adultery became punishable by death, and in at least four cases this sentence was actually imposed. Not caring for bishops, he appointed 11 regional military commanders known as the "Major Generals," to enforce "the suppressing of vice and encouragement of virtue" at the point of the bayonet.[14]

Ten years of theocracy was all England could stand. When Cromwell died, virtually no one wanted his brand of government to continue, and Charles I's son was quickly restored to the throne. Cromwell and two of his associates were dug up and posthumously executed, by hanging and then decapitation, on the twelfth anniversary of the execution of Charles I.[15]

The reaction against Cromwell's theocracy and 150 years of religious war spawned a new school of thought, called "deism," whose adherents did not deny the existence of God but did doubt how much the experts knew about him. A Christian clergyman put it aptly:

Deism is what is left of Christianity after casting off everything that is peculiar to it. The deist is one who denies the Divinity, the Incarnation, and the Atonement of Christ, and the work of the Holy Ghost; who denies the God of Israel, and believes in the God of nature.[16]

One of the first published deists was the Englishman Charles Blount, who starting in the late 1670s kept up a barrage of criticism against all revealed religion and Christianity in particular. Blount argued passionately that only natural knowledge was possible, and that all true or correct belief had to be based on perceivable evidence.

Anthony Collins wrote a series of books and tracts defending the use of reason. He found fraud in the Church of England's statement of faith, attacked clergy of all denominations, argued that the Bible commanded free inquiry, and denied any relationship between Old Testament prophecies and the life of Jesus.[17]

Though England's deists were not a large group, they touched a nerve. One of Collins' pamphlets inspired 35 outraged refutations. Matthew Tindal's *Christianity as Old as the Creation*, sometimes called the "Deist's Bible," was vilified by more than 150 published responses. Sometimes the response to deist writings was more robust. Thomas Woolston and Peter Annet were imprisoned for their freethinking pamphlets. Woolston, who branded England's leading theologians "Gygantick Sons of Error, Nonsense, Incoherence and Confusion" died in prison.[18]

Deism spawned a popular culture in which plays and novels ridiculed the clergy savagely. Bishop Seeker complained that "the distinguishing mark of the present age" was "an open and professed disregard of religion," reflected in "dissoluteness and contempt of principle in the higher part of the world" and in "profligate intemperance and fearlessness of committing crime" in the lower.[19]

The Princess

England was not the only country where religious warfare and its aftermath had exposed the moral bankruptcy of the God experts. Throughout Europe, doubt grew among readers of Erasmus, Spinoza, and others inspired by them. We have already seen the decline of religion in de Witt's Holland. In Russia, Peter the Great's modernization campaign at the turn of the eighteenth century involved subjugating the Orthodox church to the state—when the patriarch died in 1700 Peter declined to name a successor, and instead appointed government bureaucrats to manage the church. In France, Pierre Bayle's 1695 *Historical and Critical Dictionary* fanned the flames of skepticism, with outrageous observations such as "It is no more strange that an atheist should lead a virtuous life, than that a Christian should commit any kind of crime."[20]

In Germany, freethinking prevailed at the salon of Sophie Charlotte, the first queen of Prussia. Instead of jousting tournaments, she staged intellectual combats, with Jesuits pitted against Calvinists, agnostics against theologians, egging them on when the conversation became too agreeable. Drinking it all in was a young princess named Caroline, from the tiny Bavarian state of Ansbach. Her father had died at the age of 32—of smallpox. Her mother remarried, but her stepfather died a few years later—of smallpox.[21]

Caroline blossomed into the most celebrated princess of Europe. Not only was her intellect sharpened under the tutelage of Sophie Charlotte, but her long blond hair, fair skin, and what was described as "a bosom of exemplary magnitude" held a certain appeal as well. The Prussian king was thrilled when he made for her the best match imaginable: the Habsburg archduke of Austria, who was in line to become the Holy Roman Emperor. The archduke was excited as well; all Caroline had to do was agree to become a Catholic.[22]

This, however, she would not do. An eminent Jesuit was dispatched to Berlin to instruct Caroline on how to obey the pope. They argued long into the night, but ultimately Caroline gave up her chance at empire rather than acquiesce. The king was livid. It was bad enough that anyone should thwart his will, but for a slip of a girl to do so for the most foolish of reasons was more than he could bear. Caroline, approaching a bleak spinsterhood at age 22, wound up back in Ansbach.[23]

One day in 1705 a gentleman caller arrived, with a letter of introduction as "Mr. de Busch." He was duly entertained to music, cards, and elaborate suppers for several days. Caroline may well have suspected the truth: Mr. de Busch was actually Prince George Augustus of Hanover, who if everything worked out right was third in line to the English throne. George was smitten, and after their marriage remained so for the rest of his life.[24]

It was not at all a foregone conclusion that George and Caroline would ever make it to the English throne. Had Queen Mary borne children rather than dying (of smallpox) in 1694, George would have remained in Hanover. Had Duke William, the only child of Mary's successor Queen Anne, not died (of smallpox) in 1700, the same result would have occurred. Moreover, supporters of a competing dynasty were everywhere, and staged two nearly successful invasions of England.[25] Nevertheless, Caroline's luck held, and her father-in-law was crowned George I in 1714.

Upon arriving in London, Princess Caroline took up where her mentor Sophie Charlotte had left off, discreetly encouraging deism and freethinking. A voracious reader (Erasmus being one of her favorites), her books overflowed the space allotted to them in the palace, so she oversaw the construction of a library on the spot where now sits the London museum. Political realities of a new dynasty with only a tenuous hold on power constrained what she could do, but she pushed the envelope as far as she could. For example, she honored at court Isaac Newton, whose work was reviled by the Calvinists as "built on fallible phenomena and advanced by many arbitrary presumptions against evident testimonies of Scripture."[26]

Another guest at Caroline's court was a young French exile who had just assumed the name "Voltaire," who will be explored further in the next chapter. Voltaire himself was enthralled with both Caroline and the English atmosphere of intellectual freedom she encouraged. He wrote and later published a series of "Letters on England" that contributed to his legal troubles with the French government. Caroline sponsored an edition of Voltaire's epic poem criticizing the French religious war of the sixteenth century; she not only accepted Voltaire's offer to dedicate the work to her, but sent him her portrait and awarded him a pension in grateful appreciation.[27]

Behind the scenes, Caroline worked assiduously with Prime Minister Robert Walpole to re-align the Church of England along more deist lines by advancing the careers of clerics who advocated a milder, less intrusive religion in opposition to the zealots. She especially took up the cause of Dr. Samuel Clarke, a heretic who had the audacity to question the existence of the Trinity itself. When she announced that "Dr. Clarke shall be one of my favorites; his writings are the finest things in the world," the Bishop of London thought it his duty to pay her a visit to teach her the facts of England's established religion.

Furious, she told her assistant to "Send him away civilly: though he is very impertinent to suppose that I, who refused to be empress for the sake of the Protestant religion, don't understand it fully."[28]

She tried mightily to secure the repeal of the Test and Corporation Acts, which denied civil rights to those who failed to toe the theological line of the Church of England. Ultimately, the hierarchy's opposition prevailed, and repeal was delayed for another century. Still, she was one of the most influential royal spouses in English history; popular doggerel of the day ran: "You may strut, dapper George, but 'twill all be in vain; We all know 'tis Queen Caroline, not you, that reign."[29]

Inoculation

Promoting freethinking wasn't Caroline's main job, though. Her main job was producing offspring (preferably male) to perpetuate the dynasty. At this she was equally talented. Her first child, born after only 18 months of marriage, had the good sense to be a boy; eight more children followed, only one of whom died at birth.

Bearing children was one thing; keeping them alive, especially faced with the menace of smallpox, was more difficult. Smallpox had killed both her father and her stepfather, but Caroline had no need to experience its horrors vicariously. She contracted the disease herself six months after her son was born. So did her solicitous husband, no doubt from her. Both survived the ordeal, though Caroline did so only barely, and lost much of her physical beauty as a result.[30]

Thus Caroline, always fascinated by new ideas, listened intently to the reports brought back by Lady Mary Wortley from Turkey. Lady Mary had been the great belle of George I's court; rumor had her bedding the king himself. That is, until smallpox ate away most of her face, after which she wore a veil in public.[31] Still, she married well, and accompanied her husband when he was appointed ambassador to the Ottoman Empire.

In Constantinople, Lady Mary learned some interesting facts. Smallpox was not nearly as widespread in Turkey as it was in England because of the widespread adoption of a peasant custom of deliberately infecting children with pus taken from smallpox sores, in the hopes that they would contract a mild version of the disease. Everyone knew that smallpox never afflicted a victim twice; surviving your first bout meant you were safe for life. After consulting an English physician, the headstrong Lady Mary decided in 1718 to try the procedure on her own son. An incision was made on his arm, and pus from a recovering victim was rubbed into it–a procedure that came to be known as "inoculation." Just as hoped, he developed an easily manageable rash that disappeared after a few days; the antibodies he developed protected him for the rest of his life. (The young man didn't view the outcome as entirely positive, though. Once when he ran away from boarding school, the identifying scar where the inoculation had occurred helped the headmaster recover him.)[32]

It wasn't just Turkish peasants who practiced inoculation. In America, people noticed that when smallpox ravaged a town, African slaves were often untouched. Upon questioning, they revealed that the benefit of inoculation was widely known in Africa. Everyone knew about inoculation, it seemed, except Europeans who lived under the thumb of the anti-science Christian church.[33]

Caroline hesitated. But after her daughter Anne was stricken by smallpox and barely survived, she swung into action. Employing what she had learned of the scientific method, she conducted a field trial. Five prisoners from London's Newgate prison who had never suffered from smallpox volunteered for the new procedure in the summer of 1721. All of them, as hoped, developed mild cases—so mild that some skeptics doubted they were actually smallpox. Five orphans were then inoculated, all of whom survived (though it later turned out that one had lied about not having smallpox before, in order to get the reward).[34]

A sample size of 10, with one failure, would probably not satisfy today's FDA. It was enough for Caroline, though. With the king's approval and no public announcement, in April 1722 she had Lady Mary's doctor perform the procedure on her other two daughters. When they responded as hoped, she sent the doctor to Hanover, where her eldest son the heir to the throne was then living, and had him inoculated as well.[35]

There's nothing like starting at the top. Royal acceptance gave inoculation the most tremendous head start imaginable. As experience grew, doctors learned that inoculation carried risks; a small percentage of those inoculated developed symptoms serious enough to result in death. Still, that was better than the 10 to 25 percent mortality rate smallpox normally carried, and demand for the procedure grew rapidly.[36]

So rapidly, in fact, that many God experts became alarmed at this threat to their dominance. Typical was London's Rev. Edmund Massey, who preached a sermon in 1722 proving inoculation to be the work of Satan. This was evident from the Book of Job: "So went Satan forth from the presence of the Lord, and smote Job with sore boils from the sole of his foot unto his crown."[37] Satan had deliberately infected Job with smallpox; any doctor who similarly infected his patient with smallpox was following Satan.

Whether or not Satan had inoculated Job, Massey argued that inoculation implicitly rejected the quiet acceptance of God's will that characterized a good Christian:

> And when it shall seem good to him to call us forth, into the rough Paths of Suffering; if He shall please to minish and bring us low; the Example of our Text will teach us, not to behave unseemly, or charge God foolishly, but with Patience and Meekness, and Resignation, and Contentedness, take what He lays upon us.[38]

Smallpox and other diseases were an earthly punishment for sin, a downpayment on the punishment sinners would receive in Hell after death. "Diseases are sent," explained Massey, "if not for the Trial of our Faith, for the Punishment of our Sins. Bad as the World is, it would be still worse, if the Wickedness of Mankind should be so successful as to meet with no more Rebuke than it would willingly suffer."[39]

Widespread inoculation, Massey warned, would plunge the earth into a cesspool of sinfulness:

> Should all Restraints of this Sort be taken away, were there no

161

fear of Punishment in this Life, nor belief of any in the next … we may conjecture from present Disorders, how mightily they would encrease, and irremoveably be established; so that we have good Reason to bless and praise Almighty God for the wholesome Severities ordained for Offenders, without which, the World would be a much more uncomfortable Place to live in, than it is at present … The Fear of [smallpox] is an happy Restraint upon many People, who seem not so sensible of superiour Obligations, to keep themselves in Temperance and Sobriety, and want no other Encouragement to give a Loose to their Inclinations, than to be free from Apprehensions of this uncertain Visitor. … We ought then to look upon this, and all other Discouragements to Sin, with a thankful Eye, and bless that wise Providence which has mercifully set such Checks upon Iniquity, that we may not run smoothly on unadmonished to our Ruin.[40]

Humanists put people at the center of their concerns; Massey did not.

Could then these bold Practitioners lessen the Severity of this Disease; could they entirely secure Men from Danger under it … I do not see what Good Mankind would get in the main; they would, 'tis true, have one Danger less to fear, but that would be no real Kindness; forasmuch as it would be the Occasion of their running into a great many more, and if they should happen to be *more healthy*, 'tis a great Chance but they would be less *Righteous*.[41]

At bottom, what Massey couldn't abide was the thought of men relying on themselves rather than on God, through the medium of experts like himself:

There is also a Tempting of the Lord our God, when Men rely too much upon themselves, and put their Truth in one another, without calling upon God for his Assistance, or praying to him to guide and direct them. … Let me ask the Apostle's Question: Do we provoke the Lord to Jealousy? Or are we stronger than he? Shall we presume to rival him in any instance of Providence, find Fault with his Administration, take the Work out of his Hands, and manage for our selves? A dangerous Experiment this! And not to be made with Impunity, unless we thus pretend to be wiser, we prove ourselves mightier than he.[42]

Massey damned doctor and patient alike:

Let the Atheist, and the scoffer, the Heathen and Unbeliever, disclaim a Dependance upon Providence, dispute the Wisdom of God's Government, and deny Obedience to his Laws; Let them Inoculate, and be Inoculated, whose Hope is only in, and for this Life! ... Let us not sinfully endeavour to alter the Course of Nature by any presumptuous Interposition. Let us bless God for the Afflictions which he sends upon us, and the Chastisements wherewith he intends to try or amend us; beseeching him to grant us Patience under them, and in his good Time a happy Deliverance from them.[43]

Massey lost his battle. The practice of inoculation spread, despite formal condemnation by the Catholic theologians of the Sorbonne, and in a few decades an even safer procedure was discovered—vaccination—using a bovine virus similar to smallpox that normally produced only weak symptoms in humans. The effects were dramatic: in Copenhagen alone, during the 12 years before the introduction of vaccination in the latter part of the eighteenth century, 5,500 persons died of smallpox; during the next 16 years only 158 persons died of smallpox throughout all of Denmark.[44]

Caroline did not live to see the benefits of vaccination. In 1737 she died from the complications of a previously ruptured womb, after lingering for 10 days in intense pain. At no point did she ask to see a priest, causing so much consternation in political circles that the prime minister had to beg to allow the archbishop to visit her, to preserve appearances. "Pray, Madam, let this farce be played. The archbishop will act it very well. ... It will do the queen no hurt, no more than any good, and it will satisfy all the wise and good fools, who will call us all atheists if we don't pretend to be as great fools as they are." Visits were one thing, but she flatly refused to be subjected to any sacrament. George was shattered by Caroline's death: "I never yet saw a woman who was fit to buckle her shoe."[45]

The First Ending

Large portions of the clergy continued to resist; a clever inoculator in Thessaly persuaded the local priests that the Blessed Virgin had appeared and explained the process, making it acceptable so long as proper prayers were also administered. In 1885, a smallpox epidemic broke out in Montreal. The Protestant community was largely spared because it was vaccinated; the Catholic population was decimated because the priests insisted that vaccination was sinful. Abbé Filiatrault declared in a sermon that "If we are afflicted with smallpox, it is because we had a carnival last winter, feasting the flesh, which has offended the Lord; . . . it is to punish our pride that God has sent us smallpox." Soviet efforts to vaccinate the population against smallpox in the 1920s were confounded by Russian Orthodox teaching that "vaccination is the seal of Antichrist."[46]

Despite widespread vaccination, smallpox killed three hundred million people in the twentieth century, mostly in the Third World. In 1967 the World Health Organization launched a massive campaign to render it extinct, with great success. In 1974 a Hindu God expert in the southern Indian state of Bihar refused to allow his followers to be vaccinated on the grounds that smallpox was the rightful scourge of God; in the end, he and his family were vaccinated by force. Final victory was declared on October 26, 1979.[47]

So smallpox is vanquished. Or is it? By conscious decision, two small research samples of the virus remain, one in the United States and one in Russia, under closely supervised conditions. In 2002, though, Vice President Cheney convinced himself that Saddam Hussein had somehow obtained smallpox as one of his weapons of mass destruction, and was preparing to devastate a now-vulnerable American population. He strenuously advocated a crash program to prepare hundreds of millions of doses to vaccinate the entire country. When the doctors who had led the eradication program in the 1970s pointed out that even the minuscule proportion of vaccinations that resulted in complications would cost hundreds of lives and affect thousands of others, President Bush took the rare action of overruling Cheney, and limiting the program to the military and healthcare workers. But by the time the doses were ready in 2004, it was clear that Saddam had no smallpox, so even that limited program was cancelled. Bush himself was vaccinated, but Cheney chose not to be.[48]

Some speculations are too horrific even for London bookmakers to take bets on. If smallpox ever does return, the odds are high that a God expert of some stripe will have been involved.

> Vaccination is still an issue today, with many Christians opposed to vaccination against cervical cancer—apparently because the risk of cancer is supposed to deter young women from having sex. Then there is embryonic stem cell research. What would Caroline have had to say about that? Share your thoughts on this and the other questions you'll find at **dgc.humanistpress.com**!

Notes:

1 Encyclopædia Britannica Online, *Smallpox.*
2 Carrell, *Speckled Monster*, xiii; Baker-Smith, *Royal Discord*, 34.
3 Behbani, *Smallpox*, 458; Carrell, *Speckled Monster*, xiv, 365.
4 Colossians 2:8; Lindberg, *Christian Attitudes*, 51-52.
5 Peters, *Inquisition*, 245; White, *Warfare*, 285; Freethought Press, *Inquisition*, 460; Gillooly, *Adam and Eve*, 125.
6 Freeman, *Western Mind*, 66.
7 White, *Warfare*, 313.
8 Ellerbe, *Dark Side*, 42, 132; White, *Warfare*, 386; Freethought Press, *Inquisition*, 470.
9 II Chronicles 16:12-13.
10 White, *Warfare*, 325; Aronson, *Mercy*, 26.
11 Jerome, *Hilarion*; Lecky, *European Morals*, vol. 2, 108; Livermore, *Portugal*, 147; Faludy, *Erasmus*, 243.
12 MacCulloch, *Reformation*, 485.
13 MacCulloch, *Reformation*, 516; Chadwick, *Reformation*, 433-434.

14 Hutton, *British Republic*, 42, 48; MacCulloch, *Reformation*, 529; Gaunt, *Cromwell*, 190.

15 Gaunt, *Cromwell*, 3-4.

16 Holmes, *Faiths*, 39.

17 Emerson, *Latitudinarianism*, 25-26; Holmes, *Faiths*, 41.

18 Cragg, *Church*, 161; Berman, *Deism*, 63; Woolston, *Free Gift*, 35.

19 Cragg, *Church*, 127, 129.

20 Cragg, *Church*, 113; Labrousse, *Bayle*, 52.

21 Quennell, *Caroline*, 5; Arkell, *Caroline*, 5-6.

22 Baker-Smith, *Royal Discord*, 11; Arkell, *Caroline*, 11.

23 Baker-Smith, *Royal Discord*, 10-11.

24 Baker-Smith, *Royal Discord*, 11; Arkell, *Caroline*, 18, 27.

25 Carrell, *Speckled Monster*, 6, 11; Arkell, *Caroline*, 82.

26 Quennell, *Caroline*, 52, 134; Arkell, *Caroline*, 231, 287; White, *Warfare*, 143.

27 Quennell, *Caroline*, 84; Meyer, *Voltaire*, 70.

28 Quennell, *Caroline*, 136; Arkell, *Caroline*, 76, 194, 231.

29 Arkell, *Caroline*, 149, 197.

30 Arkell, *Caroline*, 39.

31 Carrell, *Speckled Monster*, 57.

32 Tronchin, *Inoculation*; Carrell, *Speckled Monster*, 57; Aronson, *Mercy*, 11.

33 Aronson, *Mercy*, 8; Carrell, *Speckled Monster*, 177.

34 Arkell, *Caroline*, 120, 135; Carrell, *Speckled Monster*, 275; Tronchin, *Inoculation*.

35 Arkell, *Caroline*, 135; Carrell, *Speckled Monster*, 345.

36 Arkell, *Caroline*, 135; Carrell, *Speckled Monster*, 356; Aronson, *Mercy*, 8.

37 Job 2:7; Massey, *Sermon*, 3.

38 Massey, *Sermon*, 5.

39 Massey, *Sermon*, 12.

40 Massey, *Sermon*, 14, 27.

41 Massey, *Sermon*, 27.

42 Massey, *Sermon*, 24, 31.

43 Massey, *Sermon*, 20, 32.

44 Aronson, *Mercy*, 20; White, *Warfare*, 339, 342.

45 Baker-Smith, *Royal Discord*, 96; Quennell, *Caroline*, 239; Carrell, *Speckled Monster*, 396.

46 Tronchin, *Inoculation;* White, *Warfare*, 343-344; Gabel, *Lenin*, 355.

47 Weisberg, *Fishing*; Carrell, *Speckled Monster*, 394; Behbani, *Smallpox*, 498.

48 Weisberg, *Fishing.*

Voltaire

CHAPTER 10

VOLTAIRE VS. THE JESUITS

Loyola

In 1534, on the hill of Montmartre overlooking Paris, a former soldier named Ignatius Loyola and a group of friends established an organization known as the Company of Jesus–the Jesuits.[1]

While recovering from battle wounds, Loyola experienced visions in which God gave him a special mission to fight on his behalf. Realizing that an uneducated grunt could do little, Loyola proceeded to educate himself at the University of Paris, during a time where he undoubtedly crossed paths with John Calvin and Erasmus–three men who definitely had no use for each other.[2]

Loyola built the Jesuits into an ultra-disciplined elite corps of counter-revolutionaries with a single mission: support the pope, God's mouthpiece on earth, in his struggles against Protestant heretics.[3]

Shrewdly, Loyola and his successors sought to maximize their leverage by influencing the hearts and minds of the nobility and the monarchs, starting at a tender age. By the middle of the seventeenth century, nearly the entire higher education system of Catholic Europe was in Jesuit hands. Cementing relationships with the future rulers they tutored, Jesuits worked their way into the position of "confessors"—priests who heard the sins of the kings, forgave them on God's behalf, and whispered in their ears what God wanted them to do. They developed a reputation for laxity on matters of morality, overlooking the sexual foibles of the powerful who did their political bidding. Father Benzi, for example, wrote that "It is only a slight offense to feel the breasts of a nun." What God really cared about was eradicating those damned Protestants who were rejecting the pope, stealing church property, and making a nuisance of themselves.[4]

The Jesuit strategy of indoctrinating a future monarch from a tender age and then guiding him toward use of force against rebellious Protestants bore its most notable fruit with Ferdinand II of Austria, who swore that "I would rather rule a country ruined than a country damned." A highly devout Catholic seen as under the spiritual thumb of his Jesuit confessors, Ferdinand got the first half of his wish by launching what became the Thirty Years War in 1618. The devastation wrought in the heart of Europe by this overt attempt to annihilate Lutheranism by force wiped out from 20 to 40 percent of central Europe's population, a far larger proportion than did the wars of the twentieth century.[5]

Though Jesuits didn't use "the end justifies the means" as a mantra, they may as well have. One Jesuit document noted that "Actions intrinsically evil, and directly contrary to the divine laws, may be innocently performed by those who have so much power over their own minds as to join, even ideally, a good end to the wicked action contemplated." Loyola himself wrote that: "We must see black as white, if the church says so."[6]

Jesuits were encouraged to lie, whenever doing so would advance their cause. For example, suppose someone had killed a fellow named Peter, and is being questioned about it. "A man may lawfully say he did not kill Peter, meaning privately another man of that name, or that he did not do it before he was born." Enterprising Spanish Jesuits busied themselves in fabricating ancient documents and relics to make Spain's Catholic heritage appear far more embedded in its culture than it really was. When the pope in 1680 ordered the Jesuits to stop teaching this doctrine, the Superior General didn't even communicate the pope's decree to his subordinates.[7]

Another theme was the superiority of the laws of God (as determined by Jesuits) over the laws of man; it was not only permissible, but required, to violate civil laws when doing so furthered the cause of God. The logical result of this kind of thinking was the systematic assassination of rulers who failed to obey God's representative the pope, such as William the Silent of the Netherlands in 1584. The Jesuit Father Busembaum wrote that "It is lawful to kill any prince excommunicated by the pope, of whatsoever country because the whole world belongs to the pope; and that whoever accepts of or executes such a commission does a meritorious and charitable act."[8] Queen Elizabeth of England nearly fell to this thinking; English Jesuits organized an assassination plot against her that progressed quite far before collapsing in 1585. Jesuits were also involved in the Guy Fawkes plot to blow up king and Parliament in 1605, the foiling of which is still celebrated as a national holiday in England.[9]

The Jesuits in France

In France, a series of Jesuit-inspired civil wars dominated the latter decades of the sixteenth century. Though blood was shed all over France, the events of Toulouse in 1562 are especially significant. A group of pious Catholics snatched the corpse of a recently deceased Protestant, intending either to desecrate her body or claim it as a Catholic convert. Protestants responded badly, and fighting broke out. A truce was negotiated; but when the Protestants laid down their arms, the Catholics fell on them, killing some four thousand in a single day. Pope Pius IV issued a decree authorizing an annual two-day celebration of this blessed event.[10]

After a decade of violence, a deal was negotiated involving the marriage of the leading Protestant prince, Henry of Navarre, to the sister of the king. Everyone who was anyone, on both sides of the divide, attended the lavish wedding amidst hopes for lasting peace. Those hopes were not shared, though, by the Jesuit-inspired "Catholic League," heavily influenced by the thinking of the Jesuit Father Juan Mariani: "It is a glorious thing to exterminate the whole of this pestilential and pernicious [Protestant] race from the community of mankind. Limbs, too, are cut off when they are corrupt, that they may not infect the remainder of the body." The Jesuits refused sacraments to those who would not support the League.[11]

The plan was simple: just kill every prominent Protestant leader

171

present in Paris in one fell swoop, in what would become known as the "St. Bartholomew's Day Massacre." The killings of the leaders went so smoothly that King Charles IX then ordered the extermination of every Protestant in France. The Jesuits did their part; in Bordeaux, the slaughter was kicked off by the sermons of the Jesuit Father Auger: "Who executed the divine judgments at Paris? The angel of God. Who in Orleans? The angel of God. Who in a hundred cities of this realm? The angel of God. And who will execute them in Bordeaux? The angel of God, however man may try to resist him." Though there is no accurate body count, historians put the number of victims in the tens of thousands. The pope wrote to Charles that "We rejoice with you that with the help of God you have relieved the world of these wretched heretics."[12]

Charles was succeeded by another staunch Catholic, Henry III, who vigorously enforced laws keeping Protestants out of all preferred positions in the country. That didn't satisfy the League, though; apparently under Jesuit influence, a Dominican friar named Jacques Clement was induced to assassinate Henry III in 1589. Jesuit school grammars thereafter included the theme "Jacques Clement has done a meritorious act inspired by the Holy Spirit."[13]

The thinking behind this assassination may well have been to reignite a war that could result in a "Final Solution" for French Protestantism—for next in line to the throne was Henry of Navarre, the same Protestant whose wedding had occasioned St. Bartholomew's Day. Unfortunately for the Jesuits, the man now known as Henry IV proved to be a capable commander, and was able to bring most of France under his control. Paris, though, proved a tough nut to crack; thousands died of starvation rather than yield to the siege of a heretic. The story that Henry actually said "Paris is worth a Mass" may be apocryphal, but he in fact decided to end the strife by publicly converting to Catholicism, thus ushering in a period of peace and prosperity for his country. In 1598 Henry signed the "Edict of Nantes," granting nearly complete freedom of worship to France's Protestants in perpetuity.[14]

The church was stunned. The pope called it "the most cursed Edict that I could imagine, . . . whereby liberty of conscience is granted to everyone, which is the worst thing in the world." In 1610 a former Jesuit named François Ravaillac succeeded where others had failed, murdering Henry IV with a knife.[15]

Thereafter, incessant Jesuit whispering in the royal ears yielded a steady tightening of the screws on France's Protestants. One of the most efficient techniques, called the *dragonnade*, involved the quartering of soldiers, not all of them nice young men, in the homes of Protestants until they decided voluntarily to convert to Catholicism.[16] In 1685 Louis XIV bowed to Jesuit pressure by repealing the "perpetual" Edict altogether, resulting in the exodus of some four hundred thousand Protestants from France.[17]

Voltaire

Two decades later, a Jesuit school in Paris enrolled an undersized 10-year-old boy named François-Marie Arouet, the youngest child of a middle-class notary. At the age of four, François' mischievous godfather had taught him stanzas of the *Moissade*, an irreverent poem featuring Moses as a charlatan. His more stoic father wanted the Jesuits to train the precocious child to be a lawyer; but Arouet had other ideas and left school after a few years to become a poet. This seemed just as preposterous to his father as it would to many parents today. But Arouet was headstrong, and after a series of false starts he produced a hit play on the Paris stage—even his father liked it.[18]

This success punched his ticket to the fashionable salons of Paris, where his cheeky wit made him a star attraction. It also landed him in the Bastille for 10 months, after he told a joke about the regent to a fellow who turned out to be a police spy. After his second arrest, he was advised by the authorities that some country other than France might be a good place to live.[19]

Arouet arrived in London in 1726, during the reign of Queen Caroline. In an effort to change his luck, he had started calling himself "Voltaire," derived from his childhood nickname meaning "the little volunteer." There he published his first epic poem, the *Henriade*, much of which he had composed while in prison. A smaller edition

173

had previously appeared in France—illegally, since the censor had banned it. The hero of the composition was none other than Henry of Navarre, of "Paris is worth a Mass" fame. The poem traced the history of persecution through the ages, drawing uncomfortable parallels between the Greeks practicing human sacrifice, the Romans throwing Christians to the lions, and the massacre of St. Bartholomew's Day.[20] As noted in the last chapter, Caroline was enthralled with the work, which Voltaire dedicated to her.

After a few years, Voltaire felt it safe to return to Paris. At a dinner party, he heard a mathematician describe flaws in a complicated new lottery scheme designed to refinance the debt of the City of Paris: anyone who could purchase all the tickets would be certain to make a fortune. Other guests laughed; Voltaire began organizing a syndicate to do exactly that. The lottery organizers balked at first, but a successful lawsuit forced them to turn over the winnings. Voltaire's share as organizer of the scheme was five hundred thousand livres. He was set for life financially thereafter, and thus free to write what he chose—if he could stay off the scaffold.[21]

For Voltaire, that was a big "if." From Caroline's England, he had written a number of lengthy letters to friends about the marvelously free land where deism prevailed and censorship was nearly unknown, and where Caroline had introduced inoculation into common practice. "It has taken seas of blood," he wrote, "to drown the idol of despotism, but the English do not think they bought their laws too dearly." When these letters were published (without Voltaire's permission), the French government was furious. The secretary to the chancellor of France advised his boss that "Voltaire ought to be shut up in a place where he could have neither ink nor paper. That man has a mind which could destroy a state." In 1734 the Parliament of Paris condemned the *Letters from England*, the public hangman burned it, and the printer was slapped into the Bastille. Voltaire dodged arrest by slipping out of the country.[22]

Voltaire delighted in finding novel ways of getting into hot water. As if history, geography, parody, and municipal finance were not enough, Voltaire turned to pure science, by popularizing the work of Isaac Newton in France. It is to Voltaire, in fact, that we owe the popular story of Newton and the apple, which he learned from Newton's niece. Voltaire not only wrote a commentary on Newton, but spent several years absorbed in his own scientific experimentation. His Newton book was banned in France as well—new ideas of any kind were deeply suspect. As Voltaire observed, "When once a nation begins to think, it is impossible to stop it."[23]

He even incurred official wrath for disparaging the enemies of Christianity. In 1742 Voltaire's play *Mahomet* delighted Paris audiences—for three nights, before it was shut down by the Solicitor-General, who had not seen it but heard negative reports. The play depicts the prophet of Islam as an impostor, who poisons the lover of a woman he desires, while making the death appear to be a miracle. "I wished to show in it," said Voltaire, "to what horrible excess fanaticism can bring feeble souls, led by a knave." French censors decided that the play was actually a subtle attack on Christianity, using Islam as a metaphor; one sharp analyst pointed out that "Mahomet" and "Jesus Christ" had the same number of syllables! "I have never made but one prayer to God," Voltaire said, "a very short one: 'O Lord, make my enemies ridiculous.' And God granted it."[24]

What finally forced Voltaire out of France for good was his most ambitious production, *Essays on the Minds and Manners of Nations.* In several large volumes, Voltaire expounded upon the history of the world as he saw it: not a catalog of names and dates, but of the forces that shaped man's destiny. By far the most powerful negative force, in all times and places, was organized religion, culminating with the tyranny of Catholicism: "Rome has always decided for the opinion which most degraded the human mind and most completely annihilated human reason." By contrast, Voltaire wrote: "The happiest period, and the one most worthy of respect which there has ever been on this earth, was the one which followed [Confucius'] laws." This time Voltaire dealt not with a petty censor, but King Louis XV himself, who announced that Voltaire, who was traveling, had better not return to France. He didn't, until after Louis XV died two decades later of smallpox, after the Sorbonne condemned inoculation.[25]

Voltaire purchased an estate just across the French border, in Switzerland. With good reason, he feared that the Calvinist authorities of Geneva might prove just as meddlesome as the French censors, and wanted to be able to escape from the frying pan back to the fire, if necessary. This was wise; when Voltaire published what is today his most well-known satire, *Candide*, the Genevan authorities ordered it burnt. Voltaire took the shrewd if ignominious course of denying authorship: "People must have lost their senses to attribute to me that pack of nonsense."[26]

The Calas Case

Voltaire was now 65 years old, quite wealthy, and enjoying the most relaxed existence of his adult life on his Swiss estate. Most men would have begun to take life easy at that point; Voltaire instead embarked on a new crusade. His first target was the Jesuits, the tip of the Catholic sword. Voltaire had mixed feelings about the Company of Jesus; he remembered his Jesuit teachers fondly, and he respected an adversary worthier than the imbecile Parisian censors. He even housed a Jesuit on his estate, with whom he frequently played chess— Voltaire is said to have been quite the sore loser. But when a Parisian Jesuit named Father Berthier published an attack on the works of Voltaire and other French humanists, Voltaire declared war. He even adopted a battle cry, which he attached to everything he wrote thereafter: "Écrasez l'infâme!", or "Crush the infamy!"[27] What exactly was "the infamy"? Voltaire, prudently, was never too specific, but "God expert power" is a fair summary.

His first salvo was a wicked satire: *The Narrative of the Sickness, Confession, Death, and Re-appearance of the Jesuit Berthier*, in which the priest is condemned to 333,333 years in purgatory, which can be cut short only if another member of his order is found who is humble, peaceable, non-litigious, and non-boring. This was followed by *Narrative of the Journey of Brother Garassise*, describing the search for someone tedious enough to fill the late Father Berthier's shoes.[28] But the fun and games stopped with Voltaire's next move, which changed France forever.

The city of Toulouse had not relaxed its hatred of Protestantism since the massacre of 1562, which it commemorated with a joyous procession and fireworks every year. Planning was underway for an extravaganza to celebrate the bicentennial, when cries were heard from the house of a modest Protestant cloth merchant named Jean Calas.[29]

Calas, age 63, was never a troublemaker. He employed a Catholic maidservant for decades, and made no protest when one of his sons decided to convert to Catholicism. His eldest son, though, was a difficult case. Moody and depressed, Marc-Antoine had been barred from practicing law because of his Protestant faith. At the age of 29, going nowhere fast, Marc-Antoine became obsessed with the literature of suicide, including the soliloquy of Hamlet. One night his lifeless body was found hanging in a storeroom after a family dinner. A crowd gathered, and a rumor circulated that Marc-Antoine must have been killed by his father, probably because he must have been planning to convert to Catholicism.[30]

Not a scintilla of evidence supported this conjecture; a mountain of circumstance and consistent testimony pointed to suicide. None of that mattered. The chief magistrate, David de Beaudrigue, felt that he knew how evil Protestants were, and knew that Calvin taught that parents of apostate children were supposed to punish them by death. He also knew how much Paris appreciated firmness in dealing with heretics. The entire family—including the Catholic maid—was clapped into prison that very night, charged with the murder of Marc-Antoine.[31]

The local hierarchy jumped in with both feet. The first step was to prejudge the case by giving Marc-Antoine a magnificent funeral in the cathedral, honoring his martyr's death. Suicides were not allowed to have funerals at all. Prayers seeking his intercession were said to have resulted in the working of miracles. Then the church published a "monitory," ordering all Catholics to come forward with evidence to prove "this crime of detestable character," on pain of excommunication.[32]

Some 150 witnesses came forward, but none had any evidence

other than hearsay, and none of the stories matched. Under the bizarre French law of the day, though, it was possible to aggregate "half-proofs," "quarter-proofs," and the like into a full-blown proof to establish guilt. De Beaudrigue also succeeded in frightening off the lawyer who had been appointed to defend the family, forcing him to make public repentance for agreeing to take the case. No witnesses favorable to the family were permitted to testify. "I take all the responsibility," de Beaudrigue said. "It is in the cause of religion."[33]

After months dragged by without discovering a smoking gun, and with his fellow magistrates beginning to express doubts, de Beaudrigue finally rammed through a solution. Jean Calas would be subjected to unspeakable torture, known as "breaking on the wheel," during which he would confess the guilt of his co-conspirators before being released to death. The torture part of the program proceeded smoothly, for hours on end. But Calas steadfastly refused, right up to his dying breath, to say anything other than that his son had committed suicide. A frustrated de Beaudrigue then had to acquiesce in the release of the remaining family members.[34]

When Voltaire first learned of the Calas case, he was unimpressed. He despised the Puritanism of the French Calvinists even more than he did Catholicism, which could be quite agreeably decadent. His first reaction was that Jean was probably guilty.[35] Then he met the youngest Calas son, who had escaped arrest by not being in the house that night. Voltaire was moved by his demeanor, and investigated further; his contacts in Toulouse assured him that the Jean Calas they knew could not have murdered his son. After he interviewed another Calas son who had been present at the house and endured the months of imprisonment, Voltaire became convinced that a horrible injustice had been done.[36]

As a law school dropout, Voltaire had failed to learn his limitations. (Famous twentieth century litigator Clarence Darrow later remarked that "Even Voltaire's father could not make a lawyer out of a genius."[37]) Without any basis or precedent, Voltaire began demanding that the case be reopened by the central government in Paris so that the honor of the Calas family could be restored. Toulouse responded, probably correctly, that Paris had no authority to overrule its decisions, even had there been any matters still in dispute.[38]

Realizing he could never win on the technicalities, Voltaire took the battle to the court of public opinion: "It is only the voice of the public that can help us to obtain justice, the forms of which have been invented to ruin innocents." Over the decades he had developed a vast network of contacts all over Europe; at Voltaire's behest people as powerful as the king of Prussia, the king of Poland, the queen of England, and the czarina of Russia began pressuring the French government about how such an injustice could be allowed to stand. "All possible means must be combined, all voices joined in unison," he insisted. One of his most telling arguments was that the verdict as a whole could not possibly be correct: if Jean were guilty and the rest of his family innocent, that meant that a frail 63-year old had managed to subdue and kill by hanging a strapping 29-year- old, all by himself. "Let them produce the procedure; all the nations are interested."[39]

Voltaire even wrote a book, his *Treatise on Tolerance*, tracing the evil history of religious persecution to soften the public mood: "Tolerance has never yet excited civil wars, whereas its opposite has filled the earth with slaughter and desolation." It was promptly banned.[40]

Most of the French establishment wanted Voltaire to butt out. The Duc de Choiseul, the king's principal minister, cautioned Voltaire that "When one arrives at a certain age, it is wise to use one's wits for the furthering of one's own happiness and that of one's friends. So I say to you, let the world wag its own way, since it is not your responsibility to change the order of things." But nothing official Paris could do would shut him up. After nearly a year of pestering, including a decisive victory in winning over the powerful mistress of the king, Voltaire finally got the King's Council to agree to review the case. The review was delayed for months because of Toulouse's reluctance to turn over a copy of the transcript; when the magistrates whined about the expense of preparing the copy, Voltaire offered to pay the cost himself.[41]

On March 9, 1764, three years to the day after Jean Calas' conviction, a Paris tribunal by a vote of 40-0 reversed the verdict and declared the entire family "perfectly innocent" and grievously wronged, while demanding that the annual celebrations of the 1562 massacre cease. The king himself made a gift of money to Calas' widow, in partial compensation for her lost income. Jean Calas became the last Frenchman ever "broken on the wheel." David de Beaudrigue lost his sanity and jumped to his death. Though Louis XV couldn't bring himself to do it, one of the first acts of his successor ended most legal restrictions on the practice of Protestantism in France.[42]

Fall and Rise of the Jesuits

David de Beaudrigue wasn't the only victim of Voltaire's astonishing victory. Timing is everything, and for the Company of Jesus the timing of the Calas fiasco could not have been worse. The Catholic monarchs of Europe were growing increasingly weary of Jesuit intrigues. In 1759, after Jesuits were implicated in a plot to assassinate the king of Portugal, the chief minister succeeded in obtaining a decree banishing the Company from Portugal and its colonies, and burning one of its chiefs at the stake.[43]

If Portugal could do it ...

Loyola had prescribed vows of poverty for his followers, but after Pope Gregory XIII gave the Company the right to engage in banking and commerce it grew immensely wealthy, with its fingers in commercial enterprises around the globe. In 1760 a Jesuit slave-trading business on the Caribbean island of Martinique became unable to pay its bills. Angry creditors back in Marseilles did not appreciate being offered satisfaction in the form of a Mass; they filed a lawsuit against the Company itself, claiming it was a single entity, responsible for the bills of each of its subsidiaries. Though the Jesuits argued that their Martinique representative was acting beyond his authority, and that anyway they were doing God's work and should be considered above petty commercial law, they lost. They then committed the extraordinary blunder of appealing the verdict to the Parliament of Paris, even though they knew it to be sympathetic to a faction within the church that Jesuits had been persecuting for decades.[44]

The Parliament of Paris proceeded to launch a thorough investigation of the hitherto secret governing documents of the order, ostensibly to determine just how independent the Martinique operation really was. Revelation after revelation piled up, not only about Jesuit business operations but about their disdain for government officials who did not carry out God's will as they saw it. The ultimate outcome was a shocker. After Parliament confirmed every claim of the Marseilles merchants, a special council concluded that for promoting "a doctrine authorizing robbery, lying, perjury, impurity—all passions and crimes; inculcating homicide, parricide, and regicide; overturning religion, in order to substitute in her stead superstition; and thereby sanctioning magic, blasphemy, irreligion, and idolatry," the Jesuit order must be banned from France. Its schools would be closed, its wealth nationalized.[45]

When their hearts resumed beating, French Jesuits assured themselves that the king would never allow this order to stand. As indeed he would not have—but for the fact that precisely at this moment, a fellow in Switzerland was bombarding Paris with letters, pamphlets, and books about the horrendous evil "l'infâme" had committed in Toulouse, and getting the opinion-makers of Europe to join in his campaign. Even though the Company actually had little or no involvement in the Calas case, it drowned in the tsunami of abuse Voltaire launched against religious intolerance, and the demonstration that it was indeed possible for common sense to prevail over even the most powerful of God experts. A visiting German princess wrote that "At Paris, among the clergy or laity, I do not believe there are a hundred persons who hold the true faith." The king let the dissolution order stand.[46]

Voltaire expressed his views on the Jesuit controversy quite clearly in his *Treatise on Tolerance*:

> In like manner, if these latter have been found to teach the most reprehensible doctrines, and if their institution appears contrary to the laws of the kingdom, it becomes necessary to abolish their society, and of Jesuits to make them useful citizens; which, in fact, so far from being an oppression upon them, as has been pretended, is a real good done for them; for where is the great oppression of being obliged to wear a short

coat instead of a long gown, or to be free instead of being slave? In time of peace whole regiments are broken without complaining. Why, then, should the Jesuits make such an outcry, when they are broken for the sake of peace?[47]

A few years later, even Spain kicked the Jesuits out, after they were caught inciting riots in Madrid. In 1773 Pope Clement XIV dissolved the Company of Jesus altogether.[48]

After Louis XV died, Voltaire finally felt it safe to return to Paris. His reception was tumultuous—a conquering hero, crowned with a laurel wreath. Nothing gratified him more than hearing people say "That is the man who saved the family of Calas!" Everyone wanted a piece of the 83-year-old Voltaire; the demands overtaxed his constitution, and two months after his arrival in 1778, he died.[49]

The hierarchy was adamant: no burial in consecrated ground for the greatest enemy the church had known since the days of Emperor Julian. A sympathetic parish priest, though, acted quickly to bury Voltaire under the floor of his church before the official order could reach him. There Voltaire remained until 1791, when the revolutionary government celebrated his memory with a grand procession and reinterment in the newly dedicated Pantheon, housing the remains of the heroes of France. Some six hundred thousand lined the streets for a glimpse of his catafalque, on which was inscribed "He taught us to be free."[50]

In 1814, when the Catholics returned to power, Voltaire's body was removed from the Pantheon, dumped in a pit and dissolved in quicklime. That same year, the pope reinstated the Company of Jesus.[51]

As for the memory of Jean Calas, here is what the online *Catholic Encyclopedia* has to say: "Some historians, carried away perhaps by too great a desire to bring the innocence of Jean Calas to the fore, assert that Marc-Antoine committed suicide. But there are weighty reasons to doubt the father's innocence. ... The responsibility of the condemnation in no way rested with the ecclesiastical authorities."[52]

> "When once a nation begins to think, it is impossible to stop it." Was Voltaire over-optimistic in light of what seems to be a resurgence of religious power in America in the past 30 years? How exactly does one go about getting a nation to think? Share your thoughts on this and the other questions you'll find at **dgc.humanistpress.com**!

Notes:

1 Boehmer, *Jesuits*, 57.

2 Boehmer, *Jesuits*, 31, 52, 90; Ridley, *Jesuits*, 144.

3 Boehmer, *Jesuits*, 75, 106; Ridley, *Jesuits*, 109.

4 Boehmer, *Jesuits*, 68, 74, 76, 110, 121, 185; Paris, *Secret History*, 25, 65; Perkins, *France*, vol. 2, 209.

5 Parker, *Thirty Years*, 39; Johnson, *Christianity*, 302; Paris, *Secret History*, 37; MacCulloch, *Reformation*, 485.

6 Duff, *Jesuits*, 11; Paris, *Secret History*, 26.

7 Duff, *Jesuits*, 14; MacCulloch, *Reformation*, 422; Boehmer, *Jesuits*, 126-130.

8 Boehmer, *Jesuits*, 109; Ridley, *Jesuits*, 235; Voltaire, *Tolerance*, Chapter 6, note 2.

9 Duff, *Jesuits*, 22; Baird, *Huguenots*, vol. 1, 285; Castelli, *Parry Plot*; Encyclopedia Britannica, 1911 edition, *Jesuits*.

10 Nixon, *Calas*, 23.

11 Perkins, *France*, vol. 2, 207; Paris, *Secret History*, 46; d'Alembert, *Destruction*, 23; Encyclopedia Britannica, 1911 edition, *Jesuits*.

12 White, *Massacre*, 451; Baird, *Huguenots*, vol. 2, 530; Ellerbe, *Dark Side*, 98.

13 Paris, *Secret History*, 46; Encyclopedia Britannica, 1911 edition *Jacques Clement*; Baird, *Huguenots*, vol. 1, 282; Baird, *Huguenots*, vol. 2, 155.

14 Baird, *Huguenots*, vol. 2, 469; MacCulloch, *Reformation*, 469-471.

15 Chadwick, *Reformation*, 167; MacCulloch, *Reformation*, 471.

16 Cragg, *Church*, 20; Labrousse, *Bayle*, 8; Catholic Encyclopedia, *François d'Aix de la Chaise*; Baird, *Huguenots*, vol. 1, 779.

17 Labrousse, *Bayle*, 10; d'Alembert, *Destruction*, 52; Perkins, *France*, vol. 2, 209; Baird, *Huguenots*, vol. 1, 921; Encyclopedia Britannica, 1911 edition, *Jesuits*; Paris, *Secret History*, 48; Nixon, *Calas Case*, 25.

18 Meyer, *Voltaire*, 13, 18, 37.

19 Parker, *Voltaire*, 23; Meyer, *Voltaire*, 31, 57.

20 Tallentyre, *Voltaire*, 35, 51-52; Parker, *Voltaire*, 38; Meyer, *Voltaire*, 52.

21 Meyer, *Voltaire*, 79; Parker, *Voltaire*, 65; Sharpes, *Outcasts*, 242.

22 Arkell, *Caroline*, 137; Meyer, *Voltaire*, 88, 101; Tallentyre, *Voltaire*, 93; Perkins, *France*, vol. 2, 367; Sharpes, *Outcasts*, 242; Darrow, *Voltaire*, 15.

23 Perkins, *France*, vol. 2, 360; Tallentyre, *Voltaire*, 71, 124; Jimack, *Voltaire*, 134; Meyer, *Voltaire*, 126.

24 Parker, *Voltaire*, 106, 216; Meyer, *Voltaire*, 144-146; Tallentyre, *Voltaire*, 168.

25 Meyer, *Voltaire*, 203, 239; Creel, *Confucius*, 261; Perkins, *France*, vol. 2, 351; Tallentyre, *Voltaire*, 337-338, 570.

26 Perkins, *France*, vol. 2, 203; Sharpes, *Outcasts*, 244; Parker, *Voltaire*, 158; Meyer, *Voltaire*, 204.

27 Meyer, *Voltaire*, 194; Tallentyre, *Voltaire*, 430, 489; Jimack, *Voltaire*, 147.

28 Parton, *Voltaire*, vol. 2, 308.

29 Voltaire, *Tolerance*, chapter 1; Nixon, *Calas*, 24.

30 Perkins, *France*, vol. 2, 200; Jimack, *Voltaire*, 146; Cragg, *Church*, 242.

31 Nixon, *Calas*, 48, 83.

32 Perkins, *France*, vol. 2, 201; Voltaire, *Tolerance*, chapter 1; Nixon, *Calas*, 37, 60, 67.

33 Nixon, *Calas*, 50, 93 178; Parker, *Voltaire*, 172; Tallentyre, *Voltaire*, 470.

34 Parker, *Voltaire*, 176; Nixon, *Calas*, 99, 108, 111.

35 Ingersoll, *Voltaire*, 28; Tallentyre, *Voltaire*, 474.

36 Jimack, *Voltaire*, 147; Meyer, *Voltaire*, 201; Nixon, *Calas Case*, 28, 133-134, 146.

37 Darrow, *Voltaire*, 8.

38 Nixon, *Calas*, 171.

39 Nixon, *Calas*, 152-155, 164; Tallentyre, *Voltaire*, 478.

40 Nixon, *Calas*, 178, 192; Voltaire, *Tolerance*, chapter 5; Parker, *Voltaire*, 183.

41 Cragg, *Church*, 205; Parker, *Voltaire*, 176; Nixon, *Calas*, 140, 159, 169, 175.

42 Meyer, *Voltaire*, 221; Nixon, *Calas*, 193, 198, 215, 217; Tallentyre, *Voltaire*, 497; Baird, *Huguenots*, vol. 2, 548.

43 Cragg, *Church*, 212-213; Perkins, *France*, vol. 2, 217.

44 Paris, *Secret History*, 29; Cragg, *Church*, 198-199; d'Alembert, *Destruction*, 67, 83; Perkins, *France*, vol. 2, 214-215.

45 Duff, *Jesuits*, 5; Paris, *Secret History*, 69; Perkins, *France*, vol. 2, 217, 223.

46 Perkins, *France*, vol. 2, 219, 224, 401, 404.

47 Voltaire, *Tolerance*, Chapter 18.

48 Cragg, *Church*, 213-214; Boehmer, *Jesuits*, 189.

49 Tallentyre, *Voltaire*, 602; Perkins, *France*, vol. 2, 205; Behrens, *Ancien Régime*, 135.

50 Ingersoll, *Voltaire* 61; Parker, *Voltaire*, ix; Tallentyre, *Voltaire*, 334, 617, 623.

51 Darrow, *Voltaire*, 62; Perkins, *France*, vol. 2, 225.

52 Catholic Encyclopedia, *The Calas Case*.

Thomas Paine

CHAPTER 11

PAINE VS. TALLEYRAND

Paine

Shortly before his last illness in Paris, Voltaire met the famous American Benjamin Franklin. The two exchanged effusive compliments: "If I were 40," said Voltaire, "I should go and settle in your happy country." It is likely that Franklin's thoughts turned to a 41-year-old Englishman whom he had helped do exactly that only four years earlier, whom he now called "his adopted political son."[1]

Thomas Paine would have been the first to admit that his first 37 years were a succession of failures, both professional and personal. Near the end of his rope, he met with Franklin, then in London, and begged for an introduction to prospective employers in America. Whether Franklin saw something that others didn't, or was simply a soft touch, in 1774 he recommended Paine to a Philadelphia publisher.[2]

Though Paine had little education as a writer, he quickly became managing editor of the *Pennsylvania Magazine*. One of his first articles was a denunciation of slavery, which he called "monstrous." Franklin himself formed the first anti-slavery organization in America a few weeks later, with Paine as a charter member.[3]

Slavery, though, was not the hot-button American issue of 1775. A series of disputes with mother England had erupted into warfare that April, and by the end of the year a great deal of blood had been shed.

By all accounts, most Americans at the dawn of 1776 did not favor independence from England. They wanted greater local autonomy, but not outright independence. They didn't appreciate being shot at by their benevolent masters, though, and at this "teachable moment" a little pamphlet by Paine, written at Franklin's suggestion, took America by storm.[4]

Common Sense was written in the unflowery language of a non-professional educated in the school of hard knocks. Among simple colonists it struck a nerve, arguing not only for independence, but for the even more radical idea of not having a divine-right king at all, but a republic governed by elected representatives of the people. More than five hundred thousand copies of *Common Sense* were printed—not bad when the total population was 2½ million, and by far the number one American seller of the entire eighteenth century. It changed people's minds. Washington himself wrote that the "sound doctrine and unanswerable reasoning" of *Common Sense* was working a "powerful change ... in the Minds of men." Even John Adams, never a Paine ally, admitted that "without the pen of the author of *Common Sense*, the sword of Washington would have been raised in vain." Quite unlike the sharp businessman Voltaire, Paine never made a penny on *Common Sense*—he donated the copyright to support the war effort.[5]

Common Sense was not Paine's only contribution to the cause. An article he wrote called *The Crisis* so moved General Washington that he had it read aloud to the nervous troops preparing to cross the Delaware and mount their surprise Christmas Eve attack on the Hessians at Trenton, the victory that saved the nearly defunct American cause: "These are the times that try men's souls. ..." In the second piece in *The Crisis* series, Paine coined another phrase that has become rather well-known: "the United States of America." Serving under General Greene, Paine fought the British with arms as well as with words. He also helped to organize the "Bank of North America" to finance the war effort.[6]

After the victory, Paine did not achieve a prominent position in the new government as one might have expected. This was partly due to his non-aristocratic background, and partly due to his annoying habit of not mincing words. In particular, he made enemies by exposing fraud in the supply contracts for the Continental Army, and refusing to let the matter drop when it implicated some well-connected politicians. So Paine returned to England in 1787, intending to stir up another revolution there—a purpose rather contrary to the desires of the king's government. After Paine published *The Rights of Man*, a cogent attack on the institution of monarchy, his arrest was ordered by a government fearing an imminent outbreak of revolution. He fled, setting sail just 20 minutes before soldiers with an arrest warrant arrived. Printers and retailers of his books who did not escape were jailed left and right over the next decade.[7] Paine instead landed in France—where a revolution had started without him.

Talleyrand

France was broke. There are lengthier explanations for what led to the revolution of 1789, but the inability of the government to pay its bills was the ultimate tipping point. The biggest reason why France was broke was the power of the Catholic Church, which owned as much as 10 percent of the land in France, often the choicest parts. Not only did the church itself pay no tax, but it siphoned off tithes from the peasants and artisans who did, thus diminishing their ability to support the government. In Beauvais, for example, tithe payments consumed 18 percent of the peasants' crops.[8] Add to that the hopeless governmental inefficiency arising from the political power of the church, and the wonder is that France stayed solvent as long as it did.

Charles-Maurice de Talleyrand-Perigord was born in Paris in 1754. As the scion of a wealthy aristocratic family, Talleyrand would have had a military career had not a childhood accident crippled his leg. As a fallback, he was steered toward the church. The fact that he had not the slightest interest in affairs of the spirit mattered not, nor did his youthful idolizing of Voltaire; the church was the path to wealth and influence, so that is the path he followed. Though he routinely ignored his vow of celibacy, he was awarded a wealthy abbey, and then made bishop of the diocese of Autun.[9]

Unlike many of his fellow bishops, Talleyrand was politically shrewd; some call him the most brilliant politician ever produced by

France. He made sure to get himself elected to the Estates-General that the king convened in 1789, consisting of the nation's leading nobility, clergy, and commoners and charged with the task of putting the government on a sounder financial footing. Rounding up the necessary votes to be elected to this august body was the impetus for Talleyrand's one and only lifetime visit to the diocese where he served as bishop.[10]

After the storming of the Bastille by a crowd chanting "Vive Voltaire!" Talleyrand perceived which way the wind was blowing. He maneuvered himself into a leadership role among those pressing for change, rather than simply being a nay-sayer. Meanwhile, he was secretly urging the king's brother to send in troops to shut down the Estates-General before it could achieve any real progress.[11]

Nonetheless, as a bishop ostensibly on the side of the revolutionists, Talleyrand carried the same counterintuitive cachet as a conservative gay or a liberal soldier today. His reputation was solidified when he secured the nationalization of church assets, in exchange for the government's undertaking to pay the salaries of the clergy—a distinctly unpopular idea among his fellow bishops. Archbishop Boisgelin wrote to his mistress that: "All is lost. I will have 30,000 livres annually, and nothing more. Nothing for all my abbeys, nothing unless I reside in my diocese, nothing but dependency on the municipal government."[12]

Nearly as bad for the hierarchy was the "Civil Constitution of the Clergy" adopted by the National Assembly, which abolished all power of the pope over the French Church. Bishops were now to be elected by the people, who could only vote after hearing Mass and taking an oath that in voting they would consider only the interests of religion. Every candidate for bishop must previously have served 15 years in a parish, and only clergy who had directly served the people's needs would be eligible. What the Civil Constitution did not do was make any change at all in the liturgy or doctrines of the church. No one had objected to the substance of the Catholic religion; the Assembly simply wanted to root out the corruption.[13] Talleyrand was one of only four bishops to support the Civil Constitution. He was promptly excommunicated, and then elected president of the revolution's National Assembly.[14]

The Civil Constitution was bad enough, but Article 18 of the "Declaration of the Rights of Man and the Citizen" was even worse: "No one can be disturbed for his opinions, even religious ones, provided that their expression does not infringe the public order declared by the law." That put the Catholic Church on the same level as every other supernatural belief. Not long afterward, all legal disabilities were removed for Protestants, and later even for Jews.[15]

The church's response was straightforward: massive resistance, both inside and outside of France. The pope ordered the clergy not to take an oath of loyalty to the government, and excommunicated those who did. Most senior clergy fled France with all the loot they could grab, and then worked ceaselessly (and successfully) to induce foreign governments, especially that of Catholic Austria, to invade France and crush the upstarts. Priests loyal to the pope who did not flee went underground, doing all they could to foment dissent and armed rebellion against the new official church.[16]

The enormous Catholic resistance is by far the biggest reason why the French Revolution took a path different from the revolution in America. Although some one hundred thousand defeated Tories (who had been led primarily by Anglican ministers) abandoned America after the war, they had never been nearly as rich or powerful as the bishops of France.[17] By contrast, a well-informed neutral handicapper in 1791 would have given short odds to the proposition that the French Church would come roaring back.

One very well-informed neutral handicapper was Talleyrand. He did not flee, but stayed behind to use his inside information to make money in bond speculation as fast as he could. All the while he was serving as an official in the revolutionary government he was actively corresponding with its enemies, assuring them that he would help them however he could.[18]

The Age of Reason

Paine's reception in France was quite different than it had been in England. Not only was he acclaimed as a hero, but he was esteemed as a revolution expert, who could guide France down the successful path

America had followed. Without trying, he was elected to represent Calais in the National Assembly—not an easy assignment for a man who didn't speak French, and seemed unable to learn it. But Paine did his best, and was instrumental in drafting the *Declaration of the Rights of Man*. Within the Assembly, Paine aligned with the moderate bloc, who sought the ascendance of tolerant middle-class values as then were prevailing in America.[19]

In the early years of the revolution, this moderate viewpoint prevailed, and France made astonishing progress with very little bloodshed.[20] Unlike in America, though, the moderates were squeezed by the recalcitrant Catholics on one hand, who stimulated a radical opposition on the other. The radicals were intent on replacing the Catholic Church with their own brand of God expertise—either outright atheism, or a bizarre "Cult of the Supreme Being" launched by the radical revolutionary dictator Robespierre with its own hymns, prayers, and the exaltation of an actress as the "Goddess of Reason." Although de-Christianization was popular in large areas of France, the newfangled religion was not. Typical was the response of the women of Le Puy, who at a solemn moment during a Supreme Being liturgy turned about and mooned the Altar of Liberty.[21]

Paine could see a smashup coming as well as Talleyrand could. Talleyrand's approach was to deal under the table with all sides, so he could land on his feet whatever the outcome. Paine's approach was to analyze the root of the problem, using the same common sense approach as he had in, well, *Common Sense*.

The resulting book, *The Age of Reason*, may be the most profound statement on religion the world has yet seen. From the outset, Paine rejects the atheist certainty that no supernatural force exists. "I believe in one God, and no more."[22] Yet he spends most of the book debunking the Christian Bible, doing a more thorough job than Spinoza in pointing out its inconsistencies and absurdities. The Gospel story "has every mark of fraud and imposition stamped upon the face of it. ... [I]t is impossible to conceive a story more derogatory to the Almighty, more inconsistent with His wisdom, more contradictory to His power, than this story is."[23]

Paine finds God not in the glibness of the God experts, but in the world around us:

> It is only in the CREATION that all our ideas and conceptions of a word of God can unite. ... It is an ever existing original, which every man can read. It cannot be forged; it cannot be counterfeited; it cannot be lost; it cannot be altered; it cannot be suppressed. ... It preaches to all nations and to all worlds; and this word of God reveals to man all that is necessary for man to know of God.[24]

He then dwells on the evil that God expert power has done the world across the centuries: "All national institutions of churches, whether Jewish, Christian or Turkish, appear to me no other than human inventions, set up to terrify and enslave mankind, and monopolize power and profit." Paine instead stresses reason and morality, eliminating idle theological speculation. But he shrewdly identifies the political difficulty of this simple approach:

> But pure and simple deism does not answer the purpose of despotic governments. They cannot lay hold of religion as an engine but by mixing it with human inventions, and making their own authority a part; neither does it answer the avarice of priests, but by incorporating themselves and their functions with it, and becoming, like the government, a party in the system. It is this that forms the otherwise mysterious connection of church and state; the church human, and the state tyrannic.[25]

When the king was caught trying to escape to join the invading armies of Catholic Austria, the radicals gained the upper hand. What became known as "the Terror" was launched in late 1792, during which something on the order of 20,000 suspected counter-revolutionaries, including some 2,000-3,000 Catholic clergy, were given summary trials and then sent to the guillotine. No doubt, many of those executed actually were conspiring against the government, an activity which has at all times in all places carried risk. But the Terror was ultimately self-defeating; even though approximately half of those accused were acquitted, it wrecked the public confidence in the new institutions that was necessary to sustain them. Meanwhile, unknown thousands of supporters of the revolution were being slaughtered by church-inspired rebels in the countryside, without any benefit of trial.[26]

Ironically, one of the victims of the Terror was Paine himself. The radicals who seized control had no use for moderates, especially their most glamorous advocate. Paine was imprisoned in December 1793, largely because he opposed the execution of the king. Talleyrand voted to execute.[27]

Paine had been working on *The Age of Reason* intermittently for years, intending it as a final testament. As his arrest grew imminent, he hastily finished a working draft and arranged to have it published, since he did not expect to emerge from prison alive. He had good reason to be pessimistic. Seven months later, Robespierre signed Paine's death warrant, to be carried out immediately.[28]

It has never been clear how Paine survived. The best answer seems to be a simple administrative foul-up by uneducated jailers in an overcrowded prison. In any case, Paris had grown tired of Robespierre's excesses; a few days after signing Paine's death warrant, Robespierre himself was beheaded.[29]

Still, Paine remained in jail, where he developed an abscess in his side that nearly killed him. Day after day, he seethed at the failure of the American authorities to heed his pleas for help. In fact, President Washington had asked the American ambassador in France, Gouverneur Morris, to use his influence to get Paine released. Morris, though, detested Paine, whom he called "a mere adventurer from England, without fortune, without family or connections, ignorant even of grammar." Morris had been among the faction Paine accused of war profiteering and he vehemently disagreed with Paine's views against slavery and monarchy, which Morris called "a moral influenza." So Morris simply lied to the American Secretary of State that he was doing all he could, adding snidely that "Thomas Paine is in prison, where he amuses himself with publishing a pamphlet against Jesus Christ." Ultimately Paine spent 10 months rotting away, until a new ambassador—future President James Monroe—easily secured his freedom by establishing Paine's American citizenship, and then taking him into his own home to nurse him back to health.[30]

In 1797 Paine and several others founded one of the world's first ethical societies, known as the "Theophilanthropists," to promote a deistic religion without superstition or priesthood, celebrating instead the work of humanists like Confucius. When an official enthusiastically presented a paper on the subject, Talleyrand scoffed: "For my part I have only one observation to make. Jesus Christ, in order to found his religion, was crucified and rose again—you should have tried to do as much."[31]

Though Paine and Talleyrand must have crossed paths, there is nothing in the writings of either man describing a direct encounter with the other. It is interesting, though, that Gouverneur Morris and Talleyrand did share the same mistress, on amicable terms; whether the two men spent time commiserating about the stubbornness of Paine we'll never know.[32] It is possible that Paine had a certain ex-bishop in mind when he wrote in *The Age of Reason* that:

> When a man has so far corrupted and prostituted the chastity of his mind, as to subscribe his professional belief to things he does not believe, he has prepared himself for the commission of every other crime. He takes up the trade of a priest for the sake of gain. And, in order to qualify himself for that trade, he begins with a perjury. Can we conceive anything more destructive to morality than this?[33]

Napoleon

When the Terror struck, Talleyrand bolted for England. The radicals were deeply suspicious of him, even before documents surfaced proving him to be in league with the enemies of the republic.[34] Talleyrand was banished from France—not that he had any inclination to return, as he witnessed people far less guilty than himself fall victim daily to the guillotine.

But the English government didn't trust Talleyrand either, so in 1793 he set sail for the United States. The fresh democratic spirit of

1790s America made the aristocratic Talleyrand positively ill.[35] He was thus relieved to learn in 1795 that the radicals were out, and their more moderate replacements were anxious for Talleyrand to return and put his considerable skills of diplomatic intrigue at their disposal.[36]

They got more than they bargained for. Though Talleyrand was a clever diplomat, his intrigues extended to domestic politics as well. He soon latched onto a young general, Napoleon Bonaparte, as his ticket for stamping out democratic untidiness and putting superior beings like himself back in charge. Talleyrand was heavily involved in every aspect of the machinations of 1799 that put Napoleon in power, first as a "Consul," then as "First Consul." Napoleon immediately issued a proclamation: "Citizens, the revolution is now sealed with the principles that first set it afoot. It is over."[37]

Napoleon relied on troops who believed they were fighting for themselves as free citizens, rather than for a divine right monarch, and quickly overran most of Europe, giving him the power to treat the church as he wished. Unlike Frederick II, who had balked at the gates of Rome, Napoleon had actually taken Pope Pius VI prisoner. Even better yet, Pius had died while in custody, presenting Napoleon with a perfect opportunity to bring the church to heel by announcing that there would be no more popes, as many people thought he would.[38]

That's what Napoleon and Talleyrand could have done, as neither had any sincere belief in Christianity. Napoleon claimed to have abandoned faith at the age of 11; at 17, he wrote an essay calling Christianity a menace to the state. He once bragged that "It was by making myself a Catholic that I won the war in the Vendee, by making myself a Muslim that I established myself in Egypt, by making myself an ultramontane that I turned men's hearts towards me in Italy. If I were to govern a nation of Jews I would rebuild the Temple of Solomon."[39]

But instead of seizing the opportunity to écrasez l'infâme, Napoleon and Talleyrand tried to have their cake and eat it too by restoring the church's prestige while leaving it under Napoleon's thumb. Throughout the lengthy negotiations over the "Concordat" negotiated by Talleyrand to re-establish the framework of relationships between France and the church, the representatives of the newly consecrated pope kept their eyes on the prize: not a prize having anything to do with spirituality, but with the pope's rights as a dictator over central Italy, revenues from which maintained the hierarchy's lavish lifestyle. The church also restored to power the bishops who had fomented rebellion against the government of France during the revolution years. What Napoleon and Talleyrand got in exchange was God's approval for their reign of theft and brutality, most visibly when Napoleon decided to crown himself emperor in 1804, with Pope Pius VII, whose election he had allowed, in attendance as a decoration.[40]

The pope was so delighted that he rescinded Talleyrand's excommunication.[41] Indeed, the revolution was now truly over: the starry-eyed vision of *Common Sense* that people could govern themselves was discarded and replaced with the old corrupt bargain between the God experts and the might-makes-divine-right monarchs.

Whether it was really necessary for Napoleon to accommodate the church at all is debatable. Cardinal Consalvi, who came to Paris to negotiate the Concordat on the pope's behalf, reported the French attitude toward religion as "indifferent for the most part, entirely so in the towns, and to an appreciable degree in the countryside," and that Napoleon was the only prominent Frenchman who wanted a Concordat. But Napoleon wanted to use the church to legitimate his rule: "No worship, no government," he told his brother Lucien. "Skillful conquerors have not got entangled with priests. They can both contain them and use them."[42] Shortly after his coronation, the church ordered French children to memorize the following catechism in their Sunday schools:

Question: What are the duties of Christians towards the princes who govern them, and what, in particular, are our duties towards Napoleon I, our emperor?

Answer: Christians owe to the princes who govern them, and we, in particular, owe to Napoleon I, our emperor, love, respect, obedience, loyalty, military service, and the taxes ordered for the preservation and defense of the empire and his throne; we also owe him fervent prayers for his safety and for the spiritual and temporal prosperity of the state ... because God, who creates empires and apportions them according to His will, by heaping His gifts upon [Napoleon], set him up as our sovereign and made him the agent of His power and His image on earth. Thus it is that to honor and serve our emperor is to honor and serve God Himself.[43]

Throughout his time in power, Talleyrand negotiated dozens of agreements, both with those France defeated and those willing to become its satellites. On every such deal Talleyrand took a large bribe, payable for his having been so reasonable during the negotiation. Even before his rise to prominence, a French revolutionary leader astutely noted that "[Talleyrand] would sell his soul for money; and he would be right, for he would be exchanging dung for gold."[44] The one nation that resisted this arrangement was the *Common Sense* United States he so detested. Indignant American negotiators publicized the secret demand for a payment of "tribute" to a party documented only as "XYZ," and an undeclared naval war broke out over what was called the "XYZ Affair." Historians today have little doubt that "XYZ" was Talleyrand.[45]

Another difference between Paine and Talleyrand involved slavery. Paine, as we saw, was among the very first Americans to come out against it. Before he returned to Europe, he was employed briefly on the staff of the Pennsylvania legislature, where he drafted what became the first abolition law in the United States. Revolutionary France followed suit, in 1794. But when Talleyrand and Napoleon restored the church to power, they restored church doctrine allowing slavery as well, at least in the French Caribbean colonies where it was economically beneficial.[46]

Restoration

Talleyrand's reputation as a brilliant politician may be overrated. We've seen how his double-dealing cost him his position with the revolutionary government. After a few years, his protégé Napoleon tired of his intrigues and pocket-lining as well, and began freezing him out of important decision-making processes.

Talleyrand was forced out as foreign minister, retaining only a high-paying ceremonial post, from which he began conspiring against Napoleon himself. He repeatedly committed treason by advising France's foreign adversaries on the best tactics to use against it, and by conspiring with the exiled Louis XVIII (the executed king's brother) for his return to power. Talleyrand once characterized "betrayal" as being merely "a question of dates."[47] Napoleon confronted him at a cabinet meeting:

> You are a thief, a coward, and disloyal. You don't believe in God. ... You have deceived and betrayed everyone. Nothing is sacred to you. You would sell out your own father if you found it profitable. I have heaped benefits, veritable fortunes on you, and yet there is nothing you are incapable of carrying out against me.[48]

As for Napoleon, he came to have reason to regret his failure to liquidate the church when he had the chance. Continued disputes with the pope resulted in his excommunication in 1809. A Catholic-inspired guerrilla war in Spain bled France dry; Catholic hostility as he crossed Poland was a major factor in the ill-fated Russian campaign that ultimately brought his downfall.[49] Napoleon boasted of using the church, but it ended up using him.

By 1814, it was time for one more Talleyrand backstab. Napoleon had no army left after squandering the lives of two million Europeans (a hundred times more than were killed in the Terror) in pursuit of ego gratification. Although the conquerors of France were dubious, Talleyrand jumped at the chance to bring back the good old days of the Catholic monarchy; by all accounts, Talleyrand was the single most important player in the restoration of Louis XVIII, with whom he had been conspiring for years. The Restoration was accompanied by a "White Terror" in which the religious took their revenge on the humanists, rivaling the worst days of the revolution's Terror.[50]

Pope Pius VII was also restored to political power in central Italy.

One of his first acts was to reinstate the Jesuits, followed promptly by decrees reviving the ban on smallpox vaccination and ordering Rome's Jews back into the ghetto.[51]

For the next 15 years, France sunk back into a theocracy to make Augustine proud. Marriages contracted by civil officials—as were most marriages during the 1790s—were declared null and void, and the couples were considered as living in the state of sin. Divorce laws disappeared from the code. The church was given total control of education. Paupers who could not prove they were faithful Catholics were denied state aid. The theater was censored before performances were allowed. Christian burial was refused even to believers, if they were suspected of heresy. Late in the period, the king appointed as his chief minister Jules de Polignac, who made decisions based on advice he received from visions of the Virgin Mary.[52]

Naturally, the brilliant politician Talleyrand assumed that he would be pulling the strings in the new regime, and he did at the outset. After only two months, though, the king decided for some reason that he just couldn't trust Talleyrand, who was dumped once again.[53] Did Talleyrand use the church, or did the church use Talleyrand?

Paine's end

Paine finally returned to America in 1802, after condemning Napoleon as "the completest charlatan that ever existed." He found an America quite different from what he had left. Revivalism spread like wildfire, with preachers outdoing one another in showmanship and wild new theologies in order to pack in a paying crowd. On one point they all agreed: the author of *The Age of Reason* was the devil incarnate. One critic, who had not actually read the book, assured his readers that "Like Judas, he will be remembered by posterity; men will learn to express all that is base, malignant, treacherously unnatural, and blasphemous by the single monosyllable of 'Paine.'" When the British government banned *The Age of Reason* for blasphemy, the same lawyer who had defended Paine's *Rights of Man* switched sides and led the (successful) prosecution of a seller of the book, whose publisher spent more than nine years in prison.[54]

Vote-counting politicians came to realize that even if the Paine-haters were a minority, there was no point in alienating them; no one would touch Paine with a 10-foot pole. A Boston newspaper called him "that lying, drunken, brutal infidel, who rejoiced in the opportunity of basking and wallowing in the confusion, devastation, bloodshed, rapine, and murder, in which his soul delights." Things were bad when a coachman refused to drive the demon Paine from Trenton to New York. They were worse when the local elections board refused to allow Paine to vote. Even the Quakers rejected him, when he sought permission to be buried in their cemetery.[55]

So when Paine died in 1809, he was buried on his own farm. A zealous Christian manufactured a tale of his dying words: "If ever the devil had an agent on earth, I am that man!" A few years after Voltaire's body was stolen from the Pantheon, a group snuck onto the farm at night and dug up Paine's bones, intending to cash in by displaying them back in England. When interest failed to materialize, the bones were discarded, inspiring a bit of doggerel:[56]

Poor Tom Paine! There he lies:
Nobody laughs and nobody cries.
Where he has gone or how he fares,
Nobody knows and nobody cares.

> Historical counterfactuals are unrewarding, because you can never prove who is right. But they're fun! So what if Napoleon had said in 1799, "That's it—no more popes. People can believe what they want, but I'm not going to tolerate some mini-God judging my every action and telling Europe whether it's ok with heaven for me to continue exercising political power or not." What happens then? Share your thoughts on this and the other questions you'll find at **dgc.humanistpress.com**!

Notes:
1 Tallentyre, *Voltaire*, 591; Fruchtman, *Paine*, 177.
2 Fruchtman, *Paine*, 16; Sharpes, *Outcasts*, 54.

3 Sharpes, *Outcasts*, 54; Fruchtman, *Paine*, 51; Jacoby, *Freethinkers*, 38.

4 Vale, *Paine*, 75.

5 Fruchtman, *Paine*, 63; Vale, *Paine*, 82.

6 Fruchtman, *Paine*, 92-94, 98; Vale, *Paine*, 123; Jacoby, *Freethinkers*, 38.

7 Encyclopedia Britannica (1911), "Thomas Paine"; Fruchtman, *Paine*, 249, 291; Vale, *Paine*, 175, 186, 192.

8 Cragg, *Church*, 201; Aston, *Religion*, 105.

9 Schom, *Napoleon*, 241; McCabe, *Talleyrand*, 8, 20; Cooper, *Talleyrand*, 12, 15, 18, 31.

10 Aston, *Religion*, 126; McCabe, *Talleyrand*, 57-59.

11 Cooper, *Talleyrand*, 36; McCabe, *Talleyrand*, 65.

12 O'Dwyer, *Papacy*, 13; Cooper, *Talleyrand*, 38; McCabe, *Talleyrand*, 74; Aston, *Religion*, 133-134, 148.

13 Vidler, *Church*, 16; O'Dwyer, *Papacy*, 13; Aston, *Religion*, 141, 200.

14 Schom, *Napoleon*, 241; Cooper, *Talleyrand*, 41-42; McCabe, *Talleyrand*, 84.

15 Aston, *Religion*, 128-129, 236, 245.

16 Aston, *Religion*, 165, 168.

17 Eaton, *Tory Clergy*, 31, 96, 100; Nelson, *American Tory*, 3.

18 Cooper, *Talleyrand*, 47, 65.

19 Fast, *Citizen*, 253; Fruchtman, *Paine*, 247, 272, 308.

20 Fruchtman, *Paine*, 218.

21 Aston, *Religion*, 260, 272, 275; Hales, *Pio Nono*, 45.

22 Paine, *Age of Reason*, 290-291.

23 Fruchtman, *Paine*, 326.

24 Paine, *Age of Reason*, 317, 322.

25 Fast, *Citizen*, 282-283; Paine, *Age of Reason*, 290-291, 448.

26 McCabe, *Talleyrand*, 107; Aston, *Religion*, 187; Fruchtman, *Paine*, 312, 335.

27 Jacoby, *Freethinkers*, 41; Fruchtman, *Paine*, 237, 295, 317; Vale, *Paine*, 195; Schom, *Napoleon*, 192.

28 Fast, *Citizen*, 282-283; Fruchtman, *Paine*, 314, 317, 324; Paine, *Age of Reason*, 273; Vale, *Paine*, 203, 275.

29 Vale, *Paine*, 207, 213.

30 Fruchtman, *Paine*, 115, 122, 193, 323-324, 331, 346.

31 McCabe, *Talleyrand*, 127; Fruchtman, *Paine*, 380, 383; Vale, *Paine*, 227; Cooper, *Talleyrand*, 96.

32 Cooper, *Talleyrand*, 45.

33 Paine, *Age of Reason*, 290-291.

34 Cooper, *Talleyrand*, 59; McCabe, *Talleyrand*, 109.

35 McCabe, *Talleyrand*, 114-116.

36 Cooper, *Talleyrand*, 77, 84.

37 Cooper, *Talleyrand*, 94, 121; McCabe, *Talleyrand*, 149; Schom, *Napoleon*, 217.

38 O'Dwyer, *Papacy*, 28; Aston, *Religion*, 286.

39 Aston, *Religion*, 316; Johnson, *Christianity*, 362; McCabe, *Talleyrand*, 164; Hales, *Napoleon*, 7, 58.

40 Hales, *Napoleon*, 51, 57, 70; McCabe, *Talleyrand*, 170, 181; O'Dwyer, *Papacy*, 50, 83.

41 McCabe, *Talleyrand*, 170.

42 O'Dwyer, *Papacy*, 57; Aston, *Religion*, 276, 321.

43 Hales, *Napoleon*, 89.

44 McCabe, *Talleyrand*, 162; Schom, *Napoleon*, 247; Cooper, *Talleyrand*, 28, 126.

45 Cooper, *Talleyrand*, 89; McCabe, *Talleyrand*, 132.

46 Fruchtman, *Paine*, 124; Thomas, *Slave Trade*, 523.

47 Cooper, *Talleyrand*, 157, 162, 176, 213, 252; McCabe, *Talleyrand*, 227; Schom, *Napoleon*, 201.

48 Schom, *Napoleon*, 491-492.

49 Hales, *Napoleon*, 101, 115, 164, 176, 192; O'Dwyer, *Papacy*, 101; Aston, *Religion*, 346.

50 Bodart, *Losses*, 133; Cooper, *Talleyrand*, 224, 227; Wolf, *France*, 36; Schom, *Napoleon*, 696.

51 O'Dwyer, *Papacy*, 127, 135.

52 Wolf, *France*, 62, 68; McCabe, *Talleyrand*, 280; Woodward, *Three Studies*, 249.

53 McCabe, *Talleyrand*, 235, 258; Cooper, *Talleyrand*, 273.

54 Vale, *Paine*, 251; Jacoby, *Freethinkers*, 36; Fruchtman, *Paine*, 342; Paine, *Age of Reason*, 286-287.

55 Fruchtman, *Paine*, 386; Jacoby, *Freethinkers*, 36; Vale, *Paine*, 270; Fast, *Citizen*, 336.

56 Fruchtman, *Paine*, 433, 441; Johnson, *Christianity*, 372; Fast, *Citizen*, 341.

Joseph Smith, Jr.

CHAPTER 12

HARRIS VS. SMITH

Free Enterprise in Religion

The Constitution written by America's founding fathers in 1787 was unique because it deliberately made no mention of God. This was no oversight; the framers intended America's government to be a human institution, deriving its authority from "We the People" rather than from any god. The first order of business of the first Congress in 1789 was to adopt a Bill of Rights, including First Amendment prohibitions against government "establishing" any religion.

Those who thought the new legal regime might weaken religion underestimated the power of the free market forces the First Amendment unleashed. Economists today are not surprised that when a government-backed monopoly is pushed aside, and entrepreneurs are allowed free entry to a potentially lucrative market (with modest start-up costs), a thousand flowers will bloom. While most of the startups will fail, those that succeed will be the ones with a combination of energy, organization, and a product that intrigues the market.

This is exactly analogous to what happened in America after the First Amendment came into being. Methodism went from being a blip on the radar to a major force, as camp revival meetings provided a social outlet for isolated American farmers.[1] The Shakers, first established by Ann Lee in 1774, grew rapidly despite their doctrine that all sex was sinful; for some reason, they died out after a few decades. The Millerites took America by storm with their prediction that the world would end on October 22, 1844. One might think that a spectacularly failed prophecy would have consigned them to oblivion; instead, they became known as the Seventh-Day Adventists, with some 14 million adherents today.[2]

America's most successful God entrepreneur by far, though, was Joseph Smith, Jr. of Palmyra, New York. In 1827, Smith claimed he found a "Golden Bible" (later called the "Book of Mormon") buried near his home, telling how the lost tribes of Israel had actually sailed to then unpopulated America, making America's Indians actually Jewish. It's worth exploring this book in further detail, but for now, fast forward to 1830, when Smith and a handful of followers established a new "Church of Christ" in Palmyra, now called the Mormons. They didn't remain in Palmyra long, though, because Smith was well-known in the community but not well-trusted. So they decamped for Kirtland, Ohio, where another evangelical entrepreneur named Sidney Rigdon turned over his customers to Smith.[3]

Over time, the new religion took on some bizarre theological notions, starting with the idea that multiple gods had formed the world. Better yet, every good male Mormon can become a god himself, by producing enough Mormon offspring; once you reach godhood, you get your own planet to be the god of, just like the people who live on the sun and the moon have their own gods. This teaching was the main theological justification for the Mormon practice of polygamy: a man could crank out offspring a lot faster with multiple wives than he could with just one.[4]

The offspring produced after attaining godhood are initially thought to be spirits, waiting for a child to be conceived by humans; a spirit then moves into this "tabernacle." But while they are waiting to be born, some spirits supposedly do things to offend God; this explains why some people are born black, signifying God's curse, while the spirits who obeyed God pre-birth come out nice and white. The twentieth century Mormon *Juvenile Instructor* explains that "We understand that when God made man in his own image and pronounced him very good, that he made him white."[5]

Wanderings

After arriving in Kirtland, Smith began relieving his congregation of its money in various ways, especially involving land speculation—buying land cheaply then selling it to newly arrived converts at inflated values. Most of the transactions were done on credit, and Smith soon decided that he needed to own a bank. After his application for a bank charter from the State of Ohio was denied because he had neither capital nor banking expertise, Smith developed a ruse. He opened an institution that issued engraved notes looking just like bank notes—except if you looked hard, you would see just before the large word "Bank" of Kirtland the tiny, faint word "Anti-," and just after it the tiny, faint words "ing Society." So the notes of the "Anti-Banking Society of Kirtland" were used as currency just as ordinary bank notes, with uneducated pioneers not knowing the difference. Smith also attracted deposits to his Anti-Banking Society by showing customers his vault filled with crates of silver coins. No one noticed that the crates actually contained a thin layer of silver coins on the top concealing gravel underneath.[6]

When the fake bank failed, Ohio issued a warrant for Smith's arrest. So Smith fled in the dead of night for Independence, Missouri, which God told him was the location of the Garden of Eden. Smith even identified a pile of rocks he found there as an altar built by Adam himself.[7]

Missouri was convenient because it bordered on Indian Territory, and Smith's plan was to unite with these descendants of the lost tribes of Israel to build himself a power base. This initiative never impressed the Indians, but it did succeed in upsetting the non-Mormon settlers of western Missouri.[8]

What bothered the Missourians more, though, was that the stream of Mormon immigrants boasted about their intention of achieving political dominance through sheer force of numbers and using it to set up a theocratic state. God's revelation to the Mormons called Missouri "the land of your inheritance, which is now the land of your enemies." Mormons announced they would "claim Jackson County by force if necessary." Smith swore that "We will trample down our enemies and make it one gore of blood from the Rocky Mountains to the Atlantic Ocean. I will be to this generation a second Mohammed, whose motto in treating for peace was 'the Alcoran or the Sword.' So shall it eventually be with us— 'Joseph Smith or the Sword!'"[9]

This was not a wise challenge to fling at the Missourians, hard men who still heavily outnumbered the Mormons. What is now called the "Missouri Civil War" broke out, pitting the Mormons against the state militia. The Mormons took the worst of it; Smith surrendered in October 1838, and was thrown into jail. While the prosecution was assembling its treason and murder case, Mormons bribed jail guards into allowing Smith's escape to Nauvoo, Illinois.[10]

The Mormons in Nauvoo went about the theocracy-building process in a much savvier manner than they had in Missouri. They sent lobbyists to the state legislature to win a charter for the city allowing them to control it, and to create a military outfit under Smith's command called the "Nauvoo Legion." There was also a paramilitary group of thugs called the "Danites," one of whom recalled a Jesuit-like instruction that in Nauvoo it was "the duty of all men to obey the leaders of the church, and that no man could commit sin so long as he acted in the way that he was directed by his church superiors."[11]

By 1844, Nauvoo had become the second largest city in Illinois, and the 4,000-man Nauvoo Legion was nearly half the size of the entire U.S. Army. But rapid expansion was accompanied by growing pains, in the form of dissent against the prophet Joseph Smith. Some people were upset about his continued shady business dealings; some thought that the proclamation of Smith as "King of the Kingdom of God" went too far. Others had reservations about Smith's Talmud-like teaching that stealing from non-Mormons to support the church was perfectly ok.[12] But Smith's biggest headache was his inability to conceal the growing illegal practice of polygamy, both for himself and members of his inner circle. He steadfastly lied about what he was doing: "What a thing it is for a man to be accused of committing adultery, and having seven wives, when I can only find one. … I can prove them all perjurers." At the time he spoke, he had at least 33 wives, including a mother-daughter pair, three sets of sisters, and quite a few who already had husbands.[13]

On June 7, 1844, dissident Mormons (led by the husband of a woman Smith had attempted to seduce) published the first edition of a newspaper called the *Nauvoo Expositor*, laying out the details of Smith's polygamy, criticizing his political ambitions (Smith had just announced he was running for President of the United States), and scorning his claim to royalty: "We will not acknowledge any man as king." The paper also proclaimed its intention to "oppose with uncompromising hostility any union of church and state."[14]

The first issue of the *Expositor* was also the last. Three days later, after Smith announced that "We have a Judas in our midst," the Nauvoo Legion on orders of the City Council attacked and destroyed its offices and printing press. These Gestapo style tactics snapped the patience of Illinois officials, who sent a constable to arrest Smith on a charge of riot. Smith responded by arranging a hasty trial before a magistrate he had appointed, who immediately declared him innocent. Correctly fearing that this might not end the matter, Smith declared Nauvoo under martial law, put the Legion on full alert, and fled into hiding across the Mississippi. There he changed his mind and decided to return to face his accusers.[15]

After he was jailed in Carthage, Illinois, Smith decided not to trust the justice system after all, and smuggled out an urgent message to the Legion to come and "break the jail, and save him at all costs." For reasons still unknown, the officer who received this order did not respond immediately; he was later murdered by Mormons for dereliction of duty. Although there is no evidence that the citizens of Carthage knew of this message, after Smith's escapes from justice in Ohio and Missouri they decided not to trust the system either. On June 27, 1844, a crowd stormed the jailhouse and murdered Joseph Smith.[16]

That ended the story of Joseph Smith, though not the story of Mormonism. Within a year, federal agents were sent to arrest Smith's successor Brigham Young for counterfeiting; he emulated Smith's example by fleeing, this time all the way to Utah. There he set up a *de facto* independent nation, with himself proclaimed as king, boasting that "I live above the law, and so do this people."[17] Full-scale war nearly broke out against an Army expedition sent out in 1857 to arrest criminals Young was harboring. In a last-minute compromise the Army agreed to abandon its mission if Young would at least pay lip service to federal sovereignty.[18]

Today the largest Mormon denomination, officially called "The Church of Jesus Christ of the Latter-Day Saints," is one of the wealthiest institutions of any kind in the United States. A 2000 estimate put the church's $25-$30 billion of assets (including landholdings the size of Delaware) at No. 243 on the Fortune 500. It boasts some 13 million members and 45 thousand missionaries worldwide.[19] Yet the whole Mormon phenomenon came perilously close to never happening at all because of a single stubborn woman, who refused to take matters on faith.

Money Digging

"Mormonism, as it is called, must stand or fall on the story of Joseph Smith. He was either a prophet of God, divinely called, properly appointed and commissioned, or he was one of the biggest frauds this world has ever seen. There is no middle ground." Those are not the words of an anti-Mormon critic, but of Joseph Fielding Smith, tenth president and prophet of the Mormon Church.[20]

America at the turn of the nineteenth century was a wide open land of economic opportunity for white people willing to work hard. Joseph Smith, Sr., the father of the Mormon prophet, was not counted among this group. He much preferred dabbling in get-rich-quick schemes, often involving the occult, which never actually made him rich. As a result he lost his farm in Vermont where Joseph, Jr. was born, and wound up moving to Palmyra, New York.[21]

Joseph, Jr. was very much his father's son. As a young man, he specialized in the art of "money digging": searching for spots where pirates, Indians, or Spaniards had buried treasure and then forgotten it. Experts in this field understood it was necessary to have a magic "seer stone," enabling the trained user to scan below the surface of the ground like an X-ray. Joseph, Jr. was lucky enough to possess more than one such stone, and became well-known over a wide area for his attempts to sell his magical services.[22]

It was always better to dig at night; his brother-in-law noted that Smith let others do the manual labor with the shovels, while he buried his face over the stone in his hat, so that he could get a clearer picture of the treasure's location. One night he and his clients came terribly close to unearthing a chest—they could hear the sound of their shovels hitting something harder than dirt. Smith saw through his stone, though, that the chest was under enchantment, and kept sinking deeper into the ground. To ward off the evil spirits that created such problems, Smith developed a ritual involving animal sacrifice at the site of the excavation, sometimes killing a dog.[23]

In 1826, neighbors filed a criminal complaint against Joseph Smith, Jr. for being "a disorderly person and an impostor." After a trial, Smith was convicted, although the remaining records do not indicate a sentence. For over a century, the Mormon Church insisted that no such trial ever occurred, but documents discovered in a courthouse basement in 1971 prove otherwise.[24]

At about the same time as his conviction, Smith fell in love with a young woman from Pennsylvania named Emma Hale. Emma's father absolutely did not approve of Smith and his money digging shenanigans. So the two lovers eloped, which did not make Emma's father any happier. Smith tearfully promised his new father-in-law that he would begin to earn an honest living, and at least for a brief time tried to do so. That must have seemed awfully dull work for Smith though; and it wasn't long before he hit upon the idea of finding an ancient book.[25]

Smith gave widely varying accounts about how he discovered the Book of Mormon. One neighbor testified that he had never told the same story twice. In any event, Smith did not claim to discover an actual book, but a set of golden plates, written in a language he called "Reformed Egyptian." At first, the book was billed as just an interesting original record of the continent's oldest inhabitants; only later, as Smith observed the effects on his potential marks, did it become more religious in character.[26]

Martin Harris

What made the book idea especially appealing was the presence in Palmyra of a fellow named Martin Harris. Unlike Joseph, Sr., Martin's father had been highly industrious, bequeathing one of the most prosperous farms in that part of the state, the value of which increased dramatically because of its good fortune in lying near the path of the Erie Canal. But Martin's interests lay elsewhere. Neighbors complained that "on moral and religious subjects, he was perfectly visionary—sometimes advocating one sentiment, and sometimes another." He had lengthy conversations with Jesus and the devil, whom he said looked somewhat like a jackass.[27] A contemporary noted that:

> Martin Harris is what may be called a great talker, an extravagant boaster; so much so, that he renders himself disagreeable to many of his society. The money he has expended, and the great things he has done, form a considerable topic of his conversation; he understands all prophecies, and knows every thing by the spirit, and he can silence almost any opposer by talking faster, and louder than he can; or by telling him, "I know every thing and you know nothing; I am a wise man and you are a fool."[28]

Smith was drawn to Martin (whom he privately called a "damn fool") and his money like a moth to a flame. Encountering him on the street one day, a wide-eyed Smith told Martin of a vision he had received, that he should ask the next person he saw for a gift of $50 (a very large sum in those days). Martin fell for it, and handed him the money—the first of many such gifts, including buying Smith an expensive new suit.[29]

For Smith's scheme to work, someone had to front the money to publish the book. To reel Martin in, Smith asked for his help in "translating" the plates he said he had found. Of course, Martin would not be allowed to see the plates themselves—an angel had said as much. So each day, a blanket would be strung across the room, with Smith and Martin on opposite sides. Smith would stare at the seer stone in his hat as an aid to translation, and then when he had each sentence worked out he would dictate it to Martin, who would write it down. For weeks on end the labor continued, with Martin growing more convinced by the day that Smith was onto something.[30]

Lucy Harris

One person who was not convinced, though, was Martin's wife. We know very little about Lucy Harris, other than that she was also Martin's cousin, nine years younger than he, and that she gave him five children. She no doubt thought that she had made a fine catch of a prosperous husband, but as Martin sunk deeper into Smith's scheme, she began to fear that more than his time was at risk. There is no indication that Lucy objected to the anti-Christian theology of Mormonism; the point she kept returning to was simply, "Where are the plates? Why can't I see them?"[31]

Smith's mother recorded one fascinating confrontation:

> Mrs. Harris made her appearance and as soon as she was well seated she began to importune my son relative to the truth of what he had said concerning the Record, declaring that if he really had any plates, she would see them, and that she was determined to help him publish them. He told her she was mistaken—that she could not see them, for he was not permitted to exhibit them to any one except those whom the Lord should appoint to testify of them. "And, in relation to assistance," he observed, "I always prefer dealing with men, rather than their wives." This highly displeased Mrs. Harris, for she considered herself altogether superior to her husband and she continued her importunities.[32]

Lucy may even have heard gossip in town; two of Smith's acquaintances later swore affidavits that he had chuckled with them about making up the story of discovering the plates. According to Smith's mother (who detested her), Lucy even ransacked the house and grounds where Smith was staying, trying to find the plates.[33]

Religions everywhere make their followers take certain things on faith. But Lucy could see no reason why she needed to take on faith the existence of golden plates with strange writing on them, if in fact the plates were hidden within a few feet of where she was standing. A *battle royale* ensued in the Harris household, with Lucy exhausting her vocabulary of synonyms for "stupid" and "dupe." What was far, far worse than mere embarrassment in Lucy's eyes, though, was her growing realization that Joseph was angling to get Martin to spend money—lots of it—to print his book. Money that should be spent on her and her family. Martin tried to appease her with a response having little to do with God's will. A neighbor records that "In conversation about Mormonites, [Lucy] observed, that she wished her husband would quit them, as it was all false and a delusion. To which I heard Mr. Harris reply: 'What if it is a lie; if you will let me alone I will make money out of it.'" Lucy also testified that she was whipped, kicked, beaten, and turned out of her house.[34]

Martin, of course, wanted to see the plates as well, if for no other reason than to shut Lucy up. Smith's father-in-law wrote that:

> Martin Harris informed me that he must have a greater witness, and said that he had talked with Joseph about it—Joseph informed him that he could not, or durst not show him the plates, but that he [Joseph] would go into the woods where the Book of Plates was, and that after he came back, Harris should follow his track in the snow, and find the Book, and examine it for himself. Harris informed me afterwards, that he followed Smith's directions, and could not find the Plates, and was still dissatisfied.[35]

Not dissatisfied enough to admit to Lucy that he was wrong, though. The father-in-law was then genuinely astonished as the "translation" work proceeded, with Smith looking at the seer stone in his hat, while the plates were still hidden in the woods! He concluded that "The whole 'Book of Mormon' (so called) is a silly fabrication of falsehood and wickedness, got up for speculation, and with a design to dupe the credulous and unwary—and in order that its fabricators may live upon the spoils of those who swallow the deception."[36]

Since he could not see the plates, Martin had another idea. He had Smith copy some of the characters onto a piece of paper, which he then took to a professor of ancient languages in New York. Lucy insisted on accompanying him, but he snuck out without telling her—she had to visit the Smith household to discover his whereabouts. The professor told Martin that the characters were gibberish ("Greek and Hebrew letters, crosses and flourishes, Roman letters inverted or placed sideways") and that he was being swindled.[37]

Smith was ready for this. When Martin returned, he simply pointed him to Isaiah 29:11: "And the vision of all is become unto you as the words of a book that is sealed, which men deliver to one that is learned, saying, Read this, I pray thee: and he saith, I cannot; for it is sealed." The fact that the professor could not read the characters *proved* that the Book of Mormon must be divinely inspired, and that Martin himself was the subject of a biblical prophecy![38]

The Theft

After words, tears, and possibly flying objects failed to remove the stars from Martin's eyes, Lucy had an idea. If her suspicions about Smith were correct, then he could be easily exposed by filching the sole copy of the manuscript, and asking him to start over again. If he could reproduce the first few pages verbatim by re-translating the golden plates, Lucy would be persuaded. If he could not, then even mule-headed Martin might agree he had been tricked. At least that's what many people thought, when the first 116 pages of the manuscript, which Joseph had allowed Martin to take home, mysteriously disappeared. According to one report, Lucy told her husband that "If this be a divine communication, the same being who revealed it to you can easily replace it."[39]

Lucy denied involvement in any theft, which is hardly surprising. But neighbors tell of her conspiring with one Flanders Dyke, a young man enamored of Lucy's eldest daughter, to allow him to come courting if he would do Lucy the favor of removing the manuscript from a locked drawer.[40] No one knows today for certain what happened; we do know that Martin's most precious possession vanished, and that Lucy had motive, opportunity, and every reason to believe that she was doing vastly more good than harm. Smith's mother was adamant: "There is no doubt but Mrs. Harris took it from the drawer, with the view of retaining it until another translation should be given, then to alter the original translation, for the purpose of showing a discrepancy between them, and thus make the whole appear to be a deception."[41]

Martin was devastated: "I have lost my soul!" The only person who felt worse than Martin was Joseph himself. According to Joseph's mother, he exclaimed "All is lost! All is lost! What shall I do?" "Sobs and groans, and the most bitter lamentations filled the house. ... Joseph was more distressed than the rest, as he better understood the consequences."[42] He had not the slightest ability to re-create the first 116 pages, or even the first page alone, any more than you could now recite the first page of this book. Finally, he hit upon a scheme that seemed too audacious to succeed, but did. A communication from the angel, after chastising him for lending Martin the manuscript in the first place (even though the angel had authorized it), told Joseph that God in his wisdom had anticipated this problem, and had conveniently incorporated a summary of the missing 116 pages elsewhere in the plates. So there was no need to attempt a re-translation, or risk an embarrassing comparison with his first effort. "Thus I will confound those who have altered my words," the Lord told Joseph. "I will not suffer that they shall destroy my work; yea, I will shew unto them that my wisdom is greater than the cunning of the Devil." A discussion of the theft of the pages appeared in the preface of the Book of Mormon, as a hedge against the day they might turn up.[43] They never have.

Somehow, this dog-ate-my-homework tale was accepted—first by Martin, who was too humiliated to resist anything Joseph might say, and later by the first converts to Mormonism. In fact, Martin felt so terrible that he mortgaged his farm to pay for the printing of the book—exactly the fate Lucy had feared. She was so terrified at the prospect of losing her home that she emptied it of furniture and valuables, even the linens, storing them with friends for protection from potential creditors. It took a special revelation from God addressed directly to Martin to accomplish this: "I command thee that thou shalt not covet thine own property, but impart it freely to the printing of the Book of Mormon. … And misery thou shalt receive if thou wilt slight these counsels; yea, even the destruction of thyself and property. … Pay the printer's debt! Release thyself from bondage." When the first edition of *The Book of Mormon* finally appeared, it listed Joseph Smith, Jr. as "Author and Proprietor" of the work, not "translator." More importantly from Lucy's standpoint, revenues from the book's sale wound up with Joseph, not with Martin, who was unable to pay the mortgage and lost the farm. He also abandoned Lucy and his children at this time. Lucy died five years later, at the age of 44.[44]

In 1831, Martin followed Smith to Ohio, where Smith continued to soak him for money, even though his principal asset was now gone. A special revelation from God commanded that "It is wisdom in me that my servant Martin Harris should be an example unto the Church, in laying his moneys before the bishop of the church. And let him repent of his sins, for he seeketh the praise of the world."[45] Lucy wrote that "The man has now become rather an object of pity; he has spent most of his property, and lost the confidence of his former friends. If he had labored as hard on his farm as he has to make Mormons, he might now be one of the wealthiest farmers in the country. He now spends his time in travelling through the country spreading the delusion of Mormonism, and has no regard whatever for his family."[46]

While still married to Lucy, Martin claimed in 1831 to have had a revelation to go to Missouri, and "obtain a Lamanite [Indian] squaw for a wife to aid them in propagating Mormonism." On the way to Missouri with a party of Mormons, after invoking the power of God for protection, he presented his bare foot to a snake he encountered in the road—which promptly bit him. In 1832, Martin submitted a written declaration that "I do hereby assert and declare that in four years from the date hereof, every sectarian and religious denomination in the United States shall be broken down, and every Christian shall be gathered unto the Mormonites, and the rest of the human race shall perish. If those things do not take place, I will hereby consent to have my hand separated from my body."[47] In 1837, Martin was excommunicated from the Mormon Church for complaining too much at the time of the Kirtland bank fraud. He later briefly dabbled with

Shakerism.[48]

Most of the other heroes in this book are philosophers, statesmen, and scholars. Lucy Harris was a housewife. She didn't want to change the world; she wanted to live her life and raise her family in peace, enjoying the fruits of working hard and playing by the rules. When a threat arose in the form of a ne'er-do-well con man, she acted. Her mind wasn't irreversibly closed to the possibility that Joseph Smith had a supernatural mission—she just wanted to see the plates. After this simple request was denied, she conceived a bold scheme that by rights ought to have led to exposing Smith for what he was—if only the rest of the world had half the sense of this noble woman. Standing up for the evidence of your senses against the bellowing of the God experts, just like the little boy in the story who cried "But the emperor isn't wearing any clothes!" is an act of heroism to be treasured.

The Mormons I know are for the most part fine, hard-working, upstanding members of the community. How does this flow from such a bizarre set of beliefs and a history that is practically a situation comedy? Share your thoughts on this and the other questions you'll find at **dgc.humanistpress.com**!

Notes:

1 Noll, *Mammon*, 4-6, 11, 19, 82.

2 Howe, *Mormonism*, viii; Maxwell, *Magnificent*, 47; Abanes, *One Nation*, 95.

3 Johnson, *Christianity*, 434; Ostling, *Mormon*, 29; Abanes, *One Nation*, 1. The official name of the principal branch of the Mormon Church today is "The Church of Jesus Christ of the Latter-Day Saints," some times abbreviated as "LDS."

4 Ankerberg, *Behind the Mask*, 100; Tanner, *Changing World*, 173; Abanes, *One Nation*, 288, 290.

5 Ankerberg, *Behind the Mask*, 283, 419; Abanes, *One Nation*, 101; Tanner, *Changing World*, 208; I Nephi 12:23.

6 Brodie, *No Man*, 198; Ostling, *Mormon*, 32; Abanes, *One Nation*, 101, 136.

7 Brodie, *No Man*, 207; Taves, *Trouble Enough*, 118; Abanes, *One Nation*, 142, 147.

8 Howe, *Mormonism*, 146; Abanes, *One Nation*, 107.

9 Abanes, *One Nation*, 105; Ostling, *Mormon*, 32; Brodie, *No Man*, 230-231.

10 Brodie, *No Man*, 239-240; Taves, *Trouble Enough*, 147; Abanes, *One Nation*, 169.

11 Taves, *Trouble Enough*, 157; Abanes, *One Nation*, 180.

12 Taves, *Trouble Enough*, 187; Ostling, *Mormon America*, 13; Abanes, *One Nation*, 182, 211.

13 Tanner, *Changing World*, 259; Brodie, *No Man*, 305, 335-336; Abanes, *One Nation*, 194.

14 Brodie, *No Man*, 362; Taves, *Trouble Enough*, 199, 202.

15 Brodie, *No Man*, 374-377, 385; Taves, *Trouble Enough*, 199, 204, 206; Abanes, *One Nation*, 198.

16 Brodie, *No Man*, 392; Abanes, *One Nation*, 199, 213; Taves, *Trouble Enough*, 213.

17 Abanes, *One Nation*, 217, 219, 222; Ankerberg, *Behind the Mask*, 423.

18 Abanes, *One Nation*, 165, 228, 231, 263.

19 Ankerberg, *Behind the Mask*, 14; Ostling, *Mormon America*, xvii, 118, 127.

20 Ankerberg, *Behind the Mask*, 25.

21 Howe, *Mormonism*, 11, 246; Brodie, *No Man*, 6.

22 Brodie, *No Man*, 32; Ostling, *Mormon America*, 25.

23 Howe, *Mormonism*, 237; Taves, *Trouble Enough*, 18, 21; Abanes, *One Nation*, 31, 42.

24 Taves, *Trouble Enough*, 18; Abanes, *One Nation*, 46.

25 Brodie, *No Man*, 31-32; Howe, *Mormonism*, 235.

26 Ankerberg, *Behind the Mask*, 294; Howe, *Mormonism*, 254-255; Taves, *Trouble Enough*, 28; Abanes, *One Nation*, 52, 69.

27 Tuckett, *Martin Harris*, 10, 15; Howe, *Mormonism*, 14, 254-255.

28 Howe, *Mormonism*, 183.

29 Howe, *Mormonism*, 236, 246; Abanes, *One Nation*, 54; Tuckett, *Martin Harris*, 20.

30 Brodie, *No Man*, 53-54; Taves, *Trouble Enough*, 40; Tuckett, *Martin Harris*, 25; Howe, *Mormonism*, 14; Tanner, *Changing World*, 132.

31 Smith, *History*, 114; Tuckett, *Martin Harris*, 10, 31; Ankerberg, *Behind the Mask*, 66.

32 Smith, *History*, 117.

33 Brodie, *No Man*, 38; Howe, *Mormonism*, 236; Smith, *History*, 121.

34 Tuckett, *Martin Harris*, 31; Howe, *Mormonism*, 254-255.

35 Howe, *Mormonism*, 265.

36 Howe, *Mormonism*, 265-266.

37 Taves, *Trouble Enough*, 36; Smith, *History*, 119; Abanes, *One Nation*, 54; Howe, *Mormonism*, 271.

38 Taves, *Trouble Enough*, 39.

39 Brodie, *No Man*, 53-54.

40 Howe, *Mormonism*, 22; Howe, *Mormonism*, 31.

41 Smith, *History*, 131.

42 Taves, *Trouble Enough*, 40; Smith, *History*, 129.

43 Brodie, *No Man*, 55; Taves, *Trouble Enough*, 41-42; Howe, *Mormonism*, 22; Tuckett, *Martin Harris*, 34.

44 Smith, *History*, 123; Taves, *Trouble Enough*, 50-51; Abanes, *One Nation*, 1; Howe, *Mormonism*, 14, 20; Tuckett, *Martin Harris*, 41, 49, 60.

45 Doctrines and Covenants 58:35.

46 Howe, *Mormonism*, 54; Howe, *Mormonism*, 256.

47 Abanes, *One Nation*, 131; Howe, *Mormonism*, 14, 159.

48 Taves, *Trouble Enough*, 116; Tuckett, *Martin Harris*, 65; Abanes, *One Nation*, 149.

Émile Zola

CHAPTER 13

ZOLA VS. DRUMONT

Catholic Anti-Semitism

For the 20 years preceding 1870, France was ruled by the Emperor
Napoleon III, a clever politician who obtained backing from the hierarchy by paying Catholic clergy as employees of the state, while
giving military support to continued papal governance over portions
of central Italy. French troops garrisoned in Rome enabled Pope Pius
IX to continue to rule a population that overwhelmingly wanted to
join the rest of newly united Italy. Until 1870, that is, when the emperor stumbled into a disastrous war against Prussia. The moment
the French departed Rome for the front, Italian troops entered, to
a tumultuous welcome: after 1,400 years, Italy was reunited at last.[1]

Pius IX was not a good sport about this, despite the fact that the
Italian government offered the church complete physical protection
and freedom to operate as it wished. For the next several decades,
the central preoccupation of the church was to manipulate European
politics in an effort to get its governmental authority over central Italy
back. No stone was left unturned. The church soon discovered that
one of the most powerful themes at its disposal was to revitalize its
age-old campaign against the Jews.[2]

Jews, after all, were the biggest beneficiaries of the new regime.
For centuries, popes had locked Jews into walled ghettos at night,
while enforcing their subhuman status with a myriad of other legal
indignities—the Nazis borrowed the idea of forcing Jews to wear a
yellow badge on their clothing from a 600-year-old Catholic Church

rule. Jews were barred from owning land, so they flocked to the cities—where they were barred from most professions. Marriage between Jews and non-Jews was strictly forbidden; for that matter, so was "familiarity or conversation." Jews were forced to endure Catholic sermons every Saturday, and jeered by Catholics on their way to and from these humiliations.[3] As the French author Edmond About put it:

> The church undertakes to keep Jews alive and miserable. It makes enclosures for them as we do for curious animals in the zoo. They are allowed to circulate throughout the city, to show Christians how dirty and degraded a man is when he is not a Christian, but when night comes, they are put under lock and key.[4]

Officially, the rules were intended to induce Jews to convert to Christianity. But not all the rules had that aim. For example, Spanish statutes ratified by the pope in 1555 prohibited even devout Catholics of Jewish ancestry from holding high church or government offices: "All of their descendants ... are as if born with polluted blood. Therefore they are denied all honors, offices, and titles ... the abomination of their ancestors will cling to them forever." The Jesuits flatly refused admission to anyone who had a Jewish ancestor within the preceding five generations—a rule that remained in place until 1946.[5]

In 1870, with Pius IX driven from governmental power, the Jews were made legally equal with everyone else. As the pope bemoaned to a Catholic women's organization in 1871, before the time of Jesus, the Jews "had been children in the House of God ... [but] owing to their obstinacy and their failure to believe, they have become dogs. ... We have today in Rome unfortunately too many of these dogs, and we hear them barking in all the streets, and going around molesting people everywhere." The official Catholic line never wandered far from linking the downfall of the pope to the machinations of the Jews; the Vatican newspaper claimed exactly that in 1890, while the Jesuits contemptuously referred to the Italian state as "a kingdom of Jews."[6]

In 1880, the Jesuit newspaper *Catholic Civilization* launched a vicious campaign against the Jews. A series of 36 articles appeared over the next 40 months, making the case for "exceptional laws for a race that is so exceptionally and profoundly perverse." The way to prevent anti-Semitic violence, argued the Jesuits, was to herd Jews back into ghettos, where the pope had confined them before he was unceremoniously removed from power.[7]

One particular tactic employed in the new anti-Jewish campaign was revival of the "blood libel": the myth that Jews routinely murdered Christian children to drain their blood. Rumors to this effect began to surface in the twelfth century. Frederick II, always interested in empirical data, convened a committee of scholars and Jewish converts to Christianity to examine the claim, which was found to be entirely without merit; both the Old Testament and Talmud, in fact, flatly banned consuming blood of any kind. But the images were too vivid for Catholic propagandists to ignore, and when the decision was made to move Jews to the top of the hit list, the blood libel returned with a vengeance. From 1887 to 1891 alone, at least 22 Jewish ritual murder accusations were widely reported in the press. The Jesuits explained that on Passover, Jews required great quantities of Christian blood, and only that of a small child would do. "If you ever wondered why some matzah is labeled kosher for Passover," the *Catholic Civilization* series explained, "now you know—it is because such matzah contains a Christian child's blood."[8]

Jews were attacked from all sides. The fact that about a quarter of France's leading bankers were Jews, even though only a tiny percentage of Jews were bankers, tarred them all with the brush of being greedy capitalists. When a Catholic-oriented bank failed in 1882, wiping out the savings of thousands, Jewish bankers were wrongly blamed for plotting its demise.[9]

In France, the Assumptionist religious order led the anti-Semitic charge. Its chief vehicle was *The Cross*, with a readership in the hundreds of thousands, including at least 25,000 members of the clergy: "the most anti-Jewish newspaper in France, the one that bears Christ, the sign of horror for all Jews."[10]

France's *Mende Religious Reader* warned that:

> We are being pillaged, dishonored, exploited, and emptied by the Jew. ... Servile, slithering, artful, filthy, and vile when he is the weaker one, he becomes arrogant when he has the upper hand, as he does now. The Jew is our master. ... When one of these vultures swoops down on the finances of a people, he pilfers, ransoms, tears, flays, strangles.[11]

France's *Catholic Bloc* newspaper deplored "the Jewish race, that parasitical and vampire race, always and everywhere scorned and shunned, that wandering race, witness over the centuries of the curse which weighs upon it. ... The Church of Satan is incarnated in the Jewish race."[12]

Drumont

In 1881, a struggling Parisian journalist named Édouard Drumont correctly sensed the unfriendly turn the populace was taking, and resolved to take its lead. Drumont spent the next five years assembling a mass of material, including nearly every bullet in the anti-Semitic arsenal, for a book he called *Jewish France*. His salary during this period was paid by a newspaper owned by a prominent Jewish family.[13] *Jewish France* could not be accused of subtlety:

> The principal signs by which a Jew may be recognized are thus: the famous hooked nose, frequently blinking eyes, teeth tightly together, ears sticking out, fingernails that are square rather than almond-shape, a torso too long, flat feet, rounded knees, extraordinarily protruding ankles, the limp and melting hand of a hypocrite and traitor. They frequently have one arm longer than the other.[14]

Of course, the differences articulated were more than simply physical; the Jew is "greedy, intriguing, subtle, tricky," whereas the Aryan is "enthusiastic, heroic, chivalrous, disinterested, forthright, confiding to a fault." Drumont analyzed the Jewish blood thirst in detail. "Ritual murder," he explained, "is a type of monomania linked more to the physiology [of the Jews] than to their religious history." Drumont relied heavily on material previously published by the Jesuits, and had the Jesuit Father Stanislas du Lac review *Jewish France* carefully before its publication to purge it of "errors."[15]

Most of France's troubles of the nineteenth century he laid squarely at the feet of the Jews, sometimes defining the term rather broadly, Even Napoleon, for example, had Jewish origins according to Drumont. "Today, the entire might of the State is placed at the service of the Jewish monopoly," Drumont concluded. His straightforward solution was that all Jewish property should be confiscated, and the Jews themselves deported, he cared not where. This became exactly the policy of the clerically backed Vichy regime half a century later.[16]

Jewish France ultimately ran through more than 200 editions, and became the best-selling French book of the entire nineteenth century, even though it was a two-volume tome running to 1,200 pages.[17]

Drumont was idolized in the Catholic press. The *Catholic Observer* noted:

> Drumont fights the Jews, as we fight them, not out of any caste or personal hatred, but rather because they are the vampires of humanity, monopolizers, usurers, speculators; they are dishonest, implacable, destroyers and slanderers, exploiters of Christian blood. It is a [matter of] defense ... an act of patriotism, of charity, of religion.[18]

Drumont struck a populist pose, resulting in occasional friction with the French hierarchy when he accused them of catering too much to wealthy Jews—especially after they backed a rival candidate in Drumont's first bid for political office in 1890. The hierarchy never complained about Drumont's bigotry; instead, it returned his volley in kind: "To prevent Drumont or others from being able to produce a truly and effectively anti-Jewish newspaper, Jewish gold has intervened to have Drumont's pen and his newspaper in its exclusive power."[19]

Once book sales leveled off, Drumont parlayed his notoriety into the launch of a political organization called the "Anti-Semitic Society" and an anti-Semitic newspaper, called *The Free Word*. Subscriptions were brisk at first, including some 30,000 priests, but after a couple of years they began to decline since there was little new for Drumont to say.[20] Then in 1892 Drumont helped uncover a scandal in French politics, involving bribery of politicians and the press during a botched attempt to construct a Panama canal. To Drumont's delight, three of the most culpable central figures in the scandal were Jews—further evidence of evil Jews lining their own pockets at the expense of France. "It seems that all of Jewry, high and low, congregated beneath the udder of this milch cow," Drumont concluded. "In the disaster that cost so many French their savings and so many good deputies their reputations, one encounters Jews wherever one turns."[21]

Dreyfus

Ultimately, the Panama frenzy dwindled, and subscriptions to *The Free Word* faded with it. So Drumont launched a new campaign, targeting Jewish influence in the army, singling out "the spy who shamelessly traffics in the secrets of national defense ... with the Cohens, the Dreyfuses, and all their other coreligionists."[22] This accusation fit within official Catholic teaching of the treasonous tendencies of all Jews. The Jesuits' *Catholic Civilization* had warned in 1890 that the Jews "formed a foreign nation in the nations where they resided, a sworn enemy of the nation's well-being. Although they may live in France, in Germany, in England, they never become French, or German, or English, but remain Jews and nothing but Jews."[23]

In 1894, Drumont struck gold. French counter-intelligence discovered a letter in which someone had offered to sell important military secrets to France's mortal enemy, Germany. The top brass had been under fire from *The Free Word* for allowing too many Jews into high ranking positions, so suspicion immediately fell on the first and only Jew to serve on the general staff, Captain Alfred Dreyfus. Even the Captain's name was perfect: the pages of *The Free Word* had vilified Jews with the family name of Dreyfus nearly as often as Jews with the name of Rothschild. Dreyfus' handwriting was somewhat similar to that of the incriminating letter, so he was immediately thrown into solitary confinement.[24]

The evidence against Dreyfus was thin, because on close analysis his handwriting was not all that similar to that of the letter. When the handwriting expert from the Bank of France told the generals that Dreyfus was innocent, they found an anti-Semitic handwriting expert to give them a better answer. So after all the evidence was presented to the jury in the ordinary course, the prosecution secretly approached the judge with some additional items, which had been deliberately forged by Major Hubert Henry—more than enough to seal a guilty verdict, especially since the defense was not even informed this was occurring.[25] Dreyfus was publicly stripped of his insignia of rank before a crowd of thousands screaming "Death to the Jews!" then shipped to the brutal hardship of life imprisonment on Devil's Island. The official Vatican newspaper observed that: "The Jewish race, the deicide people, wandering throughout the world, brings with it everywhere the pestiferous breath of treason. ... And so too in the Dreyfus case. ... [I]t is hardly surprising if we again find the Jew in the front ranks, or if we find that the betrayal of one's country has been Jewishly conspired and Jewishly executed."[26]

In fact, Dreyfus was completely innocent. France had actually been betrayed by ne'er-do-well Commandant Walsin Esterhazy, who was perennially in need of money because he maintained an expensive mistress. Fifteen months after Dreyfus was sent to Devil's Island, more secret correspondence with the Germans was discovered and traced to Esterhazy. In studying the Esterhazy file, it suddenly dawned on the new head of French intelligence, Lt. Col. Georges Picquart, that he had seen handwriting like Esterhazy's before—on the letter that launched the Dreyfus case. Picquart was no friend of the Jews, but he was above all an honest patriot.[27] Meanwhile, rumors had leaked to the public about the extraordinary secret evidence provided to the Dreyfus jury. The worried French command responded decisively by transferring Picquart to a combat zone in Tunisia, and having Col. Henry (who replaced him as intelligence chief) forge more evidence tainting Picquart himself. Drumont offered a constructive suggestion: "I do not believe that outside the Synagogue there would be many tears in France if an 'intelligent bullet' suppressed a cursed being who ... has been the disgrace and scourge of his country."[28]

By the end of 1897, Picquart's supporters generated enough heat that the army felt compelled to try Esterhazy at a court martial. Friends of Dreyfus, whose strength was fading fast in his searing tropical prison, were overjoyed that justice was finally about to be done. That was not the script, though. After a perfunctory trial, Esterhazy was acquitted, following a deliberation of three minutes. Cries of "Death to the Jews!" and "Hats off to the martyr of the Jews!" rang through the courtroom.[29]

Game over. Dreyfus had been duly convicted, Esterhazy had been duly acquitted, and there was nothing left for the French legal system to do. As Prime Minister Jules Méline put it, "There is no Dreyfus Affair."[30] Except for one man, for whom the battle had just begun.

Zola

Émile Zola had been a struggling Parisian journalist like Drumont, but had followed a different path to success. The two men knew each other, and long before the Dreyfus affair there is evidence they did not get along. Both men wrote fiction, although Drumont billed his fiction as fact. Zola wrote novels, most famously a collection of 20 novels about the extended Rougon-Macquart family that is regarded as one of the great achievements of French culture. He launched an entirely new school of literature, sometimes called "naturalism," depicting the often sordid reality of everyday life rather than the flowery "morally uplifting" content previously in vogue.[31]

By 1894 Zola was at the pinnacle of his fame, quite comfortable financially, and able to do exactly as he pleased. What he pleased was to follow in Voltaire's footsteps by taking on the Catholic Church, which he feared as the greatest enemy to an unstable French Republic that was only 24 years old. Since the overthrow of the emperor in 1870, the Republic had inched steadily away from church control: secular schools grew in strength, freedom to work on Sundays was granted, and parliamentary sessions no longer opened with a prayer.[32]

The Republic had barely survived a church-backed plot to reestablish the monarchy under the auspices of a popular general in 1889, but Zola believed that even the excesses of the various revolutions served France far better than monarchy ever had:

> If we counted the stranglings, poisonings, massacres, and all the miseries which have served to fertilize and fatten the monarchy, we could then see that it is the republicans who are the amateurs when it comes to crime, and that a burnt Paris weighs less in the balance of eternal justice than a France pillaged and murdered over the centuries.[33]

Zola launched his "Three Cities" trilogy with *Lourdes*, an exposé of the cynical preying on superstition at France's most celebrated pilgrim destination. The "hospital" at Lourdes, for example, deliberately provided no medical treatment, the better to verify which pilgrims had been cured by the power of Our Lady alone. On the day Drumont broke the Dreyfus story, Zola was in transit to Italy, to research his novel *Rome* about the backstabbing bureaucracy of the Catholic hierarchy. In *Paris*, the final piece of the trilogy, Zola's protagonist declares that "For 1,800 years now Christianity has been impeding mankind's march towards truth and justice. This march will only be able to continue when Christianity is abolished ... and is no longer seen as the absolute and definitive moral-religious code."[34]

Zola was as convinced of Dreyfus' guilt as most Frenchmen at first, but as events unfolded he grew more and more troubled. Like most in the Dreyfus camp, he was dumbfounded at the Esterhazy acquittal, which augured abandonment of the rule of law in France.[35] Zola in 1898 was prosperous, famous and happy—just as Voltaire had been in 1762. He could have just shook his head and clucked at the unfairness of it all. Instead, he devised a plan for sacrificing himself to forestall France's slide back into the Middle Ages.

"I Accuse!"

The plan was straightforward: commit libel against the entire

French high command, so sensationally, from such a prominent source, that it would have no choice but to respond with legal action, thus resurrecting a matter that was officially dead. Such a trial would be held in civil court, not military court, giving Zola a fairer chance than Dreyfus had. By winning a verdict based on the truth of his accusations, he would force an extraordinary reopening of the Dreyfus case, just as Voltaire had forced an extraordinary reopening of the Calas case 130 years earlier. Indeed, Dreyfus was being cast by his defenders as "a new Calas."[36]

"I Accuse!" screamed the banner headline in *Dawn*, a newspaper published by future prime minister Georges Clemenceau, who had himself been victimized by forged documents during the Panama affair. And accuse Zola did, in a nearly 5,000-word open letter to France's president, worded as bitingly as France's most gifted writer could conjure. He even helpfully cited the sections of the French Code he could be prosecuted under, closing with "Let them dare, then, to bring me before a court of law and let the enquiry take place in broad daylight! I am waiting." Clemenceau plastered the city with 300,000 extra copies of the edition, which caused a sensation. Like Paine, Zola accepted no payment from Clemenceau for his work.[37]

The first part of the plan succeeded. The army brought a libel action against Zola, triable in a civil court. Well-coordinated rioting broke out across France after Mass on the day before the trial opened. Windows of Jewish-owned shops were smashed by demonstrators screaming "Death to the traitors!" and "Kikes to the water!" "This is the people's noble fury," observed Drumont's *The Free Word*, whose circulation had soared to 500,000. "If there's one thing that must smell bloody awful, it's grilled kike."[38]

Zola's lawyer thwarted the prosecution's intention to avoid re-trying the Dreyfus case through a series of shrewd tactical maneuvers. At one famous moment, he asked "Will you permit me then, Mr. President, to ask in our common interest, what practical means you see by which we may ascertain the truth?" "That does not concern me!" snapped the judge.[39] At another point Zola himself suddenly interrupted the proceedings:

I demand to be allowed the same rights accorded to thieves and murderers! They can defend themselves, summon and question witnesses, but every day I am insulted in the street; they break my carriage windows, they drag my name through the mud, and the gutter press treat me like a crook. I have the right to prove my good faith, my integrity and my honor.[40]

Zola wound up getting most of his witnesses in. By mid-trial, internal reports showed the army bracing for defeat. Officer after officer then paraded to the stand, pontificating about the honor of the army, the threat to the nation, and the Jewish conspiracy undermining all that true Frenchmen held dear. The Minister of War assured the court that "I had the most crushing proof of the guilt of Dreyfus in my hands, but that proof was of such a nature that to have divulged it would inevitably have led to war. ... On my honor as a soldier, Dreyfus was a traitor who was justly and legally condemned." Another general threatened the mass resignation of the entire general staff, leaving the nation defenseless.[41] With a surly crowd surrounding the courtroom, Zola was convicted on a 7-5 vote, and sentenced to the maximum penalty of a fine and one year in prison. Clemenceau later commented that "If Zola had been acquitted that day, none of us would have left there alive."[42]

Zola appealed on a technicality, and won a new trial. When preliminaries commenced, it became apparent he would have much less of an opportunity to mount a defense than he had at his first trial. Zola's lawyer advised that the best strategy for surviving to fight another day would be to hide, to avoid being served with the paperwork necessary to complete the second trial.[43] Ignominious? Degrading? Yes, but necessary; with one more adverse result the affair really might be over. Zola left for England that very night, where he lived in hiding for the next 11 months—not an easy task for a man whose picture graced the bookshops of every city. Financially, he was devastated; his lawyers had not worked for free, sales of his books fell off dramatically, and theaters refused to produce his plays, slashing his income by two-thirds.[44]

Buying time, though, actually worked. Unbeknownst to Zola and his lawyers, while they were tangling with the procedures for the second trial, the Minister of War was requesting that the Esterhazy file be put in order, to bulletproof it against nasty rumors of forged documents. Unfortunately, the officer in charge of that process inconveniently discovered incontrovertible proof that Col. Henry had manufactured some of the evidence. Henry was hauled before three generals, where he broke down and admitted his falsifications, including those secretly provided to the jury in the first Dreyfus trial. That night, he took his own life.[45]

Drumont defended Henry on the grounds that he had forged the documents simply because he knew Dreyfus was guilty. He took up a collection for Henry's widow that attracted thousands of subscriptions, hundreds from Catholic clergy. Some donors added comments, such as that of Father Cos, who sought a "bedside carpet made of kikeskin" so that he might trample it morning and night. *The Cross* took a different tack, claiming that Henry had actually been murdered by Jews.[46]

In the ensuing uproar, Esterhazy admitted writing the original letter attributed to Dreyfus. He claimed he did so at the request of the army, which knew the Jew was a traitor but had nothing specific to pin on him. So now the case against Dreyfus had completely vanished. The original incriminating letter was admitted to be written by someone else, and the other documents against him were admitted to be forged. The government had to free Dreyfus now, didn't it? Not at all, said President Felix Faure. The courts had spoken, the army could not stand further disruption, and one rich Jew who was nearly dead anyway mattered little in the overall scheme of things.[47] Once again, game over.

Except, once again, it wasn't. On the night of February 16, 1899, President Faure suffered a heart attack and died, *in flagrante delicto* with a woman half his age. Drumont, of course, claimed that the lady was in the pay of Jews.[48] By now the political movement Zola had unleashed made its weight felt, and the parliament elected a pro-Dreyfus senator as the new president. He had to survive a right-wing coup attempt during Faure's state funeral, egged on by *The Cross*: "On all sides, people clamor for a strongman who would risk his life to tear France from the clutches of traitors, from the sectarians and imbeciles who are handing them over to the foreigner. ... Ah! Who will deliver us from this pack of brigands?" But soon afterwards Dreyfus was granted his long-awaited new trial, provoking more violence across France.[49]

Justice at last? No. Once again, Dreyfus was convicted (after his lawyer, who had also represented Zola, was shot in the back at a critical moment). This time the jury was not unanimous, and reduced his sentence to 10 years because of "extenuating circumstances."[50] The verdict was nonsensical. If Dreyfus had sold military secrets, he deserved the severest punishment; if he had not, he deserved freedom. Zola, along with most of France other than the hardest core Catholics, was "thunderstruck."

> And it is no longer anger, the wish for vengeance, the need to cry out about the crime, to demand the appropriate punishment for it in the name of truth and justice; it is, rather, amazement, sheer terror in a man who sees the impossible happen, rivers suddenly flowing backwards up to their sources, the earth trembling beneath the sun. And what I am crying out about is the distress of our generous and noble France, it is the fear of the abyss towards which she is now heading.[51]

France's president ended the nightmare a few days later by granting Dreyfus a pardon. Not until 1906 did yet another court finally clear his name.[52]

Meanwhile, Zola (who was also pardoned, along with all the actually guilty parties including Esterhazy and Henry's accomplices) started on a new series of four novels, deliberately patterned after the four Gospels—the heroes were to be named Matthew, Mark, Luke, and John. The third volume, called *Truth*, was based loosely on the story of the Dreyfus case, with elements of Calas and the blood libel mixed in.[53]

Separation

After completing *Truth* in 1902, Zola returned to Paris from his summer home. On their first night back, he and his wife went to bed after coals were lit in the fireplace to ward off an early autumn chill. In the middle of the night, both became ill. Zola rose to open a window, which proved his undoing because odorless carbon monoxide fumes already filled the air. Before reaching the window he passed out and fell to the floor, where the higher concentration of the gas killed him. His wife, who had not risen, barely survived. Once the authorities determined that the cause of death was carbon monoxide asphyxiation, they stopped investigating. A question left unresolved was how a chimney that had been cleaned regularly and worked normally on a subsequent test happened to malfunction the night Zola returned.[54]

The lack of investigation is especially puzzling because Zola had received hundreds of death threats. A bomb had been found in his carriage only 15 months earlier. In fact, no one really wanted to discover the truth. A finding of foul play would have risked further violence in a nation already teetering on the brink of insurrection.[55] Twenty years later, a right-wing activist named Henri Buronfosse confessed to a journalist that he had blocked the chimney shortly before Zola's return, and unblocked it during the commotion surrounding the discovery of the bodies.[56] There is no certainty he was telling the truth, but in the overall context of the times, the theory of a preposterous act of vandalism that just happened to succeed seems more persuasive than that of an inexplicable accident.

Zola's legacy was the church-state separation bills working their way through the parliament at the time of his death, which became law from 1900 through 1906. Disgust at the outrageous scheming of the army and the church led to an exceptionally high turnout at the elections of 1902, during which a Jesuit campaigner exhorted the pilgrims at Lourdes to "wield the sword, the electoral sword that separates the good and the wicked. ... At the next elections there will be two candidates, Barabbas and Jesus Christ. ... Will you vote for Barabbas?" The voters chose Barabbas, giving an overwhelming victory to parties committed to a secular revolution at the national election of April 1902.[57]

Tens of thousands of priests, monks, and nuns were removed from the state payroll. The Assumptionists who published *The Cross* were disbanded, seminaries and schools run by unauthorized religious associations were shut down, religious liberty was guaranteed to all, and diplomatic relations with the Vatican were severed.[58] The citizens of France expressed their heartiest approval, giving the coalition that sponsored the separation bills an even greater majority at the next national election in 1906.[59]

At the conclusion of his trial, Zola had exclaimed that "I may be condemned, but some day France will thank me for having helped to save her honor."[60] In 1908, the government acted to move Zola's body to the Pantheon, where the greatest heroes of France are enshrined. Dreyfus was in attendance; at the conclusion of the ceremony, an enraged Catholic shot him twice as "a personal protest." Though the shooter was apprehended immediately, he was never prosecuted. Dreyfus survived, rejoined the army, and served France with distinction during World War I.[61]

Adolf Hitler was born to a strict Catholic family in Austria in 1889, so he was in his early teens when Dreyfus fever and the Catholic anti-Jewish campaign were at their peak. How fair is it to blame the Holocaust on the Catholic Church? Share your thoughts on this and the other questions you'll find at **dgc.humanistpress.com**!

Notes:

1 Halperin, *Italy*, 104-107; Wolf, *France*, 418; Kertzer, *Unholy War*, 129.

2 Kertzer, *Unholy War*, 126; Kertzer, *Prisoner*, 86.

3 Isser, *Antisemitism*, 28; Kertzer, *Unholy War*, 9-11, 28, 29, 63, 79.

4 Isser, *Antisemitism*, 64.

5 Kertzer, *Unholy War*, 207.

6 Kertzer, *Unholy War*, 129, 130, 144, 150.

7 Kertzer, *Unholy War*, 134, 137.

8 Kertzer, *Unholy War*, 152, 156, 160.

9 Agulhon, *French Republic*, 69; Bredin, *Affair*, 28; Brown, *Soul of France*, 72; Benbassa, *Jews*, 105, 137, 139.

10 Agulhon, *French Republic*, 99; Benbassa, *Jews*, 138, 141; Bredin, *Affair*,

29; Kertzer, *Unholy War*, 171.

11 Brown, *Soul of France*, 173.

12 Kertzer, *Unholy War*, 211.

13 Bredin, *Affair*, 26; Busi, *Pope*, 16.

14 Bredin, *Affair*, 30.

15 Busi, *Pope*, 46, 54, 61; Kertzer, *Unholy War*, 178, 217.

16 Brown, *Soul of France*, 75; Busi, *Pope*, 65, 67.

17 Busi, *Pope*, 4, 47; Benbassa, *Jews*, 105, 140.

18 Kertzer, *Unholy War*, 165.

19 Busi, *Pope*, 96-100; Kertzer, *Unholy War*, 178-180.

20 Benbassa, *Jews*, 141; Busi, *Pope*, 92; Kertzer, *Unholy War*, 178.

21 Busi, *Pope*, 130; Brown, *Soul of France*, 161, 171, 173; Kedward, *Dreyfus*, 5.

22 Busi, *Pope*, 137; Kedward, *Dreyfus*, 55.

23 Kertzer, *Unholy War*, 144.

24 Schom, *Zola*, 161; Busi, *Pope*, 75, 90; Brown, *Soul of France*, 177-178; Kedward, *Dreyfus*, 5-7.

25 Schom, *Zola*, 161; Brown, *Soul of France*, 178.

26 Hemmings, *Zola*, 282; Benbassa, *Jews*, 141; Kertzer, *Unholy War*, 184; Brown, *Soul of France*, 183, 216.

27 Schom, *Zola*, 162; Benbassa, *Jews*, 142; Kedward, *Dreyfus*, 8; Agulhon, *French Republic*, 82; Brown, *Soul of France*, 190-191.

28 Agulhon, *French Republic*, 84; Benbassa, *Jews*, 142; Schom, *Zola*, 162; Brown, *Soul of France*, 186, 191-192; Busi, *Pope*, 142.

29 Bredin, *Affair*, 241; Agulhon, *French Republic*, 85; Brown, *Soul of France*, 203.

30 Agulhon, *French Republic*, 84.

31 Hemmings, *Zola*, 14, 52-60, 164; Schom, *Zola*, 29, 66; Kedward, *Dreyfus*, 8.

32 Hemmings, *Zola*, 238; Agulhon, *French Republic*, 20-21; Wolf, *France*, 378, 391-392; Schom, Zola, 63.

33 Brown, *Soul of France*, 118; Schom, *Zola*, 93.

34 Brown, *Soul of France*, 175; Hemmings, *Zola*, 265, 273; Schom, *Zola*, 154-156, 158.

35 Friedman, *Zola*, 38, 41; Hemmings, *Zola*, 283-285; Schom, *Zola*, 164.

36 Bredin, *Affair*, 229; Brown, *Soul of France*, 209.

37 Zola, "I Accuse!"; Bredin, *Affair*, 198, 250; Brown, *Soul of France*, 205; Hemmings, *Zola*, 289; Benbassa, *Jews*, 143.

38 Schom, *Zola*, 168; Kedward, *Dreyfus*, 11; Bredin, *Affair*, 260.

39 Hemmings, *Zola*, 287; Schom, *Zola*, 179.

40 Schom, *Zola*, 179.

41 Brown, *Soul of France*, 210; Schom, *Zola*, 181; Bredin, *Affair*, 268;

Friedman, *Zola*, 49.

42 Agulhon, *French Republic*, 88; Brown, *Soul of France*, 212; Kedward, *Dreyfus*, 91; Bredin, *Affair*, 270; Schom, *Zola*, 189-190.

43 Agulhon, *French Republic*, 90; Benbassa, *Jews*, 143; Brown, *Soul of France*, 212; Schom, *Zola*, 193.

44 Friedman, *Zola*, 54; Schom, *Zola*, 195, 198, 211, 216, 223.

45 Friedman, *Zola*, 54; Brown, *Soul of France*, 214; Agulhon, *French Republic*, 91; Schom, *Zola*, 230.

46 Benbassa, *Jews*, 145; Kedward, *Dreyfus*, 83; Bredin, *Affair*, 337, 350; Busi, *Pope*, 147.

47 Schom, *Zola*, 210; Brown, *Soul of France*, 208, 221.

48 Schom, *Zola*, 214; Busi, *Pope*, 147.

49 Kedward, *Dreyfus*, 93; Brown, *Soul of France*, 217-220; Agulhon, *French Republic*, 92-93; Schom, *Zola*, 216, 228.

50 Schom, *Zola*, 230; Brown, *Soul of France*, 225, 227; Kedward, *Dreyfus*, 9; Agulhon, *French Republic*, 96.

51 Schom, *Zola*, 230.

52 Kertzer, *Unholy War*, 185; Benbassa, *Jews*, 144; Lefèbvre-Filleau, *Zola*, 180.

53 Kedward, *Dreyfus*, 114; Schom, *Zola*, 231; Hemmings, *Zola*, 295, 299.

54 Lefèbvre-Filleau, *Zola*, 149, 150, 156, 158, 170; Hemmings, *Zola*, 302.

55 Hemmings, *Zola*, 303-304; Lefèbvre-Filleau, *Zola*, 158-161, 172.

56 Hemmings, *Zola*, 303; Lefèbvre-Filleau, *Zola*, 162-163.

57 Bredin, *Affair*, 454.

58 Agulhon, *French Republic*, 103, 108; Bredin, *Affair*, 394-395, 469; Wolf, *France*, 415, 418.

59 Bredin, *Affair*, 475.

60 Kedward, *Dreyfus*, 40; Schom, *Zola*, 188.

61 Friedman, *Zola*, 61; Agulhon, *French Republic*, 18, 124; Brown, *Soul of France*, 230; Schom, *Zola*, 19; Lefèbvre-Filleau, *Zola*, 182-183.

Kemal Mustafa Atatürk

CHAPTER 14

ATATÜRK VS. THE RED SULTAN

Ottoman Decline

In the fourteenth century a new dynasty known as the Ottomans began seizing control of the Middle East. Relying heavily on converted Christian troops from the Balkans, they surrounded what remained of the Roman Empire, finally ending it with the capture of Constantinople in 1453. Ottoman rule also moved south into the Arab heartland and across Muslim North Africa. By the beginning of the seventeenth century, Ottoman sailors raided as far as the southern coast of England.[1]

Like their predecessors, the Ottomans relied on Islam as an instrument of social control. The standard and cloak of the Prophet Muhammad were transferred to Istanbul (as Constantinople was renamed) to symbolize its status as the new capital of the Muslim world. The Ottoman sultan called himself "Caliph of the World," the title of the first four successors of Muhammad.[2] The power of the Muslim clergy grew inexorably. Muslim clergy were exempted from taxes and from confiscation of property for wrongdoing. These privileges were made hereditary, thus creating an unassailable clerical nobility that endured for centuries. Between 1550 and 1622, the number of clergy in hierarchy positions nearly tripled, with political back-scratching rather than objective need accounting for most of the increase. The chief Muslim cleric even had the power to confirm or deny the sultan's fitness to rule.[3]

The need to find more and more paid positions for the relatives of important clergy not only hurt the state's finances directly, but also had insidious indirect effects of bumping out competent officials in the outlying provinces and replacing them with dysfunctional parasites. As the quality of government receded, so did the people's respect for it. One "solution" to the problem of clerical incompetence was an institution known as *arpalik*, or payment to the clergy for not working. With advancement not based on earthly merit but on God's will, venality at court reached the point where every official appointment in the state was obtainable only through influence and purchase, with a tariff fixed in advance. Even the sultan himself accepted bribes.[4]

In Umayyad and even Abbasid times, Muslim scientific achievements had matched, and possibly outstripped, those of Europe. Even modern defenders of Muslim culture admit that after the twelfth century, though, there was a notable decline in Muslim science. The theologian Ibn Hazam had stressed that "Any fact whatsoever which can be proved by reasoning is in the Koran or in the words of the Prophet, clearly set out." Al-Ghazali, the greatest Muslim philosopher, taught that God was the only cause of all events, and could alter patterns of cause and effect when he felt like it; therefore, the proper subject for study was God, not science.[5]

The first printing press in any Muslim country was not installed until 1727—nearly 300 years after Gutenberg invented it—and over the bitter opposition of a religious establishment concerned about what it might produce. Between 1729 and 1745 that one press churned out works on history, linguistics, magnetism, and European modernization. But after its owner's death in 1745, the press was dismantled; there was no more printing in the Muslim world for nearly 40 years, when Europe's Industrial Revolution was well under way.[6]

The "knowledge gap" with Western Europe had a telling effect on the battlefield, as smaller but better-equipped European forces began to defeat the previously invincible Ottomans with regularity. Religion even affected the navy. When a Russian fleet sailed around Europe in 1770 to attack Turkey from the Mediterranean side, many Ottomans were astonished. According to their understanding of geography, such a feat should not have been possible.[7]

By the early nineteenth century, many Ottoman officials realized that things would have to change for the empire to survive. Accomplishing major change against the vested interest of the clergy, though, proved nearly impossible. Sultan Selim III, for example, ordered the army to equip itself in the European style; for his efforts, he was deposed and assassinated. When an official tried to stimulate the economy in 1841 by adopting a new commercial code based on the French model, the High Council had one question: whether it conformed to Muslim law. The official's reply that "The holy law has nothing to do with such matters" earned him immediate exile, and the new code was abandoned.[8] In 1853, the Russian czar coined the phrase "the sick man of Europe" to describe the deteriorating empire. The overriding issue of European diplomacy in the latter half of the century was how to carve the empire up in a manner that did not unduly upset the balance of power among other nations.[9]

Abdulhamit

In 1876 a coup was launched by the liberal Minister of War, Midhat, against an erratic and often drunken sultan who was pronounced insane and replaced by his brother, new Sultan Abdulhamit II. Abdulhamit declared his willingness to accept a constitution written largely by Midhat that would allow an elected assembly to rule the country, with full freedom of religion and the press.

That lasted a year, until members of the new assembly made the mistake of criticizing Abdulhamit for the conduct of a war which saw Russian troops nearly capture the capital in Istanbul.[10] The sultan responded by suspending the constitution he had just granted—though supposedly "temporary," the suspension would last for 30 years. "I have made a mistake," he announced. "From now on I shall follow in the footsteps of my grandfather, Sultan Mahmud, who understood that it is only by force that one can move the people with whose guardianship Allah has now entrusted me." Force is what he used with Midhat, the "father of the constitution," by exiling him and then having him strangled.[11]

Since reverting to business as usual left the empire with the same mountain of problems it always had, Abdulhamit tried a new strategy called "Pan-Islamism" to slow the European advance. Pan-Islamism was the attempt to unite all the world's Muslims under the political banner of the caliph of Islam, the successor of Muhammad. European powers that offended Turkey would then have to deal with angry Muslims all across Africa and Asia. Vast sums—borrowed from Europe—were used as propaganda to weaken European influence from Sudan to India. But Pan-Islamism as a foreign policy tool worked better on paper than in practice, as most non-Turkish Muslims were unwilling to pay it more than lip service.[12]

At home, Pan-Islamism translated into renewed power for Muslim God experts, with higher salaries and stricter censorship of everything the more humanistic West had to offer. Among other things, the teaching of evolution was banned from the schools, which were ordered instead to make students memorize the Koran in Arabic. Not trusting the judgment of his censors, the sultan banned the use of specific words, such as "liberty" and "constitution," along with everything ever written by authors such as Voltaire and Zola. Ultimately, all fiction was banned because it "stimulated the imagination."[13]

Abdulhamit spent borrowed money on new Muslim schools designed to inculcate piety and obedience. Between 1880 and 1907 the budgets for the navy and the police declined by more than a third, while the budget for the state-paid clergy increased by 50 percent.[14] When one official suggested that philosophy and political economy should be included in the curriculum of a new university, Abdulhamit demurred that such knowledge would be like putting a sharp knife into the hands of a child. Muslim superiority was the mantra; one book popular at court opened with the words, "The bases of contemporary civilization are nothing but the actions and traditions of Muhammad." Electricity, which terrified the sultan, was virtually unknown in Istanbul throughout his reign.[15]

Meanwhile, the Christian-majority areas under Ottoman rule continued their drive for independence, abetted by the Ottoman "millet" system under which God experts of each of the minorities under Turkish rule (Armenian Christians, Orthodox Christians, Jews, etc.) were given political power over marriages, inheritance, and other matters in their own religious communities—a system which ultimately helped tear the Empire apart. Greece, Serbia, and Bulgaria had all broken free earlier in the nineteenth century; to the east, Christian-majority Armenia agitated for independence as well.[16] Perhaps because Armenia was further away from Western press scrutiny, perhaps because he was simply tired of losing territory, or perhaps because he lost control over more zealous operatives on the scene, Abdulhamit presided over the first round of religiously organized rape, pillage, and murder that became known as the "Armenian genocide" during the mid-1890s. An exact body count will never be known, but it is estimated that tens or even hundreds of thousands of Christian Armenians were slaughtered in order to prop up Abdulhamit's rule, while thousands more fled or converted to Islam. One insider quoted Abdulhamit as saying that the only way to eliminate the Armenian problem "was by eliminating the Armenians themselves." It is this episode that earned Abdulhamit the sobriquet "the Red Sultan," a term coined by Georges Clemenceau three years before he published Zola's "I Accuse!" letter.[17]

As the years passed, Abdulhamit grew more paranoid and reclusive, rarely venturing out of his palace. He carried a revolver at all times, and used it to kill a gardener who crossed his path when he thought he was alone. He also shot dead a little slave girl who had strayed from her mother and was found playing with one of his jeweled firearms.[18]

1908

Abdulhamit's paranoia was not completely unfounded. However, the real danger came from the army, whose officers had been well-educated in modern schools. In 1908, a spontaneous minor mutiny in Macedonia brought down the Ottoman house of cards. Abdulhamit overreacted, and volunteered to turn over the government to a cabal of army officers known as the "Young Turks" and reinstate the suspended constitution if he could be spared as a figurehead. Power changed hands with almost no bloodshed.[19]

As in 1876, though, Abdulhamit had not finished playing his hand. Though the new rulers made no decisive moves against the clergy, there was suspicion that someday they might. In April, 1909, a revolt led by the "Society of Islamic Unity" broke out in the streets of Istanbul, sparked by a demonstration of religious students, aimed at revoking the constitution and restoring Abdulhamit and the clergy to absolute power.[20]

Serving in a military district not far from Istanbul when the trouble broke out was a 28-year-old officer named Mustafa Kemal, later known as "Atatürk." Atatürk was a politically active officer who had spent time in Abdulhamit's prisons for suspected disloyalty. He was serving at a faraway outpost when the mutiny broke out in 1908, freezing him out of a political role in the Young Turk regime.[21] He had no use for Abdulhamit, though, and when the counter-revolt erupted Atatürk immediately began organizing troops to crush the uprising, putting down the attempt to restore Abdulhamit with little difficulty. Abdulhamit was forced to abdicate, and comfortably imprisoned with 13 wives in a palace at taxpayer expense thereafter. He died a natural death in 1918.[22]

The son of a low-level bureaucrat, Atatürk grew up in Salonika, a heavily Jewish town that was a center for descendants of the adherents of Shabbetai Zevi who had followed him into Islam. He had been raised as a devout Muslim, but lost his faith while attending military school. A student of the French language, he devoured French newspapers during precisely the turn-of-the-century period when the news from Paris was dominated by Dreyfus, Zola, and the battle for separation of church and state.[23]

Though the Young Turks appreciated Atatürk's swift action in 1909, they still did not give him the government position he desired. Nor were they inclined to lead any social revolution in the empire. Their principal political idea was that they, rather than Abdulhamit, should be in charge, and that a representative assembly per the 1876 Constitution would solve all the empire's problems.[24] Whether they were right will never be known because the empire was soon plunged into a series of devastating wars lasting over a decade. The Young

Turks sided with Germany in World War I, a move Atatürk opposed. Atatürk's fame soared, though, when he led the successful defense of the Gallipoli Peninsula, the key to all of southeast Europe. Both the Germans he fought with and the British he defeated lavished praise on Atatürk's performance.[25]

The Ottoman Empire surrendered shortly before Germany did, and the long-discussed plans for carving it up began to unfold despite U.S. President Woodrow Wilson's promises to the contrary. Greece was to be awarded the west, Italy the south, Britain and France the Arab territories, and an independent Armenia the east. The Turks would retain for themselves only the barren central plateau.[26] The sultan who succeeded Abdulhamit and his hangers-on were ready to accept this, as it would maintain their accustomed lifestyle. But Atatürk and millions of his fellow Turks were not, and launched a guerrilla war against foreign occupation and "the treachery of the sultan-caliph." The sultan responded by signing a death warrant for Atatürk, but he had no means to enforce it since the vast body of Turkish opinion had swung to Atatürk's side.[27]

From the outset of the war for independence, Atatürk insisted that only the Turkish nation, and not a clique of military commanders, could counter the overwhelming strength of the Allies. So in the midst of combat, he convened a Constituent Assembly, with representatives elected from all over Turkey, in the primitive but centrally located town of Ankara.[28]

Atatürk inspired his troops to hang on grimly against the overwhelming military might of England, France, Italy, and Greece. Though they enjoyed both numerical and weaponry superiority over the Turks, the allies were soundly defeated by Atatürk's superior generalship. Turkey thus became the first eastern nation to make a successful stand against Western imperialism, and a model for many others to follow. Jawaharlal Nehru, whom we will see in Chapter 18 leading the Indian struggle for independence, was one Asian who was so inspired: "Kemal Atatürk ... was a hero of mine in my younger days. ... Even in prison, we followed avidly the news of [his] activities and his struggles to free Turkey from foreign rule and influence."[29]

The Atatürk Revolution

When the Allies finally agreed to leave Turkey to the Turks, a victorious Atatürk, now named president, turned on the perfidious sultan, who fled on a British battleship. In what turned out to be a short-lived compromise, Atatürk's government retained the position of caliph, or spiritual ruler of the Muslims, and appointed the heir to the absconding sultan's throne as caliph.[30]

As might have been expected, the office of the caliph served as a magnet for God experts who wished to undermine the new republic and return to the good old days of Ottoman rule. The new caliph demanded a bigger budget and the right to lavish dress to inspire awe among the faithful, while conferring with foreign Muslims intent on interfering with Turkish politics. He was stepping on the wrong toes; in less than a year, Atatürk pushed through the Assembly a bill to abolish the institution of the caliphate ("this tumor of the Middle Ages"), while banishing all members of the imperial family from Turkish territory. For the first time since its founding, the Islamic world was left without a recognized leader, a situation that continues today— the terrorist Osama bin Laden called the ending of the caliphate "the tragedy of 89 years ago."[31]

The clergy did not take the abolition of the caliphate lying down. The following year, a religious revolt arose in the southeast, with the self-styled "Commander of Warriors for the Faith" declaring his purpose to restore strict Islamic rule and rid the nation of Atatürk's secularism. After crushing the rebellion, Atatürk set about disassembling the entire infrastructure of Muslim control over Turkish society, consciously following in the footsteps of the French separation of church and state in Zola's time. He understood that it was Islam, more than anything else, that was holding Turkey back, and that there could never be progress so long as the nation remained under the thumb of a religion whose very name meant "submission." He was relentless in his scorn for the clergy, telling an audience that it was thanks to "selfish and ignorant people like these that the Turkish people had for centuries lived in huts made out of mud and rushes, with their bare feet exposed to the merciless attacks of snow and rain."[32]

The schools of Islam were shut down, and religious references were removed from oaths. The societies of dervishes, similar to the old Christian monasteries but far more powerful—the revolt had been organized by one of them—were abolished as well, while clergy were banned from wearing clerical costume out of doors, and many were pensioned off. The vast landholdings of religious establishments were nationalized, with their revenues diverted to purposes of the state. The ban on alcohol was repealed. The religious courts were shut down in favor of civil courts. By 1928, the Turkish Constitution was amended to remove all references to Islam, while every citizen was given the right to practice "the philosophical creed, religion, or doctrine to which he may adhere."[33]

Separation of religion and government could not have been made more rigorous than it was in the penal code of 1928:

> Those who make use of religion, of religious sentiments, or of things considered as sacred by religion, to stir the people to acts of a nature to bring injury to the security of the state in any fashion or quality whatever, as well as those who organize associations for this purpose, will be punished by heavy prison sentence, even if these excitations and organizations have achieved no results. ... It is forbidden to form political associations based on religious sentiments and opinions. Associations of this kind will be dissolved, and those who have formed them, as well as their members, will be punished.[34]

Though Atatürk led the charge capably, it must be acknowledged that conditions were ripe for his success. Nothing soured Turks more on the caliphate than their recollection that even though the sultan-caliph had declared World War I a jihad of Islam, the empire had been stabbed in the back by Muslim Arab nationalists rebelling to seek independence for Ottoman-controlled Arab territories–with themselves in charge, of course–and by hordes of Indian Muslim troops under British command. It might be understandable for Balkan or Armenian Christians to rebel, but if that was the way fellow Muslims were going to respect the caliph, then it was better not to have a caliph at all.[35]

Just as interesting is the road Atatürk did not take. Before he abolished the caliphate, many were suggesting that he be appointed caliph himself. If Atatürk had been primarily interested in his own power, that would have been enticing; instead, he regarded the idea as ridiculous.[36] Then in 1924 a commission began work on a plan to reform Islam itself, to bring it more in line with Christianity through devices such as pews, shoes, and instrumental music. Though the learned theologians spent four years developing these plans, Atatürk's government dismissed them in 1928 as being "as useless as a graft on dead wood." "I have no religion," Atatürk boasted, "and at times I wish all religions [were] at the bottom of the sea. He is a weak ruler who needs religion to uphold his government. … My people are going to learn the principles of democracy, the dictates of truth, and the teachings of science. Superstition must go."[37]

Modernization

Women's equality was a favorite theme of Atatürk throughout his career. "If a society does not march towards the same goal with all its men and women it will be futile to wait for any progress towards civilization." Even before the war for independence had been won, Atatürk showed his cards, by counting women in the census for the first time. Women were given the right to vote in Turkey in 1934—long before other "civilized" countries such as France (1944), Argentina (1947), and Canada (1950). With Atatürk's support, 17 women were elected deputies to the Assembly.[38] Polygamy and child marriage were banned. All marriages and divorces were performed by secular officials, and women were given equal rights in divorce and inheritance.[39]

Laws were important, but Atatürk knew that culture was even more so. "If henceforward women do not share in the social life of the nation, we shall never attain to our full development. We shall remain irremediably backward, incapable of treating on equal terms with the civilizations of the West." He showed off his bareheaded wife, an independent and outspoken woman, on a honeymoon tour through southern Turkey. He even danced with a woman in public—a first in the history of Turkey—while encouraging women to dance with men who were not their husbands at balls he attended.[40] Women began to appear in public without male escorts, to work alongside men, to play tennis. The first Turkish beauty queen was crowned in 1929.[41]

Seemingly more trivial was Turkish men's habit of wearing the fez, a brimless cylindrical cap. Though there was nothing sacred about the fez, which had only been popular for the previous hundred years, it set Turks apart from the rest of western civilization. Moreover, its lack of a brim facilitated the Muslim ritual of touching the forehead to the ground during daily prayers. Atatürk was intent on dragging Turkey into the western civilized world; so without any warning, in 1925, he announced that the fez would have to go, and all Turkish men would have to start wearing European-style hats.[42] The most important effect was psychological: the fez gave Turks a way to think of themselves as being different from the rest of Europe, and the wearing of hats made Turks think of themselves as being the same. Clergy-inspired riots broke out over the anti-fez law, but the well-prepared government suppressed them ruthlessly.[43]

Atatürk wanted to change women's headgear as well, but was unable to persuade the Assembly to ban the Muslim practice of veiling. Still, he made an enormous difference by ending police enforcement of veil-wearing and constantly urging women to dress in the western manner.[44] He commented on the practice:

> In some places I have seen women who put a piece of cloth or a towel or something like it over their heads to hide their faces, and who turn their backs or huddle themselves on the ground when a man passes by. What is the meaning and sense of this behavior? Gentlemen, can the mothers and daughters of a civilized nation adopt this strange manner, this barbarous posture? It is a spectacle that makes the nation an object of ridicule. It must be remedied at once.[45]

The government did ban the wearing of headscarves in official premises, including schools.[46]

Atatürk ruled with a firm hand at the same time that dictators in Italy, Germany, Russia, and Spain were threatening the peace of the world. But unlike his neighbors, Atatürk had not the slightest interest in territorial conquest. He felt particular contempt for Mussolini, who strutted about in gaudy military uniforms despite never having led troops in battle, correctly predicting that "He will be hanged by his people, one of these days." After reading Hitler's *Mein Kampf*, Atatürk expressed horror at "the meanness of his language and the madness of his thoughts." He brought Turkey into the League of Nations at the earliest opportunity, and supported the embargo against Italy following its invasion of Ethiopia.[47]

Even while the outcome of the war for independence was still in doubt, Atatürk realized that education was the key to modernizing Turkey, and organized a conference to plan reform. "If 80 percent of the people of this country are illiterate the fault is not in us. The fault is to be found in those who failed to estimate the character of this nation and chained our minds. This is the time to correct the mistakes of the past. And the mistakes will be corrected." After shutting down all the state-run religious schools, the government took over sole responsibility for the primary schools, and squeezed religion completely out of the curriculum. In 1933, the Faculty of Theology at the University of Istanbul was merged out of existence.[48]

A more educated populace meant a more contentious populace. At one famous presidential palace dinner party in 1932, a perhaps drink-emboldened Dr. Reşit Galip criticized the current education minister harshly. When Atatürk suggested he be more respectful, Galip refused, and Atatürk asked him to leave the table. "No," said Galip, "this is not your table, it belongs to the nation." "In that case," replied Atatürk, "I shall go myself"—which he did. In an earlier age, Dr. Galip's life expectancy could then have been measured in minutes; shortly afterward, though, Atatürk decided he admired Galip's bluntness so much that he had him appointed as the new education minister. During Galip's administration, staff positions at Istanbul University were filled by Jews escaping the Nazis.[49]

Years before Atatürk came to power, he wrote in his diary that:

> If I obtain great authority and power, I think I will bring about by a coup—suddenly in one moment—the desired revolution in our social life. Because, unlike others, I don't believe that this deed can be achieved by raising the intelligence of others slowly to the level of my own. My soul rebels against such a course. Why, after my years of education, after studying civilization and the socialization processes, after spending my life and my time to gain pleasure from freedom, should I descend to the level of the common people? I will make them rise to my level. Let me not resemble them: they should resemble me.[50]

That turned out to be his style, nowhere more than in his reform of the Turkish alphabet. Due to the influence of Islam, the Turkish language had previously been written with Arabic letters, a practice that made literacy a far more difficult achievement than it ought to have been. Atatürk personally supervised the work of experts preparing the new Latin-based alphabet, for example deciding that Q was a useless letter that could be discarded in favor of increased use of the K (a boon to rookie Turkish Scrabble players ever since). When his advisors proposed a five-year phase-in for the new alphabet, Atatürk shrewdly replied that people would simply continue to use the old script, and commanded instead that "The change will happen in three months or it will not happen at all." It happened, on schedule, with Atatürk leading a patriotic crash campaign for ordinary Turks to learn the new alphabet, then teach it to their neighbors. The number of schools in Turkey doubled during Atatürk's rule; so did the Turkish literacy rate.[51]

Atatürk knew that the Muslim legal code had to be swept away, and replaced with laws based on what worked best in practice, not what some expert said his god wanted. He was also in a hurry; as his Minister of Justice asked, "Why waste our time trying to produce something new when quite good codes are to be found ready made?" Rather than waste valuable time in constructing such an edifice from scratch, Atatürk simply borrowed from the laws of other countries.

253

The new civil code, for example, was copied from Switzerland, along with all the commentaries to guide in its application. No attempts to pick it apart were permitted; the code in its entirety became the law of Turkey in February 1926. A new penal code was copied from Italy, and a new commercial code was copied from Germany.[52] Atatürk's Minister of Justice, Mahmud Essad, explained that:

> States whose laws are based on religion become incapable after a short lapse of time of satisfying the exigencies of the country and the nation. For religions express unchanging precepts. Life goes ahead, needs change rapidly. Religious laws, in the presence of life which constantly progresses, are no more than words void of sense and forms without value. ... It is indubitable that our laws, which came out of the changeless precepts of religion and which ensured a permanent place to divine elements, have been the most powerful and the most effective factor which, in modern times, has enslaved the destinies of the Turkish nation to the mentalities and institutions of the Middle Ages.[53]

Atatürk's democracy was not perfect. He attempted, twice, to foster a "loyal opposition" party on the western model; each time, religious reactionaries seized the opportunity to undermine the republic itself, which Atatürk would not countenance.[54] What one biographer calls Atatürk's "enlightened authoritarianism" allowed far greater freedom of the press than Turkey had ever enjoyed before, but again with limits when he felt the core of the revolution itself was threatened. Atatürk was also responsible for the killing of at least a small number of political opponents. This is reprehensible under standards of a full-blown democracy—but Turkey was not a full-blown democracy, and the number of such deaths was in the tens, not in the tens of thousands (or more) as was happening in so many other countries at the time. To a group of schoolteachers who asked him whether, as certain writers maintained, he was really a dictator like Hitler and Mussolini, he replied, "If I were, you would not be allowed to ask me that question."[55] Within a dozen years after his 1938 death (half of which were taken up with World War II), Turkey not only developed a second political party that accepted the value of secular government, but saw that party win an election and peacefully succeed to power.[56]

A compelling case can be made that Atatürk's Turkish Revolution is the greatest revolution in human history, reforming all at once political institutions, social relations, religion, family, economic life, customs and even the moral bases of society, all in a 15-year span, with far more profound positive change and less bloodshed than that of its American, French, Russian, or Chinese counterparts.[57]

Once a Muslim teacher, in the course of an oration, asked angrily, "What does this word 'modern' mean?" Atatürk replied, "It means being a human being, teacher. It means being a human being."[58]

> Inch by inch, Turkey today is forgetting Atatürk and sliding back into Islamism. Western politicians and media seem to think this is just great, because it's based on "democracy." But how praiseworthy is democracy when large numbers of voters are swayed by the fraud and emotional coercion of God experts? Share your thoughts on this and the other questions you'll find at **dgc.humanistpress.com**!

Notes:

1 Sonn, *Islam*, 78; Lapidus, "Sultanates," 373-374; Smith, "Islam," 342.

2 Zilfi, *Politics*, 23; Lapidus, "Sultanates," 382; Kinross, *Ottoman*, 170, 552.

3 Schacht, *Islamic Law*, 89; Kinross, *Ottoman*, 211; Lapidus, "Sultanates," 381; Zilfi, *Politics*, 27, 94.

4 Zilfi, *Politics*, 69, 111; Bisbee, *New Turks*, 7; Warraq, *Not a Muslim*; 275; Lapidus, "Sultanates," 391.

5 Warraq, *Not a Muslim*, 136; Dhanani, "Islam," 85, 88.

6 Kinross, *Ottoman*, 381; Clog, "Attempt"; Vitrine Library, "Kâtip Çelebi."

7 Kinross, *Ottoman*, 335; Zilfi, *Politics*, 117.

8 Afetinan, *History*, 5; Kinross, *Ottoman*, 431, 476; Allen, *Turkish Transformation*, 5.

9 Afetinan, *History*, 16; Kinross, *Ottoman*, 408-412.

10 Allen, *Turkish Transformation*, 7; Haslip, *Sultan*, 57, 71-80, 101; Macfie, *Atatürk*, 19; Afetinan, *History*, 1, 146; Shaw, *History*, 167, 175, 187.

11 Hovhannisyan, *Armenian*, 45; Mango, *Atatürk*, 14; Shaw, *History*, 216; Macfie, *Atatürk*, 20; Haslip, *Sultan*, 100, 151, 183; Bisbee, *New Turks*, 13.

12 Lee, *Origins*, 279; Allen, *Turkish Transformation*, 7; Haslip, *Sultan*, 174, 180; Shaw, *History*, 260; Mango, *Atatürk*, 16.

13 Allen, *Turkish Transformation*, 91, 93; Shaw, *History*, 216, 245, 252; Bisbee, *New Turks*, 225.

14 Shaw, *History*, 226, 260; Mango, *Atatürk*, 216.

15 Kinross, *Ottoman*, 553; Haslip, *Sultan*, 245; Shaw, *History*, 230.

16 Bisbee, *New Turks*, 48-49; Allen, *Turkish Transformation*, 74; Haslip, *Sultan*, 90; Hovhannisyan, *Armenian*, 52.

17 Allen, *Turkish Transformation*, 74; Kinross, *Ottoman*, 560; Haslip, *Sultan*, 217, 222; Hovhannisyan, *Armenian*, 45, 53-54. An even bloodier outbreak occurred in 1915, while Atatürk was defending Gallipoli. Turks today claim there was brutality on both sides.

18 Haslip, *Sultan*, 137, 210.

19 Shaw, *History*, 31, 266; Mango, *Atatürk*, 77; Afetinan, *History*, 53; Haslip, *Sultan*, 258; Kinross, *Ottoman*, 573; Allen, *Turkish Transformation*, 8.

20 Allen, *Turkish Transformation*, 8; Haslip, *Sultan*, 271-272; Kinross, *Atatürk*, 43; Shaw, *History*, 279.

21 Macfie, *Atatürk*, 19, 23. Mustafa Kemal was not renamed Atatürk until many years later, but to avoid confusion I refer to him as Atatürk throughout.

22 Afetinan, *History*, 57; Haslip, *Sultan*, 294; Kinross, *Atatürk*, 44, 65; Shaw, *History*, 271, 282.

23 Shaw, *History*, 265; Kinross, *Atatürk*, 10, 16; Afetinan, *History*, 51; Mango, *Atatürk*, 31, 45, 56.

24 Allen, *Turkish Transformation*, 9; Kinross, *Ottoman*, 585; Mango, *Atatürk*, 88; Bisbee, *New Turks*, 15; Kinross, *Atatürk*, 38.

25 Sonyel, *Atatürk*, 5-6; Shaw, *History*, 317; Afetinan, *History*, 59-65; Kinross, *Atatürk*, 78, 111.

26 Sonyel, *Atatürk*, 10; Bisbee, *New Turks*, 51; Kinross, *Atatürk*, 164; Afetinan, *History*, 3.

27 Macfie, *Atatürk*, 97, 284; Shaw, *History*, 332, 356; Mango, *Atatürk*, 276; Sonyel, *Atatürk*, 17, 51; Afetinan, *History*, 30, 43, 74; Kinross, *Atatürk*, 185, 248, 256.

28 Afetinan, *History*, 75.

29 Mango, *Atatürk*, 307, 315; Afetinan, *History*, 95; Kinross, *Atatürk*, 340; Sonyel, *Atatürk*, 91, 212.

30 Sonyel, *Atatürk*, 96; Afetinan, *History*, 110, 127; Allen, *Turkish Transformation*, 56-57; Kinross, *Atatürk*, 396, 401.

31 Marshall, "Importance," xi; Kinross, *Atatürk*, 438; Shaw, *History*, 281;

Mango, *Atatürk*, 366, 401; Allen, *Turkish Transformation*, 61; Afetinan, *History,* 137, 150.

32 Shaw, *History*, 284; Mango, *Atatürk*, 423, 534; Kinross, *Atatürk*, 55, 417, 454, 467.

33 Baldick, *Mystical Islam*, 159; Sonyel, *Atatürk*, 119; Allen, *Turkish Transformation*, 49, 171-180; Kinross, *Atatürk*, 439, 467; Mango, *Atatürk*, 403, 407, 463; Macfie, *Atatürk*, 136; Shaw, *History*, 378, 385, 388; Bisbee, *New Turks*, 132.

34 Allen, *Turkish Transformation*, 179.

35 Macfie, *Atatürk*, 136; Sonyel, *Atatürk*, 8; Allen, *Turkish Transformation*, 9, 41.

36 Kinross, *Atatürk*, 439; Sonyel, *Atatürk*, 96; Mango, *Atatürk*, 407.

37 Crandall, *Gender*, 164; Allen, *Turkish Transformation*, 180; Mango, *Atatürk*, 463, 535.

38 Afetinan, *History,* 170, 176; Mango, *Atatürk*, 501; Kinross, *Atatürk*, 477, 479; Shaw, *History*, 379; Interparliamentary Union, "Women's Suffrage."

39 Sonyel, *Atatürk*, 117; Afetinan, *History*, 173-174; Macfie, *Atatürk*, 144; Mango, *Atatürk*, 438; Shaw, *History*, 385.

40 Mango, *Atatürk*, 473; Macfie, *Atatürk*, 144; Kinross, *Atatürk*, 390, 419, 478.

41 Bisbee, *New Turks*, 37; Sonyel, *Atatürk*, 117; Shaw, *History*, 287.

42 Mango, *Atatürk*, 433; Kinross, *Atatürk*, 472.

43 Bisbee, *New Turks*, 22; Kinross, *Atatürk*, 473.

44 Sonyel, *Atatürk*, 113; Bisbee, *New Turks*, 23; Afetinan, *History*, 178; Allen, *Turkish Transformation*, 139; Shaw, *History*, 385.

45 Kinross, *Atatürk*, 478.

46 Mango, *Atatürk*, 434.

47 Shaw, *History*, 376; Kinross, *Atatürk*, 522; Sonyel, *Atatürk*, 162; Mango, *Atatürk*, 504.

48 Afetinan, *History*, 181, 188; Shaw, *History*, 385; Mango, *Atatürk*, 403; Bisbee, *New Turks*, 140; Allen, *Turkish Transformation*, 96, 100, 182.

49 Mango, *Atatürk*, 481-482; Sonyel, *Atatürk*, 162.

50 Macfie, *Atatürk*, 132.

51 Allen, *Turkish Transformation*, 126; Kinross, *Atatürk*, 502; Afetinan, *History*, 187, 190; Bisbee, *New Turks*, 28; Mango, *Atatürk*, 465, 467; Shaw, *History*, 387.

52 Allen, *Turkish Transformation*, 89; Macfie, *Atatürk*, 136; Shaw, *History*, 385; Sonyel, *Atatürk*, 116.

53 Allen, *Turkish Transformation*, 34.

54 Kinross, *Atatürk*, 510-513; Mango, *Atatürk*, 471, 476; Shaw, *History*, 381-382; Bisbee, *New Turks*, 218.

55 Mango, *Atatürk,* 426, 450-451, 536; Bisbee, *New Turks,* 19; Kinross, *Atatürk,* 497.
56 Kinross, *Atatürk,* 569; Mango, *Atatürk,* 531.
57 Allen, *Turkish Transformation,* 85; Mango, *Atatürk,* 453.
58 Kinross, *Atatürk,* 432.

Clarence Darrow

CHAPTER 15

DARROW VS. BRYAN

The Ticket

Somewhere there must exist a piece of political memorabilia I would love to have, or at least see: an 1896 poster or handbill endorsing Democrats William Jennings Bryan for President and Clarence Darrow for Congress in a district in Chicago.

Bryan, at the time, was a two-term Congressman from Nebraska, at age 36 barely meeting the constitutional qualification for the presidency. He was a brilliant orator, perhaps the greatest in American history. His "Cross of Gold" speech took the 1896 Democratic convention by storm, and overwhelmed delegates made the previously unknown Congressman their nominee. Throughout his career, Bryan assured audiences that God was on his side; as for his opponents, "The Bible speaks of certain persons who love darkness rather than light ... because their deeds are evil." "There is only one side to a moral issue," he loved to say, "and that is the moral side."[1]

Clarence Darrow had become politically well-connected in Chicago by serving as city attorney, and after moving to private practice landed the plum of all clients, the Chicago and Northwestern Railway. When the great Pullman strike broke out in 1894, though, Darrow found himself sympathetic to the strikers and unable in good conscience to fight against them in court. So he resigned from the cushiest of jobs, and began representing the workers instead.[2]

Darrow was as smitten by Bryan's convention performance as everyone else. Before broadcast media, one of the most effective means of spreading a campaign's message was to send out speakers to town meetings across the country. Darrow barnstormed for Bryan all across the midwest, despite the fact that he had been nominated for Congress in Chicago. He never campaigned in his own district because the conventional wisdom had it as safely Democratic. When Republican money poured into Darrow's district the week before election day, though, the conventional wisdom failed; Bryan lost the district badly (and the country), and Darrow lost by less than 100 votes.[3] He went on to become one of the most outstanding litigators of the twentieth century.

Darrow's brilliance as a lawyer led him to understand that if the words of the law were not in his client's favor, he needed try Plan B, which meant appealing instead to the jury's decency and common sense. What is truly astonishing is that Darrow defended some 60 clients at trial facing a possible death penalty, and not one was ever executed.[4]

Race

Darrow parted company from Bryan on three major issues: race, prohibition, and evolution. Bryan's core of support came from the solidly Democratic south, which in the 1890s was busily enacting the "Jim Crow" laws to deny black people the right to vote, to attend white schools, to drink from white water fountains, etc. Bryan firmly endorsed the Jim Crow movement and opposed a federal anti-lynching law, calling white supremacy "a doctrine absolutely essential to the welfare of the South." He warmed up his crowds with jokes about the "colored brothers," and berated President Theodore Roosevelt for inviting Booker T. Washington to dine at the White House, while angrily denying the rumor that he had ever served colored men in his own home. When a black lawyer wrote to complain about his support for segregation, Bryan icily replied that "Your letter ... confirms my views and I shall be glad to preserve it as evidence of what the colored race would do if they had the power to legislate for the whites, although I think it would be an injustice to attribute to the average colored man the malignant spirit which your letter manifests."[5]

In the 1920s, a rejuvenated Ku Klux Klan became an enormously important force in American life. Re-established by a Methodist minister, its first public march was in Atlanta in 1920, celebrating the dawn of Prohibition. The 1920s Klan was an overwhelmingly Protestant organization; two-thirds of its national lecturers were Protestant ministers, who recruited as many as 5 million members and seized control of the state governments in Oregon, Indiana, and Colorado.[6]

The Klan's sudden rise generated a powerful opposite reaction among humanists and others who despised its teaching of hate. At the 1924 Democratic convention, a motion was offered to put the party on record as condemning the Klan. To its defense sprang the old Jim Crow warrior, William Jennings Bryan. Bryan shouted himself hoarse against efforts to damage party unity by criticizing its stalwart supporters in the Klan. On the final tally, Bryan won a victory for bigotry: the motion to condemn the Klan was defeated by a margin of one vote out of more than a thousand cast. As always, he credited God: "It must have been the Lord's work; I would not have been willing to risk so small a margin."[7]

Darrow took the opposite approach. His sympathies were always with the downtrodden; a third to a half of his professional time over his long career was devoted to clients from whom he collected nothing. Many times Darrow not only represented black defendants free of charge, but paid the court costs out of his own pocket. On the lecture circuit, he traveled to the heart of Alabama to attack the lynch laws.[8]

Darrow's most celebrated black defendant was Oliver Sweet, a distinguished medical doctor who moved into an all-white Detroit neighborhood in 1926. Immediately, the neighborhood formed a Klan-like "Improvement Association," the sole purpose of which was to force Sweet back to a black neighborhood where they thought he belonged. As angry crowds swarmed in front of his home shouting threats and insults, Sweet and a group of friends and relatives inside became convinced that a lynching was imminent. Shots rang out, and a white man lay dead in the street, victim of an unknown but obviously terrified member of Sweet's band of defenders.[9]

Everyone in the house was arrested, and there was little doubt about the outcome—senseless violence was exactly why whites didn't want coloreds in their neighborhood in the first place. Enter Clarence Darrow, at the behest of the National Association for the Advancement of Colored People. The defense was exceedingly difficult because it was virtually impossible for Darrow to get any of the dozens of white witnesses to concede that Sweet had any reason to be afraid of what was billed as entirely innocent activity—just people walking down the street. As Darrow later put it, "Fifty or seventy-five white persons came into court and deliberately testified that there was practically no one along the street corner that night."[10]

The conventional wisdom is that lawyers are supposed to flatter their jurors. Darrow did just the opposite, launching his seven hour closing argument by insulting them instead. He coolly told them they were all prejudiced, and he could prove it. "How many of you jurors, gentlemen, have ever had a colored person visit you in your home? How many of you have ever visited in their homes? How many of you have invited them to dinner at your house? Probably not one of you. Now, why, gentlemen?" But even though they were prejudiced, Darrow wanted them to set that aside and be fair anyway, and try to view this case as they would if a white family had been trapped inside its home by angry Negroes. He won a hung jury. On re-trial, he won an outright acquittal.[11]

Prohibition

The movement to ban consumption of alcohol in America began in 1812, led by Methodist and Baptist preachers convinced that rum was the tool of the devil. They were discomfited only slightly by the biblical reports that Jesus and his friends were drinkers; they knew what God wanted, Bible be damned. Some 30,000 churches participated in "Temperance Sunday" in 1907, and by 1917, 25 states had some form of prohibition.[12] The loudest voice was that of revivalist Billy Sunday, who called the liquor traffic the "most damnable, corrupt institution that ever wriggled out of hell and fastened itself on the public":

The saloon will take off the shirt from the back of a shivering man. It will take the coffin from under the dead. It will take the milk from the breast of the poor mother who is the wife of a drinking man. It will take the crust of bread from the hand of the hungry child. It cares for nothing but itself—for its dirty profits. It will keep your son out of college. It will make your daughter a prostitute. It will bury your wife in the potter's field. It will send you to hell.[13]

Sunday was widely regarded as a buffoon, as when he leapt to the top of the speaker's desk when given the opportunity to address a joint session of the New Jersey legislature.[14] What the movement needed was a seasoned politician of stature to help it achieve the dream of a constitutional amendment to ban alcohol.

Enter William Jennings Bryan. While running for Congress in 1890, Bryan opposed Prohibition, primarily because of an important distillery in his district. In the 1908 presidential campaign, he denied that prohibition was a "national question" at all. After he lost the 1908 race, though, Bryan began joining forces with his friend Billy Sunday in the national prohibition campaign.[15]

In 1915, Bryan began championing Prohibition on a nearly full-time basis. America's entry into World War I in 1917 provided a pretext for the Prohibitionists: grain should be used for food, not for alcohol, and soldiers and war workers needed to remain sober. Bryan as president of the "National Dry Federation" raced across the country as frenetically as he had in 1896, with Billy Sunday covering the spots he could not. One vaudeville comic invented the Bryan Cocktail: "It's made of grape juice and a nut."[16]

In 1918, Bryan had the last laugh, when the final necessary state ratified the Eighteenth Amendment. It was not self-enforcing, though; Congress in 1919 enacted the Volstead Act, which banned beer and light wine along with the hard stuff. Billy Sunday exulted that "The reign of tears is over. The slums will soon be only a memory. We will turn our prisons into factories and our jails into storehouses and corncribs. Men will walk upright now, women will smile, and the children will laugh."[17]

Trouble was, most Americans had not the slightest intention of changing their personal habits just because Congress said they should. Prohibitionists were thus faced with the daunting challenge of getting government to enforce the new laws. In 1920, the Prohibition Party attempted to nominate Bryan for president and Billy Sunday for vice president on a platform of vigorous enforcement, but both men declined the honor. By 1929, over half a million federal arrests had been made for various Prohibition violations. The government got important help from the Klan, which had its own methods of dealing with suspected moonshiners. This help was needed because one out of every 12 Prohibition Bureau agents wound up getting fired for bribery or other corruption. In San Francisco, the jury in a bootlegging trial was indicted for drinking the evidence.[18]

As Prohibition unfolded, one of its most vociferous opponents became Clarence Darrow, who toured the country giving speeches against what he saw as the only amendment to the constitution ever adopted that restricted personal freedom, rather than expanding it. "If senators and representatives had voted as they drank," he pointed out, "no such legislation would ever have disgraced America." In his widely circulated book, *The Prohibition Mania*, Darrow argued that "To legislate as if the citizens were irresponsible children, incapable of moderation, would mean a degradation of the whole country. With the same justice we might prohibit every sport because it becomes ruinous to the organism if carried to an excess."[19] "This question is not a question of statistics or facts," he told audiences:

> I have been in a statistics factory. I know how they are made. It is, as Dr. Holmes has stated, a pure question of the philosophy of government. ... Take out of this world the men who have drunk, down through the past, and you take away all the poetry and literature, practically all the works of genius that the world has produced. What kind of poem do you suppose you would get out of a glass of ice water? ... This Prohibition law has filled our jails with people who are not criminals, who have no conception or feeling that they are doing wrong. It has turned our Federal Courts into Police Courts, where

important business is put aside for cases of drunkenness and disorderly conduct. It has created new spies and detectives, snooping around doors and windows. It has made informers of thousands of us. It has made grafters and boodlers of men who otherwise would be honest. It is hateful, it is distasteful, it is an abomination, and we ought to get rid of it, and we will if we have the courage and the sense.[20]

Han Yü and the Umayyad princes would surely have agreed.

Six years after Darrow wrote, Prohibition was dead.[21] Darrow does not deserve all the credit for this, but he certainly fought the good fight.

Evolution

The greatest battle between Darrow and Bryan, though, remains the 1925 "Monkey Trial" of John T. Scopes, centering on the teaching of evolution. The idea of evolution was not new; Voltaire's collaborator Denis Diderot was imprisoned for writing about it in the middle of the eighteenth century. But it was British naturalist Charles Darwin who fleshed out the idea of natural selection as the mechanism for evolution and assembled the evidence for it in a systematic way, which he did in his *On the Origin of Species* in 1859.[22]

Darwin's work shook religion to its core. It flatly contradicted the creation stories in Genesis, thereby undermining the credibility of the Bible itself. It also undermined the "intelligent design" argument that there must be a god because the complexity of earthly life could not have happened without guidance. Darwin demonstrated that given a long enough period of time, today's life could indeed have happened without a guiding hand, one little change at a time, with the positive changes enduring and the negative changes disappearing—and had very probably done so.[23] That didn't necessarily rule out a god, but it did tend in that direction.[24] Darwin himself began adult life as a passionate Christian, and ended it as an agnostic.[25]

Many God experts resisted Darwin's theory passionately from the outset. A representative of the the American Episcopal Church wrote in the American Church Review in 1865 that "If this hypothesis be true, then is the Bible an unbearable fiction ... then have Christians for nearly two thousand years been duped by a monstrous lie. ... Darwin requires us to disbelieve the authoritative word of the Creator." Subtle Billy Sunday snarled that "I do not believe that my great-great-grandfather was a monkey with a tail wrapped around a tree. If you believe your great, great grand-daddy was a monkey, then you take your daddy and go to hell with him."[26]

Others, though, appreciated the force of the evidence, and began to seek ways to reconcile Christianity with Darwinism. Some thought God could have just set in motion the whole evolutionary process, knowing where it would lead. That was unsatisfactory to many because natural selection is an enormously wasteful and cruel process, utterly antithetical to notions like "Blessed are the meek."[27] Still, it was better than giving up altogether, especially if one avoided thinking about it too hard. By the turn of the twentieth century, religious opposition to Darwin had largely petered out in Europe, and was headed in that direction in America.[28]

But not for one man. William Jennings Bryan grew increasingly agitated as he toured the country on his campaigns and on the lecture circuit over the decline of religious faith. After failing three times to be elected president, Bryan turned more seriously to religion, and began making money publishing and delivering sermons. "My power in politics is not what it used to be," he wrote to a friend, "and, therefore, my responsibility is not so great. While my power in politics has waned, I think it has increased in religious matters." He even became one of the world's first radio evangelists, with sardonic columnist H. L. Mencken nicknaming him "the Fundamentalist Pope."[29]

Bryan called evolution "at present the only serious attack upon the fundamental fact of God and upon the great and controlling influences that rest upon belief in God." Revealingly, he wrote that "The objection to evolution, however ... is not, primarily that it is not true. ... The principal objection to evolution is that it is highly harmful to those who accept it." "The hypothesis to which the name of Darwin has been given—the hypothesis that links man to the lower forms of life and makes him a lineal descendant of the brute—is obscuring God and weakening all the virtues that rest upon the religious tie between God and man."[30]

The people who irritated Bryan the most were not his outright opponents, but the backsliders among the religious majority who sought to reconcile evolution with the Bible. "Theistic evolution may be described as an anesthetic which deadens the pain while the patient's religion is being gradually removed, or it may be likened to a way-station on the highway that leads from Christian faith to No-God-Land." He shared this aversion with Billy Sunday, who said that any minister who believes and teaches evolution is a "stinking skunk, a fraud, a hypocrite and a liar."[31] In 1923 Bryan sought to reverse the trend within his own Presbyterian denomination by running for the position of "moderator" of the national Presbyterian Assembly. He was defeated by the pro-evolution president of Wooster College by a handful of votes—with the margin of defeat provided by black delegates. He then lost again on a resolution he advanced condemning the teaching of evolution at church-sponsored colleges.[32] But as Darrow once put it, "No matter how often he was beaten, he had the same confidence that the Lord was on his side."[33]

Bryan's legislative strategy copied that of Prohibition. First, with the help of the Klan, get states to pass laws against the teaching of evolution, just as many individual states had gone dry before the passage of the Eighteenth Amendment. Then, push for an amendment to the federal constitution. Oklahoma was the first success; the governor told Bryan that "But for the influence of the KKK, I doubt if it could have carried in either House." Bryan then personally appeared before the legislature in Kentucky, where the bill was defeated by a single vote. In March 1925, Tennessee became the first state to enact a criminal penalty for teaching evolution by an overwhelming majority in both houses of the legislature.[34]

The Scopes Trial

The American Civil Liberties Union (ACLU), then only five years old, sought a test case to challenge these laws in court. It fell to the tiny town of Dayton, Tennessee, to produce a young biology teacher—John Scopes—willing to flout the new law and endure the trauma of a trial. Local politicians were anxious to put their town on the map as well; Judge John Raulston even violated procedure by convening a special grand jury to indict Scopes before another town could beat Dayton to the punch, despite the fact that a regular grand jury was scheduled to be called a short time later.[35]

Bryan immediately volunteered his services to the prosecution, even though he had little experience as a litigator. "The contest between evolution and Christianity is a duel to the death," Bryan said. "If evolution wins in Dayton, Christianity goes—not suddenly of course, but gradually—for the two cannot stand together. … In an open fight the truth will triumph."[36]

The prospect of an "open fight" enticed Darrow, a confirmed agnostic, to volunteer for the defense. As Darrow put it, "Scopes isn't on trial; civilization is on trial. The prosecution is opening the doors for a reign of bigotry equal to anything in the Middle Ages. No man's belief will be safe if they win." Later he wrote that "Scopes was trying to do for Dayton, Tennessee, what Socrates did for Athens."[37] It's too bad there was no Darrow around in 399 BCE.

Zealots of every stripe descended on Dayton, as did hundreds of representatives of the national and international press. There was no question that Scopes had taught his students Darwinian evolution— he proudly admitted it. Indeed, the ACLU felt the real battle would be fought in the state or federal Supreme Court. But Darrow had a couple of tricks up his sleeve. First, he thought he could exploit an inconsistency in the wording of the statute, which prohibited teaching "any theory that denies the story of the Divine Creation of man as taught in the Bible, and to teach instead that man has descended from a lower order of animals." The first part of the sentence, at least, made it a crime to teach against the Bible—but many theologians, disagreeing with Bryan, found no necessary contradiction between evolution and the text of Genesis. Darrow lined up theologian expert witnesses to testify to that point.[38] Depending on how you interpret "and," that might have sufficed.[39]

More importantly, Darrow was a master at appealing to the sense and humanity of jurors, beyond the narrow strictures of the statutory language. "I never liked technicalities," he wrote. "I believe that few cases are ever won that way; I preferred to take the outstanding facts and do the best I could with what was obvious to all."[40] The Tennessee Constitution said that "Knowledge, learning, and virtue being essential to the preservation of Republican institutions ... it shall be the duty of the general assembly in all future periods of this Government to cherish literature and science." All Darrow had to do was to persuade even a few of these jurors—who knew nothing about evolution other than that the God experts said it was wrong—that evolution in fact made sense, and that the ambiguous statute should be interpreted consistently with the pro-science stance of the Tennessee Constitution. Thus, he assembled in Dayton a collection of some of the most distinguished scientists in the country, and worked on the best way to present their story in a manner that would impress the uneducated but not unintelligent members of the jury.[41]

This is not as farfetched as it sounds. Natural selection is not really a difficult concept to grasp, especially for farmers who work with nature every day. There were occasions in the trial when Mencken and others sensed that the defense was scoring points with the audience; in a fair fight, Darrow might well have pulled off an upset. One fellow who wanted to hear Darrow's expert witnesses was Rep. John Washington Butler, the state legislator who had sponsored the anti-evolution law. "The Judge ought to give 'em a chance to tell what evolution is," Butler said. "Course we got 'em licked anyhow, but I believe in being fair and square and American. Besides, I'd like to know what evolution is myself."[42]

The argument about whether to allow the experts to testify provided Bryan his one opportunity to speak at length during the trial. He spent his time addressing "my friends" in the audience rather than the judge, ridiculed the education of the scientific experts, and linked belief in evolution to anarchy and German atrocities in World War I. It was left to Bryan's co-counsel to put matters succinctly: "That which strikes at the very foundations of Christianity is not entitled to a chance."[43]

An "open fight" over the truth of evolution was the last thing on Judge Raulston's mind, though. Over defense objections, he insisted on starting every court session with a prayer, and for a time allowed the trial to proceed under a giant banner that said "Read your Bible daily." Those were side issues; far more important was Raulston's flat refusal to allow the jury to hear any of the expert witnesses Darrow had so carefully assembled, thus erasing his entire case. In Raulston's view, if Scopes had taught that evolution was true, he had broken the law, and none of the witnesses could change that.[44] There was really no point to having a trial at all, other than to let Raulston himself bask in Bryan's glow and advertise himself as the judge who stood up for the Bible.

For the first time in his illustrious court career, Darrow lost his cool, reacting bitterly to the judge's ruling. When Raulston said "I hope you don't think the court is trying to be unfair," Darrow shot back "Why, Your Honor has the right to hope." He was immediately cited for contempt, and would have served time in the Dayton jail had he not offered a groveling apology when court reconvened.[45]

That appeared to be the end of the drama, but Darrow tried one last desperate tactic in an effort to exploit a chink in the prosecution's armor: Bryan's love affair with the sound of his own voice. The defense called Bryan himself to the stand as a witness, purportedly to testify as to what the Bible said about evolution. There were many reasons why admitting Bryan as a witness was absurd, not least of which that he was prosecuting the case. But Bryan quickly waived all objections of his co-counsel: "I am simply trying to protect the word of God against the greatest atheist or agnostic in the United States. I want the papers to know I am not afraid to get on the stand in front of him and let him do his worst. I want the world to know."[46] The judge, as always, did whatever Bryan asked.

The *New York Times* called the next two hours "the most amazing court scene in Anglo-Saxon history." Darrow proceeded to dismember Bryan—gently at first, then stridently, with both old men shouting and shaking their fists at one another. Most importantly, Darrow swung the crowd (and the press) over to his side.[47] As Darrow walked

Bryan through the most ludicrous parts of the Old Testament, such as Jonah being swallowed by the great fish and Joshua making the sun stand still in the sky, the crowd hooted at every Bryan stammer and squirm.[48] Finally Darrow reached the tale of Adam and Eve, where God condemned the serpent to crawl on his belly as punishment:[49]

> DARROW: Do you think that is why the serpent is compelled to crawl upon his belly?
>
> BRYAN: I believe that.
>
> DARROW: Have you any idea how the snake went before that time?
>
> BRYAN: No, sir.
>
> DARROW: Do you know whether he walked on his tail or not?
>
> BRYAN: No, sir. I have no way to know. (Laughter)[50]

That was enough for Judge Raulston, who had no intention of letting the trial that was to propel him to stardom veer in unplanned directions. He banged his gavel and declared a recess; when court reconvened, he refused to allow Bryan back on the stand. Having been denied the opportunity to present its case, the defense then waived its closing argument—a nasty trick because it meant the prosecution would be denied the opportunity to make a closing argument as well, and Bryan had spent his entire time in Dayton working up a three-hour masterpiece which he was now unable to deliver.[51]

The jury, which had been excluded from nearly the entire trial, duly found Scopes guilty, and he was fined $100. Darrow led the appeal at the Tennessee Supreme Court, which reversed the verdict because of a technical error in the way the fine was imposed—thus neatly cutting off any possible appeal to the national Supreme Court.[52] Not until four decades later did a ban on teaching evolution reach that court, which found such a law in Arkansas to be unconstitutional.[53]

So who won? On balance, the answer would have to be that Darrow won. Aside from the mundane fact that his client never had to pay his $100 fine, Darrow's performance tarnished the reputation of the anti-evolution forces and ruined their campaign to spread Tennessee-like laws to enough states to presage a national constitutional amendment. Just a few weeks after the trial ended, the legislature of Georgia, for example, defeated such a bill, and only two more states (Mississippi and Arkansas) ultimately enacted one.[54] Judge Raulston was defeated when he ran for re-election; he was beaten again when he tried to run for governor. The county superintendent of schools also ran for statewide office on the slogan of "Prosecutor of John Scopes," but was defeated as well.[55]

Mencken wrote that "Few Americans have ever done so much for their country in a whole lifetime as Darrow did in two hours. ... When he confronted Bryan at last, the whole combat came to its climax. On the one side was bigotry, ignorance, hatred, superstition, every sort of blackness that the human mind is capable of. On the other side was sense. And sense achieved a great victory."[56]

Bryan's impact should not be underestimated, though. He died a few days after the trial ended—not from mortification, but from complications of diabetes. His son attempted to carry on his work through his presidency of the "Anti-Evolution League," but he had none of his father's commanding presence.[57] But many textbook publishers and local school boards were sufficiently terrified of a fundamentalist backlash that they removed all references to evolution from their student materials, thus crippling biology education in America for decades.[58]

Had Bryan never taken up the fundamentalist cause, it is highly likely that belief in evolution among average Americans would be far greater than it is today. Among western nations, America ranks only above Turkey in acceptance of evolution at 40 percent; in Denmark, Sweden, and France the figure is above 80 percent.[59] Bryan appears to have also been right about the direct linkage between acceptance of evolution and abandonment of religion; by most measures, America remains far more religious than most of the countries of Western Europe.[60] Darrow's victory was of too slender a margin.

What would you think of a politician today who held up William Jennings Bryan as the paragon of how politics and religion ought to be intertwined? (Hint: you may want to look at Chapter 20 before answering.) Share your thoughts on this and the other questions you'll find at **dgc.humanistpress.com**!

Notes:

1 Kazin, *Godly,* 61, 70; Levine, *Defender,* 120.

2 Darrow, *Story,* 58; Weinberg, *Attorney,* xix; Harrison, *Darrow,* 59, 69, 71.

3 Darrow, *Story,* 91; Stone, *Darrow,* 100.

4 Stone, *Darrow,* 56; Harrison, *Darrow,* 237-238; Darrow, *Story,* 425.

5 Levine, *Defender,* 257; Kazin, *Godly,* 114, 122, 161-162, 227, 278.

6 MacLean, *Mask,* 8, 9; Jackson, *Klan,* 3-6, 31, 156, 207, 228; Pegram, *Battling,* 170.

7 Kazin, *Godly,* 284; Levine, *Defender,* 312-313.

8 Stone, *Darrow,* 69, 424; Harrison, *Darrow,* 71, 82; Time Magazine, "Negroes."

9 Jackson, *Klan,* 140; Darrow, *Story,* 304; Harrison, *Darrow,* 331, 337.

10 Harrison, *Darrow,* 332, 339; Darrow, *Story,* 308.

11 Harrison, *Darrow,* 340-346; Darrow, *Story,* 311.

12 Harding, *Magnificence,* 74-75; Hohner, *Prohibition,* 108-109; Darrow, *Prohibition Mania,* 157-158; Pegram, *Battling,* 120; Hintz, *Farewell,* 27.

13 Bruns, *Billy Sunday,* 161-163, 167.

14 Bruns, *Billy Sunday,* 175.

15 Kazin, *Godly,* 26, 172-173; Levine, *Defender,* 108-109.

16 Hohner, *Prohibition,* 108; Levine, *Defender,* 111, 118-119, 121, 124; Kazin, *Godly,* 256-257.

17 Hintz, *Farewell,* 31; Pegram, *Battling,* 149; Levine, *Defender,* 128.

18 Levine, *Defender,* 170; Bruns, *Billy Sunday,* 269, 291; Jackson, *Klan,* 96, 187; MacLean, *Mask,* 139; Pegram, *Battling,* 159-160, 170.

19 Harrison, *Darrow,* 284; Darrow, *Story,* 295; Darrow, *Prohibition,* 138.

20 Harrison, *Darrow,* 285.

21 Hintz, *Farewell,* 81.

22 Moore, "Charles Darwin," 213; Conkin, *Gods Trembled,* 20; Dennett, *Darwin's,* 18, 33.

23 Conkin, *Gods Trembled,* 40, 45, 59; Dennett, *Darwin's,* 18, 28, 42;

Brooke, "Natural Theology," 171.

24 Conkin, *Gods Trembled*, 40.

25 Moore, "Charles Darwin," 214; Brooke, "Darwin," 197, 201, 204; Bryan, *Menace*, 44.

26 White, "New Chapters," 146; Bruns, *Billy Sunday*, 126.

27 Conkin, *Gods Trembled*, 45; Bowler, "Evolution," 224; Brooke, "Darwin," 199; Ruse, "Belief," 376.

28 Conkin, *Gods Trembled*, 31, 49; Harrison, *Darrow*, 298.

29 Levine, *Defender*, 237, 272, 295; Kazin, *Godly*, 263, 272; Conkin, *Gods Trembled*, 50.

30 Bryan, *Menace*, 4, 17; Levine, *Defender*, 281.

31 Conkin, *Gods Trembled*, 45; Kazin, *Godly*, 276; Bryan, *Menace*, 5; Bruns, *Billy Sunday*, 128.

32 Conkin, *Gods Trembled*, 67; Kazin, *Godly*, 277, 279; Levine, *Defender*, 283-284.

33 Darrow, *Story*, 94.

34 Jackson, *Klan*, 60; Kazin, *Godly*, 280; Conkin, *Gods Trembled*, 76-81; Levine, *Defender*, 278, 326; Stone, *Darrow*, 427, 433.

35 Darrow, *Story*, 254; Conkin, *Gods Trembled*, 83; Levine, *Defender*, 328.

36 Conkin, *Gods Trembled*, 84; Levine, *Defender*, 330, 339.

37 Hecht, *Doubt*, 445; Darrow, "Agnostic," 51; Conkin, *Gods Trembled*, 84; Levine, *Defender*, 330; Stone, *Darrow*, 426, 437; Darrow, *Story*, 261.

38 Conkin, *Gods Trembled*, 84; Harrison, *Darrow*, 301.

39 Weinberg, *Attorney*, 174; Stone, *Darrow*, 438; Conkin, *Gods Trembled*, 80, 85; Harrison, *Darrow*, 301.

40 Darrow, *Story*, 427.

41 Harrison, *Darrow*, 304; Stone, *Darrow*, 439, 446; Conkin, *Gods Trembled*, 85.

42 Mencken, "Law," 194; Mencken, "Malone," 198; Mencken, "Bryan," 209; Levine, *Defender*, 325; Stone, *Darrow*, 454; Conkin, *Gods Trembled*, 86, 88.

43 Conkin, *Gods Trembled*, 91, 100; Levine, *Defender*, 344; Mencken, "Malone," 199, 201.

44 Weinberg, *Attorney*, 188; Conkin, *Gods Trembled*, 89; Harrison, *Darrow*, 304, 310, 312, 325.

45 Stone, *Darrow*, 448; Harrison, *Darrow*, 310-311.

46 Conkin, *Gods Trembled*, 95; Weinberg, *Attorney*, 200, 218.

47 Stone, *Darrow*, 457; Conkin, *Gods Trembled*, 95-97; Harrison, *Darrow*, 321; Levine, *Defender*, 348; Darrow, *Story*, 267.

48 Kazin, *Godly*, 294; Levine, *Defender*, 349.

49 Genesis 3:13-15.

50 Weinberg, *Attorney*, 227; Linder, "Scopes trial."

51 Conkin, *Gods Trembled*, 97; Weinberg, *Attorney*, 228; Larson, *Scopes*, 293; Levine, *Defender*, 347, 351; Darrow, *Story*, 260.

52 Conkin, *Gods Trembled*, 97; Jacoby, *Freethinkers*, 208.

53 Conkin, *Gods Trembled*, 98.

54 Levine, *Defender*, 353; Conkin, *Gods Trembled*, 107; Numbers, "Creationism," 280; Mencken, "Round Two," 212.

55 Darrow, *Story*, 271.

56 Mencken, "Aftermath," 218.

57 Numbers, "Creationism," 280; Conkin, *Gods Trembled*, 107; Stone, *Darrow*, 464; Levine, *Defender*, 331.

58 Jacoby, *Freethinkers*, 250-251; Numbers, "Creationism," 283.

59 Ker, "U.S. Lags."

60 Smith, "Beliefs."

President Manuel Azaña

CHAPTER 16

AZAÑA VS. MUSSOLINI

Two Apostates

Manuel Azaña and Benito Mussolini were born to Catholic families in heavily Catholic territories, three years apart. Both became writers who moved into politics; both rejected the church as young adults. Within a few years, though, they led nations at war with one another, largely over the role of the Catholic religion.

Azaña was born just outside of Madrid in 1880, and after losing his parents at an early age was sent to be educated by the monks of the Escorial. He hated it. As an adult, he wrote a book called *The Garden of the Monks*, condemning the anti-intellectual discipline he experienced there. "I have dreamed of destroying all this world," he wrote. He studied in Paris during the time of the Dreyfus affair and the separation of church and state, and translated works of Voltaire into Spanish. He mocked the church's obsession with relics in a short story about El Cid, in which bones thought to be El Cid's are examined by a doctor and determined to be those of a horse; the archbishop, unconvinced, insists instead that El Cid must have been a giant.[1]

Azaña didn't hate Catholics—he married one, and each respected the other's views throughout their years together. But as his writing turned more toward politics, he found religion contrary to the necessary virtues of a responsible citizenry in a republic: "Pure faith is unsociable; it is not useful in the republic, whose sovereignty it neither strengthens nor defends." Catholicism, in which people owe a loyalty to the pope superseding what they owe the state, was for Azaña especially problematic.[2]

Benito Mussolini's mother insisted that he be sent to a Catholic boarding school run by Salesian monks, away from the influence of his irreligious father. Nonetheless, he spent enough time in his father's blacksmith shop to pick up a disdain for religion that lasted well into adulthood. Like Azaña, Mussolini began his career as a writer before turning to politics. In 1908 he dismissed priests as "black microbes who are as fatal to mankind as tuberculosis germs," and he wrote a lurid novel called *The Cardinal's Mistress*. "When will the day of vengeance come" he asked, "when the people free themselves from tyranny and from religion, that 'immoral disease of the mind'?"[3]

In 1910 Mussolini introduced a resolution urging members of his party to "avoid religious marriage and the baptism of their children." In 1920, he railed against what he called the "rival Vaticans" of Moscow and Rome. "We are the heretics of both religions. We have torn to pieces all the revealed truths, we have spat upon all the dogmas, rejected all the paradises, scoffed at all the charlatans—red, white and black—who market miraculous drugs to give happiness to mankind."[4]

Azaña's Spain was dominated by the Catholic Church for centuries, as exemplified by the Inquisition established in the fifteenth century. Though the Inquisition's original purpose was to crack down on Spain's Jews, it proved ideally suited for crushing the outbreak of the Protestant Reformation as well. Hundreds of thousands passed through its torture chambers; as a result, the destruction of the overwhelming political power of the Catholic Church that occurred in places like England and Germany never happened in Spain.[5]

This left Spain so out of step with the rest of Europe—and so economically backwards—that it ultimately lost the last of its colonies to America in 1898. By 1931, the jig was up; the king decided to abdicate, and Spain belatedly joined its neighbors in allowing the people to decide how they wished to be governed.[6]

The people's choice, at the first elections in 1931, was to end the tyranny of the Catholic Church. A coalition led by Manuel Azaña's party swept to power, committed to ending taxpayer subsidies for the church and breaking the church's stranglehold on education. Azaña became prime minister, and one of the principal drafters of a constitution for the new republic.[7]

Though the church controlled as much as a third of the country's capital wealth, two-thirds of Spaniards rarely attended Mass.[8] The constitution Azaña helped produce pointedly refused to recognize Catholicism as the official religion of the state. On the contrary, it infuriated the church through its explicit toleration of all varieties of religious belief. Control over marriage, cemeteries, and education was transferred from the church to the civil government, payments to priests were suspended, and church doctrine was further violated by allowing women full rights of citizenship, including the right to divorce. The Jesuits were dissolved once more. As Azaña said on the floor of the Cortes: "Spain has ceased to be Catholic."[9]

Only five years earlier, the church had been strong enough to induce the government to imprison a woman for saying that the Virgin Mary bore other children after Jesus.[10] Those days were over—at least for a while.

Mussolini and the Lateran Treaty

Meanwhile, in equally Catholic Italy, Mussolini disdained the democratic path to power. Using the excuse of anarchic conditions which its own thugs did much to create, Mussolini's Fascist Party led a "March on Rome" in 1922 that frightened the king into dissolving the government and putting Mussolini in charge. Despite Mussolini's anti-clerical writings, his coup was quietly backed by the Catholic Church, which bet that Fascism's drive for lockstep unity as the ultimate goal of social organization would result in the church being invited in rather than squeezed out. The church abandoned its prior strategy of relying on Catholic political parties to advance its aims in favor of alliance with those who would crush secularism by force; thus it persuaded Italy's Catholic political party to disband rather than to oppose Mussolini.[11]

The church guessed right. One of Mussolini's first acts was to re-install crucifixes in classrooms and courtrooms, and to make religious teaching in the schools compulsory. In 1926, secret negotiations commenced over a series of agreements that ultimately included a "treaty" in which Italy recognized the 109-acre Vatican City as an independent country, a concordat establishing Catholicism as Italy's official religion and granting the church enormous power, and a financial "settlement" in which the taxpayers of Italy forked over millions of lire—equivalent to well over $1 billion in today's money—to compensate for Pope Pius XI's anguish over his predecessor's loss of church-controlled lands when Italy had united as a nation in 1870.[12]

Mussolini viewed it as simply paying extortion so that the church would support his Fascist unity; only by pacifying all dissent at home could he move forward with his dream to re-create a Roman Empire. Like Talleyrand, Mussolini concluded that co-opting the church was easier than confronting it.[13]

Not that the church minded being bought. Pius XI gloated that "We have given back God to Italy, and Italy to God." According to a shrewd German observer named Adolf Hitler, "The fact that the Curia is now making its peace with Fascism shows that the Vatican trusts the new political realities far more than it did the former liberal democracy, with which it could not come to terms." The French press gloomily agreed with Hitler's assessment, warning that the agreements represented "the alliance of the two Romes against the France of 1789."[14]

The treaties put Catholic indoctrination back into the public schools, recognizing the right of the Catholic bishops to remove any government-paid teacher of religion at will. Priests who committed crimes could be punished only by the church, not by the state. Church control over marriage replaced the regime of civil marriage that had been in force since 1860. Criticism of the Catholic Church was made a penal offense.[15]

Mussolini also used tax money to pay for the salaries of the clergy and the repair of church buildings. When you pay for something, of course, you own it; the treaty made it clear that the church could not appoint a bishop without Mussolini's advance approval. "In the Italian state," he bragged, "the church is not sovereign; it is not even free."[16]

Dictatorship works best when the public reveres the dictator. In Italy and around the world, the Catholic Church did everything it could to promote that reverence. The pope called Mussolini "the man sent by Providence," and the cardinal of Milan referred to him as "the new Constantine." Cardinal O'Connell of Boston, who received a high Fascist decoration, exalted him as "a genius in the field of government, given to Italy by God."[17] Catholic newspapers filled their pages with official propaganda against democracy and praise for the Italian warlike spirit, reminding the faithful that Jesus himself had said "Think not that I am come to send peace on earth: I came not to send peace, but a sword." Fascism permeated Italian religious life down to the smallest detail: the protocol of Catholic processions was modified to match that of Fascist parades, and Catholic publications displayed the year of the regime alongside that of the Christian era. Mussolini returned the adulation, declaring in 1931 that "I wish to see religion everywhere in the country. Let us teach the children their catechism … however young they may be."[18]

The reason why Mussolini was so insistent on totalitarian unity at home was to strengthen Italy's hand abroad. His first major foreign adventure was the invasion of Ethiopia in 1935. The church could barely contain its enthusiasm; the cardinal of Milan crowed that "The Italian flag is at the moment bringing in triumph the cross of Christ in Ethiopia, to free the road for the emancipation of the slaves, opening it at the same time to our missionary propaganda." The Archbishop of Torano intoned that "The war against Ethiopia should be considered as a holy war, a crusade" that would "open Ethiopia, a country of infidels and schismatics, to the expansion of the Catholic faith." On a specially proclaimed "Day of Faith" priests turned over their offertory collections to support the war.[19]

Catholic press and political parties around the world vigorously supported Mussolini's crusade, and denounced even the weak League of Nations sanctions against it. During the League's debate on sanctions, the pope insisted that "the hopes, the rights, and the needs of the Italian people should be satisfied, recognized, and guaranteed with justice and peace."[20] Church support never wavered when the Italian army started using mustard gas against the tribesmen, nor when it massacred 30,000 prisoners and civilians in retribution for a failed attempt to assassinate the military governor. The victims included 300 monks at a "schismatic" monastery of the Ethiopian Orthodox Church, considered its holiest spot; Catholic missionaries poured in to replace them, in an effort to convert the Orthodox to become loyal subjects of the pope.[21]

The world paid no heed when Ethiopia's emperor warned the League of Nations that "Today it is Ethiopia's turn, tomorrow it will be you." The war and subsequent repression ultimately took more than 750,000 Ethiopian lives.[22]

War in Spain

Back in Spain, the church did not take Azaña's victory lying down. Only two weeks after the 1931 parliamentary election, the Catholic primate was already condemning the triumph of "the enemies of the Kingdom of Jesus Christ." The Catholic press began trumpeting the success of the Fascists in Italy and the Nazis in Germany as models for Spain to follow.[23]

The Catholic politician Gil Robles, after returning from a Nazi rally at Nuremberg, proclaimed:

> We must reconquer Spain. ... We must give Spain a true unity, a new spirit, a totalitarian polity. ... We must found a new state, purge the fatherland of Judaizing Freemasons. ... What does it matter if we have to shed blood! ... When the time comes, either parliament submits or we will eliminate it.[24]

A coup planned by General Jose Sanjurjo, to have been signaled by the assassination of Azaña, nearly succeeded.[25]

Politics being what it is, the liberal and secularist parties that took control in 1931 squabbled among themselves once in power. In the 1933 elections they were defeated by a right-wing combine, subsidized by Mussolini, that sought to follow in his footsteps.[26] This was not at all what most Spaniards wanted. In October 1935, after being released as a political prisoner on a trumped-up charge, Azaña told the largest crowd that had ever assembled in Spain:

> All Europe today is a battlefield between democracy and its enemies, and Spain is not an exception. You must choose between democracy, with all its shortcomings, with all its faults, with all its mistakes or errors, and tyranny with all its horrors. … In Spain one hears frivolous and vain talk of dictatorship. We find it repugnant not only by doctrine, but by experience and through good sense.[27]

When the next elections were held in February 1936, the secular side reunited. Again it scored a decisive victory, despite the church's circulation of a catechism declaring it a mortal sin to vote for any candidate who supported freedom of religion, the press, or education.[28] After this defeat, the Catholic side gave up on the ballot box. Left to their own devices, Spaniards would never support continued control by God experts. Great Fascist-style rallies were held at which Gil Robles was hailed with the cry "¡Jefe! ¡Jefe!" (the Spanish equivalent of "Führer") in the hope he might start a Mussolini-style "March on Madrid" to seize power. Just as in Italy before the "March on Rome" and in Germany before the accession of Hitler, fascists and communists fought each other in the streets while committing tit-for-tat assassinations (including an attempt on Azaña), reducing the country to near anarchy.[29]

But it was not a politician who ultimately acted. It was General Francisco Franco, the recently demoted Army chief of staff, who launched a rebellion in July 1936, after failing to incite a coup immediately after the election results were tallied. Franco claimed to be fighting against Communism; in fact, Azaña had excluded all Communists and even Socialists from his government even though they had contributed to his coalition's success.[30]

Most of the army quickly joined Franco's revolt, but there was a problem. The bulk of Franco's forces were in Spanish Morocco and could not easily cross back to Spain because sailors of the Spanish navy remained loyal to the elected government. The solution was an airlift provided by Mussolini, who intervened on Franco's side from the very start, keeping a promise he had made as early as 1934. Hitler jumped in as well, with the Luftwaffe perfecting at Guernica the saturation bombing techniques, followed by the aerial machine-gunning of fleeing civilians, that were to prove so effective during World War II. Ultimately, some 100,000 Italian and German troops fought in the war, many of them conscripts.[31]

Ironically, Azaña had devoted much of his energy during his first term in office to modernizing and strengthening the army, and that new-found efficiency was now being used against him. With most of the army on his side, Franco could have swept into power quickly. But speed was not Franco's intent. He sought not a coup, but a permanent revolution, in which the forces of humanism would be crippled beyond hope of recovery.[32] As he wrote to a friendly diplomat:

> I will occupy Spain town by town, village by village, railway by railway. ... Nothing will make me abandon this gradual program. It will bring me less glory but greater internal peace. That being the case, this civil war could still last another year, two, perhaps three. Dear ambassador, I can assure you that I am not interested in territory but in inhabitants. The reconquest of the territory is the means, the redemption of the inhabitants the end. I cannot shorten the war by even one day. ... It could even be dangerous for me to reach Madrid with a stylish military operation. I will take the capital not an hour before it is necessary: first I must have the certainty of being able to found a regime.[33]

The church backed Franco's revolt with every fiber of its being, with the bishop of Salamanca likening Franco's vision to Augustine's *City of God*. The cardinal of Toledo and primate of Spain called the war a "clash of civilization with barbarism, of the inferno against Christ," and condemned the "Jews and the Freemasons who poisoned the nation's soul with absurd doctrines, Tartar and Mongol tales dressed up as a political and social system in the dark societies controlled by the Semite International." The pope himself denounced the Republic's "truly Satanic hatred of God."[34]

When the southern village of Rociana was taken by the rebels two weeks into the revolt, the parish priest made a speech from the balcony of the town hall: "You all no doubt believe that because I am a priest, I have come with words of forgiveness and repentance. Not at all. War against all of them until the last trace has been eliminated!" Over the next three months, sixty villagers were shot; not enough to satisfy the priest, though, who filed an official complaint that the repression had been too lenient.[35]

Terror

One of Franco's colleagues, General Mola, spoke of the important role terror must play in the campaign: "It is necessary to spread terror. We have to create the impression of mastery, eliminating without scruples or hesitation all those who do not think as we do. There can be no cowardice. If we vacillate one moment and fail to proceed with the greatest determination, we will not win."[36]

General Queipo de Llano spread his own brand of terror on radio broadcasts: "Our brave Legionaries … have shown the Red cowards what it means to be a man. And, incidentally, the wives of the Reds, too. These Communist and Anarchist women, after all, have made themselves fair game by their doctrine of free love. And now they have at least made the acquaintance of real men, and not milksops of militiamen. Kicking their legs about and struggling won't save them."[37]

The German and Italian forces used Spain as a test-tube for terror. That seems to have been the point of the German Condor Legion's obliteration of the town of Guernica. Shortly afterward, Mussolini's henchman Count Ciano wrote that "This is the moment to terrorize the enemy. I have given orders for the aircraft to bomb Valencia." Mussolini declared his delight that Italians "should be horrifying the world by their aggressiveness for a change, instead of charming it by a guitar."[38]

When two Basque priests made their way to the Vatican to protest the fate of Guernica, the secretary of state (soon to become Pope Pius XII) showed them the door, coldly replying that "The church is persecuted in Barcelona."[39]

As wars go, the Spanish Civil War ranks high on the barbarism scale. Atrocities were committed on both sides—lots of them.[40] But that does not mean that both sides were equally to blame.

Most national leaders throughout history, confronted by the kind of revolt Azaña faced, would have assumed dictatorial powers until the emergency had ended—even U.S. President Abraham Lincoln did so during the American Civil War.[41] Dictatorship was utterly antithetical to everything Manuel Azaña stood for though, and he never gave it a second thought. His insistence on not destroying his constitution in order to save it resulted in anarchic conditions when the bulk of the army and police force deserted, allowing uncontrollable vigilantes to do their worst.[42]

They were not encouraged or condoned by Azaña; on the contrary, he did all he could to maintain order, not only because it was the right thing to do but for the selfish reason of his quest for support from the western democracies. Every time a church was burnt or a priest was shot the hope for that support diminished. Maintaining control is not an easy task, though, when you have no army or police force. Most of the killings on the Republican side occurred early in the war, when chaos reigned. By 1938, when that control was re-established, extra-judicial violence was greatly reduced.[43]

By contrast, the Catholic rebels had a conscious policy, from the top down, of using the war to exterminate humanists from Spain. One slogan was "When you kill a Red, you will spend a year less in purgatory," and propaganda circulated that an enormous portion of the enemy population was actually Jewish.[44] After the capture of the town of Badajoz, an American journalist reported on the roundup of those who had fought to defend the city:

> At four o'clock in the morning they are turned out into the ring through the gate by which the initial parade of the bull-fight enters. There machine guns await them. After the first night the blood was supposed to be palm deep on the far side of the lane. I don't doubt it. Eighteen hundred men—there were women, too—were mowed down there in some 12 hours. There is more blood than you would think in 1,800 bodies.[45]

Aside from the authorization for the killings, there is the sheer quantity. In the town of Baena, for example, leftists killed 92 clergy and other supporters of the rebellion shortly after it broke out; when Franco's forces arrived, they killed 700 civilians in reprisal. Winners write history books, and the winning Catholics never tired of mourning the 55,000 civilians killed by government supporters during the war, including nearly 7,000 members of the clergy. Since the death of Franco in 1975, though, local historians throughout Spain have explored the previously taboo subject of the killings and torture perpetrated by the Catholic rebel armies. Their best estimates put the civilian body count in the 180,000 range, many executed for crimes such as owning a radio or reading the wrong newspaper.[46]

That's just during the war. After its end, Count Ciano reported to Mussolini in the summer of 1939 that more than 200 executions were being carried out daily in Madrid, 150 in Barcelona, and 80 in Seville. The American in charge of the Spanish bureau of the Associated Press estimated that half a million supporters of the elected government were executed by the Franco regime after the war; more recent estimates reduce the figure to a still-ghastly 150,000.[47]

Another 400,000 backers were consigned to concentration camps to perform slave labor. There Major Antonio Vallejo-Najera, head of the Army's Psychiatric Services branch, carried out experiments on women prisoners in search of the "red gene" which caused them to be so obstinate; the high command was so delighted with his scientific research they promoted him to colonel.[48]

Yet another 400,000 Franco opponents, including Manuel Azaña, were driven into exile. (General Mola had proposed that "Azaña must be caged up so that special brain specialists can study perhaps the most interesting case of mental degeneration in history.") Unfortunately for them, the most logical refuge was neighboring France. A year later the Nazis, emboldened by their success in Spain, invaded France as well. Azaña died while hiding from the Gestapo, while perhaps 10,000 of his fellow refugees died in German concentration camps.[49]

Why Azaña Lost

Why did a government that enjoyed majority support lose the war? The simple reason is that it was outgunned. Franco's rebels received massive aid from Hitler and Mussolini. But the western democracies, including America, would not even *sell* weapons to the legitimate Spanish government. France did so sporadically, but turned the spigot on and off to meet the demands of domestic politics. This was part of the western strategy of "appeasement" of Hitler and Mussolini.[50] To a larger extent, though, democracies refused to help Spain because of the political influence of the Catholic Church.[51]

Throughout the world, Catholic clergy and press rallied to Mussolini's Spanish cause. German bishops issued a pastoral letter in the first weeks of the rebellion to endorse Hitler's support for Franco. The Catholic archbishop of Westminster called the war "a furious battle between Christian civilization and the most cruel paganism that ever darkened the world." Another prominent English Catholic wrote that Franco "might not be a great man, as the world judges, but he is certainly something a thousand times more important—a supremely good man, a hero possibly; possibly a saint."[52]

In the United States, Franco's Catholic champion was Father Charles Coughlin, the powerful "Radio Priest" whose pro-Fascist broadcasts would be silenced during World War II. In 1936, though, President Franklin Roosevelt had no stomach for a fight with Father Coughlin, or any other risk to his hold on the Catholic vote. Roosevelt announced a "moral embargo" on arms sales to both sides, elevating the military rebels to the same moral plane as the democratically elected government. Enforcement was selective; the pro-Nazi President of the Texaco oil company, Thorkild Rieber, received a slap on the wrist fine for supplying the rebels with millions of dollars of oil on credit, while the Martin Aircraft Corporation was prevented from shipping planes and parts that had already been purchased by the Spanish government.[53]

Roosevelt's Secretary of the Interior Harold Ickes wrote in his diary: "He [Roosevelt] said frankly that to raise the embargo would mean the loss of every Catholic vote next fall. ... This proves up to the hilt what so many people have been saying, namely, that the Catholic minorities in Great Britain and America have been dictating the international policy with respect to Spain."[54]

Mussolini was as cynical about his Spanish involvement as he was about religion itself. The nations of Europe signed a "Non-Intervention Agreement," and created a committee to police it. Italy was not only on the committee, but had responsibility for patrolling Spain's northeastern coast. Mussolini used this authority from day one to try to keep out Soviet arms shipments, while landing his own divisions with impunity. India's Jawaharlal Nehru shook his head and called the Non-Intervention Committee "the supreme farce of our time."[55]

As the aid from Mussolini and Hitler poured in, Spain turned to Russia as the only country that would reliably sell it arms, strengthening the hands of Communists in the trade unions who took the lead in the militias fighting Franco. Azaña, a proud bourgeois who had no use for communism, was furious when he learned that Spain's gold reserves had been shipped to Russia as advance payment for arms purchases. He called Russia "the man one admits to society because it is impossible to do otherwise, but who is the friend of nobody," understanding well how demoralizing Soviet domination was for the non-Communists who were simply fighting for toleration and freedom.[56]

Azaña tried to position himself above the fray, as a national unifier who could heal wounds if only the two sides would agree to a ceasefire. He devoted most of his energy during the war years to diplomacy, rather than egging on his hastily assembled forces to fight to the death. He was convinced that if he could arrange even a temporary ceasefire under international auspices, Spaniards on both sides would be loath to renew the fighting. But Franco suspected the same and never gave a ceasefire a moment's thought. In fact, Azaña had been willing to surrender many months earlier if the rebels would agree not to conduct reprisals, but Franco flatly refused.[57]

In hindsight, Azaña's strategy seems Pollyannaish, and both sides scapegoated him for "cowardice" after the war. But if resistance could have lasted even a few weeks longer than it did, he might well have been able to pull it off. Franco's armies entered Madrid in March 1939, the same month during which Hitler broke the promise he had made at Munich and rolled his tanks into Prague. England's Neville Chamberlain abandoned appeasement at that point, and immediately announced the "line in the sand" guarantee of Poland's borders that precipitated war five months later. Had the Spanish Republic remained alive at that time, it seems quite plausible that Britain and France would have reassessed their position.[58]

Roosevelt admitted to his cabinet that the embargo had been a bad idea, telling his Spanish ambassador that "We have made a mistake; you have been right all along." But it was too late. Pope Pius XII telegraphed Franco: "Lifting up our hearts to the Lord, we give sincere thanks with Your Excellency for Spain's desired Catholic victory. We express our hope that your most beloved country, with peace attained, may undertake with new vigor the ancient Christian traditions which made her great."[59]

His hopes were more than fulfilled. Massive state subsidies to the church were reinstated, and its status was re-elevated to sixteenth century glory. Insulting or ridiculing a Catholic priest or Catholic ceremony was made a crime, as part of the penal code section outlawing sedition. Sale of contraceptives was banned, and complete church control over marriage, burial, and education reinstated. Censorship of books, magazines, and movies was strictly enforced; even the King James Bible was banned for being too Protestant.[60] Spanish troops fought alongside Italian Fascists and Nazis on the Russian front during World War II, and Franco provided bases for Nazi submarines to prey on Allied food shipments. In return, the Vatican pledged every Spanish priest to say a special prayer for General Franco every day, and Franco was given control over the appointment of bishops.[61]

Mussolini is remembered today as a pompous buffoon, a light historical sentence for a hypocrite personally responsible for seven figures worth of deaths. The greater tragedy is that Azaña is not remembered at all. Forget his personal courage, his unswerving loyalty to the vision of the tolerant society that Spain finally became after Franco's death in 1975, and his leadership of one of the few truly non-violent democratic revolutions in our planet's history. Is not the man who wrote "Liberty does not make men happy; it makes them men"[62] worth remembering for that alone?

> Mussolini's Lateran Treaty legacy is the so-called "independent nation" of Vatican City and a rogue Vatican Bank that's been a Mafia money-laundering front for decades. Some people think this is a farce that should be shut down, with the Catholic Church headquarters being made subject to the civil laws of Italy just like the Mormon Church headquarters is subject to the civil laws of the United States. What do you think? Share your thoughts on this and the other questions you'll find at **dgc.humanistpress.com**!

Notes:

1 Thomas, *Spanish*, 36; Sedwick, *Tragedy*, 5, 10, 25, 41-42.

2 Sedwick, *Tragedy*, 43.

3 Kent, *Pope*, 5; Hibbert, *Mussolini*, 5, 9; Mussolini, *Rise*, 3-7.

4 Binchy, *Church*, 392; Kent, *Pope*, 5.

5 Manhattan, *Vatican*, 84; Johnson, *Christianity*, 308; Peters, *Inquisition*, 85; MacCulloch, *The Reformation*, 298-301; Aleksandrov, *History*, 99; Kent, *Pope*, 132.

6 Holt, *Carlist*, 275; Preston, *Spanish*, 37; Kent, *Pope*, 134.

7 Holt, *Carlist*, 276; Blanshard, *Freedom*, 15; Thomas, *Spanish*, 30, 70; Sedwick, *Tragedy*, 40, 84, 76.

8 Manhattan, *Vatican*, 88; Thomas, *Spanish*, 47, 50.

9 Blanshard, *Freedom*, 18; Preston, *Spanish*, 53-54, 60, 88; Kent, *Pope*, 139-140; Thomas, *Spanish*, 73; Sedwick, *Tragedy*, 101; Manhattan, *Vatican*, 90.

10 Blanshard, *Freedom*, 62.

11 Hibbert, *Mussolini*, 29-31; Kent, *Pope*, 1; Blanshard, *Freedom*, 278; Jemolo, *Church*, 199; Johnson, *Christianity*, 281; Manhattan, *Vatican*, 77, 111-113.

12 More, *Peter's City*, 81; Jemolo, *Church*, 205; Kent, *Pope*, 7; Binchy, *Church*, 308; Cornwell, *Hitler's Pope*, 114.

13 Jemolo, *Church*, 225, 231.

14 More, *Peter's City*, 22; Cornwell, *Hitler's Pope*, 115; Kent, *Pope*, 60.

15 Blanshard, *Freedom*, 280; More, *Peter's City*, 220-236; Jemolo, *Church*, 267-268; Binchy, *Church*, 397; Manhattan, *Vatican*, 117.

16 Jemolo, *Church*, 268; Binchy, *Church*, 375, 387.

17 Jemolo, *Church*, 270; Blanshard, *Freedom*, 279; Hibbert, *Mussolini*, 76.

18 Jemolo, *Church*, 269-270; Matthew 10:34; Manhattan, *Vatican*, 119.

19 Barker, *Civilizing*, 60; Binchy, *Church*, 313, 702; Cornwell, *Hitler's Pope*, 175; Manhattan, *Vatican*, 123-124; Jemolo, *Church*, 260.

20 Barker, *Civilizing*, 198; Jemolo, *Church*, 260; Manhattan, *Vatican*, 18, 122, 124.

21 Barker, *Civilizing*, 60, 221; Lentakis, *Ethiopia*, 61-62, 64, 68, 78.

22 Lentakis, *Ethiopia*, 52; Barker, *Civilizing*, 275, 293.

23 Kent, *Pope*, 135; Blanshard, *Freedom*, 16; Preston, *Spanish*, 49.

24 Thomas, *Spanish*, 104; Preston, *Spanish*, 64.

25 Sedwick, *Tragedy*, 115; Preston, *Spanish*, 60.

26 Thomas, *Spanish*, 102; Kent, *Pope*, 142; Blanshard, *Freedom*, 19; Preston, *Spanish*, 44-45; Holt, *Carlist*, 280.

27 Sedwick, *Tragedy*, 151; Thomas, *Spanish*, 139, 142.

28 Thomas, *Spanish*, 145, 148; Kent, *Pope*, 144; Preston, *Spanish*, 81-83; Sedwick, *Tragedy*, 144, 153, 195.

29 Preston, *Spanish*, 70, 89; Manhattan, *Vatican*, 92-94; Thomas, *Spanish*, 104, 153, 163, 198.

30 Thomas, *Spanish*, 151, 204; Preston, *Spanish*, 94; Sedwick, *Tragedy*, 153.

31 Thomas, *Spanish*, 123, 342, 580, 609; Preston, *Spanish*, 117, 119, 154, 172, 193, 267, 270.

32 Sedwick, *Tragedy*, 80, 105; Thomas, *Spanish*, 499; Preston, *Spanish*, 47-48, 208.

33 Preston, *Spanish*, 274.

34 Preston, *Spanish*, 220-221; Thomas, *Spanish*, 386.

35 Preston, *Spanish*, 109.

36 Thomas, *Spanish*, 249; Preston, *Spanish*, 103.

37 Preston, *Spanish*, 206.

38 Thomas, *Spanish*, 609, 701, 785, 809.

39 Thomas, *Spanish*, 610.

40 Sedwick, *Tragedy*, 145, 161; Preston, *Spanish*, 184, 194.

41 Lincoln Institute, "Lincoln and Maryland."

42 Sedwick, *Tragedy*, 92; Preston, *Spanish*, 230, 232.

43 Preston, *Spanish*, 161; Sedwick, *Tragedy*, 171; Thomas, *Spanish*, 217, 257, 265, 268, 424, 521, 758.

44 Preston, *Spanish*, 125; Thomas, *Spanish*, 704, 736, 740.

45 Preston, *Spanish*, 121.

46 Blanshard, *Freedom*, 20; Thomas, *Spanish*, 246, 259; Preston, *Spanish*, 124, 202, 232, 301, 303.

47 Preston, *Spanish*, 320; Blanshard, *Freedom*, 21; Thomas, *Spanish*, 899.
48 Preston, *Spanish*, 309-310.
49 Preston, *Spanish*, 295, 320; Sedwick, *Tragedy*, 211, 234; Thomas, *Spanish*, 272, 923.
50 Preston, *Spanish*, 125, 157, 290; Thomas, *Spanish*, 375, 783, 803; Sedwick, *Tragedy*, 188, 196, 224.
51 Blanshard, *Freedom*, 20, 284.
52 Manhattan, *Vatican*, 98; Sedwick, *Tragedy*, 224; Preston, *Spanish*, 222; Blanshard, *Freedom*, 284; Thomas, *Spanish*, 349, 675, 677.
53 Thomas, *Spanish*, 210, 404, 559, 677, 916; Preston, *Spanish*, 139, 145, 222, 287; Manhattan, *Vatican*, 96.
54 Blanshard, *Freedom*, 179.
55 Preston, *Spanish*, 158-159; Thomas, *Spanish*, 717.
56 Preston, *Spanish*, 134, 150, 166; Sedwick, *Tragedy*, 57, 155, 176; Thomas, *Spanish*, 435, 688, 703, 795.
57 Preston, *Spanish*, 161; Sedwick, *Tragedy*, 181, 203; Thomas, *Spanish*, 169, 662, 749, 765, 800, 809, 823, 870, 910.
58 Hibbert, *Mussolini*, 101; Sedwick, *Tragedy*, 185, 216; Thomas, *Spanish*, 870, 887.
59 Preston, *Spanish*, 145; Thomas, *Spanish*, 853, 894; Blanshard, *Freedom*, 21.
60 Crandall, *Gender*, 147; Blanshard, *Freedom*, 34-39, 87, 96, 107, 113, 135, 144.
61 Chadwick, *Christian Church*, 187; Thomas, *Spanish*, 922; Manhattan, *Vatican*, 103; Preston, *Spanish*, 316; Blanshard, *Freedom*, 30-33.
62 Sedwick, *Tragedy*, 58.

Jawaharlal Nehru

CHAPTER 17

NEHRU VS. GANDHI

Gandhi

Most of the conflicts in this book are between people who loathed one another, such as Darrow and Bryan. Not so with Jawaharlal Nehru and Mohandas Gandhi. Not only did they struggle together for a common goal, but they had a deep bond of affection, likened by many to a father-son relationship.[1] Yet they differed profoundly on the role of religion. Gandhi's insistence, over Nehru's objections, on casting the Indian independence movement in religious terms led to one of the greatest tragedies in all of Indian history, with consequences still reverberating.

Mohandas Gandhi was born in 1869. He earned a law degree in England, but when he returned to India to practice law he was a dismal failure. Desperate for money, he took a job in South Africa, where he wound up involved in the political struggles of Indian expatriates. When normal methods of political persuasion failed, he turned to tactics of nonviolent resistance, with moderate success.[2]

Gandhi did not invent the idea of nonviolent resistance. In fact within India, the Sikh Ram Singh had pioneered the nonviolent resistance technique decades earlier. But Gandhi's model was none other than Socrates, who refused both to fight and to cooperate with a system he viewed as unjust. In 1908, Gandhi told the story of Socrates in *The Story of a Soldier of Truth*, telling readers that "We must learn to live and die like Socrates."[3]

In 1915, Gandhi returned to a hero's welcome in India. He was so taken with his own success that he viewed nonviolent resistance as not just a useful tactic but as a divine essence. The Hindi word he used to describe it was *satyagraha*, which translates roughly as "truth force." Gandhi began casting about for ways to apply *satyagraha* to Indian conditions, for example helping indigo farmers get better wages. He did not initially advocate independence from England, and in 1918 toured India on behalf of the British government, recruiting troops to serve in World War I.[4]

Opinions hardened in 1919, after a British general responded to a peaceful protest by opening fire, killing 379 and wounding 1,200 in an enclosed plaza from which there was no escape. Gandhi scorned the victims for attempting to flee, which marked them as mediocre *satyagrahis*. Yet he rode the wave of indignation to unofficial leadership of the pro-Independence Congress Party since even his limited record of success was better than the track record compiled by Indian politicians over the years, whose speeches and petitions fell on deaf British ears. In September 1920, Gandhi electrified India with a simple promise: a *satyagraha* campaign of a single year would produce independence.[5]

Nehru

One of Gandhi's most important lieutenants in the 1920 campaign was 31-year-old Jawaharlal Nehru, son of Motilal Nehru, India's most prominent lawyer. Coming from a Hindu family in largely Muslim Kashmir, Motilal disdained all religion, and brought up Jawaharlal to share that view:[6]

> The spectacle of what is called religion, or at any rate organized religion, in India and elsewhere has filled me with horror, and I have frequently condemned it and wished to make a clean sweep of it. Almost always it seems to stand for blind belief and reaction, dogma and bigotry, superstition and exploitation, and the preservation of vested interests.[7]

Over his father's objections, Nehru latched onto Gandhi's nonviolence for the hardheaded reason that it promised success: "This was the politics of action, not of talk." Motilal could not imagine anyone in his prestigious family being sent to jail; but in a touching case of father being influenced by son, he ultimately came around, giving up his own home and luxuries to spend years in British prisons.[8]

The Nehrus, and millions of others, were also moved by Gandhi's undoubted courage and his self-deprecating personal charm. Once he was asked by reporters whether he was appropriately dressed when he turned up at a royal reception wearing only a loincloth and shawl; Gandhi replied that His Majesty was wearing enough for both of them.[9]

The 1921 campaign was micromanaged by Gandhi. Only specific forms of disobedience were authorized: boycotts of elections, schools, and law courts. Still, the novelty and promise of success swept the nation, catching the British off-guard. The entire British presence in India consisted of a few thousand soldiers and bureaucrats, who well understood that they could not govern a nation of 300 million who did not consent to be governed.[10]

This is exactly what began to happen in 1921. As the campaign gathered momentum, the scope of non-cooperation widened, and Gandhi's collaborators were arrested for inciting Muslim soldiers to sedition. Gandhi himself raised the rhetoric level: "It is sinful for anyone, either as soldier or civilian, to serve this Government, which has proved treacherous." English-made clothing was burned, to the dismay of those who thought India's poor could use some of those clothes.[11] Bureaucrats wrung their hands over whether to arrest Gandhi or not; one official wrote that "He is not a mere politician in the eyes of the masses. He has all the sanctity of a holy man attached to him, and therein lies, to my mind, the secret of his hold and also the danger of it." India's masses viewed Gandhi as a religious messiah: the Governor of Bengal was told "that it is being widely stated in the villages that 'Gandhi Raj' has come and that there is no longer any necessity to pay anything to anybody. They are consequently not only refusing to pay rent and taxes but are repudiating their debts." The viceroy cabled home that "Religious and racial feeling at the same time is so bitter that the Government of India are prepared for disorder of a more formidable nature than has in the past occurred, and do not seek to minimise in any way the fact that great anxiety is caused by the situation." Britain had already granted substantial self-governance not only to South Africa, Australia, and Canada, but even to southern Ireland, a few miles off its shores; there seemed little doubt that India would be next.[12]

Then came a *deus ex machina* that would have embarrassed any writer of fiction: in February 1922, Gandhi simply changed his mind and called the whole thing off.[13]

The reason he cited was that in the remote village of Chauri Chaura, civil disobedience got out of hand: a crowd killed 22 policemen who had opened fire on them, thus violating Gandhi's *satyagraha* ground rules.[14] In fact, what drove Gandhi all along was religion, not politics. He saw politics not as a means for bettering people's lives, but as a tool to bring their souls more in line with his own view of the divine will. "My bent is not political but religious and I take part in politics because I feel that there is no department of life which can be divorced from religion and because politics touch the vital being of India almost at every point."[15] It simply didn't matter enough to Gandhi that independence was in his grasp, and he tossed it away. Nor did it matter enough that thousands who had dutifully followed his orders—including both Nehrus—were languishing in British prisons, their lives and families utterly disrupted. Their sacrifice was now in vain, thanks to Gandhi's whim. A relieved governor of Bombay wrote that "He gave us a scare. Gandhi's was the most colossal experiment in world history, and it came within an inch of succeeding."[16]

Nehru was dumbfounded. "What troubled us even more," he wrote, "were the reasons given for this suspension and the consequences that seemed to flow from them. ... If it was the inevitable result of a sporadic act of violence, then surely there was something lacking in the philosophy and technique of a non-violent struggle. ... Must we train the three hundred and odd millions of India in the theory and practice of non-violent action before we could go forward?" But with the messiah of the movement demanding its abandonment, there was no practical way to carry on without him.[17] Nehru ultimately spent over nine years of his life in British prisons carrying out Gandhi's ideas, at one point contracting typhoid—far more time than Gandhi himself spent. "I did a lot of reading and writing," he dryly observed.[18]

Gandhi's Muslim allies were furious as well, believing that Gandhi's refusal to consult with them first betrayed his true motives, and accusing him of a plan for "making 70 million of Indian Muslims dependent on the Hindu Mahasabha." This sparked tremendous Hindu-Muslim antagonism; in the 22 years after 1900 there had been 16 religious riots throughout India; in the 3 years after 1923, there were 72.[19]

Descent into darkness

For the next several years, Gandhi carried on his true passion, the perfection of souls, while India continued to chafe under foreign rule. One cause he championed was celibacy, including between married couples. Gandhi hated sex, period.[20] Though he sired five children, he warned his followers:

> Take it from me that there is no happiness in marriage. ... I cannot imagine a thing as ugly as the intercourse of man and woman. That it leads to the birth of children is due to God's inscrutable way. ... I refuse to believe that the sensual affinity referred to here can at all be regarded as natural. No, I must declare with all the power I can command that sensual attraction even between husband and wife is unnatural.[21]

One thing Gandhi did like was cuddling naked with teenage girls. The idea, he explained to critics, was to condition himself to an absence of desire even in the most trying of circumstances. He insisted that if he could achieve that, the resulting burst of holiness energy would be powerful enough to free India of British rule.[22]

Nor was his asceticism limited to sex; it also covered things like modern medicine. He urged the avoidance of all pharmaceuticals; he allowed his wife to die rather than let her have a shot of penicillin. How could she be sick, after all, when Gandhi himself had written about the great health benefits of celibacy?[23]

Gandhi instead promoted a treatment called "Ramanama," which consisted of repeating the name of the god Rama over and over for hours on end. At various times, Gandhi insisted that Ramanama was "a sovereign remedy for all our ailments," "a most powerful remedy" with "miraculous powers," and "a panacea for all our ills." Getting down to cases, Gandhi revealed that "Ramanama is the unfailing remedy for eradicating malaria" and that "Ramanama is an invaluable remedy for mental illness."[24]

Gandhi rejected not only modern medicine, but modern concepts of human equality as well. He was a strong proponent of India's caste system, in which social interaction, choice of occupation, and choice of spouse were strictly regulated by accident of birth: "Prohibition against inter-marriage and inter-dining is essential for a rapid evolution of the soul." At least, for everyone other than himself; he was born into a caste of grocers, but saw no difficulty in moving into fields of law and theology traditionally reserved for the highest Brahmin caste.[25]

Gandhi cratered a promising London conference on Indian self-rule in 1931 over his adamant refusal to set aside parliamentary seats for India's "Untouchable" caste. The following year, Untouchables successfully lobbied for the right to elect their own members to the colonial parliament, as the Muslims did. Gandhi was so upset he undertook a "fast unto death," relenting only when the Untouchables agreed to continue voting in the same category as the higher-caste Hindus who had treated them as subhuman for thousands of years.[26]

Though Gandhi did urge upper-class Hindus to treat Untouchables more humanely, he flatly opposed legal measures akin to American civil rights laws on their behalf. The net result of Gandhi's campaign, according to India's leading Untouchable, Bhimrao Ambedkar, was that "after a short spurt of activity in the direction of removing untouchability by throwing open temples and wells, the Hindu mind returned to its original state."[27]

Though Nehru was a Brahmin, he urged that all caste distinctions be set aside, and made sure a ban on discrimination against Untouchables was enshrined in India's 1950 constitution. "A caste-ridden society," wrote Nehru, "is not properly secular."[28]

Economically, Gandhi preferred the Bronze Age to the aviation age; as Nehru characterized his views, "The railways, telegraphs, hospitals, lawyers, doctors and such like have all to go." Gandhi preached that to possess more material goods than the minimum needed to survive (*e.g.*, to possess a chair) was the same thing as "theft." However the Hindu monastery where Gandhi and his disciples lived was financed by the generous donations of Indian industrialists. As one party leader put it, "You will never know how much it has cost the Congress Party to keep that old man in poverty."[29]

Where did Gandhi get these bizarre ideas from? Apparently, he dealt directly with God, who instructed Gandhi by means of what he called "the Voice." For example, in 1933, the Voice ordered him to launch a 21-day fast. "What a terrible example to set!" fumed Nehru.[30]

Indians demanded to know more about this Voice. Gandhi replied that it was:

> Like a Voice from afar and yet quite near. It was as unmistakable as some human voice definitely speaking to me, and irresistible. I was not dreaming at the time I heard the Voice. The hearing of the Voice was preceded by a terrific struggle within me. Suddenly the Voice came upon me. ... Not the unanimous verdict of the whole world against me could shake me from the belief that what I heard was the true Voice of God.[31]

Nehru repeatedly quarreled with Gandhi over the evils of mixing religion with politics. As Gandhi put it, "Those who say that religion has nothing to do with politics do not know what religion means." Nehru countered that "Religion as practised in India has become the old man of the sea for us, and it has not only broken our backs but stultified and almost killed all originality of thought and mind." Their arguments grew so intense that at one point Gandhi wrote Nehru that "The differences between you and me appear to me to be so vast and radical that there seems to be no meeting ground between us." Yet Nehru realized he had no choice but to associate with Gandhi because of his hold on the Hindu masses, so (at least until 1947) he always backed down.[32]

Gandhi's problem was that while most Indians thought him a holy man, they had little interest in celibacy, abandoning possessions, or

Ramanama. What they wanted was to rid themselves of their arrogant white rulers. Reluctantly, Gandhi turned again to political action. In 1930 he launched a *satyagraha* campaign against the British monopoly on salt, a commodity essential to existence everywhere. He led a 241-mile "March to the Sea," where he deliberately defied the British law against unauthorized manufacture of salt. The campaign quickly mushroomed into multiple demands for reform, including total prohibition of alcohol. Once again British control over India teetered on the brink, as 90,000 *satygrahis* filled the jails, and Indian soldiers began ignoring their officers' orders.[33]

Yet the British knew their man, discerning that he was really after fame as a spiritual leader, not actual political power for the Indian people. They flattered Gandhi by flying him in for a one-to-one negotiating session with the viceroy. What emerged was a "compromise," 95 percent in Britain's favor, which didn't even affect the salt monopoly. Another bullet dodged. The director of the Intelligence Bureau had written that "I regard the situation now confronting the government of India as the gravest I have known in the course of some 20 years' contact with the revolutionary movements in this country."[34]

Nehru was again devastated, all the more because the rigors of the latest prison term had sent Motilal to his death. "Was it for this that our people behaved so gallantly for a year? Were all our brave words and deeds to end in this?" He sent Gandhi the most cutting insult he could: "If Motilal were here, it wouldn't have happened." Worse yet, Gandhi begged Nehru himself to sell the deal to a Congress Party furious over the betrayal. Nehru agonized till the last moment, then agreed to the dirty job, sacrificing his pride to maintain unity in the face of the British.[35]

Jinnah

Early twentieth-century India was approximately 75 percent Hindu and 25 percent Muslim, with a smattering of Christians and Zoroastrians. There was occasional inter-religious strife, but nothing as excessive as what was to come. Secularized Britain could be counted on for even-handed treatment of its Hindu and Muslim subjects. As agitation for self-rule mounted, though, a question gnawed at India's Muslims: how would they fare under a democracy in which Hindus would be in the majority?[36]

Early on, Muslim leaders believed this was a problem they could solve. Mohammed Ali Jinnah, like Motilal Nehru, was a highly successful British-educated lawyer. His commanding stature gave him a preeminent position within India's "Muslim League," which he used to press for a common political front with the Hindus.[37]

Jinnah spent the early part of his career urging cooperation between Muslims and Hindus to establish a unified independent state, promoting resolutions that "the political future of the country depends on the harmonious working and co-operation of the various communities in the country," while warning against the danger of dividing India into "two watertight compartments." In 1916, Jinnah proclaimed that "I believe all thinking men are thoroughly convinced that the keynote of our real progress lies in the goodwill, concord, harmony and cooperation between the two great [Hindu and Muslim] sister communities." He and Motilal engineered the "Lucknow Pact" with the Hindu-dominated Congress party in 1916, a joint call for a secular India with separate electorates for Hindus and Muslims to guarantee minority rights.[38]

It is stretching a point to call Jinnah a "Muslim." Though his family was Muslim, he was as thoroughly secularized as the Nehrus. He married a non-Muslim, and enjoyed his distinctly un-Islamic whiskey and cigars. Jinnah is best viewed as a "non-Hindu," whose life mission was to assure that people like himself were under the thumb neither of the British nor the Hindu majority.[39]

All of which explains why Jinnah viewed Gandhi first with distrust, then with outright loathing. Gandhi stood for rule by spiritual caprice and secret voices; Jinnah, a lawyer's lawyer, stood for human-constructed law and its continued adaptation to changing circumstance.[40] Gandhi's idea of Hindu-Muslim cooperation was to join in a quixotic campaign to urge the restoration to power of the Ottoman sultan, who was ultimately exiled by Atatürk; Jinnah disdained this as a red herring. To Jinnah, Gandhi's constant references to "Rama

Raj" as the golden age of Hindu rule to be restored overshadowed his pledges of fair treatment for non-Hindus.[41] A tipping point occurred at a public meeting in 1920, when Jinnah was shouted down by a Hindu mob for opposing a resolution offered by "Mr." Gandhi without referring to him as "Mahatma" ("Great Soul"). Within a year, Jinnah began criticizing Gandhi's program as "an essentially spiritual movement" based on "destructive" methods "opposed to the nature of an ordinary mortal like the speaker himself."[42]

Early in 1922, when the wave of Gandhi's first *satyagraha* campaign was at its peak, the viceroy extended a secret offer through Jinnah and other moderates to negotiate "full provincial autonomy," which could have given India a level of self-government similar to that enjoyed by Canada. Gandhi flatly rejected the autonomy offer—then, just two weeks later, called off the whole disobedience campaign, because "God clearly spoke through Chauri Chaura."[43] Little wonder that master lawyer Jinnah felt nothing but contempt for Gandhi thereafter.

"Every time a Hindu shakes hands with me," Jinnah complained about Hindu haughtiness, "he has to wash his hands." He came to see no acceptable future for his Muslim minority other than to have its own separate state. Step by step, the Muslim League moved in that direction, ultimately adopting what became known as the "Pakistan resolution" in 1940, the word "Pakistan" meaning "land of the pure." "I have no hesitation in saying that it is Mr. Gandhi who is destroying the ideal with which the Congress was started," stormed Jinnah. "He is the one man responsible for making the Congress into an instrument for the revival of Hinduism. His ideal is to revive the Hindu religion and establish Hindu Raj in this country and he is using Congress to fulfill this object."[44]

War

When World War II broke out, the viceroy impoliticly declared India at war with Germany without bothering to consult any Indian political leaders. The differing response of the Muslim League and the Gandhi-controlled Congress party was telling. Jinnah's attitude was essentially: "Yes, we'll fight the Japanese because we don't fancy colonial rule from the East any more than we do from the West. And when we have won, and have a million trained fighters under arms, we are *going* to become independent."[45]

Nehru, a staunch democratic internationalist who had been tempted to join the international brigades fighting for Azaña's Spanish Republic, urged Congress to assume a similar stance. Instead, Congress dithered and dallied, waiting for the Great Soul to tune in the proper Voice of God.[46]

When Mussolini overran Ethiopia in 1936, Gandhi had urged the Ethiopians to "allow themselves to be slaughtered" since "after all, Mussolini didn't want a desert." After assuring his readers that "I do not believe Herr Hitler to be as bad as he is portrayed," Gandhi's advice to the British was "godly martyrdom." "Invite Hitler and Mussolini to take what they want. ... Let them take possession of your beautiful island. You will give all this, but neither your minds nor your souls."[47] Ultimately, he prevailed on Congress to adopt a bizarre "Quit India" resolution: the British must simply walk away from India in the middle of the war, leaving it "To God or to Anarchy." India would then somehow take care of itself—perhaps by "negotiating" with Japan. His reasoning appears to have been that such a massive purifying step would somehow generate enough soul-force to keep the Japanese at bay. Otherwise, he threatened a massive non-cooperation campaign, crippling the war effort.[48]

Within a matter of hours after the "Quit India" resolution was published, Gandhi, Nehru, and the entire Congress leadership found themselves in jail; the number imprisoned ultimately reached 100,000. There they stayed, until the Japanese threat subsided.[49]

Britain then moved rapidly to grant India independence. Not because of any soul force, but for the simpler reason that the empire was broke. Only strict domestic austerity measures allowed the government to avoid defaulting on its debts in 1947; the option of a massive military campaign (without American help) to maintain colonial rule over an embittered population many times the size of Britain's simply did not exist.[50]

At this point Gandhi discovered a disagreeable fact: when Jinnah said he wasn't going to subject India's Muslims to Hindu God expert rule, he *meant* it. And while the Congress leadership had spent the war staring at the ceilings of British prisons, the Muslim League had divided its time between currying favor with the British and hardening Muslim political resolve for an independent Pakistan.[51]

Had independence come in 1922, or even 1930, there would have been no separate Pakistan—the word hadn't even been invented yet. Decades of Gandhi's equating religion with politics had taken their toll, though. The most poignant exchanges must have been those between Nehru and Jinnah in August, 1946: two no-nonsense secularists who would each have been delighted to see all the religious feeling that separated them wither and die. Neither man recorded what was actually said, but Jinnah's position must have been something like "If Congress were dominated by Nehru thinking rather than Gandhi thinking, that would be one thing; but it isn't, and I am not going to gamble the future on the zebra changing its stripes."[52]

Independence

Left with no choice, Britain turned over rule to Pakistan and India as separate states. Nehru acquiesced, in part because he hoped that Pakistan would prove nonviable, and the partition would be short-lived. Gandhi did not agree, persisting in his "Quit India" fantasy in which the British would simply exit and let the Indians work things out themselves. "Let the whole nation be in flames, but we will not concede one inch of Pakistan!" But by this point Nehru and the other Congress leaders had the strength to elbow him out of the way. "No one listens to me any more," Gandhi complained. "I am crying in the wilderness." In part, this was because at the critical moment when India's fate hung in the balance, Gandhi chose to focus his energies on campaigning for a soul-purifying ban on horse-racing.[53]

All that was necessary was to draw a line between the Muslim territories and the Hindu—an impossible task, because no matter where it was drawn, millions would be left on the "wrong" side of it. What followed surpassed nearly everyone's worst fears. Mayhem broke out, egged on by politicians terrifying property owners into flight so they could claim the property for themselves.[54]

No one today really has any idea of the true scope of the violence; the best round estimates are that ten million Indians fled their homes and one million Indians died. That's a massive amount of death. Even Nehru's political opponents, though, admit that without his even-handed approach, the plight of India's Muslims would have been far worse.[55]

One of the victims was Gandhi himself, assassinated six months after independence by a radical Hindu who thought him insufficiently anti-Muslim. Though Jinnah's public reaction was polite and appropriate, he surely must have felt that his own intransigence had been vindicated. Nehru was shocked at the loss of a man he respected and loved. Yet in part Nehru may have been relieved; it was only a matter of time before Gandhi, who (for example) said he wanted to reform the Indian economy into a system of village bartering, would have begun making the prime minister's job exceedingly difficult.[56]

Jinnah emphatically did not intend Pakistan to be the sharia-dominated state it later became. He made his vision clear shortly before Pakistan's independence day:

> You are free to go to your temples, you are free to go to your mosques or to any other place of worship in this State of Pakistan. ... You may belong to any religion or caste or creed— that has nothing to do with the business of the State. ... We are starting in the days when there is no discrimination, no distinction between one community and another. We are starting with this fundamental principle that we are all citizens and equal citizens of one State. ... I think we should keep that in front of us as our ideal and you will find that in course of time Hindus would cease to be Hindus and Muslims would cease to be Muslims, not in the religious sense because that is the personal faith of each individual, but in the political sense as citizens of the State.[57]

Jinnah appointed a Hindu as Pakistan's first minister of law, and flatly rejected suggestions for adoption of Muslim sharia law (which

finally arrived in 1979). He simply wanted a land free of Hindu domination, not the place today where Christians, Hindus, and nonbeliev-
ers are routinely persecuted and harassed for violating blasphemy laws.
Unfortunately, Jinnah died of lung cancer only a few months after
Gandhi was shot. None of his descendants chose to live in Pakistan.[58]

The problem, as demonstrated throughout the twentieth century
in places as diverse as Ireland, Croatia, Lebanon, and Palestine, is
that when political borders are drawn along religious criteria it simply strengthens the power of the God experts on either side. That is
certainly what happened in Pakistan, and it would have happened in
India as well but for the steadfastness of Nehru, who called religion
"the fountainhead of authoritarianism." As Prime Minister, he fought
Congress politicians tooth and nail for fair treatment of India's Muslim minority. A rival Hindu chauvinist politician once bitterly joked
that "There is only one genuinely nationalist Muslim in India—Jawaharlal."[59] Nehru's strict secularism cut both ways, though; he had no
patience for the idea that the province of Kashmir should be awarded
to Pakistan simply because it had a Muslim majority, when the legal
process of partition had assigned it to India. For Nehru, the religion
of the inhabitants was immaterial to a truly secular government—
and he fought a war to back up that conviction. "We consider it an
absurd, obnoxious, and antediluvian theory to divide people into nations on a purely religious basis."[60]

One of his rare defeats as prime minister was over a bill he championed for years to replace the patchwork of religion-based family law
with a secular system; he ultimately had to accept a watered-down
version applicable only to Hindus in 1954. For Hindus, though, the
changes were radical, including the abolition of polygamy. He succeeded spectacularly in bringing India into the scientific age. Nehru's
India built an atomic reactor in 1957, launched a space program in
1963, and developed the second-largest pool of trained scientists and
engineers in the world. In his autobiography, Nehru wrote that "I
have no doubt, personally, that all efforts of Hindu or Muslim, to
oppose modern scientific and industrial civilization are doomed to
failure, and I shall watch this failure without regret."[61]

Jinnah surely would have found Nehru's India an acceptable home. Since Nehru's death, though, India has deteriorated into the Hindu-dominated state that Jinnah so feared, earning the dubious rating of the second-worst country on the planet for religious violence in 2009.[62] Pakistan is even worse, as a nuclear-armed, failed state, where terrorists run rampant.

Being anti-Gandhi puts me in a pretty small minority. If you want to defend him, here's your chance. Be sure to mention the way Gandhi treated his wife in your response.

Or if you'd rather talk about Nehru, do you agree with his position on Kashmir? There is little doubt that a majority of Kashmiris today would vote to leave India if they had the chance. Should they be given that chance, or was Nehru right to oppose drawing political boundaries on a religious basis? Share your thoughts on this and the other questions you'll find at **dgc.humanistpress.com**!

Notes:

1 Brecher, *Nehru*, 2.

2 Brown, *Gandhi's Rise*, 2; Keshani, "Chronology," 259; Jordens, *Gandhi's Religion*, 19; Rukmani, "Tagore," 107; Brecher, *Nehru*, 59.

3 Singh, "The Mahatma," 171; Surud, "Reading Gandhi," 113.

4 Brecher, *Nehru*, 59; French, *Liberty*, 26, 30; Jordens, *Gandhi's Religion*, 40, 224; Brown, *Gandhi's Rise*, 7, 65, 148.

5 Baird, "Convergence," 25; Brecher, *Nehru*, 63; Tharoor, *Nehru*, 32; Coward, *Indian Critiques*, 8; Keshani, "Chronology," 264; French, *Liberty*, 20, 38; Brown, *Gandhi's Rise*, 252, 307.

6 Tharoor, *Nehru*, 4; Brecher, *Nehru*, 42-45, 53, 64.

7 Sen, *Glorious*, 218.

8 Baird, "Convergence," 25-26; Brecher, *Nehru*, 65-66, 71, 75; Nehru, *Nehru on Gandhi*, 5, 11.

9 Nehru, *Nehru on Gandhi*, 48; French, *Liberty*, 17.

10 Brown, *Gandhi's Rise*, 254; Brecher, *Nehru*, 71.

11 Brown, *Gandhi's Rise*, 333; Brecher, *Nehru*, 73; Rukmani, "Tagore," 116; Coward, *Indian Critiques*, 7; Lipner, "Debate," 250; Hussein

Keshani, "Chronology," 264.

12 Brecher, *Nehru*, 74, 78; French, *Liberty*, 15; James, *Rise*, 311, 346, 382.

13 Coward, *Indian Critiques*, 8; Keshani, "Chronology," 265; Brown, *Gandhi's Rise*, 328.

14 Baird, "Convergence," 27; Brecher, *Nehru*, 77.

15 French, *Liberty*, 893; Lipner, "A Debate," 245; Brown, *Gandhi's Rise*, 160.

16 Brown, *Gandhi's Rise*, 317; Brecher, *Nehru*, 77-78.

17 Nehru, *Nehru on Gandhi*, 39; Brecher, *Nehru*, 78.

18 French, *Liberty*, 263; Brecher, *Nehru*, 91, 128; Tharoor, *Nehru*, 46.

19 Miller, "Indian Muslim," 151, 207; Tharoor, *Nehru*, 46-47.

20 Chatterjee, *Gandhi's*, 69; Collins, *Freedom*, 43; Jordens, *Gandhi's Religion*, 25.

21 Jordens, *Gandhi's Religion*, 186.

22 Jordens, *Gandhi's Religion*, 194-198.

23 Collins, *Freedom*, 61; Jordens, *Gandhi's Religion*, 25.

24 Raju, *Gandhi*, 50; Chatterjee, *Gandhi's*, 16; Jordens, *Gandhi's Religion*, 6, 180-182.

25 Raju, *Gandhi*, 260; Jordens, *Gandhi's Religion*, 97-98, 191; Brown, *Gandhi's Rise*, 10; Gorringe, "Hindu," 162; Coward, "Gandhi," 58-60; Collins, *Freedom*, 40; French, *Liberty*, 22.

26 French, *Liberty*, 86; Coward, "Gandhi," 48, 51; Brecher, *Nehru*, 180, 189; Coward, *Indian Critiques*, 12; Baird, "Convergence," 22.

27 Coward, "Gandhi," 41, 52-55, 61.

28 Balasubramanian, *Nehru*, 56, 64, 92; Brecher, *Nehru*, 94, 487, 626.

29 Raju, *Gandhi*, 58; Nehru, *Nehru on Gandhi*, 92; Chatterjee, *Gandhi's*, 69; Baird, "Convergence," 32-34; Jordens, *Gandhi's Religion*, 42, 162, 165; French, *Liberty*, 20, 25; Collins, *Freedom*, 98, 198, 369.

30 Chatterjee, *Gandhi's*, 98; Keshani, "Chronology," 260; Jordens, *Gandhi's Religion*, 206; Baird, "Convergence," 23.

31 Chatterjee, *Gandhi's*, 98; Jordens, *Gandhi's Religion*, 142-144.

32 Chatterjee, *Gandhi's*, 120; Baird, "Convergence," 19; Tharoor, *Nehru*, 61; Nehru, *Nehru on Gandhi*, 88, 93; Brecher, *Nehru*, 99, 122, 124.

33 French, *Liberty*, 58; Brecher, *Nehru*, 148-152, 155-156; Keshani, "Chronology," 266.

34 Tharoor, *Nehru*, 83; Brecher, *Nehru*, 136, 172.

35 Baird, "Convergence," 29; Tharoor, *Nehru*, 84; Nehru, *Nehru on Gandhi*, 68-69; Brecher, *Nehru*, 158, 173-175.

36 French, *Liberty*, 38, 43.

37 Hamdani, "Jinnah"; French, *Liberty*, 29; Wolpert, *Jinnah*, 34.

38 Wolpert, *Jinnah*, 36, 45; Tharoor, *Nehru*, 24; Keshani, "Chronology," 263; Brecher, *Nehru*, 55; Coward, *Indian Critiques*, 6.

39 Jalali, "Facts"; Collins, *Freedom*, 102; Wolpert, *Jinnah*, 50; French, *Liberty*, 125.

40 Hamdani, "Jinnah"; French, *Liberty*, 19.

41 Tharoor, *Nehru*, xiv; Miller, "Indian Muslim," 211; Nehru, *Nehru on Gandhi*, 32; Baird, "Convergence," 22; French, *Liberty*, 38.

42 Wolpert, *Jinnah*, 72-74; French, *Liberty*, 48.

43 Brown, *Gandhi's Rise*, 347-348; Wolpert, *Jinnah*, 76.

44 Dixit, *India-Pakistan*, 88; Collins, *Freedom*, 104; French, *Liberty*, 88; Miller, "Indian Muslim," 166.

45 Brecher, *Nehru*, 258; Dixit, *India-Pakistan*, 353; Wolpert, *Jinnah*, 162.

46 Tharoor, *Nehru*, 113; Brecher, *Nehru*, 260, 267.

47 Lipner, "Debate," 243; Wolpert, *Jinnah*, 173, 187-188; Collins, *Freedom*, 58.

48 Hitchens, *God*, 183; Brecher, *Nehru*, 285; Collins, *Freedom*, 59; French, *Liberty*, 151; Keshani, "Chronology," 269; Nehru, *Nehru on Gandhi*, 121.

49 Nehru, *Nehru on Gandhi*, 121; Coward, *Indian Critiques*, 13; Brecher, *Nehru*, 288, 291; French, *Liberty*, 155.

50 French, *Liberty*, 289, 341; Brecher, *Nehru*, 371-372.

51 Dixit, *India-Pakistan*, 106; Brecher, *Nehru*, 264, 294; Wolpert, *Jinnah*, 209.

52 Wolpert, *Jinnah*, 284; Brecher, *Nehru*, 264.

53 Collins, *Freedom*, 156; Brecher, *Nehru*, 377, 379; French, *Liberty*, 249, 278.

54 French, *Liberty*, 401; Brecher, *Nehru*, 355; Collins, *Freedom*, 216, 284.

55 Dixit, *India-Pakistan*, 108; Collins, *Freedom*, 294; French, *Liberty*, 349; Tharoor, *Nehru*, 155; Brecher, *Nehru*, 366.

56 Wolpert, *Jinnah*, 358; Brecher, *Nehru*, 386; Collins, *Freedom*, 440; French, *Liberty*, 359-360.

57 Wolpert, *Jinnah*, 339; Jinnah, "Presidential Address."

58 Hamdani, *Jinnah*; Herman, "Tough Times"; Voice of America, "US Lawmakers"; Faith Freedom, "Pakistan"; Dixit, India-Pakistan, 370; Wolpert, *Jinnah*, 371.

59 French, *Liberty*, 265, 381; Brecher, *Nehru*, 126, 315, 625.

60 Brecher, *Nehru*, 382; Baird, "Religion," 85.

61 Baird, "Religion," 83; Tharoor, *Nehru*, 213, 235, 246; Brecher, *Nehru*, 553; Balasubramanian, *Nehru*, 46, 81, 85, 91-92.

62 Telegraph, "No. 2 tag."

Gamal Abdel Nasser

CHAPTER 18

NASSER VS. BEN-GURION

Zionism

Among the crowd of onlookers when Captain Dreyfus was publicly humiliated in 1895, as described in Chapter 13, was a Jewish rights activist named Theodore Herzl. When he witnessed the hatred whipped up by Edouard Drumont in the land of Voltaire, Herzl took the lead of the budding "Zionist" movement to found a Jewish-controlled state.[1]

The idea was not a new one, even in 1895. Throughout the nineteenth century, romantics speculated about how nice it would be to see the ancient civilization of Israel rise again. In George Eliot's 1872 novel *Daniel Deronda*, for example, the title character embarks for "the East" to attempt to restore the Jewish state.[2]

Jewish God experts naturally preferred the lands that the Torah described as the divinely promised location for their state. Genesis explicitly states that: "In the same day the Lord made a covenant with Abram, saying, Unto thy seed have I given this land, from the river of Egypt unto the great river, the river Euphrates," a territory including vast swaths of Egypt, Jordan, Syria, Lebanon, and Iraq. But that was not the only choice. In 1903, the British government formally offered control over five thousand square miles of its East African territories, but the Zionists turned them down—they wanted Palestine.[3]

Unfortunately, there were only about 24,000 Jews in all of Palestine—not nearly enough with which to form a state. Thus, one of the main functions of the Zionist movement Herzl led was to encourage and facilitate Jewish migration to Palestine, while simultaneously lobbying governments to back creation of a Jewish state there. The key target was the chronically broke Red Sultan, Abdulhamit, whose territories included Palestine.[4] The sultan had lots of land and not enough money, while Europe's Jews had just the opposite.

There were two problems. First, Abdulhamit wasn't interested. Second, most European Jews were equally uninterested in uprooting themselves for a land where they would be unwelcome. By contrast, between 1880 and 1925 some 2.5 million Jews immigrated to more tolerant America. Many Jews resented being told where they should and should not live, and resented as well the impetus Zionism gave to thinking like that of Kaiser Wilhelm, the German emperor: "I am all in favor of the kikes going to Palestine. The sooner they take off the better." The standing joke was, "We Jews have waited two thousand years for the Jewish state, and it had to happen to me?"[5]

Ben-Gurion

One young Polish Jew inspired by Herzl was David Grün, from a bourgeois family in Russian Poland. Inspired by Jewish mystics with roots tracing back to Shabbetai Zevi, young Grün headed to Palestine in 1906 to pave the way for future Jewish control over the land God gave them. "Anti-semitism is caused by Jews in the Exile," he wrote. There he changed his surname to Ben-Gurion, after a leader of the failed Jewish revolt against Roman secular rule.[6]

In 1917, Ben-Gurion and the rest of the Zionist world were electrified by publication of a declaration from British Foreign Minister Balfour that "His Majesty's Government view with favor the establishment in Palestine of a national home for the Jewish people," at the same time blandly insisting that such a home must not "prejudice the civil and religious rights of existing non-Jewish communities in Palestine." Balfour's motivation had less to do with romantic notions of reviving ancient civilizations than with buttressing support for a war that wasn't going well—Napoleon had tried the same promise back in 1799. Balfour didn't really care what the Arab residents thought, writing that Jewish aspirations were "of far profounder import than the desires and prejudices of the 700,000 Arabs who now inhabit that ancient land."[7]

Balfour's seductive promise proved impossible to honor. A "national home" implied political power for the Jews and that meant "prejudicing" the rights of the vast majority of Palestine's largely Muslim populace, who viewed Zionism with violent disapproval. As early as 1899, the mayor of Jerusalem wrote the chief rabbi of France, begging him "In the name of God, leave Palestine in peace." In fact, in 1917 there were still only about 55,000 Jews in Palestine.[8]

Some of the local opposition was anti-Semitic. Islamic scripture is riddled with hatred for Jews.[9] But much of it had nothing to do with anti-Semitism, and everything to do with resisting foreign invasion. Consider another downtrodden, stateless people: the Kurds, the Gypsies, or the Hmong. Suppose the United Nations were to feel sorry for the Gypsies, and offer them, say, Missouri as a place to settle and establish their own Gypsy-controlled government. How would Missourians feel about that? Would it be primarily hatred for Gypsies, or indignation over being marginalized in their own homeland that would drive Missourian resistance? Perhaps Missourians would rise above selfishness and gracefully submit to outside takeover (though they certainly gave no indication of doing so when Mormon leader Joseph Smith arrived). The Palestinians did not. Violent rhetoric, especially from Muslim God experts, fueled increasing levels of violence throughout the 1920s and 1930s, culminating in a full-blown Arab revolt against British rule in 1936.[10]

What concerned the Arabs so much was that Ben-Gurion, who had risen to become the head of Palestine's "Jewish Agency," was increasingly successful in his efforts to create a Jewish homeland in Palestine whether the British and Arabs liked it or not, one Jewish immigrant at a time. By turning what began as a tiny minority into a majority, political power would eventually follow. With Ben-Gurion analogizing Arabs to "red Indians" and vowing to "transfer Arab populations out of the area, if possible of their own free will, if not by coercion," it is little wonder the Arabs were worried.[11]

Arab resistance came as no shock to the Zionists; in 1923, Ben-

Gurion's compatriot Vladimir Jabotinsky warned:

> Every indigenous people will resist alien settlers as long as they
> see any hope of ridding themselves of the dangers of foreign
> settlement. As long as the Arabs preserve a gleam of hope that
> they will succeed in getting rid of us nothing in the world can
> cause them to relinquish this hope, precisely because they are
> not a rabble but a living people.[12]

Ironically, Ben-Gurion and his allies received a huge boost from
the early rise of Nazism, when Hitler was abusing Jews but not yet
systematically murdering them. While a large portion of world Jewry
already viewed Hitler with horror, some rabid Zionists initially welcomed the "worse is better" notion that now more German Jews
would want to emigrate. In the ultimate "politics makes strange bed-
fellows" arrangement, Zionists collaborated with Germany's Nazis
in a complicated financial scheme called *haavara* to facilitate legal
movement of German Jews and a portion of their capital to Palestine
despite restrictions on currency transfer, by selling German manufactured goods in Palestine.[13] American Jews and labor unions had organized an international boycott of German products to protest Nazi
treatment of Jews, unions, and other disfavored groups, similar to the
international boycott that later brought down South Africa's apartheid regime. Haavara neatly undercut that by opening new markets
for Nazi output, while Zionists condemned the boycott as "un-Zion-
ist."[14] By September 1939, more than 50,000 German Jews (less than
10 percent of the total German Jewish population) had transited the
pipeline. Nazi Propaganda Minister Joseph Goebbels went so far as to
strike a commemorative medal, bearing a swastika on one side and a
Zionist star on the other. Yet, despite Zionist pressure, far more Jews
who fled Germany in the 1930s chose to live in the Americas rather
than in Palestine.[15]

Many Zionists openly admired the Fascism of Mussolini, Hitler,
and Franco—aside from its anti-Semitic component—and pledged
to emulate it in the coming Jewish state. To some extent, the feeling was mutual: Adolf Eichmann, organizer of the Holocaust, wrote

that "Had I been a Jew, I would have been a fanatical Zionist. I could not imagine being anything else. In fact, I would have been the most ardent Zionist imaginable."[16] In 1940, the leader of a Zionist military organization wrote to Hitler, offering a formal military alliance against the British to achieve a world in which Germans ran a racially pure Europe and Jews ran a racially pure Palestine. Nazis above Eichmann's level didn't want Jews running anything, though; Hitler never replied to the letter.[17]

Holocaust

As conditions for German Jews worsened, President Roosevelt convened a meeting of the Western nations at Evian, France, to develop alternatives for Jews wishing to escape Hitler's oppression. Ben-Gurion was deeply concerned, telling his colleagues that he did "not know if the conference will open the gates of other countries. ... But I am afraid [it] might cause tremendous harm to Eretz Israel and Zionism. ... and the more we emphasize the terrible distress of the Jewish masses in Germany, Poland, and Rumania, the more damage we shall cause." With little pressure for action in this direction from organized Jewry, the conference produced few concrete results, other than an easing of red tape in the United States, and an offer from the Dominican Republic to take in 100,000 refugees—which the Zionists never seriously pursued.[18] Ben-Gurion's object was not improving life for ordinary Jews of his day, but creating a powerful state for Jews in the future; his rants at American Jews for choosing comfort over the rigors of Palestine only ceased when American Jewish leaders warned that he was hurting his financial and political support among American Jews.[19]

Prior to 1942, Jews in Nazi-controlled areas were treated abominably but were not systematically slaughtered. That changed when Hitler sought a scapegoat for his own decisions that snatched defeat from the jaws of victory, ordering the extermination of Jews in territories under his control.[20] When word of the "Final Solution" trickled out, one would have thought that the focus of world Jewish activity would have been saving as many Jews as possible. Instead, the primary focus of most Jewish international organizations, at Ben-Gurion's insistence, remained on preparing a Jewish state in Palestine. Ben-Gurion put it succinctly:

> If I knew that it was possible to save all the children in Germany by transporting them to England, but only half of them by transporting them to Palestine, I would choose the second because we face not only the reckoning of those children, but the historical reckoning of the Jewish people.[21]

As the scope of the Holocaust became widely known, Ben-Gurion leveraged sympathy for the plight of the survivors into political support for creation of a Jewish state, regardless of what those survivors actually wanted. "It is possible to convert the great disaster of our people in exile into a powerful lever of redemption. A catastrophe of millions is also capable of redeeming millions. And Zionism's message … is to cast the great Jewish catastrophe in mighty molds of redemption." Besides, according to Ben-Gurion's party newspaper *Davar*, extermination was a "punishment from God" for those who had not chosen to emigrate.[22]

On one occasion, Ben-Gurion rejected a plan for a bribe that might have saved 5,000 Jewish children from Slovakia. "There are Jews in Palestine, too" he snapped. Far more Jewish Agency funds were spent on buying up land and building settlements than on rescuing Jews from Hitler's camps.[23] Even a highly pro-Ben-Gurion biographer lamented:

> Ben-Gurion did not focus on trying to stop the catastrophe as it was happening, but on making the most of what might emerge when it had run its course. As head of the Jewish Agency, the shadow Jewish government, he made no real attempt to lead a crusade—for example, to press the pope to cry out, or the Allies to bomb the gas chambers or the railroads leading to them. … Meanwhile, his party newspaper *Davar*, as well as other Hebrew papers, continued to underplay the Holocaust, even after there could be no doubt that the killings were massive.[24]

After the war, Ben-Gurion's view was simply that "The Zionist role is not to rescue the survivors in Europe, but to rescue Eretz Israel for the Jewish people." He blocked plans to transfer thousands of child Holocaust survivors in frail health from wretched camps for displaced persons to safe havens elsewhere in Europe, for fear that such resettlement "might weaken the struggle for free immigration of Jewish refugees to Palestine." The head of the mission Ben-Gurion sent to Europe to capture Holocaust survivors for Palestine complained bitterly of the "moral danger" posed by those who wished to stay put, thereby "desecrating the honor of Israel." "The majority do not want to settle here," reported a member of the Jewish Agency executive. "They want quiet, they want rest. They are not made for a war of ideals."[25]

Independence

As the war ended, Ben-Gurion unleashed a campaign of sabotage and murder, in cooperation with Jewish bomb squads, to persuade the British that maintaining their position in Palestine wasn't worth the cost. This included the bombing of British headquarters at the King David Hotel, killing nearly 100. But Zionist terrorism victimized Jews as well as Gentiles; 17 Jews died in the King David blast.[26]

A critical player was the United States. By early 1945, President Roosevelt realized that the hostility a Jewish state would engender in the Arab world made Ben-Gurion's goal untenable. He privately told Jewish leaders that he believed Jewish statehood was "impossible of achievement." Instead, he wanted to resettle up to 200,000 Holocaust survivors who wished to live in other countries in the west, as he had started trying to do at Evian. A statement to that effect was drafted by the State Department on April 12, 1945; but that morning, Roosevelt suffered a stroke and died.[27]

Harry Truman, who succeeded him, needed to deliver more than empty rhetoric to maintain the Democratic hold on the Jewish vote, and to answer to the millions of dollars of American Zionist money he received in campaign cash. "I'm sorry, gentlemen," he told his diplomatic advisers, "but I have to answer to hundreds of thousands who are anxious for the success of Zionism; I do not have hundreds of thousands of Arabs among my constituents."[28] Over strong opposition from the State Department and the Pentagon, which rightly feared a permanent backlash from the Arab world, Truman came down hard on Ben-Gurion's side, making possible the approval of a United Nations resolution partitioning Palestine into Jewish and Arab controlled areas.[29]

The resolution awarded Israel only a portion of what became its borders. This troubled Ben-Gurion not at all; his focus was on establishing a government with a powerful military, which could then conquer the remainder of the biblical land of Israel at a future time: "After we constitute a large force following the establishment of the state—we will cancel the partition of the country [between Jews and Arabs] and we will expand throughout the Land of Israel."[30]

As Roosevelt, the State Department, and the Pentagon had anticipated, the Arab world erupted with fury. Syria, Iraq, Jordan, and Egypt sent their standing armies in to crush the fledgling state, and in the early stages of 1948 nearly did so. Both sides agreed to a cease-fire in June to let diplomats work out a solution. The Israelis used the respite to rearm, and when the fighting resumed they conquered an area nearly 30 percent larger than that assigned by the UN, including territories that Truman had insisted should remain in Arab hands.[31] UN mediator Count Bernadotte pressed the Israelis to stick closer to what had been awarded them by the UN partition, and allow those Arabs who had fled the fighting (as happens in most wars) to return to their homes. Ben-Gurion rejected both ideas with scorn. Bernadotte was then assassinated by a group whose members included future Prime Minister Yitzhak Shamir.[32]

The Jewish armed forces seemed as intent on ethnic cleansing as they did on defeating the Arab armies. Ben-Gurion quoted approvingly from the book of Joshua, in which conquering Jews repeatedly murdered every man, woman, and child in the towns they captured.[33] The most infamous massacre occurred at Deir Yassin, where as many as 250 men, women, and children were lined up and shot, while the survivors were paraded in a spectacle through Jerusalem. Future Prime Minister Menachem Begin gushed: "Accept my congratulations on this splendid act of conquest. ... As at Deir Yassin, so everywhere, we will attack and smite the enemy. God, God, thou hast chosen us for conquest." A year later, Deir Yassin was renamed "Givat Shaul Bet" and occupied by Jewish residents.[34]

Jewish historian Benny Morris documents more than 20 other mass killings, some of them larger than Deir Yassin, concluding that "Ben-Gurion clearly wanted as few Arabs as possible to remain in the Jewish state." A campaign approved by Ben-Gurion called for the forced expulsion from the state of Arab villagers who resisted the Jewish onslaught. Vast tracts of land previously owned by fleeing Arabs were stolen and distributed to Jewish occupiers, with no compensation paid to the owners.[35] There were plenty of cases of Arab murder of innocent Jewish civilians as well, and there would undoubtedly have been Arab plunder of Jewish property had the Arabs prevailed, but to the victor went the spoils. Despite the mass expulsions, Jews may well have continued to be a minority in their own state, a situation rectified in part by continued expulsion of Arab residents in the years after the war ended.[36]

"The Jewish people is conscious of its moral superiority and humanitarian uniqueness, and therefore has been able to maintain its independence," Ben-Gurion explained. He often stressed that Jews were the "chosen people" and a "light to the nations" compared to the Arabs they displaced. A strongly Zionist Winston Churchill agreed that no "wrong has been done to these [Arab] people by the fact that a stronger race, a higher grade race, or at any rate, a more worldly-wise race, to put it that way, has come in and taken their place."[37]

Even the additional 1948 conquests, though, were far from satisfactory to Ben-Gurion. Shortly after the Balfour Declaration, he had modestly proposed that the Jewish state include Palestine, all of today's Jordan, and large chunks of Lebanon, Syria, and Egypt. When the fighting ended, Ben-Gurion wrote that "[A] Jewish state in part [of Palestine] is not an end, but a beginning. ... Our possession is important not only for itself ... through this we increase our power, and every increase in power facilitates getting hold of the country in its entirety." Israel's 1952 government yearbook pointedly noted that "The state has been established in only a portion of the land of Israel."[38] Ben-Gurion was fond of quoting Joshua 13:1: "Now Joshua was old and stricken in years; and the Lord said unto him, Thou art old and stricken in years, and there remaineth yet very much land to be possessed."

Ben-Gurion's Israel was a theocracy, ruled by a coalition of his Labor Party and fanatic religious parties. Periodic crises were triggered by religious issues such as the importation of non-kosher food, religious education, conscription of the ultra-Orthodox, and milking cows on the Sabbath. Israel still allows complete God expert control over personal matters such as marriage and burial. "Nothing can surpass the Bible at lighting up the manifold problems of our life," Ben-Gurion said. "There can be no worthwhile political or military education about Israel without profound knowledge of the Bible."[39]

Nasser

One of the Egyptian officers who fought with distinction in 1948 was Major Gamal Abdel Nasser, who took an Israeli bullet in the chest and whose unit was captured defending a position while supporting units fled. Nasser was, first and last, an Arab nationalist, who had previously been wounded in street demonstrations against the British domination of Egypt.[40] The son of a postal clerk, Nasser's family had at one point shared a house with a Jewish family, whose children were Nasser's playmates. At no point in his career did he indicate animosity against Jews. One of his first acts after taking power in Egypt was to pay a friendly visit to a Cairo synagogue. He did, though, resent any foreign domination of the Middle East, and saw Israel as the "vanguard of imperialism."[41]

Nasser was shamed by the inability of the combined Arab forces to defeat the Israelis, which he blamed on the corruption surrounding Egypt's British-backed king. Conspiring with other like-minded officers, in 1952 he deposed the king in a coup that established rule by a military junta. For the first time since the days of the pharaohs, Egypt was ruled by native Egyptians.[42]

America at first welcomed Nasser. In fact, shortly before the coup, an American diplomat advised his British counterparts that "We need another Mustafa Kemal [Atatürk], to secularize and Westernize his country and direct the political energies of the people away from the British towards the reconstruction of their own economy and social structure. Even so Egyptians are not Turks, and men like Mustafa Kemal cannot be ordered *a la carte*!"[43]

Nasser may not have been another Atatürk, but he was in the same ballpark. Like Atatürk, he successfully ended foreign domination of his country. Like Atatürk, he led a social revolution, including land reform to strengthen Egypt's middle class, an end to child labor, and expansion of access to healthcare and clean drinking water. Later, he added a progressive income tax and equity-sharing for industrial workers to the mix. During Nasser's rule, Egypt's industrial production quadrupled and its exports doubled.[44]

The land reform campaign soon put him in conflict with the religious establishment, which owned many of the large estates he sought to break up. Soon the Muslim Brotherhood began plotting against him; on October 26, 1954, a Muslim Brotherhood assassin fired eight shots at Nasser from close range as he delivered a speech, but somehow missed. Nasser seized the moment, crying "Each of you is Gamal Abdel Nasser! Gamal Abdel Nasser is of you and from you and he is willing to sacrifice his life for the nation!", thus cementing his hold on the popular imagination.[45]

Nasser observed the outward forms of Islam, but like Atatürk was not truly a believing Muslim. As a young student he had written approvingly of Voltaire. He blamed Islam for Egypt's backwardness, and sought with great success to remove it from the public sphere. "I really don't know how one could possibly govern according to the Koran," he revealed to an interviewer in 1953. Nasser seems to have been a deist in the Thomas Paine mold: "When I was young, I did not want to be a Muslim because my father was one. ... Since 1947, I do believe in something at the bottom of my heart. ... But I think that all religions are fundamentally the same." When an interviewer asked "What does God mean to you? Is he the language and the laws of the Koran?" Nasser answered: "No longer. For me, he means saying: because he accepts it, I do this. Because he rejects it, I do not do that."[46]

Nasser became the Muslim Brotherhood's implacable foe. Some of the means he used to suppress it were reprehensible, but he was in a war to the death that he did not intend to lose. "The real crime of the Muslim Brethren is to have tried to infiltrate the police and the army in order to seize power forcibly. What they tried to wage on us was holy war."[47] He broke Islam's stranglehold on Egyptian society, especially its women, who as in Turkey were freed from wearing the veil. He even created an extensive program of family planning services. He drove Sharia out of the court system, and clamped government control on Al-Azhar, the university that served as the most important source of Islamic theological pronouncements since Atatürk's ending of the caliphate. Religious figures were effectively banned from television, and works previously denounced as blasphemous were allowed to be published. His Arab Radio broadcasts even shamed Saudi Arabia into freeing its slaves, at the cost of bitter condemnation from Saudi-sponsored propaganda that Nasser's regime was "un-Islamic"— as indeed it was. He imprisoned and later executed Sayyid Qutb, the chief theologian of the Muslim Brotherhood, who taught that humans must be ruled only by God, not by other humans, and that no legislation beyond the existing Sharia was permissible.[48]

What ultimately undermined Nasser, though, was the steady stream of propaganda emanating from Israel, portraying him as the next Hitler on one hand and a tool of the communists on the other, despite his explicitly anti-communist writings. Nasser's youngest son tells a story that explains the Israeli fear. A British cabinet minister once assured Ben-Gurion that he had good news: Nasser was more concerned with raising the standard of living of the people of Egypt than in making war on Israel. Ben-Gurion's response: "You call that good news?" He well knew that Israel's growth ambitions could be realized only if its Arab neighbors were weak. A new Atatürk would render God's promise in Genesis far more difficult to achieve.[49]

After taking power, Nasser believed that achieving peace with Israel was both inevitable and desirable, as it would allow him to focus his energy on the economic development at the top of his agenda. He initiated secret contacts, while clamping down on the guerrilla raids that Palestinian refugees had been launching across the border.[50] But Ben-Gurion had no interest in peace, and no confidence that any Arab would, either:

> Why should the Arabs make peace? If I were an Arab leader, I would never make terms with Israel. That is natural: we have taken their country. Sure, God promised it to us, but what does that matter to them? Our God is not theirs. ... There has been anti-Semitism, the Nazis, Hitler, Auschwitz, but was that their fault? They only know but one thing: we have come here and stolen their country. Why would they accept that?[51]

Ben-Gurion commenced what would be a temporary retirement in 1953, replaced by the more moderate Moshe Sharett. Prospects for peace never looked better, as secret negotiations commenced in Washington and Paris. But on July 4, 1954, without Sharett's knowledge, Israeli intelligence activated a sleeper squad of agents in Cairo, and had them plant bombs at the U.S. Information Agency. The idea was to portray Nasser's Egypt as anti-American, undermining prospects for American support, and to derail the peace talks. They wound up getting caught, but succeeded in sabotaging the talks; Nasser was reluctant to deal with double-crossers. Many historians today are persuaded that the hidden hand behind the attack was Ben-Gurion, who was not serving in office when it occurred but who had a loyal following in the Mossad.[52]

1956

Economically, Nasser's dream was to harness the power of the Nile through construction of the Aswan High Dam, to bring vast new areas under cultivation, control floods, and provide electricity for industry. Western countries promised the financing he needed to start work, but dragged their feet when Nasser began following Jawaharlal Nehru's "nonaligned" movement in the Cold War, including his diplomatic recognition of communist China.[53]

A frustrated Nasser then made a bold move to secure funding for his dam: he nationalized the Suez Canal Company, which was owned by British and French investors, so that future tolls would be paid to Egypt. There was no question about his legal right to do so; compensation was paid to the owners, and Britain and France had already nationalized much of their own private sectors. Nor was Egypt's ability to run the canal in question; despite a sudden pullout of European engineers designed to embarrass the Egyptians, ships continued to transit the canal without a hitch. But Britain and France worried that if they let this Third World upstart push them around, they would open a Pandora's box of problems from other Third World nations.[54] So they conspired with Israel, always anxious to expand its borders to cover more of the territory God granted in Genesis. Ben-Gurion arrived in disguise at a secret war-planning meeting in Paris, where he pressed for a plan to (1) assassinate Nasser, (2) divide Jordan between Iraq and Israel, (3) give Israel a chunk of Lebanon, and (4) dump all the Palestinian (and Jordanian) refugees into Iraq.[55]

On October 29, 1956, the Israelis launched a sneak attack against Egypt, which they carried off without a hitch. They were aided immeasurably by British and French attacks which commenced shortly thereafter, ostensibly to "protect" the Suez Canal. Ironically, the canal was working just fine before the combined attacks, but as a response Nasser managed to sink ships inside it, thus blocking it for months.[56]

The most significant difference between Atatürk and Nasser was that Atatürk was a brilliant military commander, and Nasser was not. In fact, some historians suspect that Nasser deliberately kept the Egyptian military weak, so it would not become a political rival. Even Atatürk, though, could not have held off Britain, France, and Israel simultaneously. Israel occupied Gaza and the Sinai within a few days.[57]

Ben-Gurion's real agenda was not the Sinai, but to expand the war so he could seize Jerusalem and parts of Jordan. He solemnly pronounced in the Israeli parliament that the reason for war was "the restoration of the kingdom of David and Solomon" to its biblical borders.[58] But Nasser dissuaded Jordan and Syria from coming to his aid, and then a startling thing happened. World opinion, with Nehru leading the charge, swung heavily in favor of Nasser and against the three bullies ganging up on him. America's President Dwight D.

Eisenhower, who always treated the Arabs and Israelis with an even hand, had predicted to British Prime Minister Eden before the attack that "the peoples of the Near East and of North Africa and, to some extent, of all of Asia and all of Africa, would be consolidated against the West to a degree which, I fear, could not be overcome in a generation and, perhaps, not even in a century." On the phone to Eden once the attack began, Ike was blunter: "I can only presume that you have gone out of your mind."[59]

So the British and French advance quickly halted, and Ike then called for Israel to withdraw its occupying troops. "No nation," he said, "should be allowed to occupy foreign territory and be permitted to impose conditions on its own withdrawal." Ben-Gurion responded to the leader of the free world by ignoring him. This was not the best way to deal with Eisenhower; his diplomats soon threatened a cutoff of U.S. aid, a ban on sale of Israeli bonds in America, and UN sanctions that, in Ben-Gurion's words, would have been "a catastrophe for the State of Israel."[60]

Israel withdrew. Defiant Nasser emerged more popular than ever before.[61]

Israel still received secret spoils of war, though, in the form of cashing in a French promise of a nuclear reactor, which Ben-Gurion quickly converted into a facility for the manufacture of nuclear weapons. For decades thereafter, Israel hid its nuclear status while sanctimoniously promising not to be the first country to introduce nuclear weapons into the Middle East. Estimates are that today Israel possesses between 200 and 500 nuclear warheads.[62]

Nasser also demonstrated his independence in another way. When western nations refused to sell him arms, he bought them instead from the Soviet bloc. Thereafter, Britain, the American CIA, and the Saudis formulated an alternative Nasser strategy: assassinate him. Their chosen instrument was the Muslim Brotherhood, which tried everything from nerve gas to poisoned coffee. But they were inept, and Nasser was lucky.[63]

In April 1967, Ben-Gurion's successors launched a series of deft diplomatic and military maneuvers, aimed first at Syria, that ultimately resulted in a devastating sneak attack on Egypt. Nasser knew his military was years away from being ready to take on Israel. Even future prime minister Yitzhak Rabin later admitted that "Nasser did not want war." It was Lyndon Johnson's CIA that gave Israel the critical intelligence data it needed to destroy the Egyptian air force on the ground. Another future prime minister, Shimon Peres, later put it, "It took 80 minutes to execute a plan which had been in the making for 10 years."[64] This time Jordan did make the mistake of getting involved, and Israel captured the Jordanian prize Ben-Gurion had sought all along. Forty-five years later, it is clear Israel has no intention of giving it back, or of allowing its non-Jewish residents any more "sovereignty" than that enjoyed on an American Indian reservation.[65]

Nasser dramatically resigned after the 1967 debacle, but the Egyptian public wouldn't let him go, and the clamor persuaded him to rescind the resignation.[66] The first Egyptian to rule Egypt in 2,200 years was a man of the people. He knew that people do not have a divine right to rule over others, be they British, French, or Jewish; and that the Christian, Jewish, and Muslim God experts who claim to know a supernatural plan for everyone, especially in the religiously scarred Middle East, are the most dangerous frauds of all.

Had America backed Nasser's secular vision rather than Ben-Gurion's biblical vision, how different would the world look today?

> Though Nasser's Egypt had elections, they fell short of the democratic ideal because of his crackdown on communists and, more significantly, the Muslim Brotherhood. Results of the post-"Arab Spring" elections suggest how anti-democratic this must have been. But how "democratic" is it to allow a party to succeed based on the claim to be God's mouthpiece on earth, in a population brainwashed by God experts from birth? Is a period of transition to free-for-all democracy justifiable? Share your thoughts on this and the other questions you'll find at **dgc.humanistpress.com!**

Notes:

1 Bredin, *Affair*, 298; Johnson, *Jews*, 519; Bose, *Contested*, 212.

2 Johnson, *Jews*, 378.

3 Shahak, *Jewish History*, 12; Genesis 15:18; Johnson, *Jews*, 401; Kurzman *Ben-Gurion*, 58.

4 Bose, *Contested*, 215; Heller, *Birth*, 2.

5 Heller, *Birth*, 2; Benbassa, *Jews*, 136; Johnson, *Jews*, 397, 400.

6 Bose, *Contested*, 239; Segev, *Seventh*, 330; Kurzman, *Ben-Gurion*, 101.

7 Dershowitz, *Case*, 35; Nicosia, *Third Reich*, 3, 19; Finkelstein, *Beyond Chutzpah*, 9.

8 Neumann, *Case*, 41; Bose, *Contested*, 215-216.

9 *See, e.g.*, Koran 5:41, 5:51, 5:64, 5:82, 9:30, 33:26-27, 62:6; Sell, *Historical*, 464.

10 Heller, *Birth*, 4; Bose, *Contested*, 218-220.

11 Jabotinsky, "The Iron Wall," 35; Bose, *Contested*, 214, 225; Giladi, *Scandals*, 20.

12 Bose, *Contested*, 229.

13 Mendelsohn, "Report," 117; Krojanker, "Transfer," 77; Segev, *Seventh*, 21, 29-30.

14 Nicosia, *Third Reich*, 39, 195; Zionist Federation, "Address," 42; Vladeck, "Debating," 92-93.

15 Brenner, *51 Documents*, 130; Nicosia, *Third Reich*, 48; Segev, *Seventh*, 35; Shaw, "Evian."

16 Achimeir, "Diary," 42; Shahak, *Jewish History*, 71; Eichmann, "Transported," 267.

17 Stern, "Fundamental Features," 300-302; Nicosia, *Third Reich*, 114, 197.

18 Penkower, *Roosevelt*, 3; Nicosia, *Third Reich*, 158; Segev, *Seventh*, 28; Kurzman, *Ben-Gurion*, 220; Shaw, "Evian."

19 Kurzman, *Ben-Gurion*, 182, 332, 335.

20 Segev, *Seventh*, 75.

21 Finkelstein, *Beyond Chutzpah*, 117; Neumann, *Case*, 81.

22 Kurzman, *Ben-Gurion*, 246; Segev, *Seventh*, 98.

23 Segev, *Seventh*, 92, 102.

24 Kurzman, *Ben-Gurion*, 246.

25 Heller, *Birth*, 27; Finkelstein, *Beyond Chutzpah*, 117; Segev, *Seventh*, 118-120.

26 Bose, *Contested*, 230; Giladi, *Scandals*, 33; Johnson, *Jews*, 521; Heller, *Birth*, 125, 272, 275; Kurzman, *Ben-Gurion*, 262, 267; Turner, *Suez*, 80; Johnson, *Jews*, 523.

27 Heller, *Birth*, 24-25, 199; Penkower, *Roosevelt*, 14, 17-18, 21-22.

28 Johnson, *Jews*, 524; Shahak, *Jewish History*, vii; Bose, *Contested*, 231.

29 Johnson, *Jews*, 525; Dershowitz, *Case*, 64, 67; Heller, *Birth*, 22.

30 Morris, *Birth*, 24.

31 Aburish, *Nasser*, 22, 25; Turner, *Suez*, 82; Kurzman, *Ben-Gurion*, 274, 278; LaCouture, *Nasser*, 283.

32 Morris, *Birth*, 142, 151; Kurzman, *Ben-Gurion*, 299-300.

33 Morris, *Birth*, 292; Bose, *Contested Lands*, 236; Heller, *Birth*, 141, 145; Joshua 6:21.

34 Johnson, *Jews*, 528; Bose, *Contested Lands*, 236; Morris, *Birth*, 114, 193.

35 Finkelstein, *Beyond Chutzpah*, 265; Heller, *Birth*, 195; Morris, *Birth*, 63, 137, 158, 179.

36 Dershowitz, *Case*, 281; Kurzman, *Ben-Gurion*, 281; Morris, *Birth*, 246-251; Finkelstein, *Beyond Chutzpah*, 283.

37 Heller, *Birth*, 146; Segev, *Seventh*, 468; Finkelstein, *Beyond Chutzpah*, 9.

38 Finkelstein, *Beyond Chutzpah*, 280; Johnson, *Jews*, 538.

39 Heller, *Birth*, 290; Johnson, *Jews*, 550-551; Heller, "Cremation"; Kurzman, *Ben-Gurion*, 26, 334.

40 Aburish, *Nasser*, 25; Turner, *Suez*, 55, 65; LaCouture, *Nasser*, 33, 63-65.

41 LaCouture, *Nasser*, 366; Aburish, *Nasser*, 11; Turner, *Suez* , 61, 180.

42 Aburish, *Nasser*, 18, 45; Turner, *Suez*, 86, 128; LaCouture, *Nasser*, 110.

43 Turner, *Suez*, 96.

44 Aburish, *Nasser*, 46, 139; LaCouture, *Nasser*, 127, 233, 383.

45 Aburish, *Nasser*, 46; 54; LaCouture, *Nasser*, 128-129.

46 DeLong-Bas, *Wahhabi*, 257; LaCouture, *Nasser*, 28, 127-128, 364.

47 DeLong-Bas, *Wahhabi*, 257; LaCouture, *Nasser*, 127-128; Aburish, *Nasser*, 55.

48 Podeh, *Rethinking*, 285; Abou El Fadl, *Rethinking*, 83; Aburish, *Nasser*, 140, 147, 200, 237; Esposito, *Islam*, 655, 675.

49 Giladi, *Scandals*, 27, 93; Aburish, *Nasser*, 59-60; Heller, *Birth*, 102; Kurzman, *Ben-Gurion*, 340.

50 Kurzman, *Ben-Gurion*, 371; Aburish, *Nasser*, 48, 50.

51 Bose, *Contested*, 230; Neumann, *Case*, 152; Kurzman, *Ben-Gurion*, 371.

52 Giladi, *Scandals*, 24; Kurzman, *Ben-Gurion*, 372-373; Aburish, *Nasser*, 64, 67, 70-73, 98.

53 Eveland, *Ropes*, 194; Aburish, *Nasser*, 104; Turner, *Suez*, 150, 174.

54 Aburish, *Nasser*, 105, 110, 116; Turner, *Suez*, 176, 182, 204-205, 237.

55 Kurzman, *Ben-Gurion*, 386; Giladi, *Scandals*, 38-39; Turner, *Suez*, 290-291.

56 Segev, *Seventh*, 297; Turner, *Suez*, 327.

57 LaCouture, *Nasser*, 119, 299; Turner, *Suez*, 202.

58 Aburish, *Nasser*, 98; Shahak, *Jewish History*, 8.

59 Tharoor, *Nehru*, 190; Aburish, *Nasser*, 120-121; Turner, *Suez*, 246, 367.

60 Eveland, *Ropes*, 245; Bose, *Contested*, 280; Segev, *Seventh*, 298;
Turner, *Suez*, 397.

61 Turner, *Suez*, 439; Aburish, *Nasser*, 121.

62 Turner, *Suez*, 264; Segev, *Seventh*, 367; Kurzman, *Ben-Gurion*, 343;
Neumann, *Case*, 156.

63 Eveland, *Ropes*, 194; Aburish, *Nasser*, 80, 89, 128, 198.

64 Eveland, *Ropes*, 324; LaCouture, *Nasser*, 294-296; Aburish, *Nasser*,
250-260.

65 Eveland, *Ropes* 325; Carter, *Palestine*, 150-160.

66 Aburish, *Nasser*, 268; LaCouture, *Nasser*, 314.

Steven Biko

CHAPTER 19

BIKO VS. MALAN

Calvinism

Chapter 8 explored the Calvinism of Spinoza's Holland, a religion that carried humility before the Christian God to its logical conclusion. The thinking was that since God was so great and man was so small, there was nothing at all man could do to affect his own salvation; God had already decided everything from the beginning of time. The best the "elect" pre-chosen by God for salvation could do was to stick together and avoid the contamination of the damned who formed the overwhelming majority of the human species.[1]

When Spinoza was 20, a band of Calvinists belonging to the Dutch Reformed Church (DRC) established a colony at the southern tip of Africa. Their purpose was not to spread God's word, but to station the trade route to the spice islands of today's Indonesia. They were soon supplemented by parties of Calvinists fleeing from Catholic France.[2] As the little Cape Colony grew, its members discovered that life could be made vastly more pleasant by employing slaves to do the drudge work in the fields. So white South Africans built a flourishing slave economy—as explicitly permitted by their Christian Bibles and Augustine. Soon the territory had more slaves than whites.[3]

At the end of the Napoleonic wars the colony's ownership shifted to Britain, whose culture had become more secularized by the Enlightenment efforts of Queen Caroline. Britain moved to abolish slavery throughout the empire in the early nineteenth century, and in 1838 it was South Africa's turn.[4]

Abolition coupled with the lack of distinction in British common law between the rights of blacks and whites bewildered and infuriated the colonists, who had been shielded by distance from the effects of the Enlightenment. It wasn't just that equality hurt them economically; at a deeper level, it went against their god's plan. Or so the Afrikaaners, as they were now called, convinced themselves by extending Calvinist theology to cover peoples as well as individuals. God had certainly chosen the Jews, as it said in the Bible. Manifestly, he had chosen the Afrikaaners as well, leading them to a promised land just as Moses had been led. God himself placed the Afrikaaners in Africa, entrusting them with a mission to spread Christian civilization. Just as obviously, God had not chosen backwards black people for anything good at all.[5]

Lacking the strength to defeat the godless British militarily, thousands of Afrikaaners voted with their feet in what became known as the "Great Trek," heading to the interior to set up self-governing republics where they could treat blacks as they believed God intended.[6] The diary of the niece of the Great Trek leader explained that:

> It is not so much their freedom that drove us to such lengths, as their being placed on an equal footing with Christians, contrary to the laws of God and the natural distinction of race and religion, so that it was intolerable for any decent Christian to bow down beneath such a yoke; wherefore we rather withdrew in order thus to preserve our doctrines in purity.[7]

As happened a century later in Palestine, the residents did not respond well to religious invasion, but were overcome by superior firepower. At the battle of Blood River in 1838, 3,000 Zulus with only spears for weapons were slaughtered in repeated suicide charges against settlers sporting muskets and cannon, sheltered inside a tight barricade of overturned wagons; no Afrikaaners died. The DRC thereafter attributed the miraculous victory to its "covenant with God."[8]

The British didn't really mind losing these troublemakers, until the latter part of the century when diamonds and gold in fabulous quantities were discovered in the interior.[9] Suddenly, it seemed, the moral imperative of expanding British civilization came into sharper focus.

With much greater difficulty than they had expected, the British succeeded in conquering the Afrikaaner republics in a series of confrontations culminating in the 1899-1902 Boer War, during which they gave the twentieth century a new concept called the "concentration camp," where Afrikaaner civilians were interned. The Afrikaaners were led by an Enlightenment resister who denied the roundness of the earth. In many respects, though, the British won the war but lost the peace. Afrikaaners outnumbered the British colonists by a wide margin, and the British agreed to keep blacks off the voting rolls in most areas.[10] Within very few years, South Africa was run along lines far closer to those of the "defeated" Afrikaaner republics than of Enlightenment Britain.

One of the most important steps along that road was the passage of the "Native Lands Act" in 1913, purporting to restrict black land ownership to the 7 percent (later increased to 13 percent) of territory that had been "reserved" for them—a figure dramatically out of proportion to the 80 percent of the population the blacks comprised. Thousands of blacks were summarily evicted from their farms without compensation. This and other restrictive measures were enacted while Gandhi lived in South Africa, without attracting his interest. He was focused on the welfare of the country's relatively prosperous Indian minority, not the blacks whom he contemptuously called "kaffirs" (Afrikaans for "niggers").[11]

Malan

Daniel François Malan, a descendant of the original French Calvinist South African immigrants, avoided the perils of the Boer War by being safely off in divinity school, emerging as a DRC minister in 1905. Rev. Malan alienated his first congregation by preaching, like Bryan, in favor of the prohibition of alcohol. He was more successful in his second effort, where he stressed tried-and-true themes of racial superiority and anti-Semitism. He became such a skilled communicator that in 1914 he left the pulpit to become founding editor of a new anti-Semitic newspaper called *Die Burger*.[12]

Malan's prominence as an anti-Semitic journalist led him, like

Drumont, to a career in politics. He was elected to Parliament in 1918, and joined the cabinet in 1924. The worldwide depression of the early 1930s struck South Africa with particular virulence, resulting among other things in the fusion of the country's two principal political parties in an effort to maintain stability. This Malan could not stomach, any more than a rabid liberal or conservative could accept a merger of America's Democratic and Republican parties today. So Malan formed what became known as the National Party (NP), starting with only seven followers—reminding doubters that "Hitler started with seven."[13]

At first the NP achieved little success, but in 1938 it scored a coup through its sponsorship of events celebrating the centennial of the "Great Trek." This event, replete with a commemorative ox-wagon journey across the country, seized the Afrikaaner imagination. One-sixth of the entire Afrikaaner population attended the closing ceremony, many after journeying hundreds of miles.[14] There they heard Rev. Malan declaim that:

> Here at Blood River you stand on holy ground. Here was made the great decision about the future of South Africa, about Christian civilization in our land, and about the continued existence and responsible power of the white race. ... We hold this nationhood as our due, for it was given us by the architect of the universe. His aim was the formation of a new nation. The last hundred years have witnessed a miracle behind which must lie a divine plan. Afrikaanerdom is not the work of men but the creation of God.[15]

Observers likened the event to the recent Nazi rally at Nuremberg, a tie-in that was far from fanciful. There was great admiration for Hitler's racial theories among the Afrikaaners; there was also bitter opposition to the arrival of 4,000 German Jewish refugees. When war broke out in 1939, Malan and others came out forcefully against South African involvement on Britain's side, saying they preferred a Hitler victory. Many prominent Afrikaaners did more than argue; they sabotaged war industries, and plotted a coup to replace the government with one that would switch sides. Malan opposed extra-legal methods, but still was given the title *Volksleier* (similar to Führer), and pledged to deal with problems including "the surplus Jewish population."[16]

The war produced economic boom times in South Africa, which in turn created a labor shortage, filled in large part by blacks. This led to a weakening of the institutions of racial segregation, despite the best efforts of the DRC. One widely publicized incident involved DRC support for a wildcat strike by white garment workers when they learned that blacks were secretly employed in a closed-off corner of their factory. A DRC committee distributed a pamphlet entitled "White South Africa Save Yourself! Support the White Clothing Worker and the Three Afrikaans Churches in Their Struggle for the Maintenance of the Color Bar and Christendom."[17]

Through it all the DRC kept hammering home God's command for separation of the races, pressing the government to obey God's will. Hadn't God deliberately separated the nations at the Tower of Babel, they reasoned? Hadn't God forbidden race-mixing for that other chosen people in Israel? Then there was the story of Noah's bad son Ham and his progeny, cursed to be a "servant of servants." The Bible didn't say Ham was black, but the Jewish Midrash did and many Protestants believed it.[18] Former DRC minister Malan loaded his rhetoric with theology: "Afrikaanerdom is not the work of man but a creation of God. We have a divine right to be Afrikaaners. Our history is the highest work of art of the Architect of the centuries." He could also be blunt: "We want to make sure that South Africa remains a white man's country."[19]

Apartheid

Malan made his push for power in the first postwar election, in 1948, on a pledge to "Keep the kaffir in his place." The ruling party was not pro-black by any means, but it was not as strident about race as the NP. Enforcement of existing segregation rules was uneven, and at a time when world opinion was shifting toward racial equality, the government appeared lackadaisical in bucking the trend.[20] The accomplished communicator Malan simplified his message to a single word: "apartheid," a term coined by a DRC minister meaning "apart-ness" for the races. A DRC federation had explicitly endorsed the "theology of apartheid" the previous year: "Apartheid stretches over the whole area of people's lives. ... The principle of apartheid between races and peoples, also separate missions and mission churches, is well maintained within Scripture." The NP lost the popular vote, but be-cause of over-representation of rural areas achieved a small minority in the Parliament. After 30 years in politics, Malan had reached the top.[21] A wave of racial legislation and enforcement of existing race laws that had long been urged by the DRC ensued; no one would ever accuse Malan of reneging on his campaign promises:[22]

• A tightened ban on interracial marriage, soon followed by criminal penalties for interracial sex (much to the consterna-tion both of visiting sailors and existing interracial married couples).[23]

• A "Population Registration Act," requiring all residents to be tagged by race, which would be stamped on their identity passes— restricting black movement. In their peak year, the pass laws resulted in over 700,000 prosecutions.[24]

• A public accommodations law to overturn court decisions re-quiring "separate but equal" facilities, eliminating the "equal" part. Regulations imposed segregation for taxis, ambulances, hearses, buses, trains, elevators, benches, lavatories, parks, church halls, town halls, theaters, restaurants, and hotels.[25]

• A "Bantu Education Act" to shunt blacks into dead-end careers—"education for serfdom," many called it. By 1975, the government was spending 15 times as much per pupil on whites as on blacks.[26]

• A ban on strikes by black workers.[27]

• Tougher laws restricting blacks to the lands reserved for them, and eliminating the "black spots" that still soiled white lands by expropriation without compensation.[28]

Malan ran over parliamentary opposition with an irrefutable argument: "Why did the Creator make the mistake of creating countries, nations and languages? He should not have done so ... and in addition the Creator also proceeded to create different colours. I say that [opposition] is a charge against Creation and the Creator."[29]

South Africa's black majority did not take all this lying down. For the first time in the twentieth century, organized black resistance broke out, some of it modeled along the lines of Indian non-violence. Nehru's India, in fact, was among apartheid's most vocal opponents.[30] Malan's response had all the nuance of a bulldozer. Demonstrations were broken by force, thousands of dissenters were thrown in jail, and a "Suppression of Communism Act" gave the government near-limitless power to keep blacks in line. By the time Malan stepped down at the age of 80, his prisons held more inmates than did Britain's, which had four times South Africa's population.[31]

H.F. Verwoerd, whom Malan appointed Minister of Native Affairs in 1950, and who then became Prime Minister in 1958, brought more intellectual rigor to apartheid by separating blacks onto their own semi-independent "Bantustans," where they could enjoy "separate development." This fit nicely with the DRC's biblical justification for separation of the races according to God's plan.[32] It's tougher to see God's reasoning in consigning 80 percent of the population to 13 percent of the land, though, and the poorest land at that, with whites retaining all subsurface mineral rights. Some 3½ million blacks were forcibly uprooted from their homes and jammed into overpopulated "homelands" to carry out the DRC's vision.[33]

Throughout the apartheid period, there was extensive cross-fertilization between the DRC and the American proponents of segregation, then under intense challenge. In 1948, when Malan's anti-miscegenation proposal was debated in parliament, members pointed to America for support. "Is it not something for the other side to think about that in 30 out of the 48 States of the United States they have legislation on similar lines to this?"[34] The "White Citizens Councils" that formed across the south to oppose the Supreme Court's *Brown vs. Board of Education* decision were filled with Protestant clergymen who employed the same biblical arguments against race-mixing as were being used in South Africa. For example, a publication of the Mississippi Citizens' Council tract declared that "The races of man are the handiwork of God, as is everything in nature. If He had wanted only one type of man, He would have created only one." Many American Protestants, such as Rev. Jerry Falwell, explicitly supported South African apartheid well into the 1980s.[35]

Biko

The day Malan was sworn in as prime minister, he probably did not envision that an 18-month-old black baby would one day demolish the structure he was planning to erect. Steven Bantu Biko grew up in the same wretched conditions as millions of other South African black children. He managed to secure an education, though, and entered medical school. There he became involved in reform-oriented student political organizations, where he quickly came to resent the domination of liberal whites. They were well-meaning, perhaps, but the cultural notion of white superiority was so deeply ingrained that they could not avoid more than a tinge of condescension when, as Biko put it, "they made all the decisions for us." "To us it seems that their role spells out the totality of the white power structure—the fact that though whites are our problem, it is still other whites who want to tell us how to deal with that problem."[36]

Biko shocked his white friends by breaking away in 1968 and forming his own group, the South African Students Organization (SASO), for non-white students only—mixed-race and Indian students were welcome. How can we achieve an integrated society, liberals complained, when you segregate yourself? Biko's response was an exposition of what he called "Black Consciousness." The only way 20 percent of the population could so thoroughly dominate the remaining 80 percent was because the 80 percent let them do it; and they let them do it because they had, in countless ways from birth, been brainwashed with their own inferiority.[37]

As long as blacks are suffering from inferiority complex—a

result of 300 years of deliberate oppression, denigration and derision—they will be useless as co-architects of a normal society where man is nothing else but man for his own sake. Hence what is necessary as a prelude to anything else that may come is a very strong grass-roots build-up of black consciousness such that blacks can learn to assert themselves and stake their rightful claim.[38]

If ordinary black people came to accept that there was nothing wrong with them, then apartheid could not possibly survive. As Biko put it, "The limits of tyrants are prescribed by the endurance of those whom they oppress."[39]

Biko was expelled from medical school, giving him time to establish a publication called *Black Review*, a political organization called the "Black People's Convention," foundations to aid students and the families of political prisoners, and a medical clinic. He was described as having "an extraordinary magnetism. His hold on his all-black audiences was almost frightening; it was as if they were listening to a new 'messiah.'"[40]

Black Consciousness was nonviolent, though not on supernatural Gandhian grounds. Biko believed violence and satyagraha-style confrontation were inexpedient because they wouldn't work; and they were unnecessary if the 80 percent would come to believe in its own human worth. "We are not interested in armed struggle. We have stated clearly in our own documents that we are not interested either in confrontation methods, by that meaning, demonstrations which lead to definite breaking of existing laws, such that there is reaction from the System, what you call the System." Instead, it was a movement of self-help, of black-run community improvement projects and clinics. As Biko put it succinctly: "Black man, you are on your own."[41]

Friends described Biko as consistently free from any spirit of hatred, bitterness, or resentment. When questioned once about this he laughed and said these would take too much time and energy. "When there is violence there is messiness. Violence brings too many residues of hate into the reconstruction period. Apart from its obvious horrors, it creates too many post-revolutionary problems. If at all possible, we want the revolution to be peaceful and reconciliatory."[42]

In one of the worst miscalculations in history, the authorities allowed the Black Consciousness movement breathing room to establish itself and thrive. In part, this was because they despised white do-gooders, and took a sadistic pleasure in watching them squirm when the people they were trying to help spurned them—a "divide and conquer" strategy, with a vengeance. In part, it was because Black Consciousness arguably fit with the theology of racial separation.[43] Mostly, though, it was simply a colossal mistake. For Biko in fact sought a fully integrated society with equal rights for all—the antithesis of apartheid. "We are looking forward to a non-racial, just, and egalitarian society in which colour, creed, and race shall form no point of reference." He specifically rejected the idea of herding blacks into Bantustans as "a solution given to us by the same people who have created the problem. In a land rightfully ours we find people coming to tell us where to stay and what powers we shall have without even consulting us."[44]

Black Consciousness was not a difficult concept even for uneducated people to grasp, once it is explained in simple terms. In the early 1970s, it shot across South Africa like wildfire. The repression following the trial of Nelson Mandela in 1964 had reduced black protest to a whisper, but once blacks began seeing themselves as real people, the number of incidents surged, as did the number of strikes by black workers.[45]

When authorities realized that this Black Consciousness diversion was getting out of hand, the screws began to tighten, especially on Biko. In 1973 he was "banned," a severe punishment prohibiting travel outside his home town, publishing of articles, being quoted in the press, and even meeting with more than one other person at a time. Still, he had never been arrested, a fact his colleagues who had been "inside" teased him about: "I think the bastards are trying to discredit me," he laughed.[46]

That ended in 1975, when Biko was arrested and held for 137 days without being charged or tried. The same year, the government launched a lengthy prosecution of nine activists, in what the *Rand Daily Mail* admitted was a trial of Black Consciousness itself. Defendants were not accused of committing or encouraging violence, but of promoting an idea that would undermine the state. Biko himself was not a defendant because as a "banned" person he could not write for the publications at issue. But Biko's testimony in May 1976 gave him a forum to publicize his ideas he would not have otherwise enjoyed.[47]

A month later, the government's fears of where Black Consciousness might lead were realized, when student demonstrations in the shantytown of Soweto erupted into violence that soon engulfed the country, taking a thousand lives. Though Biko expressed frustration about being unable to provide the students the guidance they needed, authorities were deeply impressed by the fact that the rioters demanded negotiation with three leaders: Nelson Mandela (already in jail), Robert Sobukwe (an opposition leader since Malan's days, living under house arrest), and Steven Biko.[48]

After the Black Consciousness defendants were convicted late in 1976, the police turned their attention to the mastermind Biko, who had been arrested again after the rioting subsided and held in solitary confinement for 101 days. He was arrested again the following March, and again in July; he was out on bail when his final arrest occurred in August 1977. None of his arrests was for violence or inciting to violence; he was never convicted of any offense at all.[49]

Black Theology

Precisely because so much of the justification for apartheid was religious, Biko focused at length on issues of religion. For someone who already had quite a bit on his plate in bucking the white establishment, by far the easiest course of action would have been for Biko to leave religion alone, or to say (as some God experts did) that "God is against apartheid, so I am too." Yet take it on he did; for as Biko put it, "Too many are involved in religion for the blacks to ignore."[50]

Biko was not an atheist; but even though he was raised as an Anglican altar boy, he did not accept the main tenets of conventional Christianity, *e.g.*, the divinity of Jesus. "The most unbelievable aspects of organised religion," he wrote, "are to do with the advent and sub-sequent role of Christ on earth."[51] He condemned Christianity for its role in instilling the black sense of inferiority that Black Conscious-ness sought to erase:

> The acceptance of the colonialist-tainted version of Christian-ity marked the turning point in the resistance of African peo-ple. ... Because the white missionary described black people as thieves, lazy, sex-hungry etc., and because he equated all that was valuable with whiteness, our Churches through our min-isters see all these vices I have mentioned above not as manifes-tations of the cruelty and injustice which we are subjected to by the white man but inevitable proof that after all the white man was right when he described us as savages.[52]

It wasn't just the DRC that was bad; Biko noted that it was orga-nized religion in general:

> I've also grown to question in fact that very need for worship in an organised way. In other words do organised churches necessarily have a divine origin or should one view them as man-created institutions probably in the same category as soc-cer clubs? ... I can reject all Churches and still be Godly. I do not need to go to Church on Sunday in order to manifest my godliness.[53]

So what did he mean by "Godly?" Like Paine, Biko accepted the idea of a god, but believed man could know nothing about it, other than through examination of the universe itself: "I find it completely unnecessary for me to even contemplate the nature of the God I be-lieve in; whether he is spiritual, human, or plant-like, I find com-pletely irrelevant to the issue. ... Suffice it to trace back to him all that happens around us and out of this to begin to understand somewhat his powers."[54]

Though man knew nothing about God, man could still have "reli-gion": "If one takes religion as nothing else but what it is – *i.e.*, a social institution attempting to explain what cannot be scientifically known about the origin and destiny of man, then from the beginning we can see the necessity of religion. All societies and indeed all individuals, ancient or modern, young or old, identify themselves with a particular religion and when none is existent, they develop one"—in other words, religion as a moral code.[55]

Biko's campaign to build an integrated culture with blacks as "co-architects" extended to building a new religion as well. "If the white God has been doing the talking all along, at some stage the black God will have to raise His voice and make Himself heard over and above noises from His counterpart."[56] Specifically, the black contribution to the religion/moral code had a powerfully humanist overtone:

> One of the most fundamental aspects of our culture is the importance we attach to Man. Ours has always been a Man-centred society. ... We believe in the inherent goodness of man. We enjoy man for himself. We regard our living together not as an unfortunate mishap warranting endless competition among us but as a deliberate act of God to make us a community of brothers and sisters jointly involved in the quest for a composite answer to the varied problems of life. Hence in all we do we always place Man first and hence all our action is usually joint community oriented action rather than the individualism which is the hallmark of the capitalist approach.[57]

Most importantly, he said, "God is not in the habit of coming down from heaven to solve people's problems on earth."[58]

Biko's final arrest occurred on August 18, 1977, when he and a friend were stopped at a roadblock. What happened after that is not clear in every detail, but the apparent plan of his captors was to persuade Biko that he was not fully human, after all. He was kept completely naked at all times, chained to a wall, and allowed no books, papers, communication, or exercise. He was repeatedly interrogated by police with a deserved reputation for using more than verbal traps to extract information. Biko may or may not have tried to fight back during his interrogation on the morning of September 6, as police decades later claimed he did. What definitely did happen was that Biko received a severe injury to the head, and for the rest of that day and several succeeding days drifted in and out of consciousness, all the while naked, manacled, and chained to a grill. Doctors were brought in to look at him; having been informed by the police that he was simply "shamming," they did nothing. One doctor found blood in his spinal fluid, an extremely serious symptom, but he did nothing either.[59]

On September 11, Biko took a turn for the worse. His jailers responded by tossing him, still naked, into the back of a van, which set out on a grueling 700-mile journey to Pretoria. Biko died in his cell a few hours after arrival. Shortly afterward, the government attempted to erase Black Consciousness by outlawing all of Biko's organizations.[60]

The minister of justice, Jimmy Kruger, insisted that Biko had died of a hunger strike. He poured salt on the wound by saying of Biko's death that "it leaves me cold," then chuckling that black and white alike were given "the democratic right to starve themselves to death." An inquest revealed the true cause of death as brain injury; a highlight was the jailer who testified that "No assault charges have ever been laid against my assaulting team." He was allowed to correct his statement to "interrogation team." Even after the results of the inquest were made public, Kruger continued to stick to the hunger strike line.[61]

The government would have been better off simply murdering Biko in an untraceable manner, as it allegedly did with SASO leader Abram Tiro, killed by an anonymous a parcel bomb. As Biko had predicted, "You are either alive and proud, or you are dead, and when you are dead, you can't care anyway. And your method of death can itself be a politicizing thing. ... So if you can overcome the personal fear for death, which is a highly irrational thing, you know, then you're on the way." His death provided decisive impetus to the anti-apartheid movement worldwide. More than 20,000 mourners attended his funeral, where they were attacked by police who fractured a number of skulls.[62]

Two months later, the United Nations, which had previously labeled apartheid a "crime against humanity," slapped an arms embargo on South Africa; the only member state to violate it was Israel. Ronald Reagan, the darling of America's Christian right, opposed sanctions on South Africa while disingenuously remarking that South Africa had "eliminated the segregation we once had in our own country." But in 1986 Congress overrode his veto and slapped full economic sanctions on South Africa.[63]

The most important event of 1986, though, was that the DRC finally caved in to decades of worldwide opprobrium and announced that God really didn't demand the continuation of apartheid after all. They neither apologized nor acknowledged past error; they just admitted that things weren't working out well in practice. The critical point was that once the moral underpinnings for a system that was obscene on its face were yanked out, the system could not possibly stand. Nor did it; Nelson Mandela was freed from jail four years later, and four years after that he became South Africa's first black president.[64] Unfortunately, corruption and buffoonery have plagued South African politics since Mandela's retirement. There is no certainty that things would have been different had Steven Biko lived, but it would be nice to know what he would have done with the chance.

> Think about an issue completely different from apartheid: global warming. We have God experts taking all sorts of different theological positions on what is really a purely scientific and economic issue. Does it only matter whether the God experts happen to take a position that is the same as your own? Share your thoughts on this and the other questions you'll find at **dgc.humanistpress.com**!

Notes:

1 Poggi, *Viability*, 295-296; Moodie, *Rise*, 23; Chadwick, *Reformation*, 95; MacCulloch, *Reformation*, 195, 244.

2 Loubser, *Critical*, 10; Cornevin, *Apartheid*, 35; Kuperus, *State*, 2; Lapping, *Apartheid*, 5; Thompson, *History*, 32, 35.

3 Cornevin, *Apartheid*, 54-55; Thompson, *History*, 36.

4 Woods, *Biko*, 14; Cornevin, *Apartheid*, 56; Lapping, *Apartheid*, 12-13; Thompson, *History*, 58.

5 Lapping, *Apartheid*, 7; Kuperus, *State*, 3, 36; Moodie, *Rise*, 25; Time,

"South Africa"; Cornevin, *Apartheid*, 33, 52, 59.

6 Woods, *Biko*, 14; Moodie, *Rise*, 29; Thompson, *History*, 67, 88.

7 Loubser, *Critical*, 12; Thompson, *History*, 88.

8 Cornevin, *Apartheid*, 60; Moodie, *Rise*, 6; Lapping, *Apartheid*, 18; Thompson, *History*, 91, 198.

9 Lapping, *Apartheid*, 19; Thompson, *History*, 110.

10 Thompson, *History*, 137; Guelke, *Rethinking*, 61; Woods, *Biko*, 15; Kuperus, *State*, 26; Lapping, *Apartheid*, 32, 37.

11 Cornevin, *Apartheid*, 120; Kuperus, *State*, 28; Thompson, *History*, 163, 165, 171; Lapping, *Apartheid*, 50; Kemp, "Myth."

12 Time, "South Africa"; Cornevin, *Apartheid*, 38; Moodie, *Rise*, 84; Ellis, "Malan," 391-392.

13 Cornevin, *Apartheid*, 38; Kuperus, *State*, 53, 86; Ellis, "Malan," 391-392; Time, "South Africa."

14 Thompson, *History*, 162; Moodie, *Rise*, 177; Cornevin, *Apartheid*, 38, 61.

15 Lapping, *Apartheid*, 66; Moodie, *Rise*, 198.

16 Geldenhuys, "Head," 249; Giliomee, "Leader," 104; Guelke, *Rethinking*, 34, 76; Kuperus, *State*, 54; Time, "South Africa"; Cornevin, *Apartheid*, 38-39; Thompson, *History*, 184; Lapping, *Apartheid*, 74; Moodie, *Rise*, 167, 194, 209, 235.

17 Welsh, "Executive," 139; Thompson, *History*, 180-181; Moodie, *Rise*, 253-254.

18 Joshua 23:12-13; Genesis 9:20-26, 11:1-9; Beresith, 59; Moodie, *Rise*, 245; Kuperus, *State*, 59, 63; Cornevin, *Apartheid*, 32.

19 Loubser, *Critical*, 25; Cornevin, *Apartheid*, 41.

20 Time, "South Africa"; Guelke, *Rethinking*, 4, 25; Woods, *Biko*, 366; Kuperus, *State*, 56, 62.

21 Ellis, "Malan," 391-392; Guelke, *Rethinking*, 3; Thompson, *History*, 186; Kuperus, *State*, 58, 72; Lapping, *Apartheid*, 97.

22 Giliomee, "The Leader," 108; Loubser, *Critical*, 78; Kuperus, *State*, 87.

23 Lapping, *Apartheid*, 105; Kuperus, *State*, 78.

24 Lapping, *Apartheid*, 105; Kuperus, *State*, 77; Guelke, *Rethinking*, 29.

25 Guelke, *Rethinking*, 27; Lapping, *Apartheid*, 122; Thompson, *History*, 198.

26 Jefferson, "Rhetoric"; Woods, *Biko*, 366; Cornevin, *Apartheid*, 133; Cornevin, *Apartheid*, 93.

27 Kuperus, *State*, 77.

28 Kuperus, *State*, 77.

29 Lapping, *Apartheid*, 105.

30 Cornevin, *Apartheid*, 80; Cornevin, *Apartheid*, 130; Thompson, *History*, 188.

31 Schrire, *Leadership*, 300; Welsh, "Executive," 145-146; Thompson,

History, 208; Lapping, *Apartheid*, 121; Time, "South Africa."

32 Geldenhuys, "Head," 260-261; Welsh, "Executive," 144, 154; Kuperus, *State*, 79, 83, 94-95.

33 Biko, "Bantustans," 82; Cornevin, *Apartheid*, 26; Thompson, *History*, 194; Kuperus, *State*, 106; Lapping, *Apartheid*, 154.

34 Botham, *Almighty*, 51.

35 McMillen, *Citizens*, 171; Goldberg, *Kingdom*, 12.

36 Sharpes, *Outcasts*, 25; Bernstein, *Biko*, 8, 122.

37 Jefferson, "Rhetoric"; Thompson, *History*, 212; Bernstein, *Biko*, 8, 13, 18.

38 Biko, "Black Souls," 21.

39 Bernstein, *Biko*, 14.

40 Cornevin, *Apartheid*, 134; Bernstein, *Biko*, 8-9; Stubbs, "Martyr," 158.

41 Biko, *I Write*, 136; Bernstein, *Biko*, 6, 14; Guelke, *Rethinking*, 123.

42 Stubbs, "Martyr," 214; Woods, *Biko*, 84.

43 Guelke, *Rethinking*, 123; Stubbs, "Martyr," 158.

44 Mpumlwana, "Introduction"; Bernstein, *Biko*, 12; Biko, "Bantustans," 82.

45 Woods, *Biko*, 30; Bernstein, *Biko*, 11; Guelke, *Rethinking*, 124; Kuperus, *State*, 109.

46 Bernstein, *Biko*, 9; Stubbs, "Martyr," 161; Cornevin, *Apartheid*, 135; Woods, *Biko*, x, 90.

47 Bernstein, *Biko*, 9, 16-17; Stubbs, "Black Consciousness," 99.

48 Tinyiko, "Black God"; Pretorius, "Head," 223; Schrire, *Leadership* 302; Kuperus, *State*, 112; Stubbs, "Martyr," 194; South African, "Sobukwe"; Bernstein, *Biko*, 9.

49 Bernstein, *Biko*, 9-10, 16.

50 Tinyiko, "Black God."

51 Stubbs, "Martyr," 163, 191, 193, 211-212.

52 Biko, "Church," 56-57.

53 Stubbs, "Martyr," 210.

54 Stubbs, "Martyr," 209.

55 Biko, "Church," 55.

56 Biko, "We Blacks," 30.

57 Biko, "Some African," 41-42.

58 Biko, "Church," 60.

59 Daley, "Apartheid Inquiry"; Bernstein, *Biko*, 10, 19, 32, 35, 56, 97.

60 Sharpes, *Outcasts*, 24; Bernstein, *Biko*, 5, 99; Welsh, "Executive," 174; Stubbs, "Martyr," 208.

61 Woods, *Biko*, 214; Bernstein, *Biko*, 20, 37, 119.

62 Biko, *I Write*, 152; Woods, *Biko*, 12; Bernstein, *Biko*, 15, 25.

63 Thompson, *History*, 200, 222, 233-234; Kuperus, *State*, 123; Guelke, *Rethinking*, 1, 135, 196-197.

64 Loubser, *Critical*, 114; Kuperus, *State*, 136-138, 140, 144.

Ayaan Hirsi Ali

CHAPTER 20

HIRSI ALI VS. OBAMA

Infidel

Two children were born in the 1960s, both to well-educated east African fathers engaged in political reform movements. Ayaan Hirsi Ali and Barack Obama each rejected their family's religious backgrounds, and they each are having profound but opposite effects on the power of God experts in early twenty-first-century society.

Ayaan Hirsi Ali was raised in a devout Muslim family, in several different lands: Somalia, Saudi Arabia, Ethiopia, and Kenya. Her father, per Muslim custom, had multiple wives, leaving Hirsi Ali and her siblings to be raised by her strictly religious mother and grandmother. At the age of 5, Hirsi Ali was subjected to the monstrous ritual of female circumcision. Her education consisted largely of rote memorization of passages from the Koran, with no questioning allowed. Once, when she asked a Koran teacher a pointed question about a passage that made no sense, he responded by slamming her head against the wall, fracturing her skull.[1]

The subservient status of women in Muslim society was constantly drilled into Hirsi Ali. Women cannot leave home without a male family escort, drive a car, or choose their own spouses; those who step out of line are brought to heel with a good beating. As she grew into womanhood, she learned more about what was expected; after delivering a stern lecture to his class about sexual morality, a religion teacher tried to force himself on her.[2]

As a teenager, Hirsi Ali for a time retreated into the hijab, the tent-like full body covering with only a small opening for the face. The beginning of her rebellion from Islam had to do with hormones. Somehow she and her sister got hold of Harlequin romance novels, showing a world of freedom, excitement, and individual empowerment far different than the dull servitude of her mother's world.[3]

The more serious break came when her father turned up one day to carry out the one duty he felt important: marrying Hirsi Ali off to an acceptable Muslim husband he had chosen. This was *definitely* no Harlequin romance. The chosen groom was bald, trite, sanctimonious, and in Hirsi Ali's opinion a "pea-brain"; not a bad man, perhaps, but not Prince Charming.[4] But she had no choice; it would disgrace her entire family and (according to Muslim teaching) condemn her soul to hell if she disobeyed her father's command.

The wedding was to take place at the groom's home in Canada. The plan was for Hirsi Ali to fly to Germany to visit relatives, then head to Canada when her visa was approved. For months, Hirsi Ali was tormented by the thought that once she set foot on that airplane, her life would be over.[5] She couldn't do it. She bolted.

She chose to hide in Holland, which has a large Muslim immigrant community. Hirsi Ali blended in for a while, found a job, and began to experience the joy and aggravation of individual freedom for the first time. Her clan ultimately tracked her down and put her through an impromptu trial, in the presence of the jilted groom, whom she was forced to reject to his face. She was lucky, though, because she was merely disowned. Thousands of other Muslim women have lost their lives in honor killings for similar offenses.[6]

With more energy than many other refugees, Hirsi Ali both earned her keep and educated herself at the University of Leiden. She read Socrates, Spinoza, and Voltaire, wide-eyed that a world so at odds with the prison of Muslim womanhood could exist. At the same time, working as a translator, she dealt with Muslim women who were not as ready as she to take the leap to full personhood. They were caught in a downward spiral of obedience to religious dictates, resulting in ever more misery, and ironically strengthening their reliance on the solace of religion. The more she saw of the happiness of humanist Holland versus the misery of immigrant Muslims who refused to assimilate, the more disenchanted she became with Islam itself. Her conversion occurred shortly after September 11, 2001, when the religion whose very name means "submission" showed exactly what obedience to the whims of God experts could produce. "I was an atheist. ... And I felt relief. It felt right."[7]

Her public disenchantment with Islam began to draw attention. First, a job with a policy think-tank, then a slot on the Labor Party ticket to the Dutch Parliament. She won. Hirsi Ali was savvy enough to realize that a freshman legislator was not going to change the whole world at once, so she honed in on one issue: getting the Dutch police to maintain statistics on the number of honor killings that occurred when Muslim women defied authority, as she herself had done. There was bureaucratic resistance to doing so, as liberals objected to the politically incorrect implication that Islam could be associated with such barbarity. But Hirsi Ali's persistence was rewarded with a pilot project in a single police district; when 11 honor killings were counted there in a single year, her point was made.[8] Holland has emphasized prevention and detection of honor killing ever since.[9]

It was her extra-Parliamentary activities that brought Hirsi Ali to the world's attention. In the post-9/11 era, her public critique of Islam brought her a mounting number of death threats. Undeterred, she proceeded to produce an artsy film condemning Islam's treatment of women, directed by the irrepressible Theo van Gogh. There was little public reaction when the work (appropriately entitled *Submission*) was shown on Dutch television in September 2004. But two months later, van Gogh was knocked from his bicycle and assassinated by a devout Muslim. Pinned to his chest was a note proclaiming that Hirsi Ali would be next.[10]

Civil disorder broke out across Holland as Muslims rioted and many who despised foreigners, religious or otherwise, got in their licks in return. Hirsi Ali, who already lived under police protection, went into deep hiding. She became politically radioactive as well. Even though she had already decided to leave Parliament, the leader of her party tried to win points by nullifying her Dutch citizenship, on the grounds that she had lied on her original application for political asylum. Debate over this triggered a political crisis and a new national election, which the party leader lost.[11] Hirsi Ali then decamped for America, became a best-selling author of fascinating books about her experiences, and emerged as the world's no. 1 voice of common sense in dealing with the threat posed to Enlightenment civilization by radical Islam.

Politician

Hirsi Ali landed in an America gripped by the phenomenon known as "Obamamania." Unlike Hirsi Ali, Barack Obama grew up in a God expert-free household. His mother became an outspoken atheist in college, and was "a lonely witness for secular humanism" as Obama put it. His grandparents, who helped with the child-rearing duties, were less outspoken but had abandoned religion many years earlier. Barack himself embraced the humanist worldview—until he caught the political bug.[12]

From an early age, it appeared that Obama was primed for success in whatever field he chose. Highly intelligent, handsome, well-educated, and well-grounded in human decency by his family, Obama had the whole package. He began his career as a community organizer in Chicago. "Issues, actions, power, self-interest: I liked these concepts," Obama explained. "They bespoke a certain hardheadedness, a worldly lack of sentiment; politics, not religion." His salary was paid by a consortium of churches, though, and much of his work was done through existing church organizations.[13]

Community organizing is frustrating work, and organizers burn out quickly. Whether or not that happened to Obama, he ultimately concluded that to make a difference in people's lives, he needed to hold elective office. To win office, he needed to become either a pastor or a lawyer. He chose law school, and his natural talent got him into Harvard. His abilities shone through there as well, and he was elected as the first-ever black chief editor of the *Harvard Law Review*.[14]

At that point he had his pick of the choicest legal jobs; instead he returned to Chicago, and began building a political base by working for a small firm specializing in civil rights. In 1996 he was elected to the State Senate, after using legal means to remove all his opponents' names from the ballot. In 2000, he ran against incumbent Congressman Bobby Rush, who also happened to be an ordained minister and pastor of the Beloved Community Christian Church.[15] Here Obama encountered the first setback of his previously charmed existence, as he ran headlong into the power of organized religion. Pastor after pastor aligned with fellow pastor Rush; when one broke ranks to endorse Obama, he was besieged by complaints from his colleagues. Despite a well-financed campaign, Obama went nowhere, losing the primary by a 2:1 margin. Obama, "a very apt student of his own mistakes," seems to have resolved never to be out-religioned again.[16]

Two years later, Obama launched a daring bid for the U.S. Senate. This time he traveled with a Bible and quoted it frequently, while brownnosing every black congregation in the state. He even changed the cadence of his speech when addressing black audiences, to sound more like a preacher. "This is a campaign based on truth and honesty and based on the values that I learned in the church." So much for the values he learned from his family. He went so far as to lie about his mother, assuring an interviewer that "I was raised more by my mother, and my mother was Christian." He trumpeted his membership in the church of Rev. Jeremiah Wright, named in an *Ebony* magazine survey as the no. 2 black minister in America. One by one his opponents self-destructed, allowing Obama to win by the biggest majority in the history of Illinois Senate races.[17]

Not without more religious trauma, though. Obama's Republican opponent was devout Catholic Alan Keyes, who claimed to know God's mind exactly. "Christ would not vote for Barack Obama" he kept insisting. By his own admission, Obama dealt with these attacks poorly. He couldn't risk saying "You haven't the faintest idea what God does or doesn't want, so shut the hell up," because that might alienate the God expert support base he had so carefully cultivated. So he stammered and stumbled. Though no one can read Obama's mind, with hindsight it is easy to picture him resolving to never allow himself to be put in this kind of box again.[18]

Obama's overwhelming victory resulted in immediate clamor for a run for president in 2008. It also resulted in his staff's development of "The Plan," a strategy for maximizing Obama's political clout whether or not he ultimately took the plunge. A key component of The Plan was an embrace of religion to neutralize the "values voters" who many Democratic strategists thought had cost Democrats the 2004 election. The centerpiece was a ballyhooed speech Obama delivered in 2006, most of which was repeated in his book *The Audacity of Hope*. His campaign website later called it "the most important speech on religion and politics in 40 years."[19]

Obama commenced his ode to religion not as a believer might—by arguing that God's will is important and worth following. Instead, he began with opinion polls, arguing that championing religion is expedient, while omitting it from the political arena "is bad politics." He went on to salute leaders who have woven religion into their politics. Whom do you think he championed as the paragon of "the great reformers in American history [who] were not only motivated by faith, but repeatedly used religious language to argue for their cause?" None other than his predecessor as Democratic presidential nominee, William Jennings Bryan.[20] The same Bryan discussed in Chapter 15, whose "religious language" enabled Prohibition, the success of the Ku Klux Klan, and the taboo on teaching evolution, whom some of us regard as Exhibit A for keeping religion *out* of politics.

Obama kept up his religious grandstanding throughout the campaign. "I pray to Jesus every night" he solemnly informed Ohioans, while his campaign distributed brochures across the river in Kentucky depicting Obama beneath a giant, glowing cross. He informed another Ohio audience that same-sex civil unions were good public policy because of the Sermon on the Mount. "We do what we do because God is with us," he cried at another point.[21] Bryan never said it better. "I am a devout Christian," he assured *Christianity Today*. "I believe in the redemptive death and resurrection of Jesus Christ. I believe that faith gives me a path to be cleansed of sin and have eternal life." This was the exact opposite of what he told an interviewer in 2004: "I don't presume to have knowledge of what happens after I die." That knowledge apparently entered his brain when he announced his run for president. Yet in the same breath, Obama warned that "One of the things that's very important in this day and age is that we don't use religion as a political tool and certainly that we don't lie about religion as a way to score political points."[22]

"You cannot deny Obama's brilliance, his disciplined approach," says his former opponent Bobby Rush. "He is a very political guy, very calculating." Campaign literature pictured Obama preaching in church, even though he had earlier told an interviewer that "I think there is an enormous danger on the part of public figures to rationalize or justify their actions by claiming God's mandate."[23] Obama's ploy blew up in his face, though, when researchers began delving into the theology of his chosen pastor, Jeremiah Wright, a former Black Muslim and fan of the Jew-baiting Louis Farrakhan. Obama had joined Wright's Trinity Church as part of his political base-building after law school; it was known as a "power church," counting Oprah Winfrey among its members. As even a fawning Obama biographer put it, "A big, visible church where many upwardly mobile and politically active blacks attended was just the place he wanted to be." In the year he launched his presidential campaign, flush with book sales cash, Obama became the single biggest contributor to Wright's church.[24]

Now Wright was being shown endlessly on cable news, taunting America that the September 11 attacks were simply "chickens come home to roost," alleging that AIDS was a government plot for exterminating blacks, accusing the government of the "US of KKK" of murdering little girls in church bombings, and thundering "No, no, no! Not God Bless America. God damn America! That's in the Bible."[25]

"Why," people wondered, "did Obama choose this particular church?" "I thought I could meet more campaign contributors there" wouldn't be a good answer. As the pressure mounted, Obama claimed he never heard Wright say such things, contrary to his 2004 boast that he attended Trinity "Every week–11:00 am service." He then delivered a major speech in Philadelphia, not about pastors in politics, but about race. Obama struck a heroic pose, swearing that he would stand by his mentor and friend through thick and thin. "I can no more disown him than I can disown the black community."[26]

The press praised Obama's wisdom and courage. But well-funded campaigns do daily tracking polls, and Obama didn't like what he saw. His campaign begged Wright to stop preaching; a close friend of Obama's offered him cash to do so. A month later, Obama did disown Wright and later resigned from Trinity (without disowning the black community). His backers defended the break because "Reverend Wright made it clear he cared more about the cause of black theology than the political aspirations of his spiritual son."[27] Exactly. Obama cares more about his political aspirations than about what is or isn't true about God. Rather the opposite of Ayaan Hirsi Ali, who decided that her life should be shaped by truth, not the other way around.

The Great Kowtow

As president, Obama bent over backwards to make nice to God experts, so they wouldn't say bad things about him.

He instituted the practice of starting all his public events with a prayer from a local God expert, as no previous president has ever done. Prayers are carefully vetted by White House theologians before delivery, lest any Wright-isms should slip in.[28]

He made a great public show of appointing a "faith advisor," a 26-year old Pentecostal minister (and campaign worker) named Joshua Dubois. One of the well-publicized duties for which taxpayers pay Dubois' salary is writing a daily prayer for Obama, who would otherwise have to rely on one of the many "prayer for the day" books and websites.[29]

Obama not only continued the Bush "faith-based initiative," he expanded on it. The faith-based initiative is the program that takes money from humanist taxpayers and gives it to God expert organizations, some of whom teach that humanists deserve to be tortured in hell, forever. Obama's own faith-based advisory panel voted (narrowly) to recommend that all faith-based funds should be paid to section 501(c)(3) organizations, rather than directly to churches, to provide greater accountability and protection against improper use. But Obama rejected even this modest recommendation. There is some reason to believe that a greater proportion of faith-based funding is flowing through more accountable 501(c)(3) organizations than before, but that still doesn't address the fundamental problem. One of these 501(c)(3) groups, for example, is Catholic Charities, the "charity" that receives nearly $3 billion (62 percent of its funds) from the government, but that has cut off providing adoption services for orphans altogether rather than place a handful of them with same-sex couples.[30]

Even outside the formal faith-based initiative, Obama's administration ignored the line ostensibly separating church and state by funneling "economic stimulus" money directly to church-affiliated organizations, including ones connected to his old foe, Rev. Bobby Rush. This is not the first time legislation has explicitly earmarked funds for churches, and it is not clear whether Obama is primarily responsible for including the Rush earmarks in the bill. What is certain is that Obama has expressed no public opposition to taxpayer funding of church groups, which is hardly surprising since he himself, in his days in the Illinois legislature, was responsible for earmarking thousands of taxpayer dollars for God experts who might become politically useful to him someday.[31]

During the campaign, Obama was asked whether he would prevent recipients of faith-based grants from discriminating in their hiring practices based on religion. This followed notorious cases of the Salvation Army and other religious organizations firing low-level employees for being insufficiently Christian.[32] He responded unambiguously that he would never allow such practices to continue. Once he won the election, though, what had been a clear answer became a subject of "review," for nearly two years, by faith advisor Dubois and a task force of religious leaders. Ultimately Dubois published a restatement of the faith-based policy that was deafeningly silent on the hiring discrimination question he was supposed to be reviewing. Did that mean that discrimination would be allowed to continue unchecked?[33]

Finally, in the summer of 2011, Obama was pinned down with a precisely worded question at a town hall meeting. His response was the exact opposite of his campaign pledge. Religious outfits, he now insisted, even those on the federal dole, should be perfectly free to hire only fellow zealots.[34] White people are not free to hire only other whites; is there a good reason why Methodist churches should be given taxpayer money to hire only other Methodists, even for menial positions?

Federal law since 1954 has limited tax exempt status for churches to those that keep political endorsements out of the pulpit. In 1987, this was expanded to prohibit political attacks from the pulpit as well. The Internal Revenue Service (IRS) has enforced these rules in the past with a mix of warnings and occasional litigation against preachers who violate them, inadvertently or otherwise. In the 2004 election cycle, for example, IRS selected 110 cases for examination, issued 69 written advisories, revoked the tax-exempt status of 5 organizations and proposed revocation for 2 others, all within the 2½ year period following the election.[35]

In 2008, the pattern of violations changed dramatically, when a group of militant preachers decided to defy the law in a highly public way by ostentatiously making such endorsements and daring IRS to do something about it. They did the same thing in 2010, and again in 2011. Some even graciously submitted tapes of their endorsement sermons to IRS.[36]

IRS normally cracks down hard on tax protesters, such as those who insist that the income tax is somehow unconstitutional, because it knows that voluntary compliance is essential to orderly collection of the revenue. When it comes to enforcing the law against God experts, though, the Obama administration strategy has been to turn tail and run. None of the public protesters have been pursued by IRS. Lawyers who expected to earn big fees defending these folks are frustrated, because there are no cases to defend. Equally frustrated are pastors who scrupulously comply with the law, only to observe their scofflaw brethren walk away scot-free. Thirteen Ohio ministers complained to IRS in 2011 about their "grave concerns over the current inability of the IRS to enforce the federal tax laws applicable to churches."[37]

Why the inaction, especially in comparison to the IRS record in prior administrations? Could it be that Obama actually supports political sermons? Longtime Obama advisor Valerie Jarrett spoke to the congregation from the pulpit of Atlanta's Ebenezer Baptist Church early in 2012, taking the opportunity to blast "Republicans in Congress" for putting the jobs of police, teachers, and firefighters in jeopardy. Shortly after the religious service, the church conducted a voter registration drive.[38]

Obama's Justice Department took a shocking position in federal court that effectively nullifies the "Establishment Clause" of the First Amendment—the part that says "Congress shall make no law respecting an establishment of religion." Courts in the good old days thought this clause was important, and thus allowed citizens the right to challenge the constitutionality of any law that seemed to violate it. "No more," says the Obama administration; courts are too busy to spend time defending the Constitution, and mere citizens should have no legal standing to challenge government endorsement of religion (this particular case involved the "National Day of Prayer") or handouts to churches.[39] If American citizens aren't allowed to bring these cases, then who can?

> Some humanists look at the Obama record and say "Not great, but he isn't as bad on mixing religion and politics as Bush was." Others argue that if you're not part of the solution, you're part of the problem. Your take? Share your thoughts on this and the other questions you'll find at **dgc.humanistpress.com**!

Obama wrote movingly in *The Audacity of Hope* about his need for "an unequivocal commitment to a particular community of faith," to avoid being "alone in the same ways [my mother] was ultimately alone." So he joined Trinity Church because "I felt God's spirit beckoning me. I submitted myself to His will."[40] Yet, once he achieved his White House dream, Obama found a different way to avoid being "ultimately alone." Golf. He almost never attends church anymore—a total of four times in his first year in office, and only once in the six months after that. But by May 2011, he had played some 68 rounds of golf, each running quite a bit longer than a typical church service.[41] Despite a promise shortly before his inauguration that he would join a Washington church, he never did so. Ostensibly, this was because of concern for the disruptive effect his presence might have. But the churches themselves can assess best the tradeoff between disruption and prestige, and a number of them actively sought to bring in Obama as a member.[42] Moreover, former Presidents Jimmy Carter and Bill Clinton both attended church regularly, and Washington churches are well-accustomed to dealing with celebrities. Amazingly, when criticized for his lack of church attendance, the same fellow who put out campaign literature showing his head bowed in prayer now began insisting that his faith was a private matter.[43]

Some of us think there is nothing wrong with golf. But there is quite a bit wrong with hypocrisy. It was the always eloquent Obama who wrote that "Nothing is more transparent than inauthentic expressions of faith—such as the politician who shows up at a black church around election time and claps (off rhythm) to the gospel choir."[44]

So is Obama guilty of "inauthentic expressions of faith," or not? Only he knows. His patterns of church attendance, the Wright flip-flop, the afterlife flip-flop, the emphasis on religious findings in opinion polls, and the lies about his mother and his source of values certainly smack of someone who is not really an ex-humanist after all, but simply a salesman, telling the customer at hand whatever he wants to hear.

Innocent or guilty? If Obama had heeded his wife's advice after his defeat in 2000 and returned to private life, do you think he would still be attending Trinity Church today? Or would he more likely be the head of a local humanist organization? Share your thoughts on this and the other questions you'll find at **dgc.humanistpress.com**!

Islam

As president, Obama carried his embrace of religion over to the realm of dealing with Islam, acting at times as though he could herd Muslim God experts the same way he herded Chicago pastors.

The first stop on his Islam appreciation tour was Istanbul, where he proclaimed that "America is not at war with Islam."[45] He later ratcheted that up to say that America is not even "in competition" with Islam.[46] America values objective scientific truth, freedom of expression, freedom of belief, humane treatment of prisoners, and equal legal rights for women and men. Islam, manifestly, does not—just ask Hirsi Ali. Yet Obama insists that America is not to be in competition with Islam. Does that mean that he sees Islam's values as equivalent to those of America? Or does it mean that even though Islam's values are not equivalent to ours, he just doesn't care?

Obama went out of his way to congratulate his Turkish hosts for their "secular democracy," at a time when the Turkish government was moving steadily toward an Iranian-style Islamicization of the Atatürk achievement, with dozens of secularist politicians languishing in Turkish prisons on vague charges of "conspiring" against the Islamist regime.[47] Just a few months before Obama arrived, the Turkish government published warnings that:

> Women have to be more careful, since they have stimulants. ... [T]hey should not show their ornaments and figure and ... they should cover in a fine manner. ... His highness the prophet Muhammad did not think kindly of women who put on perfumes outside their homes and go strolling and saw this as immoral behavior.[48]

Obama delivered his centerpiece speech on Islam a few months later in Cairo, where he spoke glowingly of the "partnership between America and Islam." His speech was co-hosted by al-Azhar University, the closest equivalent to the Vatican in the Muslim world. Of all the hosts available, Obama agreed to speak at the institution that just a few years earlier had warmly endorsed the practice of female circumcision, and whose leader shortly after September 11 had announced that "Everyone who fights for his rights and explodes himself as a suicide bomber to kill his enemies is a martyr, not a terrorist."[49] After extolling al-Azhar as "a beacon of Islamic learning," Obama then went on a flight of purest fiction, crediting Islam with everything from the invention of the magnetic compass (actually invented by the Chinese, centuries before Muhammad) to printing, oblivious to the fact that no printing press was allowed to operate in the entire Muslim world until the middle of the eighteenth century.[50]

Obama even misquoted the Koran: "The Holy Koran teaches that whoever kills an innocent, it is as if he has killed all mankind; and whoever saves a person, it is as if he has saved all mankind." But the Koran does not say "kills an innocent," it says "slays a soul, unless it be for manslaughter or for mischief in the land." It then defines "mischief in the land" as opposing the messenger Muhammad.[51] The next verse prescribes the punishment for those who make such "mischief in the land": "They should be murdered or crucified or their hands and their feet should be cut off on opposite sides."

Obama touched on Islam's treatment of women, but in a curious way. Not a word about the barbarity of slicing up little girls, the pressure for women to live inside tent-like coverings, or the vast array of Muslim practices to ensure women's subservience to men–*e.g.*, wife-beating, as mandated by al-Azhar.[52] He noted only the importance of literacy for Muslim women—something that is far from being their most serious problem. Hirsi Ali was taught to read, and even in Saudi Arabia a majority of college graduates are women. As she noted after the speech, "He didn't touch upon Muslim women being confined, being forced into marriages or being victims of 'honour killings.'"[53]

Next year, it was on to Jakarta to praise Muslim Indonesia for "the spirit of religious tolerance … that remains one of the country's defining and inspiring characteristics"—despite the surge in violence against Indonesian Christians and "heretical" Muslims in the preceding few years, and ignoring the new 5-year jail term for blasphemy created by Indonesia's parliament shortly before Obama arrived.[54]

Obama then assured his listeners that religious faith is "fundamental to human progress," essentially telling humanists to take a hike. This fit perfectly in "tolerant" Indonesia, where every citizen must register as Muslim, Catholic, Protestant, Hindu, Buddhist, or Confucian; non-believers and Jews are denied legal existence.[55]

The most significant world events of Obama's presidency, at this writing, are those of the "Arab spring" uprisings that promise to upend the political culture of a critically important region, for better or worse. No greater opportunity for encouraging the spread of Enlightenment values at a "teachable moment" could be imagined. When demonstrations broke out against the rigged election in Islamist Iran in 2009, Obama did nothing: "We are going to monitor the situation and see how this plays itself out before we make any judgments about how we proceed." The movement fizzled. In Egypt, not only did we say nothing on behalf of the secularist element of the uprising, but we made a show of welcoming the Muslim Brotherhood into the political process—the same outfit we once paid so much money to try to assassinate Nasser. At this writing, it is too early to tell how the "Arab spring" will turn out; the "moderate Islamist" party that just took over Libya with the help of American dollars and bombs promises to bring back polygamy.[56]

What Obama never did was present the case for a Muslim-world Enlightenment, the kind that Hirsi Ali demands. "Democracies should foster the voices of dissent and sponsor Muslim dissidents in the West," she argues, "so that the one-sided, stultifying religious rhetoric to which millions of Muslims are subjected every day has a counterpoint."[57] It was Senator Obama, back in 2006, who pointed out that: "The United States won the Cold War not simply because it outgunned the Soviet Union but because American values held sway in the court of international public opinion, which included those who lived within communist regimes."[58] What would the world look like today if American presidents had spent 50 years praising communists for their peacefulness and tolerance?

What was the Muslim reaction to all this? Essentially, "Thanks, but no thanks." Favorability ratings for America shot up across the Muslim world immediately after the Cairo speech, then faded to Bush-era levels a few months later. It seems Muslims believe that actions speak louder than words; Obama's unflagging support for the persecution of Palestinian Muslims by Israel negated all his lofty talk.[59] Meanwhile, the government of Pakistan played the most lucrative double game in history, taking billions of American aid while busily supporting Muslim terrorists in Afghanistan and India.[60]

Hirsi Ali understands that what is needed is a "campaign of enlightenment," like that of Voltaire and Paine, which unfortunately passed the Muslim world by. She knows that people in Muslim countries are capable of moving beyond Islam, as she did; she calls giving up without trying "a racism of low expectations." Her prescription is that Islam needs "a Voltaire to call Muslims to break free of superstition, to use their minds and not their emotions, to take note, as he did … that 'Nothing can be more contrary to religion and the clergy than reason and common sense.'"[61] She especially condemns the liberal desire to avoid offense to Muslims at all cost:

> I cannot emphasize enough how wrongheaded this is. Withholding criticism and ignoring differences are racism in its purest form. Yet these cultural experts fail to notice that, through their anxious avoidance of criticizing non-Western countries, they trap the people who represent these cultures in a state of backwardness. The experts may have the best of intentions, but as we all know, the road to hell is paved with good intentions.[62]

The Road Not Traveled

Obama's apparent "good intention" on his travels to Muslim-majority countries was to improve America's image by allying America with "moderate" Muslim God experts. Atatürk could have told him that doing so was "as useless as a graft on dead wood."[63] This is evident not only in the Muslim opinion polls cited earlier, but in the continued Muslim terrorist attacks after his speeches, in the United States and elsewhere. In Cairo, where Obama delivered his most important ode to Islam, the new Muslim Brotherhood-dominated parliament is now starting to say it doesn't even want to accept American money anymore.[64]

Engaging with the people of these nations is undoubtedly important, but wasn't there a better way to go about it? Barack Obama is at his best when delivering calm, constructive criticism. He chides black men about failing to bear the burdens of responsible fatherhood. His wife, undoubtedly with his involvement, lets parents know that we're not doing a good job of controlling our children's weight. He leans on Warren Buffet to reproach the wealthy for their incessant moaning over taxes.

Islam is certainly ripe for a little constructive criticism—or according to Hirsi Ali, a lot—but there is barely a whiff of that in any of Obama's rhetoric. There is so much he could have done, without being rude to his hosts. When he went to Istanbul, Obama could have thanked Turkey for giving the world Atatürk, and devoted his "teachable moment" to encouraging Muslim-majority nations to follow the shining example he set. When he went to Cairo he could have lavished praise on Egypt's secular democratic movement—the folks now being crushed by the Muslim Brotherhood—rather than fawning over al-Azhar and misquoting the Koran. When he went to Indonesia, if he were at a loss for words, he could have recited passages from his own 2006 book:

> All of which underscores perhaps the most profound shift in Indonesia—the growth of militant, fundamentalist Islam in the country. ... Today, Islamic parties make up one of the largest political blocs, with many calling for the imposition of sharia, or Islamic law. Seeded by funds from the Middle East, Wahhabist clerics, schools, and mosques now dot the countryside. ... Islamic militants and self-proclaimed "vice squads" have attacked churches, nightclubs, casinos, and brothels. ... Indonesia feels more distant now than it did thirty years ago. I fear it's becoming a land of strangers.[65]

Four years later, as president, he served up nothing but flattery for Indonesian Islam. A colossal opportunity, missed.

Only in an alternate universe could we know for sure whether a different tone would have worked out better. Would it have earned America greater respect from people with a tradition of placing a high value on honor than Obama's obsequiousness did? Would it have had a longer term benefit, as did our decades of criticism of communism, even if it failed to improve America's image in the short run? Or would it just have made matters even worse? Share your thoughts on this and the other questions you'll find at **dgc.humanistpress.com!**

What ties together the heroes of these chapters, from Socrates through Hirsi Ali, is their *attitude* toward the God experts of their time and place. That attitude, in a nutshell, is simply: "You are just not important. You do not speak for God, and what you say God wants carries no weight against what I have thought through to be right." Such an attitude carries risks, but in the long haul it has worn down the power of irrational dogma.

Obama's attitude toward the God experts of this century, Muslim and non-Muslim alike, has been just the opposite. It's as though he were telling them: "You are *sooo* important. Here, take more money. Here, let me be bend another rule for you. Here, listen to my new rhetoric telling the world how wonderful you are. Now please like me." He is wearing down nothing. Ever since his 2006 argument that disentanglement from religion "is bad politics," he has appeared bent on leaving respect for the world's God experts greater than he found it. This is worse than not being part of the solution. It is the essence of the problem.

Rightly or wrongly, many Americans dreamed that Obama might be different. He certainly looks and sounds different from other presidents. His tone is thoughtful, sensible, and downright humanist. If America had the open-mindedness to elect someone like that, might permanent, systemic change be at hand? Not just the odd policy position that comes and goes, but sea change in process, a liberation from the dead hand of dogma that the heroes of this book fought against so valiantly.

It hasn't happened, at least not yet. Given Obama's political history, any such dreams were probably unrealistic, but the disappointment stings nonetheless.

Some argue that Obama had to show deference to religion to succeed. "If Senator Obama did not say what he said he would never get elected," said Jeremiah Wright.[66] But is this true? He won election to the state senate without groveling. In both 2004 and the fall of 2008 the breaks of the game were such that if his heart was beating, he could not possibly have lost. All he ever had to say about religion was "I believe faith is a private matter that has no bearing on which candidate is fittest to serve."

And what if he *had* lost? The earth would have continued to rotate, and Barack Obama would have continued to be an extraordinarily gifted individual, capable of improving the lives of thousands. Hirsi Ali tried elective office and voluntarily gave it up because she realized she could make a greater difference elsewhere.[67] Obama's sister tried to dissuade him from politics, as did his wife, who questioned whether politics was a place for decent people.[68]

Before he ran for office, Obama wrote that "I work mostly with churches and community groups, men and women who quietly build grocery stores and health clinics in the inner city, and housing for the poor. Every so often I'll find myself working on a discrimination case, representing clients who show up at my law firm's office with stories that we like to tell ourselves should no longer exist."[69] Is that so terrible? Obama himself mused after his 2000 defeat that "What's not clear to me is whether I should do that as an elected official or by influencing government in ways that actually improve people's lives."[70]

As a lawyer grows in stature, his cases grow in importance. That certainly happened with an earlier Chicago lawyer defeated in his own Congressional run, who was described in Chapter 15 crossing swords with Obama's hero William Jennings Bryan. Obama could have become another Clarence Darrow, the humanist voice to free black America from the grip of its Jeremiah Wright churches. Instead, he followed in the footsteps of an earlier humanist apostate, a non-believer who feigned belief to advance his own ambition, the cleverest politician of his day, who showered benefits on God experts to win their backing, who did a few good things but whose lasting impact on the advancement of humanist values at a critical moment in history was nil. Obama, thus far, is another Talleyrand.

> Obama has done quite a few things that humanists like, which are not mentioned here. His billion dollar re-election campaign can tell you all about those. On balance, when you compare Obama with a hero like Hirsi Ali, do you think I'm being too hard on him—or too soft? Share your thoughts on this and the other questions you'll find at **dgc.humanistpress.com**!

Notes:

1 Hirsi Ali, *Infidel*, xxii, 31, 48, 49, 77.
2 Hirsi Ali, *Caged Virgin*, 17-19, 163; Hirsi Ali, *Infidel*, 130.
3 Hirsi Ali, *Infidel*, 79, 85, 94.
4 Hirsi Ali, *Infidel*, 170, 173.
5 Hirsi Ali, *Infidel*, 186.
6 Butler, "Muslim Culture"; Hirsi Ali, *Infidel*, 187, 205-210, 240.
7 Hirsi Ali, *Caged Virgin*, 68, 172; Hirsi Ali, *Infidel*, 235, 248, 281-282.
8 Hirsi Ali, *Caged Virgin*, 141; Hirsi Ali, *Infidel*, 294, 296, 302, 309.
9 Islam in Europe, "Netherlands."
10 The Independent, "Theo van Gogh"; Van Gogh, "Submission"; Hirsi Ali, *Infidel*, xxi, 313-317; Hirsi Ali, *Caged Virgin*, xiv.
11 Hirsi Ali, *Nomad*, 97; Hirsi Ali, *Infidel*, 322-328, 337-339, 344-345.
12 Mansfield, *Faith*, 8, 15; Obama, *Dreams*, 17, 50; Obama, *Audacity*, 203; Remnick, *Bridge*, 25; Mendell, *Obama*, 70.
13 Mansfield, *Faith*, 23; Obama, *Audacity*, 206; Mendell, *Obama*, 65-68; Remnick, *Bridge*, 147, 155, 181.
14 Remnick, *Bridge*, 151, 198, 361, 483; Mendell, *Obama*, 82, 89, 101.
15 Remnick, *Bridge*, 244, 324; Mansfield, *Faith*, 1; Yachnin, "Lawsuits."
16 Scott, "Streetwise"; Remnick, *Bridge*, 347.
17 D'Souza, *Roots*, 142; Falsani, "Interview"; Scott, "Streetwise"; Remnick, *Bridge*, 190-191, 314, 398; Mendell, *Obama*, 77, 188, 227, 237.

18 Obama, "Keynote"; Mansfield, *Faith*, 94; Obama, *Audacity*, 211-212; Remnick, *Bridge*, 449; Mendell, *Obama*, 301.

19 Pew Forum, "In Pursuit"; Obama, "Keynote"; Mansfield, *Faith*, 87; Remnick, *Bridge*, 457, 465, 481; Mendell, *Obama*, 350.

20 Obama, *Audacity*, 214, 218; Obama, "Keynote."

21 Parker, "Controversial"; Vu, "Obama"; Foust, "Obama"; Obama, "Speech."

22 Pulliam, "Q&A"; Falsani, "Interview."

23 Remnick, *Bridge*, 365, 545; Falsani, "Interview."

24 Obama, *Dreams*, 280; Remnick, *Bridge*, 195, 581; Mendell, *Obama*, 75; Mansfield, *Faith*, 60; D'Souza, *Roots*, 108.

25 Remnick, *Bridge*, 516, 567.

26 Obama, "More Perfect"; Mansfield, *Faith*, 64; Remnick, *Bridge*, 573; Falsani, "Interview."

27 Hitchens, "Blind Faith"; Gallup Politics, "Gallup Daily"; Zeleny, "Obama"; Obama, "On My Faith"; Mansfield, *Faith*, 64; Remnick, *Bridge*, 575, 579.

28 Gilgoff, "New Tradition."

29 CNN, "Obama"; Banks, "Obama"; Kornblut, "Obama's spirituality"; Parsons, "Obama's Man."

30 Duin, "Obama"; Christianity Today, "New Director"; Marus, "Faith-based"; Brachear, "Catholic Charities"; Goodstein, "Catholic bishops."

31 Allen, "Illinois"; Smith, "Obama's Stimulus"; Judicial Watch, "Uncovers"; Day, "Obama earmarks."

32 Mooney, "Controversy"; Goldberg, *Kingdom*, 128-132.

33 Gorski, "Obama"; Associated Press, "Obama makes"; Lynn, "Faith"; Americans United, "Obama."

34 Stone, "Atheist"; Secular Coalition, "Atheist."

35 Internal Revenue Service, "Charities."

36 Associated Press, "Pastors"; Slevin, "Ban"; Slevin, "33 Pastors"; Snyder, "Pastors"; Strom, "Political."

37 Southern Poverty, "Crackdown"; Butts, "IRS"; Strom, "Political"; Byrnes, "Churches."

38 Munro, "Jarrett."

39 Associated Press, "Obama administration."

40 Obama, *Audacity*, 206, 208; Obama, "Keynote."

41 Sabar, "Obama"; Gilgoff, "For first time"; Koffler, "Obama golfs."

42 Starr, "First Lady"; Niesse, "Obamas"; Harris, "Obama"; Barakat, "Obama."

43 Brinton, "Why Obama's"; Lee, "Obama."

44 Obama, *Audacity*, 216.

45 Obama, "Turkish Parliament."

46 Obama, "New Beginning."

47 Jenkins, "Between Fact"; Agence France-Presse, "Turkish"; International Herald Tribune, "Study."

48 Tait, "Secular."

49 Obama, "New Beginning"; Williams, "Muslim"; Mikhail, *Islam*, 279.

50 Computersmiths, "History"; Kinross, Ottoman, 381; Clog, "Attempt"; Vitrine Library, "Kâtip Çelebi."

51 Koran 5:32-33.

52 Hirsi Ali, *Nomad*, 129; Trifkovic, *Sword*, 156.

53 Shahin, "Saudi"; Worthington, "Cairo"; Hirsi Ali, *Nomad*, 164.

54 Obama, "University of Indonesia"; Blake, "Indonesia"; Firdaus, "Religious."

55 Gelling, "Law."

56 D'Souza, *Roots*, 184; Klapper, "US angered"; Karon, "Tunisia."

57 Hirsi Ali, *Caged Virgin*, 33.

58 Obama, *Audacity*, 308.

59 Agence France-Presse, "Obama"; Madhani, "Obama"; LaFranchi, "Muslim world"; Kiefer, "Year."

60 Wright, "Double Game."

61 Hirsi Ali, *Nomad*, 205, 214; Hirsi Ali, *Caged Virgin*, 27; Hirsi Ali, *Infidel*, 245.

62 Hirsi Ali, *Caged Virgin*, xviii.

63 Crandall, *Gender*, 164; Mango, *Atatürk*, 535.

64 Mazzetti, "Suspect"; Associated Press, "Egypt."

65 Obama, *Audacity*, 278.

66 Remnick, *Bridge*, 581.

67 Hirsi Ali, *Nomad*, 223; Hirsi Ali, *Infidel*, xxii.

68 Obama, *Dreams*, 209; Remnick, *Bridge*, 253, 308, 367.

69 Obama, *Dreams*, 438.

70 Remnick, *Bridge*, 366.

THEREFORE

It would be entirely possible to write a book pairing 20 admirable God experts with 20 repugnant unbelievers. "Schweitzer vs. Stalin" would fit nicely in such a book. It would also be possible to bring out facts showing the heroes of this book in a less flattering light. Socrates seems to have been as obnoxious as they come. Paine's reputation for drunkenness may not have been entirely undeserved. Lucy Harris may have been a shrew. Darrow may have bribed a juror. Julian, Zhu Di, Atatürk, and Nasser didn't retain power by gentle humility.

And yet ...

There is a truth here that is illustrated if not conclusively proven by the comparisons selected. The truth is that we are all stuck here together on this little planet, and we need to get along. We're all we've got. No spirit in the sky is going to help us if we can't help ourselves. Every shred of plausible evidence bears this out.

Figuring out how best to get along in a world that only grows more complex, never simpler, is an exceedingly difficult task. It must be, since we do it so poorly. It is a task made far more problematic when we have Euthyphros, Smiths, and Gandhis running about, interrupting our collective train of thought with frenzied outbursts that God wants us to do this, that, or the other. Worse yet are the cynical politicians, who don't believe what they are mouthing but do believe that caving in to the God experts will help them to the top of the heap.

Flawed as they may have been, the heroes of this book teach us how to tune out the spiritual static and rely on our common sense. At the pace of a snail, civilization is moving in their direction. If we can pick up the pace a little bit, we just might have descendants around to thank us in the twenty-second century.

PICTURE CREDITS

All pictures are via Wikimedia Commons, unless otherwise indicated.

Chapter 1
Socrates: James Anderson

Chapter 3
Han Yü: Dr. Meierhofer

Chapter 4
Ibn Rushd: George Jackson Fisher

Chapter 7
Erasmus: Hans Holbein the Younger

Chapter 10
Voltaire: Catherine Lusurier

Chapter 11
Paine: By By Auguste Millière, after an engraving by William Sharp, after a 1792 portrait by George Romney

Chapter 13
Zola: William Feldman

Chapter 16
Azaña portrait: Enrique Segura, Collection of the Ateneo Científico, Literario y Artístico de Madrid. http://www.ateneodemadrid.com/

Chapter 17

Nehru: Kamat.com

Chapter 19

Biko: Associated Press

Chapter 20

Hirsi Ali: By Steve Jurvetson from Menlo Park, USA

Cover

Julian, lower left: Classical Numismatic Group, Inc.
http://www.cngcoirs.com

BIBLIOGRAPHY

A complete hyperlinked bibliography is available online at
www.luisgranados.com/dgcbibliography.html